From the Pages of Scripture

God's biographies reveal the secrets of warning and instruction for our daily lives. "For whatsoever things were written aforetime were written for our learning, that we through patience and comfort of the Scriptures might have hope."   *Romans 15:4*

Illustrated in the World of Nature

"But ask now the beasts, and they shall teach thee; and the fowls of the air, and they shall tell thee: Or speak to the earth, and it shall teach thee: and the fishes of the sea shall declare unto thee."   *Job 12:7-8*

Character Sketches

From the Pages of Scripture
Illustrated in the World of Nature

VOLUME II

INSTITUTE IN
BASIC YOUTH CONFLICTS, INC.

Printed in U.S.A. by Rand McNally and Company
1978

Printed in the United States of America.

Library of Congress
Catalog Card Number: 76-3050

ISBN 0-916888-02-9

Table of Contents

PART ONE • FLEXIBILITY

SENSING AND ADAPTING TO THE WISHES OF THE ONE I SERVE

CONSERVING MY TIME AND ENERGY TO COMPLETE MY PRIORITIES

REMAINING FREE TO ACCEPT THE BEST COURSE OF ACTION

CHANGING PLANS IF UNEXPECTED CONDITIONS REQUIRE IT

PART TWO • ALERTNESS

PART THREE • AVAILABILITY

PART FOUR • ENDURANCE

PART FIVE • JOYFULNESS

PART SIX • HOSPITALITY

PART SEVEN • GENEROSITY

> "He that is greatest among you shall be your servant. And whosoever shall exalt himself shall be abased; and he that shall humble himself shall be exalted."
>
> *Matthew 23:11, 12*

When the disciples of Jesus Christ disputed among themselves as to who would be the greatest in the Kingdom of Heaven, He said to them, "The kings of the Gentiles exercise lordship over them; and they that exercise authority upon them are called benefactors. But ye shall not be so; but he that is greatest among you, let him be as the younger; and he that is chief, as he that doth serve." (Luke 22:25,26)

Jesus illustrated this principle by washing the feet of His disciples. Then He said, "I have given you an example, that ye should do as I have done to you. Verily, verily, I say unto you, the servant is not greater than his lord." (John 13:15, 16)

A "NEW" APPROACH TO TRUE GREATNESS

LEARNING THE SKILLS OF SERVING

THE NEED FOR GREATNESS

Man's desire for greatness is of God, but few are aware of the price or the procedure which God has established to achieve greatness. Each one of us may describe our striving for it in different ways. One may want to be successful, another may want to be accepted, and still another may want to achieve something that will last. Whatever the description, the desire and need to be great will always exist, and the vast majority will continue to stumble in their efforts to achieve it.

> **GREATNESS IS NOT A GOAL TO BE SOUGHT AFTER BUT A BY-PRODUCT OF LEARNING HOW TO SERVE.**

For example, a man may be acclaimed as a great businessman, but nothing is said if, in the process of achievement, he sacrificed his own family. A woman may be praised as a great achiever, but only passing mention is made of the fact that she destroyed her marriage in the course of reaching her goal. A young man may be honored as a wealthy person, but no reprimand is voiced even though he achieved his wealth by violating moral standards.

It is man's ideal of greatness—not God's—that is being exalted today, but an alert Christian can detect the unhappy by-products that accompany it. Man's view of success overlooks or ignores the tragic pricetag it may require.

> **IN ORDER TO ACHIEVE TRUE GREATNESS, WE MUST FIRST DISCARD OUR OWN IDEAS OF WHAT IT IS.**

GOD'S HALL OF FAME

MEN AND WOMEN WHO ACHIEVED GREATNESS BY SERVING

DANIEL

A great counselor

Daniel's greatness began when he purposed not to defile himself, whatever the cost. His convictions were matched by his faithful prayer life and his faultless service to the king. His enemies found nothing to criticize except his fearless worship of the Lord.

JOSHUA
A great warrior

The evidence that Joshua was a faithful man is shown in his loyal service to Moses for over forty years. The secret of his courageous and successful warfare was the skill which God commanded him to practice consistently. He was to meditate upon God's Word day and night so that he would have good success.

DORCAS
A great friend

Dorcas demonstrated the unique mark of a Christian. She was "zealous unto good works." Her workmanship was of high quality, and the recipients of her service were God's special women—widows. The value of her life was indicated by the great loss felt by those she served when she died.

MAN'S WAY TO GREATNESS	GOD'S WAY TO GREATNESS
A. Focus on power	A. Focus on submission
B. Emphasis on freedom	B. Emphasis on responsibility
C. Concern for gain	C. Concern for giving
D. Desire for immediate fulfillment	D. Desire for lasting achievement
E. Yearning for the praise of men	E. Yearning for the approval of God
F. Aspiration to be served	F. Aspiration for serving others
G. Longing for self-gratification	G. Longing for self-control
H. Need for pushing ahead	H. Need for patience
I. Striving to lead men	I. Striving to follow God
J. Interest in competition	J. Interest in cooperation

SETTING OUR SIGHTS ON TRUE GREATNESS

True greatness requires that we become great in the right areas. This means that we must learn how to be great in faith, great in godly character, great in wisdom, great in self-control, great in patience, great in godliness, great in gentleness, great in love. (II Peter 1:1-10)

The first step is to become great in faith. "Without faith it is impossible to please God, for he that cometh to God must believe that He is (God lives) and that He is a rewarder of them that diligently seek Him." (Hebrews 11:6)

> **FAITH IS VISUALIZING WHAT GOD IS WILLING AND READY TO DO IN AND THROUGH OUR LIVES.**

Every man or woman who achieved a place in God's hall of fame was first and foremost a person of great faith. Faith was not a vague term to them. It was a clear picture of what God intended to do in and through their lives.

Every Christian must learn to walk by faith and not by sight. This means making decisions that are consistent with the ways of God rather than with natural inclinations which are contrary to Scripture. The following ways of God are basic to serving and vital for achieving true greatness:

1. Understanding how God builds character through the birth, death, and fulfillment of a vision

2. Realizing that all power belongs to God and that He carefully loans it to the human authorities whom we serve

3. Serving with a spirit of obedience so that we have a right basis for appealing to our authority

4. Discerning the higher purposes of God when He allows us to suffer under the hand of human authority

UNDERSTANDING HOW GOD BUILDS CHARACTER THROUGH THE BIRTH, DEATH, AND FULFILLMENT OF A VISION

A. BIRTH OF A VISION

Every Christian has the opportunity and responsibility of asking God to reveal the purpose of his life. As we are faithful in serving those whom God has placed over or under us, and as we become concerned for the work and reputation of God, we can expect Him to reveal our purpose and calling.

Nehemiah served the king. When he heard about the disgraceful condition of God's city, Jerusalem, he visualized rebuilding the walls. God worked through the king to assist Nehemiah in achieving this vision.

David visualized building a temple for God. Moses envisioned leading his people out of bondage.

Today a man may visualize a spiritual ministry with other men. A woman may have a concern to teach other women how to love their husband, how to be discreet, how to manage their homes, and how to love their children (Titus 2:4, 5).

NOAH
A great builder

Noah served for 120 years before the flood by obeying God and standing alone. A tribute to his faithful service was his ability to keep his growing family together and protect them from the destruction which God brought upon the wickedness of his day.

DAVID
A great king

The skills for David's success were learned when he made the best use of his time while performing a menial family responsibility. His flexibility was demonstrated when he went from the life of a shepherd to the position of a king's assistant and then back to the role of a shepherd.

11

MOSES

A great deliverer

The turning point for the success of Moses came when he identified with the people of God and chose to suffer affliction with them rather than enjoy the pleasures of sin which last only for a short time.

JOSEPH

A great ruler

The critical test of Joseph's serving came when he was unjustly imprisoned. Even there he continued to make those around him happy and successful. What he learned in prison about deceptive and guilty men was essential for his future leadership position and for bringing his guilty brothers to repentance.

B. DEATH OF A VISION

Our vision is usually a combination of godly concerns and human ideas. Vital Christian character must be developed in us before God can accomplish His vision through us. The value of our vision, however imperfect, is that it remains a motivation to carry us through the death of that vision. Faith is knowing that He will accomplish His vision in His own way and time. Meanwhile, He will build Christ-like character in our lives.

> THE "PRISON" IN WHICH WE FIND OURSELVES DURING THE DEATH OF A VISION WILL BE GOD'S CLASSROOM FOR THE DEVELOPMENT OF CHRIST'S CHARACTER IN US.

The vision of Moses died when he was rejected by his people and forced to flee to the desert for 40 years. Joseph's vision of being a great ruler was destroyed when he was sold by his brothers as a slave into Egypt. A father's vision of becoming a minister might be dashed by his wife and children who do not want him to leave a good business to pursue seminary training.

During this death of a vision, God desires to build the qualities of patience, meekness, self-control, gentleness, faith, purity, and love into our lives.

It is important to remember that Satan is also active during the death of our vision. His greatest deception is persuading us to fulfill God's vision with human effort. Whenever we do this, there are continuing conflicts.

God gave Abraham the vision of becoming the father of a great nation. The death of that vision came when his wife was barren. Rather than waiting for God to fulfill his vision, Sarah and Abraham tried to "help" God by having a son through Sarah's handmaid, Hagar. The result was conflict between Isaac and Ishmael and their descendants.

> WE WILL BE TEMPTED TO FULFILL GOD'S VISION WITH HUMAN EFFORT. IF WE YIELD TO THAT TEMPTATION, WE WILL EXPERIENCE CONTINUING CONSEQUENCES.

Satan may often use those closest to us to "protect" us from the death of a vision. For example, Peter tried to talk Christ out of His crucifixion, but Jesus recognized the true source of his ideas. "Get thee behind me, Satan; for thou savourest not the things that be of God, but the things that be of men." (Mark 8:33)

C. SUPERNATURAL FULFILLMENT OF A VISION

God does not just want to fulfill our vision. He wants to do so with evidence of supernatural power. When those around us know that God fulfilled our vision, we have a life-changing message and the love of Christ motivates our sharing it.

The disciples had a vision of Christ establishing His kingdom. They experienced a death of that vision when He was crucified. But the supernatural fulfillment when Christ was raised from the dead gave them the power to proclaim the Gospel boldly.

God fulfilled the vision of Moses to lead His people out of bondage by supernatural power. God will fulfill the vision of a father who wants to have a spiritual ministry. He will do so as the father learns Christ-like character and becomes more effective than other fathers in meeting the needs of his wife and children.

THE WAY OF GOD IN THE BIRTH, DEATH, AND FULFILLMENT OF A VISION

1	**2**	**3**
BIRTH OF A VISION	DEATH OF A VISION	SUPERNATURAL FULFILLMENT OF A VISION
RELATED SEQUENCE IN I CORINTHIANS 13:13		
"FAITH	HOPE	LOVE"
ILLUSTRATIONS OF SEQUENCE IN CHRIST'S TEACHING		
A grain of wheat contains the potential of becoming many grains of wheat.	The grain of wheat must first die. "Except a grain of wheat fall into the ground and die, it abideth alone." John 12:24	The potential is fulfilled after death. "But if it die, it bringeth forth much fruit." John 12:24

ABRAHAM
A great friend of God

God called Abraham to raise up the foundations of many godly generations. This required great faith and total obedience to God's Word. The test of obedience and faith came when God asked him to sacrifice his most cherished affection. His obedience earned for him a special place in God's hall of fame.

THE SHUNAMMITE WOMAN
A great hostess

The greatness of this woman was revealed as she turned the circumstances of an older husband and no children into freedom to serve others. God richly rewarded her spirit of contentment.

ANNA
A great widow

Her name might be missing from Scripture if she had not used a loss to develop spiritual power. Anna was a young widow who chose to channel her energies into significant Christian service through the house of the Lord.

JAMES
A great apostle

His mark of greatness was illustrated during a church counsel. He waited until everyone else had presented their views. When he finally spoke, he displayed a grasp of Scriptural principles and the ability to apply them. His wise service resolved a difficult conflict and brought harmony to the group.

RECOGNIZING THAT ALL POWER BELONGS TO GOD AND THAT HE CAREFULLY LOANS IT TO THE HUMAN AUTHORITIES WHOM WE SERVE

There will always be a natural resistance to authority and a desire to be our own boss. This independent spirit is the opposite of a servant's heart. Our tendency to reject authority is usually strengthened by a wrong concept of human power.

We assume that power has been claimed by a parent, a husband, a leader, or that it has been given to them by other people. This is wrong. Any power or authority that a man or woman possesses has been given to him or her by God.

> **POWER AND AUTHORITY ARE NOT CLAIMED BY PARENTS, HUSBANDS, AND OTHER LEADERS. NEITHER ARE THEY GIVEN TO THEM BY OTHERS. POWER AND AUTHORITY ARE GIVEN BY GOD.**

Pilate was confused about this fact when Jesus was brought to him for trial. Pilate said, "Knowest thou not that I have power to crucify thee, and have power to release thee?" Jesus answered, "You could have no power at all against me, except it were given to you from above." (John 19:10,11) When Pilate heard this, he sought a way to release Christ (John 19:12).

This fact is further emphasized in Romans 13. "Let every soul be subject unto the higher powers. For there is no power but of God; the powers that be are ordained of God. Whosoever, therefore, resisteth the power, resisteth the ordinance of God; and they that resist shall receive to themselves damnation." (Romans 13:1,2)

When we recognize that God gives power, we also have the faith to visualize His ability to "turn the heart of the king" and remove power from those who misuse it (Proverbs 21:1).

Even more important, we are able to understand the purposes of God through authority which provide motivation for us to learn true character. The character qualities that are essential for greatness cannot be adequately developed without the person being under authority. Even Jesus "though he were a son, yet learned he obedience by the things which he suffered." (Hebrews 5:8)

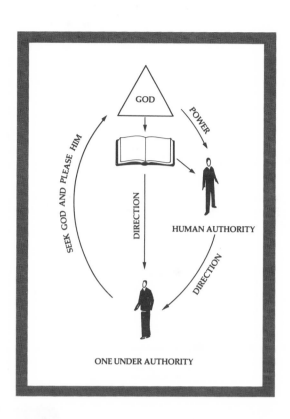

ESTHER

A great queen

The secret of Esther's ability to turn the heart of the king was more than her outward beauty. It was her spirit of submissiveness to whoever's authority she was under. Even in the matter of dress, she allowed the officer in charge to select what she should wear when she was presented to the king.

SERVING WITH A SPIRIT OF OBEDIENCE SO THAT WE HAVE A RIGHT BASIS FOR APPEALING TO OUR AUTHORITY

God gives power to human authorities so that His specific purposes can be carried out through them. The more aware we are of the purposes for which God gives power, the more able we are to appeal to those with that power. His purposes for parents are that they raise their children with Christian training and discipline (Ephesians 6:4). His purposes for a husband are to protect, to provide for, to love, and to sanctify his wife (Ephesians 5:25-28). God gives power and authority to government officials for the praise of those that do well and the punishment of those that do evil (Romans 13:3-6).

The purpose of our appeal should be to encourage and assist them to use their authority properly. We appeal when necessary because we are aware that they must give an account to God for their actions, attitudes, and leadership. They must also give an account to God for us (Hebrews 13:17).

Knowing how to appeal to those in authority is the balance to obedient service. Just as godly character will never be formed without the lessons learned from being under authority, so godly wisdom will not be perfected without learning how to appeal to those in authority.

AQUILA AND PRISCILLA

Great workers

This couple had a gracious ability to include guests in their lives and work. They were so committed and concerned for other Christians that they were willing to lay down their lives for them. Their mobility and hospitality contributed much to the growth of the early Christian church.

15

GOD'S HALL OF SHAME

MEN AND WOMEN WHO FAILED BECAUSE THEY SERVED THEMSELVES

HEROD ANTIPAS
Conquered by lust

Herod was responsible for the death of John the Baptist. He had violated God's marriage laws and was lulled into a spiritual stupor by the seductive dancing of Salome. He strove for greatness according to his natural inclinations. The more he tried to strengthen his own position and kingdom, the more insecure he became. The more he violated God's laws, the more guilt and fear he experienced. His pride prevented him from understanding the freedom that Christ came to bring, and his tortured conscience refused to allow him to enjoy the wrong marriage, temporal power, and earthly possessions to which he so futilely clung.

1. We must be in "right standing"

If we expect our authority to hear our petition, we must be under his authority and in fellowship with his spirit.

2. We must have the right basis for our appeal

The right basis of appealing to our authority involves protecting his reputation, defending his authority, and helping him achieve his stated goals.

3. We must present our appeal at the right time

The right time to present a petition is when our expectations are balanced regarding the outcome, when our authority can concentrate on the petition, and when we are willing to sacrifice for it.

4. We must give accurate information

We must know accurate information about the thoughts, desires, and goals of our authority. We must have accurate information about our own strengths and weaknesses, and we must give accurate information about the petition.

5. We must have the right attitudes

Probably more appeals are rejected because of wrong attitudes than any other reason. We must exhibit genuine love, loyalty, and a servant's spirit.

6. We must use the right words

Extreme care must be taken to select the right words for an appeal. Right words flow naturally from one with a spirit of serving and loving. Right words are gracious words. They are humble words—free from resentment.

7. We must display the right response if our appeal is rejected

The highest test of right attitudes is not when we make our appeal but when our appeal is turned down.

DISCERNING THE HIGHER PURPOSES OF GOD WHEN HE ALLOWS US TO SUFFER UNDER THE HAND OF HUMAN AUTHORITY

There may be times when an appeal is properly made, should be granted but is not. One of the following reasons may account for this:

1. God has hardened the heart of the authority because he has rejected the truth and now believes a lie. After Pharoah continued to resist God's appeal, God hardened his heart (Exodus 14:8). If a man rejects the truth, God will send him a lie (II Thessalonians 2:10, 11).

2. God has purposed to refine our lives through suffering. "If any man suffer as a Christian, let him not be ashamed, but let him glorify God on this behalf." (I Peter 4:16) See also I Peter 4:19.

3. God may want us to suffer in order to give healing or be an example to others. "(God) comforteth us in all our tribulation, that we may be able to comfort (counsel) them who are in any trouble, by the comfort with which we ourselves are comforted of God." (II Corinthians 1:4)

It is in this area of suffering for doing right that true greatness is achieved. Jesus taught His disciples to rejoice when they were persecuted for righteousness sake and be exceedingly glad because "so persecuted they the prophets before you." (Matthew 5:12) In this statement Jesus puts all those who suffer for righteousness sake on the same level as the prophets who are in His hall of fame.

WHEN WE SUFFER FOR SERVING GOD, WE DEMONSTRATE THE MARK OF TRUE GREATNESS AND CAN EXPECT HIS RICHEST REWARDS.

"And whatsoever ye do, do it heartily, as to the Lord, and not unto men; Knowing that of the Lord ye shall receive the reward of the inheritance: for ye serve the Lord Christ. But he that doeth wrong shall receive for the wrong which he hath done: and there is no respect of persons." (Colossians 3:23-25)

A further benefit of suffering for godly service is that it forces us to rethink our values and set our affections only on things above. True greatness comes in seeing God's realities in heaven and then working to bring them about upon this earth. Only as we fill our mind with heavenly truths will we be able to pray with understanding, "Thy will be done in earth, as it is in heaven." (Matthew 6:10)

GOD'S HALL OF SHAME

JEZEBEL
Conquered by greed

Her name is synonymous with wickedness, self-serving, and sensuality. She served her husband, but in so doing turned his heart to do wickedness more than any other king before him. Her service for others was prompted by evil, selfish motives. Her wickedness caused God to remove His power from her and her husband and brought about the destruction of their entire family.

DEMAS
Conquered by pleasure

Demas could have had a great name and a great reward. He served Paul during one of the most crucial times of his ministry, but Demas became weary in well doing and failed to reap the harvest of his labors. Instead, he will always be known as the man who forsook Paul, "having loved this present world." II Timothy 4:10

THE STARTING POINT OF TRUE GREATNESS

The decisions we make in life are based on the ideas we have already accepted. Wrong ideas lead to wrong conclusions. The most important decision that we will ever make involves our relationship with God and His Son, the Lord Jesus Christ. This relationship will affect every other decision we make in life.

The beginning to true greatness is recognizing that "the god of this world hath blinded the minds of them which believe not, lest the light of the glorious gospel of Christ, who is the image of God, should shine unto them." (II Corinthians 4:4) We must recognize and reject Satan's lies that would keep us from accepting and experiencing the living, eternal Son of God within our mind and life.

NICODEMUS

"How can these things be?"

"The natural man receiveth not the things of the Spirit of God: for they are foolishness unto him: neither can he know them, because they are spiritually discerned. But he that is spiritual judgeth all things. . . "
(I Corinthians 2:14,15)

"YE MUST BE BORN AGAIN"

Nicodemus was a religious ruler. He came to Jesus one night and listened as Jesus said to him, "Verily, verily, I say unto thee except a man be born again, he cannot see the kingdom of God. Nicodemus said unto him, How can a man be born when he is old?" (John 3:3, 4) Jesus explained that he was not speaking of a physical rebirth, but a spiritual rebirth. He went on to say to Nicodemus,"God sent not his Son into the world to condemn the world but that the world through him might be saved. He that believeth on him is not condemned; but he that believeth not is condemned already, because he hath not believed in the name of the only begotten Son of God." (John 3:17, 18)

	SATAN'S LIES	GOD'S TRUTH
1.	Man is basically good.	Every person is a sinner by birth and by choice (Romans 3:10, 23).
2.	The "good Lord" overlooks our faults.	The penalty of sin is eternal separation from God (Romans 6:23).
3.	If we try to do right, God will surely let us into heaven.	No man can achieve the perfection God requires to enter heaven (Ephesians 2:8-9).
4.	The pain we go through on earth is God's only judgment for sin.	God demonstrated His love for us by sending His Son to pay the eternal penalty for our sin (John 3:16).
5.	We need to have faith in ourselves.	We need only believe in the Lord Jesus Christ as our personal Savior for salvation (Romans 10:9, 10).
6.	I've always been a Christian.	Only when we put our faith in Christ do we become a genuine Christian (John 3:36).
7.	We can't really be sure of heaven.	We can know now that we have eternal life (Romans 8:16; I John 5:13).

THE FIRST STEP...

To understand spiritual truth is to pause for a moment and ask the Spirit of God to open up our spirit to the following truths from Scripture:

1. "As it is written, There is none righteous, no, not one. . . For all have sinned, and come short of the glory of God."   Romans 3:10, 23

2. "For the wages of sin is death; but the gift of God is eternal life through Jesus Christ our Lord."   Romans 6:23

3. "For God so loved the world, that he gave his only begotten Son, that whosoever believeth in him should not perish, but have everlasting life."   John 3:16

4. "For by grace are ye saved through faith; and that not of yourselves: it is the gift of God: Not of works, lest any man should boast."   Ephesians 2:8, 9

5. "That if thou shalt confess with thy mouth the Lord Jesus, and shalt believe in thine heart that God hath raised him from the dead, thou shalt be saved. For with the heart man believeth unto righteousness; and with the mouth confession is made unto salvation."   Romans 10:9, 10

6. "He that believeth on the Son hath everlasting life; and he that believeth not the Son shall not see life; but the wrath of God abideth on him."   John 3:36

7. "The Spirit itself beareth witness with our spirit, that we are the children of God."   Romans 8:16

"These things have I written unto you that believe on the name of the Son of God; that ye may know that ye have eternal life, and that ye may believe on the name of the Son of God."   I John 5:13

PAUL

"I know in whom I have believed."

Paul was also a religious leader. He zealously persecuted Christians in the early church. He claimed to be "the chief of sinners." One day "the light of the glorious gospel" broke into his heart, and he put his faith and trust in the Lord Jesus Christ for his eternal salvation.

PRAYER TO BE BORN AGAIN

A spiritual rebirth occurs when we "believe in our heart and confess with our mouth" the Lord Jesus Christ as our personal Savior from sin.

"Thank You, God, for loving me, a sinner, and for sending Your Son to pay the penalty of my sin. Right now I put my trust in His death and resurrection for my salvation and receive the eternal life that You offer me through Him. Thank You for hearing this prayer, cleansing all my sin through Christ's blood and accepting me now as Your child. Teach me and direct me through Your Word and Your Spirit to discover Your purpose and will for my life. Amen."

HOW TO USE QUIZ QUESTIONS TO CREATE INTEREST IN SCRIPTURE EVENTS

> If we are to teach the truths that Christ taught, we would do well to use the methods of teaching which He used. Among the more prominent of these methods was the use of curiosity to maintain interest. The following ideas are essential to do this:

1

BE EXCITED ABOUT WHAT YOU ARE GOING TO TEACH

The word *"enthus"* means "of God." A Christian ought to be the most enthusiastic person there is, especially when sharing the eternal truths of God's Word. A sense of enthusiasm will be communicated as we realize that the information to be taught is the most important truth that could be learned. But the true basis of enthusiasm is knowing that the information has already become a vital part of our lives.

2

CREATE INTEREST IN WHAT YOU WANT TO SAY

Scripture uses the example of "breaking up the fallow ground." It illustrates the need to prepare the mind and the heart for the seeds of truth which will be planted in them. This means winning the full attention and interest of the listener.

A. People of all ages usually enjoy demonstrating their knowledge in answering a question. The quiz questions were designed for this purpose. An opening phrase might be **"Let's see if you know the answer to this question."**

B. Emphasize that although the question is not easy, they may know the answer.

C. You may want to illustrate the value of knowing God's Word by offering a prize to the one who gives the right answer. If the prize is one that every listener wants, it will certainly build interest in the quiz question. One possibility would be, **"The first person who gives the right answer will win a dollar."**

D. Pause until everyone is ready to concentrate on the question and the Scripture event to follow. Allow interest to build while you patiently wait for everyone's attention. Arrange for tasks that might be distractions to be taken care of first.

3

CONCENTRATE ON BEING FAIR

Children have a keen ability to sense when someone is being unfair. If they do not sense fairness, they will not only lose interest in the quiz, they will react to it.

A. Become familiar with the question beforehand so that you can clearly and accurately read it. Pronounce each word and read it slowly.

B. Give rules on how the listener should respond before you ask the question. **"If you think you know the right answer, raise your hand, and wait until I call on you."**

C. Be prepared to see who raises his hand first. If you can't watch their response and read the question, too, ask someone else to help you determine whose hand goes up first.

D. Allow an equal opportunity to younger members of the family or to those who don't have as much Bible knowledge by occasionally saying, **"This time let's give the younger members of the family an opportunity to answer first. If they can't answer it, we'll let the rest of the family try."**

WELCOME AND ENCOURAGE EVERY RESPONSE THAT IS GIVEN

The purpose of the quiz is to encourage as much participation as possible. Reaction to an answer will discourage the person and may cause him to feel that you are rejecting him.

A. Think about each answer for a moment or two before indicating whether it is right or wrong. This builds suspense and adds to the interest. It also demonstrates worth to the person and to the thoughts he has given.

B. If a wrong answer is given, don't say, "You're wrong," or "That's a silly answer." Rather say positively, **"That's a good try."**

C. Use gentleness and a kind smile when you must inform a person that his answer is "not quite right."

D. Remember that the questions are general and could possibly fit several different Scriptural events. Usually one situation is the best answer, but this may not always be true. Because of this be ready to say, **"That could possibly fit, but that is not the answer to this question."**

REPEAT THE QUESTION WHEN NECESSARY

If no one guesses the correct answer, which may often be the case, or if there is a long silence, repeat the question. If someone asks you to repeat the question, make sure that you do not overlook those who are waiting to give an answer.

GIVE PROPER WARNING BEFORE ENDING THE QUIZ

After giving sufficient time for each person to answer, prepare to end the quiz. You might do this by saying, **"You have ten seconds left to give the answer."** Make it clear that when you end, the prize can no longer be earned for this quiz.

GIVE PROPER RECOGNITION TO THE WINNER

Show genuine enthusiasm for the one who guesses the right answer. Encourage others to share in his happiness. Give the prize immediately after reading the Scripture event.

DON'T GIVE THE ANSWER IF NO ONE GUESSES IT

Each quiz question has been designed to be difficult for a purpose. If no one answers it, it will be answered in the story. Their interest in the question will carry over to the Scripture event. If the right answer is given, relate it to the Scriptural event. **"Here's the background to that quiz question."**

PAUSE FOR COMMENTS AFTER THE STORY

After you finish reading the Scripture event, be silent for a few moments. This will allow each listener to think about what he has just heard. It will also allow for comments and questions which may prompt significant further discussion.

END ON A HIGH POINT OF INTEREST

Never force a discussion or continue a discussion when the listeners have lost interest. The skill of a good teacher is knowing when to end a discussion. The perfect time is when the listener has something of importance to think about and interest is high enough for them to want to do it again in the future.

HOW WELL DO YOU KNOW THE WAYS OF ANIMALS?

God established the precedent of learning the ways of animals in the account of Adam. God brought each animal to him to be named. In order to do this, Adam had to have thoroughly understood their ways.

MATCH THE FOLLOWING STATEMENTS WITH THE PROPER SPECIES ON THIS PAGE.

A. *Bison*

1. WHICH ANIMAL FINDS ITS WAY BY LISTENING?

Answer: Page 92

B. *Brown-headed Cowbird*

2. WHAT ANIMAL CAN'T TAKE PRESSURE?

Answer: Page 192

C. *Bobcat*

3. WHAT ANIMAL IS SWAYED BY THE CROWD?

Answer: Page 80

D. *Flying Squirrel*

4. WHICH ANIMAL IS PRACTICALLY UNTAMABLE?

Answer: Page 266

E. *Myotis Bat*

5. WHAT ANIMAL FIGHTS WITH ITS FEET?

Answer: Page 330

F. *Kangaroo Rat*

6. WHAT BIRD RELIES ON OTHERS TO RAISE ITS YOUNG?

Answer: Page 130

MATCH THE FOLLOWING STATEMENTS WITH THE
PROPER SPECIES ON THIS PAGE.

7. WHAT BIRD FLIES UNDERWATER?

Answer: Page 254

A. *Timber Wolf*

8. WHICH SPECIES HAS A BUILT-IN
SURGICAL KIT?

Answer: Page 216

B. *Ruby-throated Hummingbird*

9. WHAT ANIMAL WON'T BOTHER
FIGHTING IF IT CAN'T WIN?

Answer: Page 142

C. *Turkey*

10. WHAT BIRD FLIES BACKWARDS?

Answer: 42

D. *Dipper*

11. WHAT BIRD USES ACTING TO PROTECT
ITSELF?

Answer: 54

E. *Massasauga Rattlesnake*

12. WHAT ANIMAL HAS BUILT-IN
POPULATION CONTROL?

Answer: Page 66

F. *Mosquito*

13. WHAT SPECIES HAS EGGS BUT DOESN'T
LAY THEM?

Answer: Page 304

G. *Varying Hare*

H. *Bittern*

14. WHICH BIRD PREPARES FOR FASTING?

Answer: Page 154

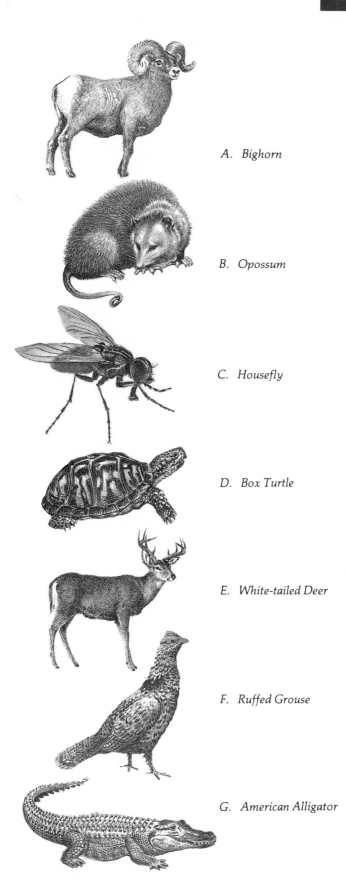

A. *Bighorn*

B. *Opossum*

C. *Housefly*

D. *Box Turtle*

E. *White-tailed Deer*

F. *Ruffed Grouse*

G. *American Alligator*

The wisdom which God gave to Solomon included a thorough understanding of the world of nature. ". . . He spake also of beasts, and of fowl, and of creeping things, and of fishes. And there came of all people to hear the wisdom of Solomon." (I Kings 4:33-34)

MATCH THE FOLLOWING STATEMENTS WITH THE PROPER SPECIES ON THIS PAGE.

15. WHICH SPECIES HAS THOUSANDS OF EYES BUT LIMITED VISION?

Answer: Page 116

16. WHICH SPECIES ASKS ITS YOUNG WHEN THEY ARE READY TO HATCH?

Answer: Page 366

17. WHAT ANIMAL CAN GO WHERE OTHERS CANNOT?

Answer 316

18. WHICH BIRD BUILDS A HOME IN THE SNOW?

Answer: Page 292

19. WHICH ANIMAL HAS A BUILT-IN NURSERY?

Answer: Page 166

20. WHAT SPECIES BOXES ITSELF IN TO GET OUT OF TROUBLE?

Answer: Page 180

21. WHICH ANIMAL HAS NO ODOR AT BIRTH?

Answer: Page 30

God assumes that we know the ways of animals. If we do not, there are many important references in Scripture which will not have significance and practical application for us.

MATCH THE FOLLOWING STATEMENTS WITH THE PROPER SPECIES ON THIS PAGE.

22. WHICH SPECIES FEEDS ITS YOUNG CAFETERIA STYLE?

Answer: Page 342

23. WHICH BIRD DEMONSTRATES THE TRUTH OF THE ADAGE, "THERE IS SAFETY IN NUMBERS?"

Answer: Page 204

24. WHAT BIRD WOULD RATHER WALK THAN FLY?

Answer: Page 104

25. WHAT BIRD ENJOYS SNOW BATHS?

Answer: Page 230

26. WHAT ANIMAL BUILDS ITS NEST ALMOST ANYWHERE?

Answer: Page 280

27. WHAT BIRD USES ITS FEET FOR A NEST?

Answer: Page 354

28. WHAT BIRD HAS ITS OWN MEAT MARKET?

Answer: Page 242

A. *Black-capped Chickadee*

B. *Emperor Penguin*

C. *Sand Wasp*

D. *American Coot*

E. *Shrike*

F. *Deer Mouse*

G. *Ring-necked Pheasant*

Flexibility

"Likewise, ye younger, submit yourselves unto the elder. Yea, all of you be subject one to another, and be clothed with humility: for God resisteth the proud, and giveth grace to the humble. Humble yourselves therefore under the mighty hand of God, that he may exalt you in due time."

I Peter 5:5,6

PART ONE

Flexibility

IS SENSING AND ADAPTING TO THE WISHES OF THE ONE I SERVE

"Servants, obey in all things your (earthly) masters . . . not with eye-service as men-pleasers; but in singleness of heart, fearing God."
Colossians 3:22

LIVING LESSONS ON FLEXIBILITY . . .

FROM THE PAGES OF SCRIPTURE

Persuading others to cooperate with our plans seems to be an inborn talent for most people. Some have developed it to a greater degree than others. The opposite skill does not come so easily—sensing the true wishes of those we serve and concentrating our energies, thoughts, and emotions to accomplish them. If a leader fails to develop this ability in his own life, he will be unable to instill it in the lives of those who follow him. This was the experience of one of the greatest leaders the world has ever known. He accomplished great things for God but might have accomplished even more if he had learned the true meaning of flexibility under a very difficult authority.

ILLUSTRATED IN THE WORLD OF NATURE

WHITE-TAILED DEER   *Odocoileus virginianus*

By the late eighteen hundreds, the white-tailed deer had dropped in numbers from fifty million to near-extinction. Public concern saved the animal, and it is now estimated that more than eight million deer inhabit the United States. In May or June the female has her young. She usually has twins, although a brood of three is not uncommon. Over a ten-year period a female and her offspring are capable of producing as many as 130 animals. Approximately fifty-one percent of all fawns born are male. They grow very rapidly on their mother's milk. The deer's milk, richer than that purchased in the store, contains twice the solids and three times the fat and protein of that of the Jersey cow. On this diet the fawn quadruples its weight in a month. As an adult it weighs between 150 and 300 pounds. In the wild it may have a life-span of ten years.

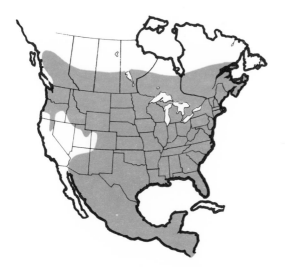

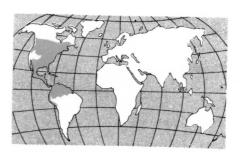

The range and habitat of the white-tailed deer

FLEXIBILITY

HOW DOES THE DEER ILLUSTRATE THE NEED TO ADAPT TO THE WISHES OF THE ONE IT SERVES?

In the east a brilliant glow burst over the treetops. Its fiery light filtered through the leaves, creating dancing silhouettes of shadow on the ground. A doe walked along the forest path on that beautiful June morning.

Normally this graceful creature would have browsed among the tender new shoots of grass. But today was different. The doe wasn't interested in food. When the morning hours passed, she quietly slipped away to a secluded place where she would give birth to a fawn.

This was the first time the two-year-old doe had gone through this experience, so the probability of having more than one fawn was remote. The birth would be over in ten minutes.

Soon it was busily licking the small, white-spotted fawn. Contentment welled up within as it washed the little one. The doe did this so vigorously that the unsteady fawn was knocked off its wobbly feet.

Hungry from the exertion of birth, the fawn began nuzzling its mother's white belly and suckled the warm, nutritious milk. When full, it dropped off to sleep. For the next three days it would remain practically motionless, lying with legs folded underneath its body and neck extended.

During this time of the young fawn's life it is provided with a special protection against enemies. It has no odor to betray its location. A predator could walk right by it, and the infant with its protective coloration would still be safe, if it remained perfectly still.

The doe concealed its young in a secluded spot, returning six or seven times each day to feed it. Thus it ensured that its own scent would not endanger the fawn by attracting enemies.

As the days passed, the fawn grew rapidly. With its growth came an increasing desire to wander. This was a dangerous matter that the mother had to deal with immediately in order to prevent it from becoming a habit. In no uncertain terms, the doe made it very clear to the young fawn that when hidden, it must stay there. Every time it was disobedient, the doe firmly pushed it back down with its muzzle. If firmer measures were needed, the doe would raise her forefoot, place it on the fawn's back, and forcefully press it to the ground. In spite of the mother's stern disciplinary actions, however, the young fawn still continued to wander on occasion.

One day a swallow-tail butterfly caught its eye. The fawn stood up to investigate. Its movement disturbed the insect, and it quickly flew away. As the fawn watched the bright wings flutter out of sight, terror and fright suddenly gripped the creature. There, just a few yards away, stood a hungry coyote on the prowl for food.

It was too late for the mother to intervene. The quick and powerful coyote had caught the movement of the fawn. With a few well-paced strides, the coyote lunged at the defenseless creature. One powerful snap of its jaws, and the fawn was dead.

The little deer had needlessly lost its life because it failed to adapt to the wishes of its mother.

SCRIPTURAL REFERENCES TO THE DEER

"As the hart panteth after the water brooks, so
panteth my soul after thee, O God."
Psalm 42:1

There are two times a deer develops a tremendous thirst for water—when fleeing from danger and when withstanding an opponent in combat. Similarly, we are to develop a spiritual thirst for God's Word by fleeing from youthful lusts and resisting the devil in spiritual combat (II Timothy 2:22; James 4:7).

"My son, if thou be surety for thy friend, if thou hast
stricken thy hand with a stranger . . . deliver thyself
like a roe from the hand of the hunter...."
Proverbs 6:1,5

Deer are very alert to danger, springing to action and remaining hidden while it exists. Surefooted, they leap over seemingly impassable barriers, and their lifted tail signals others of danger.

There are implications for a wise businessman in this verse. One is never to be a cosigner. If you are, take quick, firm action to extricate yourself honorably. Detect and avoid those who seek to gain at the expense of others.

"Rejoice with the wife of thy youth. Let her be as the
loving hind and pleasant roe...."
Proverbs 5:18,19

Tame deer are a study in gracefulness, affection, loyalty, contentedness, good grooming, and bright energy. Every woman would do well to learn these qualities and demonstrate them to her husband.

There are over thirty references to the deer, fallow deer, roe, roe buck, hart, and hind in Scripture.

CHARACTERISTICS AND PHYSICAL FEATURES OF THE WHITE-TAILED DEER

Flexibility in sensing and obeying the wishes of its mother would have saved the fawn's life. The young deer had failed to learn two basic lessons. The first was that it needed to be inconspicuous while the coordination of its legs and muscles was developing. Its weak little legs were no match for the swift coyote, and its only real protection was to learn to be quiet and still. The second lesson that it failed to learn was that it always had to be alert to danger. Chances were, had it seen the coyote first, it could have followed its natural inclination and cautiously dropped to the ground, blending with its surroundings and averting detection. From the birth of the fawn on, the mother is constantly alert to danger and through example will teach its young what it needs to know in order to survive.

WHAT IS ONE OF THE FIRST PRECAUTIONS A MOTHER TAKES AFTER THE FAWN'S BIRTH?

The mother is always alert to the danger of roving predators. In order to protect its young, one of the first precautions the mother takes is that of completely bathing the infant with her tongue. She may eat the placenta in order to eliminate any telltale sign which would betray the deer's presence.

As soon as the fawn is able to walk the doe takes a second precaution. It leads the fawn away to a place of safety. The young deer is able to stand within the first ten minutes of its life; however, it will take about an hour before it can sufficiently coordinate its wobbly legs to follow its mother to a resting place.

For the next three days, the young animal remains practically motionless with its legs tucked underneath its body, its neck stretched out, and its head pressed flat against the ground. Its odorless, spotted body blends inconspicuously with its background.

WHAT IS SIGNIFICANT ABOUT THE FOOTPRINT OF A FAWN?

Coyotes can very quickly pick up the scent of an adult deer long after it has passed by. Interdigital glands are located between the points of the hooves. These glands deposit a waxy secretion which causes the scent of the deer's tracks to be stronger than any other animal. This is not the case with young fawns. Its tracks do not have this scent, and it will not be acquired until the fawn has sufficiently developed its running skills. Because of this, a coyote, even with its keen nose, will not be able to detect the scent.

PROTECTIVE FEATURES
OF THE FAWN

The scent of a young fawn is almost impossible for a coyote to detect.

Protective coloration

Interdigital gland

The fawn's spots resemble shadows on the ground caused by sunlight filtering through leaves.

More than 300 white spots help a fawn blend in with its surroundings.

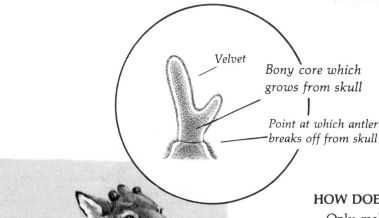

Velvet

Bony core which grows from skull

Point at which antler breaks off from skull

May

June

July

August

September

Pedicel

December to February

HOW DOES AN ANTLER GROW?

Only male deer, or bucks, grow antlers. There have been recorded cases when, due to an overabundance of hormones, a female grew antlers, but this is most unusual. The pedicel is the base from which the antlers grow. First, two little knobs appear on the buck's forehead. The skin becomes soft and velvet-like and starts to swell as calcium deposits form into antlers. Short, bristly, velvet hair covers the antlers while they are growing.

Three complete sets of arteries are needed to supply the rapidly-growing antlers with sufficient nourishment. One set grows on the inside, providing blood to the interior bone. A second arterial system is on the outside of the antler, and a third is in the velvet itself. It is for this reason the deer takes great care not to strike the growing antlers against a hard object as they are very pliable and will readily bleed if damaged.

By August the growth of the antler is completed. A cluster of cells forms at the base and grows outward to block the blood supply. The antler becomes bone hard, and the velvet shrivels and begins to peel off in strips. This peeling causes an itching sensation. To speed up the removal of this "velvet," the buck rubs the hardened antlers on sapling trees and polishes them in preparation for the mating season.

After mating season, between the end of December and February, the buck sheds its antlers. Older bucks drop them in December and younger bucks later—perhaps as late as February. They usually fall off one at a time, breaking off below the bar of the antler leaving the pedicel exposed. There will be very little bleeding, and for three to five days the pedicel will look like a raw sore. In May the process begins again.

Mice and other rodents *gnaw at discarded antlers in order to satisfy their craving for calcium and other materials. The expectant female needs these minerals to develop the tiny frames of its offspring. Left alone, the antlers weather and slowly deteriorate.*

CAN YOU TELL A DEER'S AGE BY THE SIZE OF ITS ANTLERS?

Not really. A young buck will first grow antlers when it is approximately sixteen months of age. The completed antler may have either the appearance of a spike or a small fork. The finest and most magnificent antlers, or "racks," will be grown by the six to seven-year-olds. When deer grow older than this their rack tends to regress.

HOW DO YOU COUNT THE NUMBER OF POINTS ON AN ANTLER?

The main support of the antler is called the beam. From the dorsal surface of the beam points or tines grow and point forward. The largest ones are at the back, and they become progressively smaller towards the front. A growth over one inch is considered a point.

The system to count points varies with locality. A three-point deer in one locality is considered a six-point deer in another, depending whether you count both sides of the rack or just one.

DOES THE WHITE-TAILED DEER USE ITS ANTLERS AS WEAPONS?

The deer will use its antlers as weapons only under extreme stress or in captivity. During the rutting season, the fighting between males is more of a pushing-shoving contest with their heads. Only occasionally will deer use their antlers to try to slash each other.

One weapon which the deer does use quite expertly is its lethal hooves. These are razor sharp and can inflict serious wounds on an enemy. The rattlesnake is one such enemy. The deer will readily leap into the air and pounce on the snake. Even with its poisonous fangs the rattlesnake is no match for the deer. The quickness with which the deer inflicts its blows will kill and tear the rattlesnake to shreds.

Using its tail, *the white-tailed deer will "flag" or signal its companions of danger. The deer also communicates danger by a sharp whistle.*

WHAT SPECIAL FEATURE DOES THE DEER'S EYE HAVE?

The deer has the ability to focus on both nearby and distant objects at the same time. This is of great benefit to the animal in that it allows it to concentrate on what it is eating and at the same time keep a watchful eye out for predators. Because the eyes are set high and spread wide apart, the deer can see almost completely around itself.

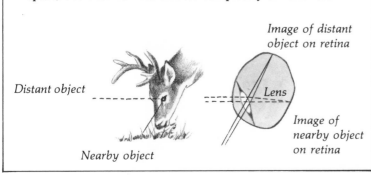

Distant object

Image of distant object on retina

Lens

Image of nearby object on retina

Nearby object

WHAT DOES THE DEER EAT?

The deer's diet is varied although it consists almost entirely of vegetation. It includes such things as mushrooms and goldenrod in the summer and the suckers and twigs of such trees as maple, yellow and white birch, willow, black cherry, juniper, white cedar, aspen, and oak. Deer are very fond of oak acorns and gorge themselves on these nuts in early fall. The white oak acorn is its favorite because it is less bitter than others. The deer gains the largest amount of weight in the shortest amount of time by eating this nut.

HOW DOES THE DEER EAT?

The fawn is weaned from its mother's milk in four months. But much earlier, at about three weeks of age, the young fawn will have begun to browse.

An adult white-tail breaks off twigs and chops up the food with its twenty-four grinding teeth. It chews the food only briefly, moistening it and passing it on to its rumen, a storage compartment. The deer fills up its rumen as quickly as possible and returns to its cover where the process of digestion is completed.

While it rests, it regurgitates the partially digested material in the rumen in the form of little cuds, chewing these for half a minute and then swallowing them again. The material then passes through sixty-five feet of intestine. Digestion and discharge of waste will be complete within a day and a half from the time it is eaten.

WILL THE DEER EAT ANYTHING OTHER THAN VEGETATION?

The white-tailed deer may sometimes be seen fishing in a creek or stream. It will go about this by skillfully pawing at fish, such as trout, until it disables one. It then secures the fish in its mouth, chews and swallows. It is not uncommon for it to eat fish as large as fourteen inches.

The white acorn—*a favorite seasonal food of the deer—must be harvested quickly. The nut sprouts and then rots in a very short time after it has fallen to the ground.*

Acorns

Buck

Doe

Fawn

MESOPOTAMIAN FALLOW DEER
Dama mesopotamica

The fallow deer was an inhabitant of Israel, particularly the forest regions of Galilee and Mount Carmel. Since Bible days its numbers have diminished. The last fallow deer seen was in the late eighteen hundreds. Under Mosaic Law it was considered a clean animal and could be eaten. The flesh was highly esteemed as food, and it was especially good during certain seasons. The buck was at its best from July to October and the doe from November to February.

HOW DOES SCRIPTURE ILLUSTRATE THE NEED TO SENSE THE WISHES OF THE ONE BEING SERVED?

Scripture instructs those who are under authority to adapt to the wishes of the one they serve. Scripture also requires everyone to obey God. The more we learn to obey God, the more we will understand the true purpose and potential of flexibility. **What man in Scripture thought he was fulfilling God's wishes by getting out from under authority?**

(Pause for a response—see page 20)

He is listed with the great men and women in God's hall of fame. He was a man of courage, faith, and conviction—one of the greatest leaders the world has ever known. These facts force us to ponder with dismay the final days of his life.

At that time he spoke to the nation which he had led. He told them that they were a stiff-necked people and warned them never to forget how they had provoked the Lord their God. He pointed out that their rebellion began the very first day they were freed from bondage, and he predicted it would continue in the future.

Immediately following the disappointing message, God told this leader that he would die without leading his people into Canaan because he had rebelled against the Lord.

It has been said that a nation will not rise above the level of its leadership. What was lacking in this man's life that prevented him from inspiring a spirit of obedience and flexibility within those he led?

The answer may be discovered in an event which took place many years before. Early in life, this man turned from riches and honor to serve the Lord. He chose to suffer affliction with the people of God rather than enjoy the pleasures of sin which last only for a season. But in his zeal to serve the Lord, he took matters into his own hands long before the Lord gave him specific steps of action.

As a young man he knew that God had chosen him to lead his people out of bondage, but at that time he was serving the very ruler whose power oppressed them. This young man decided that serving the ruler was not the way to freedom.

One day he took up an offense for a slave who was being beaten. He assumed that this was the time to fulfill the vision of leadership and liberation which had been given him. After killing the taskmaster who had beaten the slave and incurring the wrath of the ruler, he fled from the land. During the years that followed he was out from under that authority and far away from his people who continued to cry out for freedom.

By getting out from under authority he set a tragic precedent. Throughout his leadership they repeated this pattern toward him and toward God. They rebelled against God's provisions and God's laws. There were uprisings against his authority and leadership. The faith of this leader was great enough to lead his people out of bondage but not great enough to lead them into a land of blessing.

How different his example might have been if Moses had remained under Pharaoh's authority until it was God's time for him to leave Egypt. This was the example of Joseph before him and Daniel, Esther, and Nehemiah after him. Moses had great faith but even greater faith is built by adapting to the wishes of those in authority without disobeying God.

From Exodus 1:11-15 and Numbers 20:7-13

Moses may have used the equipment *of an Egyptian scribe when writing the first five books of the Bible. This arrangement served as the Egyptian symbol for the word "scribe."*

An Egyptian building brick *is stamped with the Pharaoh's seal. The wet clay was mixed with pieces of straw for strength.*

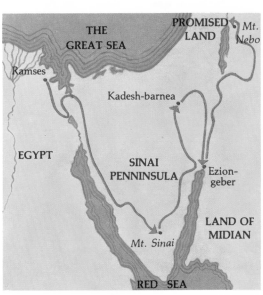

Moses was born in Egypt, *exiled to the wilderness area of Midian, and returned to Egypt at the age of eighty. He led his people out of bondage, to Mt. Sinai, and then to Kadesh-barnea. Because of their disobedience, he led them through the desert for forty more years and was finally buried on Mt. Nebo. Years later he appeared with the Lord on a mountain in the Promised Land.*

MOSES' FLEXIBILITY ALLOWED GOD TO FREE A NATION

The life of Moses can be summarized by a continuing cycle of great vision followed by frustration and finally the Lord's fulfillment of the vision in a miraculous manner.

A RULER WHO FLOATED INTO LEADERSHIP

Moses was born into a country which had banned his own birth. When his mother "saw him that he was a goodly child, she hid him three months." (Exodus 2:2) His mother had been given a vision for her new baby boy. Certainly such an attractive child had not been born merely to be drowned in the Nile River. After three months she recognized the impossibility of concealing him. She prepared a little raft for him to float on the river, realizing that—apart from a miracle—she would never see him again. Then, through a miraculous circumstance of timing, the mother's vision for her son was revived. Pharaoh's daughter found the weeping babe, adopted him as her son, and hired Moses' mother to nurse him.

A VISION GIVEN BY GOD

Moses grew to manhood as an Egyptian prince, and when he was forty years old, the Lord gave him a vision. He desired justice for his people—the mistreated Hebrew slaves. When he saw an Egyptian beat a Hebrew, he murdered the Egyptian in a rage of vengeance. When Pharaoh heard of the incident, Moses was forced to flee to the desert to escape death. His vision of helping his people was quickly extinguished. He spent the next forty years as a shepherd in the wilderness of Midian.

One day the Lord Himself appeared to Moses, rekindling his vision for his people. The Lord spoke, "I am come down to deliver them out of the hand of the Egyptians, and to bring them up out of that land unto a large and good land, unto a land flowing with milk and honey." (Exodus 3:8) This was more than Moses had ever imagined.

A STUBBORN PHARAOH REFUSES TO COOPERATE

Filled with fear and doubt, he presented the idea to the elders of Israel. "The people believed; and when they heard that the Lord had visited the children of Israel, and that he had looked upon their affliction, then they bowed their heads and worshiped." (Exodus 4:31) Moses' excitement was short-lived. After an appeal to Pharaoh, his request to let the Hebrews leave was denied and their workload doubled. His own people began to turn against him.

A miraculous series of ten judgments upon the Egyptians convinced Pharaoh to give the Hebrews permission to leave. They had been generously given gifts by the Egyptian people. It seemed as if they were finally going to be delivered. After only a few days of travel, the vision of escape was once again dimmed. Pharaoh changed his mind and sent his army after them in hot pursuit.

GOD USES A FLEXIBLE MAN AND A WOODEN ROD TO FREE A NATION

Now the Israelites were trapped by mountains, desert, Egyptians, and water. In their moment of despair the Lord commanded Moses, "Lift thou up thy rod, and stretch out thine hand over the sea, and divide it; and the children of Israel shall go on dry ground through the midst of the sea." (Exodus 14:16) The next morning, the Hebrews were safe on the Sinai Peninsula, and the Egyptian army had been drowned in the sea.

Although Moses was not allowed to lead his people into the Promised Land, he died in full view of the land as the respected leader of a free people. The Lord had used him to deliver the children of Israel out of bondage and into freedom. Moses' great vision had been fulfilled by the Lord.

MOSES CHARACTER SKETCH

WHY DID MOSES RISK HIS POSITION AND LIFE FOR A HEBREW SLAVE?

Scripture records that Moses was born into a home where faith in the Lord was still alive. "By faith Moses, when he was born, was hid three months by his parents, because they saw that he was a proper child, and they were not afraid of the king's commandment." (Hebrews 11:23) When Moses was found in the river, his sister Miriam volunteered to find a Hebrew woman to nurse him for the Pharaoh's daughter. That woman, of course, was his own mother; and Moses lived in safety in his parents' home until he was weaned. In those two or three formative years Moses' young spirit was directed toward the Lord. His parents' prayers followed him to Pharaoh's palace, and his faith continued to grow. "By faith Moses, when he was come to years, refused to be called the son of Pharaoh's daughter, choosing rather to suffer affliction with the people of God than to enjoy the pleasures of sin for a season." (Hebrews 11:24,25) His parents feared the Lord more than they feared Pharaoh, and so did their son, Moses.

HOW DID THE LORD ADAPT MOSES FOR HIS MISSION?

The Lord knows our frame and knows what His chosen servants need. For Moses it was an environment of soft beds, rich food, and loose morals in a palace utterly devoid of helpful spiritual influences. He experienced the life Egypt had to offer and discovered its emptiness. When the multitude wished to return to the delicacies of Egypt, Moses was not tempted.

In spite of this environment, Moses learned important skills. He was "learned in all the wisdom of the Egyptians, and was mighty in words and in deeds." (Acts 7:22) His curriculum involved military science, useful in his mission of organizing a group of slaves into an army. It also included writing skills, necessary for his task of authoring the first five books of the Bible.

Years in the desert of Midian taught Moses to serve his sheep, his family, and his father-in-law. Here he learned to quiet his heart in communion with the Lord. He also learned the skills of a nomadic desert dweller which would be employed when he led two million people in the Sinai Peninsula for forty years. His intellect was sharpened in Egypt; his spirit was sharpened in Midian. He was now ready for his task after eighty years of training.

DID MOSES COMPLETELY FULFILL THE WISHES OF THE GOD HE SERVED?

Moses' life ended in personal disappointment. Although he successfully led the children of Israel out of the slavery of Egypt, the Lord had forbidden him to enter the Promised Land. Although he pleaded three times for a reversal, the Lord said, "Speak no more unto me of this matter." (Deuteronomy 3:26) More than a thousand years later, however, even this desire was miraculously granted. On the Mount of Transfiguration two men talked with Jesus whose glory had been briefly unveiled. One was Elijah, and the other was Moses. They "spoke of his decease which he should accomplish at Jerusalem." (Luke 9:31) Moses had been divinely escorted into the Promised Land at last. He was one of the first to know about the Lord's marvelous plan of redemption through the death, burial, and resurrection of Jesus. Moses, who had led the Israelites out of Egypt's bondage, now knew how the Lord Jesus would lead others out of the bondage of sin.

"And the Lord said, I have surely seen the affliction of my people who are in Egypt, and have heard their cry by reason of their taskmasters; for I know their sorrows; and I am come down to deliver them out of the hand of the Egyptians, and to bring them up out of that land unto a large and good land, unto a land flowing with milk and honey."

MOSES
mō′zĕz

39

Flexibility

IS CONSERVING MY TIME AND ENERGY TO COMPLETE MY PRIORITIES

"And that ye study to be quiet, and to do your own business, and to work with your own hands, as we commanded you."

I Thessalonians 4:11

LIVING LESSONS ON FLEXIBILITY . . .

FROM THE PAGES OF SCRIPTURE

The highest praise that can be given to one who serves is that he accomplished a task with the same efficiency and quality as the one who assigned it would have. When a servant proves his ability in executing jobs of lesser importance, he becomes more and more valuable to the one he serves. One of the greatest servants described in Scripture was a man who was entrusted with a most difficult and important task. He had proven himself in years of faithful service, and God honored him in this crowning achievement by guiding him to accomplish it. This account demonstrates the importance of conserving our time and energy in order to complete our priorities.

ILLUSTRATED IN THE WORLD OF NATURE

RUBY-THROATED HUMMINGBIRD   *Archilochus colubris*

Confined to the western hemisphere, the hummingbird was virtually unknown in Europe before the voyage of Columbus. The hummingbird family (*Trochilidae*) consists of some 320 species and has the distinction of having as one of its members the smallest species of bird in the world. Of these species only one, the ruby-throated hummingbird, inhabits the eastern two-thirds of the United States. This three and one-half inch bird weighs about as much as a copper penny. The ruby-throated hummingbird has an exceptionally long migration. Its powerful little wings carry it as far north as Canada and as far south as Central America.

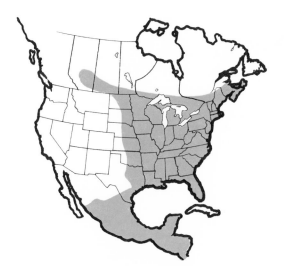

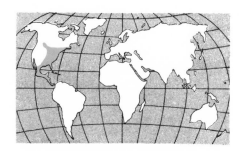

The range and habitat of the ruby-throated hummingbird

FLEXIBILITY

HOW DOES THE HUMMINGBIRD ILLUSTRATE FLEXIBILITY BY CONSERVING ITS TIME AND ENERGY TO COMPLETE PRIORITIES?

It was twilight. All the daytime birds were settled, resting in their perches for the night. All the birds rested, that is, except one, the smallest of them all—the tiny ruby-throated hummingbird. It was busily flitting from flower to flower, trying to get every last bit of food before the light was gone and it would be forced to stop.

Weeks earlier the hummingbird would have gathered this food for the purpose of sustaining itself through the night. But now its motivation was different. It was more determined. The hummingbird was about to undertake a major task which, if it wasted its resources, would prove disastrous.

Twice each year the ruby-throated hummingbird travels from southern Canada to as far south as Panama. The distance is long, but the bird can make most of it with relative ease. Along the way the voyager has many feeding stations which give it the needed strength to continue.

Gram for gram, the hummingbird has the greatest energy output of any known warm-blooded animal. The reason this tiny bird burns up so much energy is because of its very small size. Just as a teaspoon of hot water loses heat faster than a kettle of hot water, so a tiny body such as a hummingbird's will lose heat faster than a larger body. Because of this rapid heat loss the hummingbird must burn proportionately larger amounts of energy in order to keep warm.

As the bird darted from flower to flower gleaning nectar and insects, it felt the coolness of the evening. The temperature was dropping rapidly. In the morning it was going to undertake the most dangerous leg of the migration. Tomorrow's flight pattern was five hundred miles over treacherous

gulf water to Mexico. If the hummingbird ran out of fuel, it would drop into the sea and perish. There could be no turning back.

Extra energy was required for the hummingbird to maintain its body temperature during this cool night. Darkness would confine it to a perch, prohibiting it from gathering any more food. The bird had stored a certain amount of fat to serve as fuel, but if the trip were to be successful, it could not afford to take the chance of using any of the reserve now.

Although this could be a serious problem, the flexible little hummer would not let this hurdle interfere with the priority of reaching its destination. The tiny traveler would regulate its energies by a simple but effective means. It would do something very unusual for a bird. The hummer would hibernate for the night.

The bird permitted its body to go into a torpid condition. By doing so, only one-fifth to one-sixth the amount of fuel that normally would have been needed to maintain the warmth of its body was used. In this torpid condition the hummingbird became motionless—so much so that one could actually touch the bird and it would not move.

The little bird passed the night hours in this condition. In the morning when the sun rose, its warm rays penetrated the body of the little creature and the bird slowly began to stir. Soon it was back among the flowers sucking nectar and capturing small insects in final preparation for the journey.

The trip would be successful. This three and one-half inch, feathered creature had regulated its energies to allow it to accomplish the remarkable feat of flying five hundred long miles—non stop.

SCRIPTURAL REFERENCES TO THE HUMMINGBIRD

Although there are no references which specifically mention the hummingbird, there are verses which have indirect application to this creature.

"Our soul is escaped like a bird out of the snare of the fowlers...." Psalm 124:7

A bird's life is endangered by nets which are lifted into the air. Because the hummingbird is so small it is able to escape from nets which would trap larger birds. God uses the example of how large we are in our own eyes to indicate our vulnerability to the snare and destruction of pride. King Solomon was honored with wisdom when he saw himself as "but a little child." (I Kings 3:7) God chose Saul when he was little in his own sight (I Samuel 15:17).

"O that I had wings like a dove! For then would I fly away, and be at rest. Lo, then would I wander far off, and remain in the wilderness. Selah. I would hasten my escape from the windy storm and tempest."
Psalm 55:6-8

The hummingbird conserves its strength for long flights in two ways—first by taking a unique rest prior to the flight and then by making every motion count in flight. God promised to crown the efforts of the Jew with success if he entered into the rest of the Sabbath (Isaiah 58:13,14) and made the best use of each of the remaining six days (Exodus 20:9).

CHARACTERISTICS AND PHYSICAL FEATURES OF THE RUBY-THROATED HUMMINGBIRD

The flexibility which the ruby-throated hummingbird employed to conserve its energies enabled it to survive and complete a rigorous task. Unfortunately, this little creature hasn't always been so successful. In the early 19th century, the hummingbird and other members of its family were a mark of high fashion. Women sought them for jewelry and decorative ornaments for their hats. The demand was so great that during one year a London firm imported more than 400,000 skins from the West Indies. Over a period of years, millions of hummingbirds were killed. Many species have never been seen since.

HOW WAS THE HUMMINGBIRD USED AS AN ORNAMENT?

The glittering feathers of the hummingbird produce intense metallic shades of green, blue, ruby, and violet. These skins made striking accents on apparel. The gem-like feathers are usually on the gorget or the crown of the bird. The male is more elaborately adorned than the female.

IS THE HUMMINGBIRD A CREATURE OF HABIT?

Yes. When the hummingbird arrives from its migration, it carefully selects a perch which it vigorously protects. The hummingbird becomes so accustomed to this perch that if something causes it to break off, the bird has a very hard time adjusting. The little hummer just cannot believe that this has happened. Refusing to believe the perch has been lost, the little hummer will make as many as one hundred attempts to land at the spot where the perch used to be.

HOW DID THE FAMILY GET A NAME LIKE TROCHILIDAE?

It is really very appropriate. The name comes from the Greek word meaning "a bird." The hummingbird is a prime specimen with its beautiful feathers, sleek form, and skillful ability in flight. No other bird can duplicate the same feats in the air. The hummingbird can fly forward, backward, upside-down, and straight up like a helicopter. In fact, it can even remain suspended in the air. In flight the wings move so fast, that only their misty outline can be seen.

One of the features *that distinguishes the male ruby-throated hummingbird from the female is its ruby-colored gorget.*

MOVEMENTS OF THE
RUBY-THROATED HUMMINGBIRD

Forward motion

Hovering motion

Backward motion

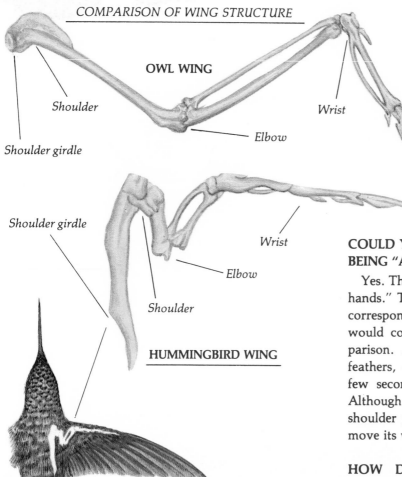

OWL WING

Shoulder

Shoulder girdle

Elbow

Wrist

Shoulder girdle

Wrist

Elbow

Shoulder

HUMMINGBIRD WING

Primary feathers

Secondary feathers

The muscles that move the hummingbird's wings are unusually large and well-developed. These muscles account for approximately 25 to 30 percent of the bird's total weight. The muscles which lift the wings—elevator muscles—are half as heavy as the depressor muscles.

There is no other bird as adept in the air as the hummingbird. The hummingbird is limited, though, in its ability to soar on motionless wings. This ability is reserved for owls and other large birds.

COULD YOU THINK OF THE HUMMINGBIRD AS BEING "ALL HANDS"?

Yes. The wings of the hummingbird are practically "all hands." That part of the wing's structure which would correspond to our arm is quite small. The part which would correspond to our hand is very large in comparison. Attached to the "hand" are ten large flight feathers, otherwise known as primaries. The relatively few secondary feathers are attached to the forearm. Although the wrist and elbow are rather rigid, the shoulder joint is so flexible that the hummingbird can move its wing in all directions.

HOW DOES THE HUMMINGBIRD CONSERVE ENERGY IN FLIGHT?

The hummingbird is extremely coordinated in flight. Ordinarily a bird will achieve lift only on the downward stroke of its wing. The upward stroke does virtually nothing to aid lift. The hummingbird, on the other hand, is able to use both the upward stroke and the downward stroke to gain momentum. By altering the angle of the wing, it can achieve both lift and propulsion. In other words, the agile hummingbird needs to work only half as hard as a normal bird in flight.

DOES A HUMMINGBIRD HAVE TO SLOW DOWN BEFORE IT STOPS?

No. The hummingbird can approach its perch at full speed, abruptly stop, and start up again as quickly as it stopped. The hummer starts flying before leaving the perch and it is practically at full speed the instant it is in the air.

The hummingbird can produce both lift and propulsion with the upstroke and downstroke motion of its wings

HOW MUCH FOOD DOES A HUMMINGBIRD EAT IN ONE DAY?

The daily food requirements of the hummingbird are somewhere between two and four grams. If a man were to match this on a pound for pound, gram for gram basis, he would have to eat approximately 300 pounds of food each day. The hummingbird needs this amount of food in order to meet the energy requirements of its daily activities. This inquisitive little bird is always on the move. Its exploratory spirit aids it in discovering new food sources.

DOES THE HUMMINGBIRD JUST EAT NECTAR?

No. The hummingbird would not survive if it lived on nectar alone. It must balance its diet with protein by eating insects such as gnats and mosquitoes.

One method of supplementing its diet is by looking out for swarms of insects, dashing through and scooping them up as it flies. The hummingbird is usually careful to pursue only those insects which it can eat whole. It does not care to tear them up and eat them piecemeal as is characteristic of some other insect-eating birds.

WHY IS THE HUMMINGBIRD'S TONGUE FRINGED?

Some thought it was caused by wear and tear from sticking it in and out of flowers. But the real purpose for this fringed effect is to allow the bird to stretch its long, slender tongue into flowers and sweep out insects which were attracted to the flower by the scent.

HOW LONG IS THE BILL OF THE BIRD?

The hummingbird's bill varies from species to species. The bill of the ruby-throat is about one-fifth of the total body length.

The bill serves many functions. It directs the tongue in reaching into crevices to draw out nectar. The female uses her bill like a needle when she constructs the nest. The hummer has gained a reputation for being a pugnacious little bird, and it will also use its bill as a threatening weapon to drive intruders away from its territory.

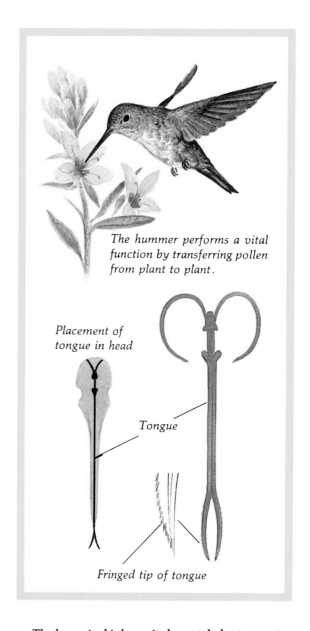

The hummer performs a vital function by transferring pollen from plant to plant.

Placement of tongue in head

Tongue

Fringed tip of tongue

The hummingbird uses its long, tubular tongue *to draw up nectar. The slender bill protects the tongue and aids the hummer in reaching into hard-to-get-at places for food.*

At 15-minute intervals the female thrusts the full length of her long bill down the throats of her young, regurgitating food for them.

The egg—shown at its actual size—produces a baby hummingbird no larger than a bumblebee.

The hummingbird—very protective of its territory—chases a song sparrow. These tenacious little birds have even been known to drive away a golden eagle.

HOW DOES THE HUMMINGBIRD HANDLE LARGE INSECTS?

It doesn't, and many times they handle the hummingbird. Accounts have been recorded of insects such as the praying mantis and dragonfly capturing the hummingbird. The mantis will quietly wait for insects to come and feed at flowers, and sometimes the unsuspecting hummingbird becomes the victim of its jaw-like clamps. Dragonflys have also been known to pursue and capture hummingbirds which have crossed into their territory.

The hummingbird has some other unusual enemies. The frog is one, and even fish are able to jump out of the water and successfully catch one of these low-flying birds. Thistle plants may also impale the delicate, little creature on their needle-like thorns.

ARE SPIDERS A FRIEND OR FOE OF THE HUMMINGBIRD?

They can be both. Sometimes the hummingbird unknowingly flies into the network of a spider's web. Of course, in order to entrap the bird, the web would have to be that of a large spider, and it would also have to be very well-constructed. Cases have been recorded, though, of it happening. While the hummingbird tries to escape, the spider injects it with its poison, waits for it to die, and entombs it with the silky threads. On the other hand, a spider web can also be a benefit to the hummingbird. The female uses large amounts of spider web to glue together various materials for its nest.

WHAT BUILT-IN FEATURE DOES THE NEST HAVE TO PROTECT THE EGGS?

The rim of the nest is constructed so it curves inward. Because of this feature, the two eggs are less apt to be shaken out. The female constructs a nest the size of half a walnut. The bulk of the nest is composed of bud scales. These scales are covered with lichen and tufts of green moss then cemented to the nest with the cobweb material.

HOW TO ATTRACT HUMMINGBIRDS

You can provide yourself with hours of entertainment by purchasing an inexpensive feeder and filling it with a solution of sugar water. The little hummer can detect when there is not enough sugar, and if the solution is too weak it will avoid the feeder. A recommended solution is one part sugar to eight parts water. Honey is not a good substitute because it has been discovered that this tends to promote the growth of a fungus harmful to the bird. This sweetened solution will only be a supplement to the diet of the hummer. The bird will need to balance this supply with the protein of insects.

HOW DOES SCRIPTURE ILLUSTRATE FLEXIBILITY BY CONSERVING TIME AND ENERGY TO COMPLETE PRIORITIES?

Jesus taught that even a cup of cold water given in His name would receive its reward. Where in Scripture did the gift of a drink of cool water result in a great reward?

(Pause for a response—see page 20)

The trusted assistant of the richest man in the country was summoned by the one he served. He listened intently as his kindly employer poured out his heart and gave him his most difficult assignment.

This wise, diligent servant was not a man accustomed to defeat, but this unusual task posed the very real prospect of failure. Carefully and respectfully he summarized his concerns, and one by one his alert questions were answered. Then he was sent on his way.

To understand the difficulty of his mission, we must realize that one of the most important decisions that any man will ever make is discerning the right life partner. An even more difficult task would be to choose a partner for someone else. Such was the responsibilty given to this servant. He was to choose a bride for his master's son.

After many years of working with people he had learned to discern vital character qualities. He now devised a plan to detect them in a young lady, and then he submitted his plan to the Lord. No sooner had he done this than a beautiful girl walked to the well by which he rested and fulfilled the very requirements of his test. At his request she offered him a drink of the water she had just drawn. Then she volunteered to draw water for his ten thirsty camels also.

He gave her a valuable reward of costly jewelry and asked if he could meet her parents. At her home he was invited to sit down for a meal, but he graciously declined and stated that he would not eat until he had finished his task.

He explained how God had answered his prayer and had also blessed the life of the one he served. He asked permission of the girl's parents and brother for her to become the bride of his master's son, heir to all the family wealth.

But the mother and brother made one request. "Let her stay here a few days, at least ten, and then let her go." He emphasized the importance of quickly completing the task that had been assigned to him so that he could fulfill the priority of the one he was serving. The parents asked the girl what her wishes were, and she agreed to go at once.

In this final request Abraham's servant was called upon to be flexible, but he knew that flexibility is only a desirable quality if it does not hinder completing the tasks and priorities which have been assigned.

From Genesis 24

"**And when she had done giving him drink,** she said, I will draw water for thy camels also, until they have done drinking. And she hastened, and emptied her pitcher into the trough, and ran again unto the well to draw water, and drew for all his camels."

"**And it came to pass,** as the camels had done drinking, that the man took a golden ring of half a shekel weight, and two bracelets for her hands of ten shekels weight of gold."

"And Rebekah lifted up her eyes, and when she saw Isaac, she lighted off the camel... and the servant had said, It is my master: therefore she took a veil, and covered herself."

BY CONSERVING TIME AND ENERGY, A SERVANT WAS USED TO SHAPE A NATION

The immediate cause of Abraham's desire to obtain a wife for his son, Isaac, is given in Genesis 24:1, "Now Abraham was old, and well stricken in age." Abraham was now 140 years old; his wife, Sarah, had died about three years before, and their only son, Isaac, was forty and as yet unmarried.

CHOOSING THE MOTHER OF A NATION

The last half of Abraham's life had centered around God's promise to bless the world through a descendant of his son, Isaac (Genesis 12:3; 17:19). Now in his old age, he felt both the urgency and the responsibility to select a wife for his son who would be worthy of being the mother of the Lord's people.

A SERVANT IS CALLED TO DO THE JOB

Abraham felt that the best wife for his son was to be found in the family of his brother in Mesopotamia. He refused, however, to let Isaac himself go and choose his wife. He knew his son well and may have felt that Isaac would be pressured into remaining in Mesopotamia instead of returning to the land the Lord had promised them. To avoid this risk, he sent his most trusted servant instead and made him swear that he would never bring Isaac into the land of Mesopotamia (Genesis 24:6).

A TRUE TEST OF LOYALTY

The name of Abraham's servant is not mentioned. All we know is that he was the "eldest servant of his house, that ruled over all that he had." (Genesis 24:2) A very strong possibility is that this servant is Eliezer, previously mentioned as the heir of Abraham's household (Genesis 15:2,3). If that is the case, Eliezer would then have been at least sixty or seventy years old and no doubt the senior servant as well. If this servant was indeed Eliezer, it is a tribute to his character that Abraham chose him for such a task. It was Isaac who had displaced him from his possible inheritance; now he was choosing a wife for him.

A THREE-FOLD MISSION

The servant began his assignment in complete dependence on the Lord (Genesis 24:12). His priorities were clear. His first responsibility was to worship the Lord. "And the man bowed down his head, and worshipped the Lord." (Genesis 24:26) His second concern was for his master, Abraham. "And he said, Blessed be the Lord God of my master, Abraham, who hath not left destitute my master of his mercy and his truth." (Genesis 24:27a) His third concern was for his own success in serving the Lord and his master. "I being in the way, the Lord led me to the house of my master's brethren." (Genesis 24:27b)

When the servant returned, having successfully completed his mission, he told Isaac all the things that he had done (Genesis 24:66). No words of commendation are recorded, but we can only imagine that Abraham's response was similar to the words the Lord will say to his faithful servants: "Well done, thou good and faithful servant; thou hast been faithful over a few things, I will make thee ruler over many things. Enter thou into the joy of thy lord." (Matthew 25:21)

ABRAHAM'S SERVANT CHARACTER SKETCH

WHY WAS THE SUCCESS OF ABRAHAM'S SERVANT SO IMPORTANT?

Abraham was concerned that his son not marry a Canaanite (Genesis 24:3). He knew that if he were to die, Isaac might be tempted to marry into one of the influential Canaanite families. That would be conducive to peace, social standing, and acceptance in a strange land. But as a man of faith, Abraham was more concerned about the spiritual prosperity of his descendants than their material and social prosperity. He wanted a wife for Isaac who would not corrupt their children with the ungodly beliefs and practices of the Canaanites. He wanted a wife who would support her husband in the worship of the Lord and teach her children the knowledge of the Lord. Abraham felt that the best wife for his son would be found among his own family in Mesopotamia where they had not entirely lost the knowledge of the true God (cf. Genesis 24:50). This strong conviction of Abraham was later expressed in national law (Deuteronomy 7:3). The reason is given, "For they will turn away thy son from following me, that they may serve other gods." (Deuteronomy 7:4)

WHY DID ABRAHAM'S SERVANT DEVISE SUCH A DIFFICULT TEST TO DISCOVER ISAAC'S APPOINTED WIFE?

It was not unusual for a girl to offer a drink of fresh water to a stranger after a long journey. But to offer to quench the thirst of ten camels was unusual indeed. As many as twenty gallons of water can be consumed by one camel in a drinking session. If the camels had been watered only the night before, they still could have easily consumed at least fifty gallons. This was no small task for a young girl.

However, the servant's test was neither spectacular nor arbitrary. It was designed to bring to light the very qualities that would best complement his master's son, Isaac—hospitality to a weary traveler, alertness to the needs of the animals, generosity and ambition in giving of herself, endurance in completing the task, joyfulness if she did the job cheerfully, and flexibility in changing from what she was doing.

WHY WAS ABRAHAM'S SERVANT SO ANXIOUS TO COMPLETE HIS ASSIGNMENT?

At two different times, the servant expressed urgency in accomplishing his task. When food was set before him he said, "I will not eat, until I have told my errand." (Genesis 24:33) Later, when asked to stay a little longer he replied, "Hinder me not, seeing the Lord hath prospered my way; send me away that I may go to my master." (Genesis 24:56)

His eagerness to return immediately is surprising under the circumstances. The trip from southern Canaan to Haran was about 500 miles. A team of freight camels averages 28 miles per day without difficulty. Hence, the trip would have taken between two and three weeks. The men were undoubtedly tired and would have normally welcomed a ten-day rest before returning. The servant knew the concern this delay would have caused Abraham and Isaac who knew the exact traveling time of the trip to Haran. A ten-day delay would have caused them unnecessary anxiety for the safety and success of their servant. Such concern may have prompted the prayer and meditation in which Isaac was involved when his servant returned (Genesis 24:63). The faithful servant had put his personal conveniences second to his master's priorities—a genuine expression of selfless love.

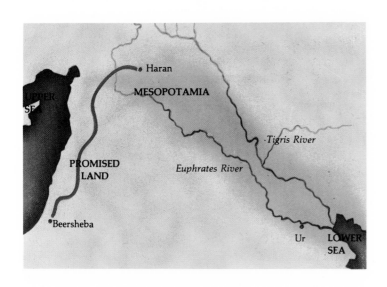

"And the servant told **Isaac** *all things that he had done.*"

ABRAHAM'S SERVANT

51

Flexibility

IS REMAINING FREE TO ACCEPT THE BEST COURSE OF ACTION

"O Lord, I know that the way of man is not in himself: it is not in man that walketh to direct his steps."

Jeremiah 10:23

"A man's heart deviseth his way: but the Lord directeth his steps."

Proverbs 16:9

LIVING LESSONS ON FLEXIBILITY . . .

FROM THE PAGES OF SCRIPTURE

The reality of God and the value of spiritual objectives seem hollow in a family that experiences continual conflict. In such a family it is all too easy for a son or a daughter to despise their family and spiritual heritage, and temptations may be strong to sacrifice future potential on the altar of momentary pleasure. Scripture records the tragic account of a young man who despised the opportunities that were his by birth and disclaimed a priceless heritage. Too late he realized the value of what he had lost and discovered that he was no longer in a position to pursue the best course of action.

ILLUSTRATED IN THE WORLD OF NATURE

AMERICAN BITTERN *Botaurus lentiginosus*

The American bittern joins with the heron family to form the *Ciconiiformes* order. In the days of Henry VII, the bittern native to Europe was highly esteemed for the flavor of its meat. Typical of other members of this family, the American bittern lives near both fresh and saltwater marshes. Because it is a solitary bird and rarely seen, many thought that it was a nocturnal feeder, but probably the only nocturnal habit it has is its migratory flight. The bird migrates in the spring between mid-March and April and in the fall between September and October. From the tip of its bill to the tip of its tail the bittern achieves a length of 27 inches and has a wingspread of 39 inches.

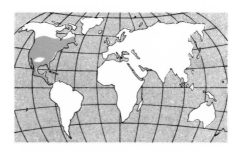

The range and habitat of the American bittern

FLEXIBILITY

HOW DOES THE BITTERN ILLUSTRATE FLEXIBILITY BY BEING FREE TO ACCEPT THE BEST COURSE OF ACTION?

It was a perfect spring day. All the senses verified it. The dampness of recently melted snow intensified the pleasant aroma of budding cottonwoods. Frogs proclaimed spring as their noisy croaking called to potential mates. The voice of a male red-winged blackbird competed for a hearing as it announced to the world the boundaries of newly-established territory.

Tender new shoots had popped up among the weathered remnants of last year's cattails. Excitement filled the air. Nature was preparing to bring forth new life.

This was the spot that a female bittern had chosen to build her nest. Last year she had raised her young in the swamp, and she was once again anticipating the same success.

She had already gathered an assortment of dried reeds and constructed a well-concealed nest one foot in diameter and a few inches high. In addition to the secluded site of the nest she had taken another precaution to ensure secrecy. She had constructed two paths—one for entering and the other for exiting. The parent birds would never fly directly to the nest itself. Instead they landed at the end of the entrance path and walked in. Similarly, the birds left the nest by walking out to the end of the exit path and then flying away.

A feeling of contentment rushed over the bittern on that beautiful spring morning. There, in the center of her nest, lay a single egg. This was the first; she would probably lay four more. But as she stood there, her contentment suddenly turned to fear and anxiety. Her preoccupation with the nest had allowed the approach of a red fox to go unnoticed. The fox was drawing dangerously close as it prowled the marsh in hope of securing an easy meal.

Any course of action would have to be executed quickly. The bittern had three choices. She could slip down the exit path and fly away. She could stand her ground and try to fight off the intruder. Her bill was a lethal weapon, extremely sharp, and could be wielded with deadly accuracy. There was a third option. Although it would seem unlikely to succeed, this was the course she chose. Pointing her bill upward, she froze. In an amazing camouflage, the light and dark stripes which cloaked her throat and breast allowed the bird to blend perfectly against the reeds.

Then the breeze stirred, and the reeds slowly began to sway in the wind. The bittern played its role to the fullest. Gently, she too, began to sway. Her whole body participated in the disguise. From the bill to the legs, each part moved to produce a sway that defied detection from the movement of the surrounding cattails.

The prowler looked in the direction of the bittern. The wind was blowing the wrong way for the fox to detect the scent of the bird and because the bittern had executed the part so well, it remained undetected. The predator moved on. By taking a few preliminary steps the bittern was flexible and free to choose the best course of action to protect her nest from the fox.

SCRIPTURAL REFERENCES TO THE BITTERN

"I will also make it (Babylon) a possession for the bittern*, and pools of water...." Isaiah 14:23

The bittern is a very shy bird which lives in quiet and solitude away from civilization. This prophecy was made when Babylon was a thriving metropolis at the height of its glory. God's judgment fell upon the city, and it became a lonely desolation. Its wreckage covered an area of over one hundred and fifty square miles. The ruins contained many pools of water which provided an ideal nesting place for the bittern.

Spiritually, Babylon symbolizes the corruption of those who oppose God's ways (Revelation 17:5,6). Like Babylon, the ways of immorality appear to prosper, but the pleasures of sin last only for a season. Afterward, they are replaced by the loneliness of separation from vital human relationships and from God.

*Some authorities translate the word *kippod* as hedgehog or porcupine rather than bittern; however, the characteristics of all three fit the prophecy. Other references are: Isaiah 34:11 and Zephaniah 2:14.

An easy way to remember the voice of the male bittern is to think of the sound made when a stake is driven into the ground.

CHARACTERISTICS AND PHYSICAL FEATURES OF THE AMERICAN BITTERN

The flexibility of being in a position to choose the best course of action enabled the bittern to elude danger and remain concealed; however, this long-legged bird isn't always content to stay secluded. In fact, in the early spring of the year the male goes to great lengths in order to tell the females its location.

WHY IS THE BITTERN REFERRED TO AS THE STAKE DRIVER?

The bittern's voice has been likened to the sound made when a stake is driven into the ground. During mating season, from February to June, the male bittern lays claim to its territory and notifies females of its location. The bird accomplishes this by the unusual sound which it makes. When the bittern serenades, its song can hardly be called musical, but one would have to admit it is unique! *Oong-ka-choonk--oong-ka-choonk--oong-ka-choonk!* Other local names which have been given to the bird are thunder-pumper, mire drum, and bog bull—to name just a few.

HOW DOES THE BITTERN PROJECT ITS VOICE?

Only the male bittern produces this unique sound by inhaling large quantities of air and then exhaling in explosive bursts. The bird lowers and raises its head when inhaling. Then with convulsive jerks it opens its mouth and throws its head forward, simultaneously exhaling the air. The bittern's voice carries well and may be heard over a mile away.

ISN'T THE BITTERN AFRAID OF LETTING ITS ENEMIES KNOW WHERE IT IS?

Not really. It is hard to gauge the distance and exact location of the bittern from its sound. It is interesting that the intensity of sound seems no louder when the bird is nearby than when it is quite a distance away. As the distance between the bittern and the listener increases, each set of syllables becomes indistinguishable as they blur together, giving the effect of a single note.

Do you know why it will be very hard for this fox to find the bittern?

WHAT DOES THE BITTERN DO WITH ITS NECK WHEN IT FLIES?

Like other species of the order *Ciconiiformes*, the bittern has a rather long neck. When flying, it compacts its neck by folding it back into a tight "S" shape. The long neck feathers of the bittern tend to cover the "S" and give the neck a shorter appearance. This practice allows an observer in the field to distinguish quickly between a bittern and a crane. Although the crane's neck is also long, it stretches it straight out when it flies.

IS THE BITTERN SAFE IN THE AIR?

When danger approaches and the bittern takes to the air, it lifts awkwardly off the ground, dangling its feet as it goes. The bird has strong, steady wing beats, but its flight is so slow that it makes an easy target for predators or sharpshooters.

IS THE BITTERN A GOOD MOTHER?

Young bitterns have many enemies. Some of the more common ones are hawks, owls, mink, raccoons, and water snakes. The mother is very aware of these dangers and always keeps a watchful eye on her young. When danger approaches, the bittern is quick to defend. She may try to bluff the enemy by arching her wings and bristling her feathers, elevating them in such a way that she has the appearance of being twice her normal size. If forced to fight, the bittern aims for the eyes of its enemy. With its lethal weapon, the bill, it makes vigorous, swift blows in an attempt to disable its opponent.

With its shorter *wingspan the bittern is able to produce stronger and quicker wingbeats than the heron. The long legs of these birds trail behind and function as rudders.*

The bittern bristling its feathers in order to appear more formidable

HOW DOES A PARENT BITTERN DECIDE WHICH OF ITS YOUNG TO FEED FIRST?

She doesn't. The young decide for her. When the female returns to the nest, the young jump at her beak until one succeeds in grasping it. As the little beak holds on at a right angle to the base of its mother's beak, a stimulus is triggered and the mother's neck goes into jerking, muscular convulsions. She lowers her head and neck on the nest for several seconds. As a result, food is regurgitated and transferred into the open mouth of the young bird. The process is then repeated by the rest of the young.

WHAT DOES THE BITTERN'S DIET CONSIST OF?

Bitterns are entirely carnivorous; they eat no vegetation. They are gluttonous and will eat just about any kind of animal matter they can find in the meadows and marshes of their home. Some of the basic items on their menu are insects, fish, frogs, crayfish, and mice.

WHAT IS ONE OF THE MOST VALUABLE SKILLS THAT THE BITTERN USES TO SECURE FOOD?

Patience. The bittern spends most of its time just waiting for its prey to come within reach. Then it suddenly darts out and captures the victim with its spear-like bill. When the bird does walk about in the marsh, it raises and replaces each foot so slowly and carefully that the movement is noiseless and almost imperceptible.

The bittern patiently waits *for a fish to swim within reach and, with amazing accuracy, impales it on its sharp, spear-like beak.*

Because the bittern is not equipped to tear its prey, *it catches only those fish that it can eat whole.*

AN UNUSUAL DELICACY

A bittern stood motionless, watching with great interest the large, painted turtle which sunned itself in the middle of the road—or so it appeared to the casual eye. The bittern stood among the tall grasses and weeds, its bill pointed upward in characteristic manner.

The bittern wasn't interested in the turtle, but it was interested in what the turtle was doing. The bird had waited for quite some time for the turtle to finish its task.

The painted turtle had left the security of a nearby lake and journeyed there to lay its eggs. She had just laid the last of the soft, leathery-shelled white eggs and was in the process of covering them so that the sun would do what she could not—incubate the eggs. When the turtle finished, she waited for a while and walked to the edge of the lake, never to return to her eggs.

The bittern marked the spot well and cautiously walked to the center of the road. Using its sharp beak, it easily probed the loose dirt, and was soon feasting on the eggs of the painted turtle—a rare delicacy for the bittern.

Least bittern

American bittern

GROOMING UTENSILS

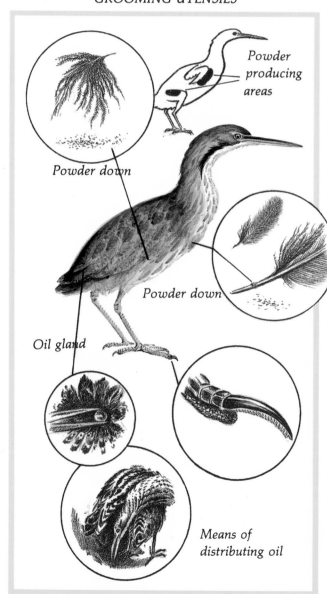

Powder producing areas

Powder down

Powder down

Oil gland

Means of distributing oil

Of the two North American species, *the least bittern is the smaller—half the size of the American bittern. This smaller bird concentrates more on insects, amphibians, and crustaceans and eats less fish than its larger relative.*

WHY DOES A BITTERN NEED TO GROOM ITSELF?

A considerable portion of the bittern's diet consists of fish. Although the bittern tries to be careful, it invariably soils its feathers with the fish's protective slime. To alleviate the problem, the bittern employs an elaborate procedure to clean and revitalize its feathers.

HOW DOES THE BITTERN COPE WITH DIRT AND GREASE?

The bittern is equipped with certain utensils and supplies which enable it to stay clean even though it has such a messy menu. It follows a definite procedure, and when it is finished the bird really sparkles.

The first step is to determine the soiled areas. Usually the head and neck are the worst. The bittern begins by rubbing special feathers located at the side of its breast which contain powder down. The bird completely covers its dirty feathers with this powder. Once the areas are covered, the powder absorbs moisture, collecting and disintegrating slime and mud. When the powder dries, it begins to flake off.

The bittern then uses another tool to remove whatever powder remains. Located on its middle toenail is a fine-toothed comb. The bird runs this comb through its feathers, freeing them of the dried powder.

After the feathers are cleaned and dried in this manner, the bittern reaches back, raises its tail vertically, and locates its oil gland. It dips its beak into the oil supply and then rubs this oil on the cleaned areas. When the bittern has completed the procedure, each feather is immaculate. The whole operation takes about two hours.

IS THERE MUCH DIFFERENCE IN APPEARANCE BETWEEN THE MALE AND FEMALE BITTERNS?

No. Their appearance is the same. The seasons cause very little change in adult plumage. In the spring the feathers appear to be slightly grayer on top and paler beneath than they are in the fall.

HOW DOES SCRIPTURE ILLUSTRATE THE NEED TO REMAIN FREE TO ACCEPT THE BEST COURSE OF ACTION?

The secret wish of many adults is expressed in the statement, "If only I had it to do over again." They are usually referring to a decision or an event that cannot be undone which has had continuing consequences. Who in Scripture wept bitter tears when he realized a decision—one which seemed unimportant when he made it—was unchangeable?

(Pause for a response—see page 20)

Only hunters understand the compelling drive that forces them to stay on the trail, and no one but this particular hunter could understand why a kill was so important on this occasion. He had been stalking his prey for several days without success. Every trick he had learned in years of hunting had failed, but the excitement of the hunt urged him on.

He had not been conscious of the great amount of energy he had used. Over each hill and beyond each thicket lay the possibility of the game he prized. That prize would replenish his strength and fulfill his real purpose.

The unspoken objective that relentlessly drove him on was the goal of maintaining his reputation as a skilled hunter in the eyes of his father. He desired his approval more than the father realized. More painful than hot days, cold nights, an empty stomach, and an exhausted body was the prospect of returning home empty-handed.

But on this occasion he had long since passed the point of caring about game. The skillful hunter of venison had become the victim of exhaustion, hunger, and a burning sun. He desired only to return for food and rest. When he finally reached his destination, he was met by the tantalizing aroma of red pottage.

The memory of his brother's specialty made his mouth water. He came in, dropped to the ground and said, "Please give me some of that red pottage." His brother seized this moment of weakness. He had been waiting for an opportunity and quickly demanded, "Sell me this day your birthright."

As the oldest son, this hunter had received certain spiritual opportunities and responsibilities in the family. This was his spiritual birthright, but where had God been when he needed Him on the hunt? His failure in the field would bring his father's disappointment and disapproval. What did a birthright matter now?

"I am at the point to die and what profit shall this birthright do me?" So he sold it to his brother. He was given a meal of bread and pottage of lentils in return. After eating his meal he went away, despising the birthright he had sold.

Years later he realized the great value of that birthright, and he wept bitter tears in front of his father, hoping to regain what he had lost. But his decision was irreversible. He had exchanged his rich heritage for a bowl of red pottage.

Why had it been easy for him to sell cheaply what was priceless? The reasons may be found in relationships within his own family. His father loved him for his hunting abilities, not his spiritual achievements. His approval and fellowship centered around tasting his son's venison rather than delighting in his son's spiritual refreshment. His mother showed favoritism toward his younger brother. Thus he was not especially close to her and missed the benefit of her spiritual insight. His brother cheapened the birthright by equating its value to a mess of pottage. By selling his birthright Esau violated the very secret of what made him successful as a hunter— maintaining a position that would allow him to choose the best course of action.

From Genesis 25:27-34

WRONG VALUES PREVENTED ESAU FROM CHOOSING THE BEST COURSE OF ACTION

The character of Esau is something of an enigma. His grandfather was Abraham; his grandmother was Sarah—both of whom are praised for their faith in the Lord (Hebrews 11:8-19). His father, Isaac, is also commended for his faith (Hebrews 11:20). His mother, Rebecca, was likewise a woman who discerned spiritual things and worshiped the Lord (Genesis 24:56-60; 25:22, 23).

FAVORED BY HIS FATHER—REJECTED BY GOD

Esau was a favorite of his father. He was an athlete of a man, a skilled hunter whose arrow never missed its mark. He was the pride and joy of Isaac, providing him with venison and other delicacies. After comparing Esau to his scheming and deceptive brother, Jacob, we are surprised to read Scripture's severe condemnation of him. "Was not Esau Jacob's brother? saith the Lord; yet I loved Jacob, and I hated Esau." (Malachi 1:2, 3) Again we read in the New Testament that Esau was a "profane person." (Hebrews 12:16)

TWO BROTHERS—TWO NATIONS

The first clue to Esau's character is given while he was still in the womb of his mother. When Rebecca conceived after twenty years of barrenness and felt unusual movements in her womb, she inquired of the Lord. She learned that she was to give birth to two nations and that one nation would be stronger than the other. She learned that the greater, or older, son would eventually serve the lesser, or younger (Genesis 25:23; Romans 9:12).

In Rebecca's zeal to help the Lord fulfill this prediction, she began her deceitful scheming. She probably instigated Jacob's theft of Esau's birthright. When she heard Isaac planning to give the family blessing to Esau, she resorted to deception in her effort to obtain the blessing for Jacob.

A PREDICTION FULFILLED BY DECEIT

We know that Rebecca loved Jacob (Genesis 25:28), but why would she blatantly deceive her own husband to seize the blessing for him? To understand this, it is necessary to understand the significance of the family blessing in patriarchal times. The head of the family was considered both its king and its priest. He made the final decisions in civil matters and led in the worship of the Lord. He was entrusted with the family's physical welfare as chief and with its spiritual welfare as priest.

The birthright was the right of the firstborn son. He also had the right to sell it, if he so desired. Under later Mosaic Law, this involved a double portion of the inheritance (Deuteronomy 21:17). The blessing was not a mere material right dependent on the order of birth but was of a more spiritual nature. Functioning in his role as priest, the patriarch would blend benediction and prediction when he gave the final blessing as he was taught by God's Spirit. He was, in effect, announcing his spiritual successor. Rebecca, aware of the unique nature of Isaac's blessing in light of God's promises to Abraham, desired this promise to be fulfilled through her younger son, Jacob.

Having agreed to his mother's plan, Jacob successfully deceived his father who pronounced the blessing on him. When Isaac realized that he had been tricked, he trembled in shock but refused to alter his words. He recognized that Jacob was the one through whom the blessing was to pass. As priest, he could only utter the words the Lord had given him (cf. Hebrews 11:20).

THE LOVE OF GOD EXCHANGED FOR THE LOVE OF MAN

We are tempted to feel sorry for Esau, having been duped by both his mother and brother. But we must not refuse to agree with the Lord's evaluation of this man "who for one morsel of meat sold his birthright." (Hebrews 12:16) Esau was a good man according to the standards of the ungodly Canaanites whose company he enjoyed, but he had rejected the better way of his fathers. He was more interested in the world he could hear, see, smell, touch, and taste than a world he could not see, "a city which hath foundations, whose builder and maker is God." (Hebrews 11:10) Unlike his fathers, he did not "desire a better country, that is, an heavenly." (Hebrews 11:16) Esau exchanged the love of God for the temporal love of men and women (Romans 9:13).

"Now therefore take, I pray thee, thy **weapons,** *thy quiver and thy bow, and go out to the field, and take me some venison.*"

"**And she put the skins of the kids of the goats upon his hands,** *and upon the smooth of his neck.*"

ESAU CHARACTER SKETCH

HOW DID ESAU DISQUALIFY HIMSELF FOR THE POSITION OF BLESSING?

The son who received the blessing would be heir to the promises given to Abraham. Not only would his descendants be "as the stars of the heaven, and as the sand which is upon the seashore" (Genesis 22:17), but they would also inherit the land of Canaan (Genesis 15:18). In the tradition of Abraham, Rebekah was concerned that these promised descendants would have God-fearing parents to teach them (Genesis 24:3,4). Esau had already married two Hittite women "who were a grief of mind unto Isaac and Rebekah" (Genesis 26:34,35). Esau had no regard for the promises of God. He had sold his birthright for a meal. He thought he had nothing to lose since his father was only a stranger in a foreign land. Jacob, on the other hand, believed the promises and knew that some day the Lord would give all of the land in which they lived to their descendants. Esau was not spiritually fit to become the family's spiritual heir.

WHY DIDN'T REBEKAH GO TO HER HUSBAND WITH HER CONCERN?

The most likely explanation is that she did not feel it would do any good. It is possible that Rebekah had lost respect for her husband's spiritual leadership. This may have begun when Isaac lied to the Philistines, claiming that she was his sister rather than his wife (Genesis 26:7). She was no doubt disappointed with his leadership when he allowed Esau to marry the ungodly Hittite women who would teach their children their abominable religious beliefs and practices. And even though the faithless Esau had despised his birthright, he remained Isaac's favorite son. The reason for this preference was based not on Esau's character, but on Esau's ability to supply him with his favorite food (Genesis 25:28). She forgot that the Lord had not appointed her to be priest of the family, and she wrongfully decided to usurp her husband's role as spiritual leader. Her lack of respect for Isaac's role may have cheapened its importance in Esau's eyes as well.

WHAT WERE THE CONSEQUENCES OF ESAU'S FAILURE TO CHOOSE THE BEST COURSE OF ACTION?

Because Esau was not interested in inheriting the land which the Lord had promised to Abraham and then to Isaac, the Lord allowed him to lose the blessing which accompanied it (cf. Genesis 26:3, 4). Esau forfeited any claim to the land of Canaan and had to settle in the nearby land of Edom, located to the southeast. Edom is a rugged, inhospitable, and mountainous country with only a few cultivable areas. The Lord said concerning Esau that he "laid his mountains and his heritage waste for the jackals of the wilderness." (Malachi 1:3) His descendants were destined to live by the sword and serve the descendants of Jacob. The only consolation was that they would have periods of freedom (Genesis 27:40). And so it was; the historical relation of Edom to Israel assumed the form of a continual cycle of servitude, revolt, and reconquest. After a long period of independence, the Edomites were defeated by Saul and enslaved by David. They revolted under Solomon and again under Joram and were later subdued by Amaziah. Not until the reign of Ahaz did they shake their yoke off completely. But the Edomites were eventually conquered again, compelled to submit to circumcision, and incorporated into the Jewish state.

INHERITANCE
OF JACOB

INHERITANCE
OF ESAU

ESAU
ē'sô

63

Flexibility

IS CHANGING PLANS IF UNEXPECTED CONDITIONS REQUIRE IT

"Be (anxious) for nothing; but in everything by prayer and supplication with thanksgiving let your requests be made known unto God. And the peace of God, which passeth all understanding, shall keep your hearts and minds through Christ Jesus."

Philippians 4:6,7

LIVING LESSONS ON FLEXIBILITY . . .

FROM THE PAGES OF SCRIPTURE

A son will often try to be strong where his father was weak; but if he is bitter, his attitudes or actions will become just like his his father's. Bitterness is the result of not recognizing the hand of God working through our enemies. A twenty-five year old king tried to be strong where his father was weak, but there was bitterness in his heart. This man viewed the enemies of his father as independent agents. They were actually individuals whom God stirred up to reprove his father who had rejected the Word and counsel of the Lord. This bitterness decreased his ability to see God's power and program and forced him to rely on his own strength. The tragic result was an inability to be flexible when conditions required it.

ILLUSTRATED IN THE WORLD OF NATURE

VARYING HARE   *Lepus americanus*

Regulated by a seven to ten-year population cycle, the numbers of the varying hare fluctuate from scarcity to abundance. This solitary, secretive animal makes its home in brushy woodlands and heavy forests of mixed conifers and hardwoods. Except for the female's slightly longer length, the male and female are identical in appearance. They average eighteen inches in length and attain a weight of three to four pounds. The animal's most common name is snowshoe rabbit; however, it has been given other names in different localities such as brush rabbit, northern hare, snow rabbit, or swamp jack rabbit.

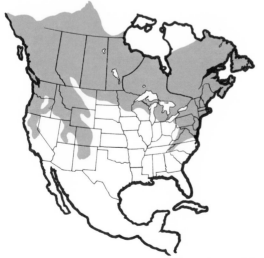

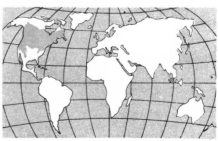

The range and habitat of the varying hare

FLEXIBILITY

HOW DOES THE VARYING HARE ILLUSTRATE FLEXIBILITY IN RESPONDING TO UNEXPECTED CONDITIONS?

Only survival was on the mind of a young snowshoe rabbit. This doe was one of last year's offspring, and now she prepared to bear young of her own. She could feel life within her but was uneasy. Nothing seemed right and she had the terrible sense that disaster lay ahead.

The winter had been long and cold. Only half of the normal amount of snow had fallen that year. The previous summer and fall had been the driest in recorded history. The drought caused dangerously low water levels in swamps, hindering new growth and threatening existing plant life. Snow was desperately needed to replenish the water supply for spring growth.

These harsh conditions and the lack of food had taken their toll among the hare population. Many were starving and others became too weak to escape the teeth of the bobcat or the sharp talons of the snowy owl.

The snowshoe rabbits depended on tender twigs and needles of the pine, white cedar, spruce and tamarack trees for their winter food supply. The shortage created intense competition among the hare and forced them to girdle the trees, stripping them of the bark and shoots within their reach.

The doe was aware that soon she would not only have to provide for herself but for her young as well. Her loss of weight was evident by her gaunt appearance. The harsh winter conditions had stripped her of needed food reserves within her body. Chances were that her young wouldn't survive under these conditions. There was also the possibility that she herself would die in the process of giving birth. There just wasn't enough food to prepare her for this undertaking.

The fact that she was not physically prepared to produce this, her first family, and the stress of securing food had triggered a process deep within her body. The three-week old embryos stopped growing. Her body responded to her condition of physical weakness with a process called resorption. The mother completely reabsorbed the embryos within her own system.

Now she was free to concentrate on replenishing her needed strength and wait until environmental conditions were favorable to allow her to raise strong, healthy young. The snowshoe rabbit had been provided with the flexibility to cope with the changing, unexpected conditions of her environment to ensure that she would bear healthy young and would have the strength to care for them.

SCRIPTURAL REFERENCES TO THE HARE

"Nevertheless these ye shall not eat of them that chew the cud, or of them that divide the cloven hoof: the camel, and the hare, and the coney; for they chew the cud, but divide not the hoof; therefore they are unclean unto you." Deuteronomy 14:7

God divided animals into two groups—clean and unclean. The division existed long before the Law was given to Moses. Noah was told to take seven pairs of clean beasts and birds and only two pairs of unclean beasts and birds into the ark (Genesis 7:2, 3).

Although man has not yet discovered all the reasons why unclean animals are not to be eaten, one study has revealed that more energy is required to digest the meat of a hare than is gained by eating it. Thus the expression, "starving to death on rabbit."

"And the hare, because he cheweth the cud, but divideth not the hoof; he is unclean unto you." Leviticus 11:6

The accuracy of Scripture has been questioned by some because their observations did not reveal that the hare chewed the cud as stated in the verse above. One acclaimed expert wrote, "Moses further stated that they (the hare) did, however, chew the cud. Anatomical analysis of the hare reveals that they do not re-chew their food. But Moses' error was a very natural one, for they gave the appearance of rumination with their constant moving of the jaws."

Further research has revealed that the hare does indeed redigest its food as the Bible states. (See page 72.)

CHARACTERISTICS AND PHYSICAL FEATURES OF THE VARYING HARE

The flexibility of the varying hare to respond to unexpected conditions of its environment also characterizes the cottontail rabbit. The hare and rabbit belong to the same order, Lagomorpha, and appear to be similar; however, there are definite distinctions which separate the two.

WHAT IS THE DIFFERENCE BETWEEN A HARE AND A RABBIT?

The most noticeable difference between the adult hare and rabbit is the hare's longer ears and larger hind legs and feet in proportion to its body size. At birth the distinctions between the two are even greater. Young hare are born with their eyes open. They are well-furred and capable of walking and hopping just hours after birth. Young rabbits, on the other hand, are born blind, naked, and helpless.

WHAT IS A BABY HARE CALLED?

Young hares are called leverets. This name comes from a French word which means a hare in its first year. A baby rabbit, on the other hand, is called a kit or kitten.

HOW MUCH DOES A LEVERET WEIGH AT BIRTH?

This furry little ball weighs about two and one-half ounces.

HOW PARTICULAR IS THE SNOWSHOE RABBIT ABOUT ITS NEST?

After a gestation period of thirty-six days the female has from two to six young. She is not particular about the construction of the nest itself; however, she is quite concerned about its location. She usually chooses a site with a slight elevation, enabling her to view her surroundings and allowing drainage to keep the bed dry. She tries to pick a spot with overhanging branches for additional protection. Here the weight of her resting body makes a small depression in the ground. This is called the "form."

At one time hare were included *in the order of rodents; however, rabbits and hares have six incisor teeth and rodents have only four. This extra pair of chisel-like incisors is small and round, located directly behind the upper set. Although they neither have a cutting edge nor particular value to the animal, these extra teeth are sufficient basis for scientists to place the hare in a separate order—the lagamorpha.*

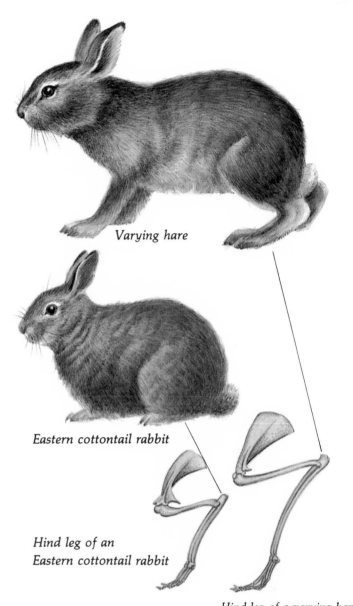

Varying hare

Eastern cottontail rabbit

Hind leg of an
Eastern cottontail rabbit

Hind leg of a varying hare

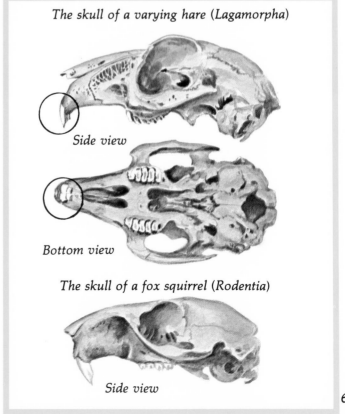

The skull of a varying hare (Lagamorpha)

Side view

Bottom view

The skull of a fox squirrel (Rodentia)

Side view

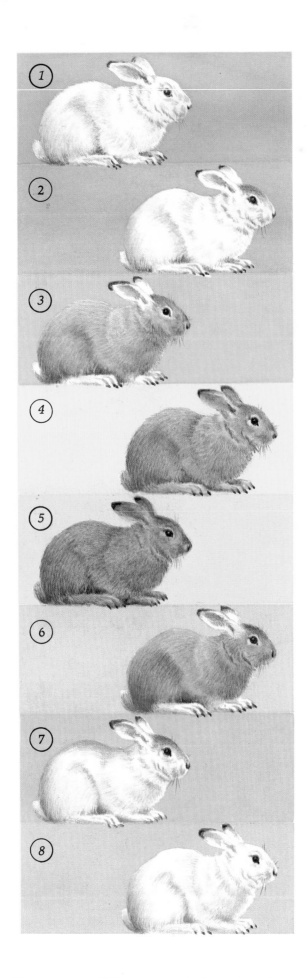

WHY IS THE ANIMAL CALLED A VARYING HARE?

Twice a year the snowshoe rabbit's fur or pelage changes color. It varies from dark brown in the summertime to white in the winter. During these times of the year the fur is either completely brown or completely white except for black fur on the ear tips.

DOES WEATHER CAUSE THE FUR TO CHANGE COLOR?

No. The variation is not due to weather, and for that matter the hair does not actually change color but rather molts, replacing old hair with new.

In late winter the stimulus of the longer day's extra light period is transmitted through the eye. This stimulus causes the pituitary gland to produce certain hormones. They in turn activate the reproductive organs and stimulate the shedding of winter's white hair and the growth of summer's brown hair.

The whole process can be artificially stimulated by either increasing or decreasing the daily photo period with an electric light bulb. That is, by gradually increasing or decreasing the hare's exposure to light for a few hours each day, one can trigger the molt.

IS THERE A PATTERN TO THE COLOR CHANGE?

There is a definite pattern. In the autumn the first evidence of change is seen in the feet. Next, the ears and side of the nose change. The color spreads to the front of the head, then to the rump, flanks, and finally to the back. In springtime the order of color change is reversed when the hare takes on its brown pelage.

WHAT DOES A SNOWSHOE HAVE THAT MOST WOMEN WOULD LIKE?

Stay-put hair. The snowshoe rabbit's fur is very fine and soft; however, the makeup of the hair is such that it resists the action of the wind, and therefore the animal always has a neat appearance.

IS THE SNOWSHOE RABBIT'S FUR VALUABLE?

Because the fur doesn't wear well it does not have high commercial value. The fur is very brittle and the hide is weak; however, it does have qualities which make it distinctive.

When used as clothing the fur allows ventilation so the wearer does not perspire even when active. It is also very light in weight. A third quality that the Indians particularly appreciated is that it makes unusually warm blankets. It took approximately 130 skins cut into strips, stretched, and woven together to make one blanket. The chickadee also appreciates the fur's soft quality. It uses discarded tufts in its nest to cradle its eggs and young.

The snowshoe rabbit's sequence of color variation *by season: 1 - winter; 2,3,4 - late winter and spring; 5 - summer; 6,7 - middle to late fall; 8 - winter*

WHAT IS THE HARE'S MAJOR DEFENSE?

Its speed. At the approach of danger the hare quickly disappears into thick vegetation. Depending on the powerful hind legs to generate speed, and relying on the forelegs to support the front end of its body, the animal has the ability to burst from a relaxed position into an instant run. Familiar with the terrain, it usually travels a well-used path, adeptly maneuvering through the thick underbrush in places most of its enemies cannot reach. It is able to clear eight to twelve feet in a single bound. At times it leaps into the air as it is running to critique its present situation.

DOES THE SNOWSHOE RABBIT REALLY HAVE SNOWSHOES?

It doesn't have snowshoes as we commonly picture them, but it does have very wide feet which accomplish the same purpose. The bottoms of its feet are padded with rectangular hairs which give traction. It is able to spread its long toes wide apart and outdistance its enemy by maneuvering over deep snow without sinking.

WHICH IS MOST IMPORTANT TO THE HARE—EYES, EARS OR NOSE?

The most important and most acute of the snowshoe's senses is that of hearing. By maneuvering its long ears the hare can detect faint noises and accurately determine the source of sound. For protection, the hare's ears are the most vital.

The nose of the hare is also sensitive and plays an important part in its survival. The hare intensively sniffs the air and all objects, especially those with which it is unfamiliar. It depends upon its nose to locate food.

The vision of the hare is poor. It can perceive little more than movement despite the fact that its laterally-placed eyes give it a wide angle of vision. It is further hindered by the inability to constrict its pupils. For this reason the snowshoe rabbit tends to be most active at dusk and dawn—periods of dim light.

The snowshoe is very fastidious *and spends much time washing its fur. It even cleans the soles of its feet!*

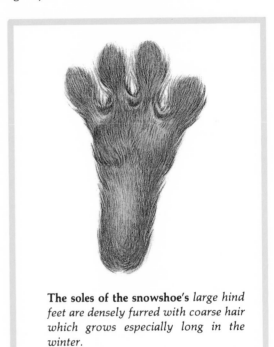

The soles of the snowshoe's *large hind feet are densely furred with coarse hair which grows especially long in the winter.*

Varying hare in the process of reingestion

Hard pellets　　　*Soft pellets*

By standing on its hind toes *the snowshoe rabbit can gather food as high as two feet off the ground.*

WAS SCRIPTURE WRONG IN CLASSIFYING THE HARE AS AN UNCLEAN ANIMAL?

"Nevertheless these ye shall not eat of them that chew the cud, or of them that divide the cloven hoof; as the camel, and the hare, and the coney: for they chew the cud, but divide not the hoof; therefore they are unclean unto you." (Deuteronomy 14:7)

Certain grazing animals such as sheep, cattle, and deer chew their cud by regurgitating partially digested vegetable matter and then grinding it in their molar teeth before swallowing for the second time. The hare does not do this. Why then does Scripture call this animal a cud-chewing mammal in the reference above?

It has been discovered that the hare does re-eat and redigest its food. The hare passes two types of pellets. One pellet is large, dry, hard and has little, if any, food value. This the animal eliminates from its body. Another pellet is soft and is encased in a moist membrane which is not permitted to touch the ground. The animal reaches over with its mouth and swallows these pellets—a process called reingestion.

The casing remains intact and the pellet does not mingle with food already in the stomach. When it dissolves several hours later, it gives nourishment and aids digestion by providing lactic acid, potassium, sodium, and phosphorus. This allows the hare to extract and utilize nutrients that it might have missed and enables the hare to survive periods of fasting.

TAMARACK TREE *Larix laricina*

The needles and inner bark of the tamarack tree are one of the main foods of the snowshoe rabbit. This unique tree is a deciduous conifer. In late September the needles turn a golden yellow and shortly afterward drop from the tree. In the early spring, before the ground thaws, the tree begins to leaf again.

The tamarack grows best in swamps where the substrate condition is either well-drained or on compacted peat. The root system of this tree is shallow but exceptionally wide. The roots rarely reach a depth of more than one and a half feet, but they may spread wider than the height of the tree. Seeds ripen in autumn and are shed from cones. They lay dormant and do not germinate until after they are exposed to the cold of winter.

As the hare feeds more and more on these trees, its flesh takes on the unpleasant taste of resin although normally its flavor is good. Rabbit is a poor source of nutrition and does not provide the needed nutrients to sustain a person to carry on rigorous activities. When the Indians were forced to eat rabbit because there was nothing else available they would say they were "starving on rabbit."

HOW DOES SCRIPTURE ILLUSTRATE THE NEED TO CHANGE PLANS IF UNEXPECTED CONDITIONS REQUIRE IT?

It is always difficult to be flexible when we have set our affections on the plans that we have made. It is even more difficult when changing plans will mean financial loss. Who in Scripture was asked to change his plans when it would cost him a great amount of money to do so?

(Pause for a response —see page 20)

A twenty-five year old son ascended to the throne of his assassinated father. He purposed that his reign as king would not be marred by the problems that caused his father's downfall, but there was bitterness in this son's heart.

Bitterness will cloud a man's ability to reason and decrease his spiritual vision. As soon as the kingdom was established, this son avenged the death of his father. Those who had killed him were clearly guilty, but there is no mention of remorse or repentance for his father's sin which had precipitated the murder. His father had conspired against and killed a faithful prophet of God. That prophet had earnestly warned the king to change his course of action so that God could prosper the kingdom.

This young son now directed his energies to the task of strengthening his kingdom. He organized the entire nation militarily. Then he hired 100,000 allied soldiers to join forces with them against an enemy. Just before the invasion, a prophet of God warned the king that he must change the plans which had been made. "Let not these men whom you have hired go with you for the Lord is not with them. If they go with you, you will fall before your enemy for God has power to help and to cast down."

The king knew that the prophet was right, but he struggled with the thought of changing his plans. They had been so carefully devised and so costly to initiate. "What about the money I have already paid to the soldiers?" The prophet assured him, "The Lord is able to give you much more than this."

It is not a small matter to send home 100,000 hired soldiers. Having set their hearts on the battle and the rewards it might bring, they were disappointed when plans were changed. Because their desire for battle and the spoils of war was great, they attacked and plundered many cities on their way home, infuriating the young king.

His own military campaign was a success without the hired troops. The enemy was conquered—ten thousand enemy soldiers were killed in battle; ten thousand were led captive to the top of a cliff and pushed over the precipice. Their bodies were broken and crushed on the rocks below.

After the king returned from the victorious campaign, he was rebuked by a prophet of God. "Why have you sought after the gods of the people, which could not deliver their own people out of your hand?"

This young king was guilty of the same sin his father had committed years earlier. He brought home the false gods of the nation he conquered and began to worship them. An angry reply revealed that he was not prepared to heed the warning. "Have you been appointed to be my counselor? Stop speaking, or I will kill you."

This proud king who was unwilling to admit that he was wrong now made plans of revenge against the nation whose soldiers he had hired earlier. The king of Israel rebuked him for making these plans of battle and advised him to stay home. But the unyielding king disregarded the warning. He persisted in his plan, engaged in battle, and was defeated. Discontent grew within his land and, like his father, he was assassinated.

This king showed promising signs of wise flexibility in his early years, but the more he turned from God the less able he was to change plans which were contrary to the will of God. Amaziah was willing to be flexible if the price wasn't too high, but in the end he lost his treasures, his kingdom, and his life by not changing plans.

From II Kings 14:1-20 and II Chronicles 25

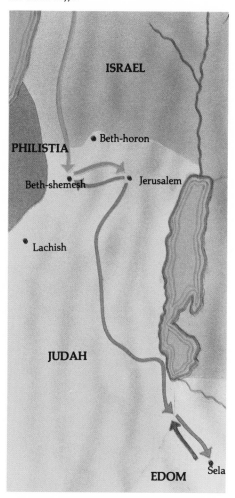

Amaziah may have taken the idols *from this great high place located on a rocky mountain in Edom. He may have thrown the Edomite soldiers down from the same cliffs.*

ISRAEL

Beth-horon

PHILISTIA

Beth-shemesh   Jerusalem

Lachish

JUDAH

EDOM   Sela

While Amaziah was defeating the Edomites *to the south, Joash of Israel invaded northern Judah. Amaziah returned to wage war against Israel at Beth-shemesh and was defeated. Jerusalem was conquered, and Amaziah was taken captive.*

UNEXPECTED CONDITIONS PRESENT A DIFFICULT DECISION FOR AMAZIAH

At the age of twenty-five, Amaziah launched his up and down, twenty-nine-year reign as the king of Judah. He began by doing "that which was right in the sight of the Lord, but not with a perfect heart." (II Chronicles 25:2) He was familiar with the Law of Moses and conformed to it outwardly; for when he avenged his father's death, "he slew not their children, but did as it is written in the law in the book of Moses." (II Chronicles 25:4) Having demonstrated his courage and fairness, he must have quickly secured the confidence and support of the kingdom.

ESTABLISHING AN ARMY

Amaziah's next job was to reorganize the war-torn army which he had inherited from his father, Joash. Because of Joash's apostasy, the Lord humiliated him and his army by sending a small company of Syrian soldiers who "destroyed all the princes of the people from among the people, and sent all the spoil of them unto the king of Damascus." (II Chronicles 24:23) As a result of this previous defeat, the number of fighting men had been greatly reduced. When Amaziah decided to number his army, he found only "three hundred thousand choice men, able to go forth to war, who could handle spear and shield." (II Chronicles 25:5)

After reorganizing his army, he must have entertained bright hopes of recovering the fortunes which his predecessors had lost. His first target was their perpetual enemy—Edom. These people had first been defeated by Saul (I Samuel 14:47) and later subjugated by David (II Samuel 8:14). The Edomites attempted a revolt under the reign of Solomon but remained subject to the kingdom of Judah until the reign of Joram, when they rebelled again(II Chronicles 21:8-10).

VICTORY BRINGS DEFEAT

Amaziah decided to reinforce his army with 100,000 mercenaries from the northern kingdom of Israel. A man of God warned the young and inexperienced Amaziah that, if he used these Israelite soldiers whom the Lord was not with, his army would be defeated (II Chronicles 25:7, 8). Amaziah hesitated over the loss of one hundred talents of silver which had already been paid, but he submitted to the prophet's counsel.

With his own army of 300,000 he defeated the Edomites and captured Seir, their capital. To the amazement and disappointment of the godly in Judah, he returned to Jerusalem with Edomite gods and began to worship them (II Chronicles 25:14). The anger of the Lord was kindled against this disobedient act, and He announced through a prophet that Amaziah would be destroyed for his rebellion (II Chronicles 25:16).

THE COST OF DISOBEDIENCE

While Amaziah was in Edom the Israelite troops, which had been dismissed from battle, spent their excess energy plundering the northern cities of Judah (II Chronicles 25:10, 13). Headstrong and lifted up in pride after his victory against the Edomites, Amaziah rashly challenged Israel to battle. The result was disaster.

In the battle fought at Beth-shemesh, Judah was utterly defeated. The defensive wall around Jerusalem was broken, resulting in total subjugation. The city was plundered, and Amaziah was taken captive (II Kings 14:11-14).

Uzziah, the son of Amaziah, began to reign in place of his captive father until Amaziah was finally released after the death of Israel's king. But the people favored the rule of Uzziah to that of his father. There was a conspiracy against his life, and so Amaziah fled to the fortified city of Lachish. "But they sent to Lachish after him, and slew him there. And they brought him upon horses, and buried him with his father in the city of Judah." (II Chronicles 25:27, 28)

AMAZIAH CHARACTER SKETCH

WHY DIDN'T AMAZIAH WANT TO DISMISS THE MERCENARIES?

When the man of God told Amaziah to fight without the hired reinforcements, the king's first protest was that the payment of one hundred talents of silver would be lost. This sizable expenditure from the already impoverished treasury would constantly remind the leaders of Amaziah's foolish and hasty decision. If they lost the battle, it would have made him look even worse in their eyes. Further, Edom had revolted before under King Jehoram who had possessed a much larger army than Amaziah. Despite an army of over one million fighting men which Jehoram inherited from his father, he still had been unable to subdue Edom (cf. II Chronicles 17:14-18). The extra 100,000 men, no doubt Israel's finest professionals, would be a boost to the Judean army's morale. The choice for Amaziah to make was between the Lord's command and his own human reasoning. Because he was willing to change his plans and obey the Lord, he won the battle.

WHY WOULD AMAZIAH WANT TO WORSHIP THE EDOMITE GODS WHICH THE LORD HAD JUST DEFEATED?

It seems incredibly foolish for a king to worship the very gods which had just failed to protect their own country. The Lord's prophet mocked Amaziah's twisted reasoning by questioning, "Why hast thou sought after the gods of the people, which could not deliver their own people out of thine hand?" (II Chronicles 25:15) This question revealed the weakness in the king's thinking. Amaziah believed that different nations were assigned different gods. He seems to have believed that the Lord was the God of Israel but not the God of Edom. He thought that by incurring the favor of the gods of Edom and worshiping them, they would allow him to rule over the allotted territory. His foolishness deserved the severe rebuke of the prophet.

WHY DIDN'T AMAZIAH CHANGE HIS PLANS THE SECOND TIME?

Amaziah's inflexible behavior defies reason. He had just obeyed the Lord and, as a result, defeated the Edomites. Now he was rebuked again, and he completely disregarded the prophet's warning. Rather than cry out to the Lord in repentance and destroy the Edomite idols he was worshiping, he prepared for war against their century-long ally. Even the godless king of Israel recognized the arrogant pride in Amaziah's heart as a result of his victory. King Jehoahaz warned him, "Lo, thou hast smitten the Edomites; and thine heart lifteth thee up to boast. Abide now at home. Why shouldest thou meddle to thine heart, that thou shouldest fall, even thou, and Judah with thee?" (II Chronicles 25:19) Amaziah again refused to consider advice. He was soundly defeated by Jehoahaz and spent the next years of his life in captivity. After he returned to his home, he was assassinated. Amaziah had tried to serve more than one master—the Lord and the gods of Edom. His life illustrated the words of the Lord, "No man can serve two masters; for either he will hate the one, and love the other; or else he will hold to the one, and despise the other. Ye cannot serve God and mammon." (Matthew 6:24)

"Now they made a **conspiracy** *against him in Jerusalem, and he fled to Lachish; but they sent after him to Lachish, and slew him there.*"

AMAZIAH
ăm-à-zī'à

Alertness

"And Jesus increased in wisdom and stature, and in favour with God and man."

Luke 2:52

PART TWO

Alertness

IS RECOGNIZING OPPORTUNITIES AND DANGERS WHICH OTHERS OVERLOOK

"Hear counsel, and receive instruction, that thou mayest be wise in thy latter end."

Proverbs 19:20

"The simple believeth every word: but the prudent man looketh well to his going."

Proverbs 14:15

LIVING LESSONS ON ALERTNESS . . .

FROM THE PAGES OF SCRIPTURE

Many parents wonder why they have problems with their sons and daughters. They don't realize that what a father allows in moderation, his children may excuse in excess. The quality of alertness involves recognizing opportunities and dangers which others overlook. Scripture gives a vivid illustration of a father who had the chance to establish a society of godly men and women but failed to exercise this aspect of alertness and, as a result, diminished the opportunity God gave him.

ILLUSTRATED IN THE WORLD OF NATURE

GREAT PLAINS BISON *Bison bison*

The buffalo of North America is not really a buffalo at all. Because it is an even-toed, hollow-horned ruminant it belongs to the family *Bovidae*. Its genus name is *bison* and its species name is also *bison*. Only in Asia and Africa is the true buffalo found. When early French explorers came to the North American continent and first saw bison, they were reminded of their oxen in Europe and named them *les boeufs*. Through mispronunciation, the English-speaking frontiersmen gradually simplified the name to *buffe* and *buffelo* and then, finally, *buffalo*. Among all wild animals of North America the bison is the largest. Although its normal weight is about a ton, a bull can weigh as much as 3,000 pounds.

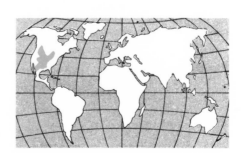

The range and habitat of the Great Plains bison

The range of the bison during the early 1800's

ALERTNESS

HOW DOES THE BISON ILLUSTRATE THE NEED TO RECOGNIZE DANGER WHICH OTHERS OVERLOOK?

A terrible, blood-curdling scream broke the silence of the plain, and the ground began to tremble and shake. Billows of dust clouded the air. Confusion reigned. As the thunderous spectacle moved forward in a compact mass no obstacle seemed large enough to stand in its way.

Only minutes before, a herd of bison several hundred in number had been feeding peacefully. The magnificent beasts, overwhelming in size, created quite a sight as they casually grazed on the grass. Some bison measured twelve feet long and six feet high. They were without question the largest of the North American land animals.

Because of its sheer size, the bison had few enemies. But the animal's peaceful coexistence with the Indians was beginning to change. The Indians were becoming more and more of a threat to this "king of the plains."

Under normal circumstances, hunting equipment of bow, arrow, and lance was no match for these swift and wary animals. Kills were few and far between. The hunters were creative, though, always looking for more effective ways to secure this vital source of food. When conditions were right, they compensated for their primitive hunting equipment by using a unique tactic.

One characteristic of this animal that the Indians used to their own advantage was the creature's poor vision. A second was its tendency to herd and stampede blindly when danger approached. The Indians had taken great preparation and precaution to ensure the success of this hunt. With the hunters strategically positioned, they needed only the cooperation of one or two animals.

Knowing that the bison couldn't see well and that it was nervous and short-tempered, an experienced Indian was elected to choose a susceptible candidate—a young bull. By using the wind to his advantage, the hunter slowly crept up to the unsuspecting animal.

At just the right time the Indian let out a blood-curdling scream. The startled animal immediately began to run in fright. Like a shock wave, panic spread through the herd of bison. A large cow—one of the leaders—noticed what was happening. She, too, followed the younger bull's example and took to flight when she saw the frightened animal. Soon the entire herd was moving in a thundering, massive stampede.

By yelling and waving wildly, the carefully positioned hunters directed the stampeding bison in the direction they wanted them to go.

Suddenly terror flashed through the cow. She hadn't been alert to her path but had blindly followed the lead of the inexperienced bull. Before she could change her course she ran off a sheer cliff, tumbled through the air, and, with a hideous thud, crashed to the ground. The others behind her also realized too late what was happening. They could do nothing to reverse their course and they, too, were plunging to their deaths.

As quickly as it began, the hunt ended. The entire group perished. If the cow had only been alert to recognize danger that the others overlooked, she might have saved herself and possibly the others as well.

SCRIPTURAL REFERENCES TO THE BISON

"Will the wild ox be willing to serve thee, or abide by the crib? Canst thou bind the wild ox with its band in the furrow? Or will he harrow the valleys after thee? Wilt thou trust him, because his strength is great? Or wilt thou leave thy labor to him?"
Job 39:9-11

Though now extinct in Israel, proof of the buffalo's existence was found when buffalo bones were unearthed in Palestine. The Biblical "wild ox" may refer to a buffalo. Outwardly the animal is placid, but attempts to harness its energy for plowing or pulling loads would be futile. It is easily aroused and must be approached with caution.

Job and his three friends knew a great deal about the world of nature, but God showed them how little they knew about many, many aspects of His creation—including the untamed nature of a wild beast.

God compares an attempt to reform the nature of a non-Christian person with trying to change the nature of an animal. Results are only temporary. "But it is happened unto them according to the true proverb, The dog is turned to his own vomit again; and the sow that was washed, to her wallowing in the mire." (II Peter 2:22)

Both sexes of the bison *have horns. The horns are not shed, and they grow as long as two feet.*

CHARACTERISTICS AND PHYSICAL FEATURES OF THE PLAINS BISON

The lead bison's lack of alertness in recognizing danger proved to be costly. The herd perished in the stampede. With the development of the plains and the advent of the horse and rifle, hunters who sought the animal only for its hide and tongue learned and exploited this weakness of the bison. If they identified the lead animals and killed them, they were able to shoot large numbers of the herd before the animals became aware of what was happening. With this kind of mounting pressure on the bison, its numbers quickly diminished. In less than twenty years, from 1865 to 1884, the population of bison herds decreased from sixty million to near extinction.

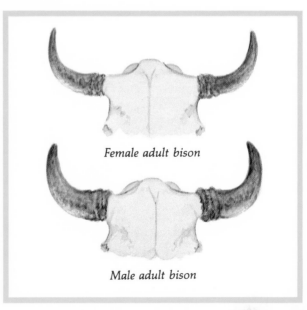

Female adult bison

Male adult bison

WHY WAS THE BISON SO IMPORTANT TO THE INDIAN?

The bison was the mainstay of the Plains Indian. As long as the bison roamed the plains, he prospered. For centuries the animal supplied thousands of Indians with food, clothing, and shelter. Through his creativity, the Indian had learned to use every part of the animal; each had its special purpose.

MEAT supplied the Indian with food. Especially in the autumn the Indian hunted bison because at that time of year the animal has its best flavor. Bison meat tastes and looks very much like beef except that it is a little darker, more tender, with closer grain and a lower cholesterol level. The Indians dried the meat by cutting it into strips and allowing it to cure. The dried meat was called pemmican and served as a substitute when fresh meat was unavailable.

SINEWS were used for binding an arrow point to its shaft, for bowstrings, thread, and webbing on snowshoes.

HIDES had many uses. They made warm, durable clothing, robes and moccasins. They provided tepee coverings for shelter and material for boats, bedding, rawhide ropes and shields. The Indians even made coffins by wrapping their dead in bison hides.

LONG HAIR was braided into rope or used for ornamentation.

STOMACHS, BLADDERS, AND OTHER INTERNAL ORGANS made suitable containers for holding nuts, berries, and pemmican.

TALLOW was molded into large balls and used for waterproofing. It also served as a hair grease.

BONES made bows, tools, scrapers, and toys for children. The ribs were even used as runners for dog sleds.

GALL OR BILE produced an important ingredient to make yellow paint.

HORNS were made into spoons and drinking utensils or used as a device to carry hot coals.

HOOVES were used to make glue.

TAILS made excellent fly swatters.

DRIED DUNG OR "CHIPS," which could be stored indefinitely, provided the Indian with fuel for hot fires.

STOMACH JUICES served in a life or death situation as a substitute for water.

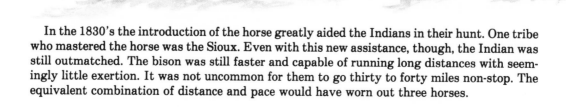

In the 1830's the introduction of the horse greatly aided the Indians in their hunt. One tribe who mastered the horse was the Sioux. Even with this new assistance, though, the Indian was still outmatched. The bison was still faster and capable of running long distances with seemingly little exertion. It was not uncommon for them to go thirty to forty miles non-stop. The equivalent combination of distance and pace would have worn out three horses.

Shields for protection

Tools for working

Pemmican or
jerky for food

"Chips" for fuel

MATERIALS THE BISON PROVIDED FOR THE INDIAN

Robes for warmth

Tepee coverings for shelter

Glue for cementing

THE PLAINS BISON *Bison bison bison*

The wood bison is larger *in size than the plains bison. Its head is placed higher on its shoulders; its coat is heavier, and, unlike the plains bison, the whites of its eyes do not show.*

THE WOOD BISON *Bison bison athabascae*

☐ *Range and habitat of the plains bison*

■ *Range and habitat of the wood bison*

Bison wallowing in the dust

WERE THERE ENEMIES BESIDES MAN THAT COULD KILL THE BISON?

Surprisingly, one of the bison's greatest enemies was ice. During the winter these large animals became accustomed to traveling fearlessly across icebound rivers and lakes. The thick ice formed a bridge and could support their weight at that time. But in the spring they would attempt to cross these same rivers on their return to a summer range, unaware of the change that had occurred. Although the ice looked the same, it had begun to melt beneath the surface, and the bison's "bridge" had deteriorated. As these one to three-thousand-pound animals ventured out onto the ice in compact herds, their weight would be too great, and thousands of helpless animals would crash through to their deaths.

Another enemy was the grizzly bear. With one powerful swipe of its paw it could break the neck of a bison. The bison was faster than the grizzly, though, and a healthy animal had little trouble outrunning this predator.

The timber wolf was another threat. Usually these animals were able to kill only the young, sick, or injured. If the herd was nearby and one of these weaker animals was threatened, other bison would huddle around it and attempt to gorge the attacker and ward it off.

WHAT IS THE BISON'S MOST ANNOYING ENEMY?

The most annoying enemies aren't large animals but rather small, biting insects. To relieve the uncomfortable itching the bison will lay down on its side and move about in the dirt, violently plowing up the ground with its horns and body. It wallows on one side, stands up and shakes itself, and does the same on the other side. It completely covers itself with mud and dirt in an effort to rid itself of the pests.

Birds such as the cowbird, magpie, and blackbird benefit from and help the bison. As many as a dozen of these birds perch on the back of a bison and aid it by ridding it of flies and insects.

Buffalo bird, or cowbird

As the bison moved *through the grass it kicked up insects. Birds were attracted to this unusual source of food and would fearlessly move in among their hooves to take advantage of the opportunity to feed.*

HOW DOES SCRIPTURE ILLUSTRATE THE NEED TO RECOGNIZE DANGERS WHICH OTHERS OVERLOOK?

The strength of a nation is in its families, and the strength of a family is in the standards of its father. What father invested an enormous amount of time, energy, and money to protect his own family but—because he was not alert to one danger—brought a curse into the very family he was protecting?

(Pause for a response—see page 20)

This man walked with God as few others have. In his early life, sin abounded on the earth; but rather than his love for God growing cold, it became greater. All around him violence multiplied at an alarming rate. The chief concern of everyone centered around satisfying their desires for eating, drinking, and sensual living.

He watched as friends and relatives corrupted themselves with wicked habits. He observed that the pleasures to which they sold themselves were not only destructive to their futures but repulsive to God.

He purposed that when he raised his own children they would escape the corruption that was in the world through lust. That meant he would have to be very alert to spiritual dangers and true to God's standards. God honored his desires and gave him a detailed plan to spare his family from the great flood that destroyed the mocking, jeering civilization which refused to be warned.

This man and his family now had the unprecedented opportunity to learn from the failures of the past and establish an entirely new civilization based on God's righteous standards. Their success would depend upon their ability to exercise alertness to spiritual dangers.

Alertness was far more important than this father realized. He, his wife, his sons, and their wives had been exposed to the godless standards of a wicked society. Like a family susceptible to a contagious disease, they needed the wise protection of an alert father.

One day he indulged in the luxury of satisfying his own personal desires. He made and became drunk on the fermented juice of grapes. One of his sons saw him in a shameful, drunken condition. His condition tempted the son to commit even greater wickedness. When that father became sober, he realized what his son had done. Guilt and anger prevented him from seeing the need of confessing his sin, asking forgiveness, and then correcting and restoring his son. Instead, he pronounced a curse upon one of his descendants.

That father was Noah, a great man of faith who found grace in the sight of God but failed in this test of alertness. He sowed iniquity, reaped vanity, and the rod of his anger brought spiritual destruction. Ironically, the curse that he gave would demand the very quality of alertness which he lacked. "A servant of servants shall you be unto your brethren."

From Genesis 10:20-29

When the flood came, *out of all mankind only Noah, his wife, his three sons, and their wives were saved in the ark. On the basis of a cubit as 18 inches, the ark was 450 feet long with a beam of 75 feet and a depth of 45 feet. These divinely given dimensions provided excellent stability for the huge craft.*

The wine press represented above *was found in Israel. Its use is demonstrated by the two men squeezing the juice out of the fresh grapes with their feet. The juice runs into the deeper pit where it is scooped out with jars. The heavy sediment remains on the bottom.*

NOAH OVERLOOKED A DANGER AND LOST AN OPPORTUNITY

We have few details about conditions during the time just preceding the great flood other than, "the wickedness of man was great in the earth, and that every imagination of the thoughts of his heart was only evil continually." (Genesis 6:5)

TWO CITIES WITH THE SAME PROBLEM

There is a possibility that people spent much of their time overeating and overdrinking at wedding feasts (cf. Matthew 24:37,38; Luke 17:26,27), but that certainly was not the cause for their destruction. The nature of their sin may be surmised from the nature of the prominent sin of two other peoples whom God completely destroyed later in history.

The first illustration is the cities of Sodom and Gomorrah. The sordid example of their wickedness given in Genesis 19:1-11 reveals the depth of the depravity to which they had descended. Even after the messengers of the Lord struck these perverse men blind, they continued to grasp for the door of Lot's house in an insane attempt to satisfy their sensual desires (Genesis 19:11). In Jude 7 the nature of the sin of Sodom and Gomorrah's inhabitants is succinctly stated. Their sin was abject sexual depravity. In God's mercy, He destroyed them to stop its influence.

Another target of God's destruction was the people of the cities remaining in Canaan. Because of their iniquities, the Lord commanded the Israelites to "smite them, and utterly destroy them." (Deuteronomy 7:2) The Lord purposed to spew the Canaanites out of the land because they had defiled it with their sexual abominations. These abominations are described in painfully explicit detail in Leviticus 18.

It is reasonable to assume that God destroyed the people of Noah's time for the same reason that He destroyed the Canaanites, namely, because of their vile sexual misconduct and degeneration. With this in mind, the seriousness of Noah's lapse and his son Ham's immoral act described in Genesis 9:20-27 becomes apparent.

A MOMENT OF WEAKNESS—A LIFETIME OF SHAME

Noah planted a vineyard and made wine. He drank the wine and became drunk. The heat generated in his body by the alcohol no doubt prompted him to remove his covering within his tent. He was in this drunken condition when Ham gazed upon his nakedness. God's spokesman on earth was no longer being influenced by God's Spirit but rather by the alcohol of wine. The one who had been spared from a generation of sensual perversion was now unwittingly tempting his son to that same type of activity. The implication is that Ham not only saw his father's nakedness, but that he looked upon it with satisfaction. He then told his brothers about their father's condition apparently in a very disrespectful way.

A CURSE FOR ONE—A BLESSING FOR TWO

When Noah awoke from his wine and knew what his son Ham had done to him, he cursed Canaan, the son of Ham. He then blessed his other two sons, Shem and Japheth, who refused to dishonor their father.

NOAH CHARACTER SKETCH

WAS NOAH AWARE OF THE DANGEROUS EXAMPLE HE WAS SETTING?

Since Scripture states that "Noah was a just man and perfect in his generations" (Genesis 6:9), some have charitably suggested that Noah was unaware of the effects of wine. The New Testament, however, states that men were "eating and drinking" before the flood (Matthew 24:38; Luke 17:27). That expression is often associated with the eating of food and the drinking of wine (cf. Luke 7:33,34; 12:19). The Bible is very honest in describing the failures of the righteous. Lot was also called "just" (II Peter 2:7), but he, too, allowed himself to become drunk with tragic consequences (Genesis 19:33).

It is conceivable that Noah chose to become drunk because he wanted to escape the reality of a situation which may have depressed him. Noah no doubt knew of his son Ham's growing disrespect for his authority and the authority of God. He may also have been aware of this rebellious spirit developing in his grandson, Canaan. Did Noah think that the flood had been in vain, merely to be repeated again and again? Had he forgotten God's promise never again to destroy all of mankind? In any case, he turned to the wrong source to find peace and joy. It is possible that the low standards of pre-flood society influenced Noah. In comparison, he may have justified becoming just a "little" drunk in the privacy of his own tent (cf. Luke 8:17). Noah probably was aware of the effects of wine, but there is no way that he could have anticipated the tragic results of his actions.

WHY DID NOAH CURSE CANAAN RATHER THAN HAM?

A principle of God's Law is, "every man shall be put to death for his own sin." (Deuteronomy 24:16) A son cannot be punished because of the sin of his father. We must conclude, therefore, that the curse on Canaan was just; it was a prophecy of the judgment that would result because of sinful acts that would be committed by his descendants. It is significant, that these sins were of the same nature as those of their ancestor, Ham (cf. Deuteronomy 5:9). Canaan's descendants were the inhabitants of Sodom, and this city is remembered by the name of its perverted sin. Centuries later, the Romans, not exactly a standard for moral purity, were surprised by the depth of depravity of the few remaining Canaanites. But only one of Ham's four sons is mentioned in the curse; only one son chose the path of complete moral depravity. The grace of God is available to all men, regardless of the sins of their parents.

WHAT SPECIAL OPPORTUNITIES DID NOAH BESTOW ON HIS OTHER SONS?

Shem and Japheth were blessed because they honored and showed respect to their father even during his lapse of faith. They were not seeking to justify and excuse their sinful actions by pointing their finger at the one who had proclaimed God's standards to them. When Shem and Japheth honored their father, they set an important example for their own children to follow. It established their respect for the teachings of their father—the principles of which would naturally cause them and their children to prosper (cf. Prov. 1:8,9). The righteous ways of Noah did not die with him, but were passed on to his sons who honored him.

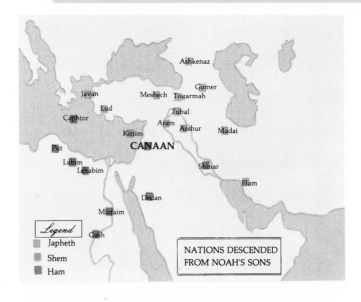

NATIONS DESCENDED FROM NOAH'S SONS

Legend
Japheth
Shem
Ham

"And Noah awoke from his wine, *and knew what his younger son had done unto him. And he said, Cursed be Canaan; a servant of servants shall he be unto his brethren."*

NOAH
nō′á

IS ACTING QUICKLY UPON SIGNALS OF DANGER

"A wise man will hear, and will increase learning; and a man of understanding shall attain unto wise counsels."

Proverbs 1:5

LIVING LESSONS ON ALERTNESS . . .

FROM THE PAGES OF SCRIPTURE

If we do not warn the wicked to turn from their wicked way, they will die in their iniquity; but their blood will be upon our hands. God repeats this warning twice in Scripture to emphasize its importance (Ezekiel 3:18, 33:8). God further instructs us to rescue those who are unjustly sentenced to death. We are not to stand idly by and allow them to die. We have a responsibility to act upon what we know. The entire Christian world has been enriched by the ministry of one man whose life was saved when an alert bystander acted quickly upon the signals of danger which he observed.

ILLUSTRATED IN THE WORLD OF NATURE

BROWN MYOTIS BAT *Myotis lucifugus*

"Flittermouse" is the name once given to this remarkable acrobat of the air. It is the only mammal capable of true flight. This little creature is approximately three and one-half inches in length and has a wingspan of about nine inches. Size is usually a good indicator of a mammal's life expectancy. For instance, a mouse lives approximately one year; a dog, twelve years; a horse, seventeen years. And yet the little bat, which is smaller than a mouse, is capable of living more than twenty years. The bat, which has been the source of many mysteries and superstitions over the years, lives in colonies of thousands. It inhabits caves, hollow trees, and buildings. It is normally nocturnal—active from dusk until dawn.

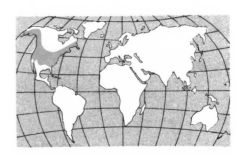

The range and habitat of the brown myotis bat

ALERTNESS

HOW DOES THE MYOTIS BAT ILLUSTRATE ALERTNESS BY ACTING QUICKLY UPON SIGNALS OF DANGER?

Beep--beep--beep--beep . . . The object moved so swiftly that it was hard to track in the blackened sky. Even when it flew within the arc of light from a lamppost, it was still difficult to detect. The creature darted in different directions at many angles as it zigzagged through the air.

When the morning light began to break, the little form made its way underneath a wooden shingle where it would rest for the day. As the sun rose and activity began, the bat's rest was about to be disturbed.

Two nights before, a heavy thunderstorm revealed a leak in the roof of the summer cottage. It just so happened that the location of the leak was beneath one of the shingles where the bat rested.

During the storm a young man had mentally marked the leaky spot. Equipped with a ladder and hammer, he climbed the rungs to expose the leak and repair it. As he lifted one of the shingles, he noticed the sleeping brown bat. Quickly he covered it, hurried down the ladder, and returned with a jar. Lifting the shingle once again, he positioned the jar and forced the bat to drop in. This little creature would provide many hours of study and entertainment.*

As the young student fed and cared for the animal, it became quite a pet. When the little bat grew more and more accustomed to its surroundings, its keeper granted it the freedom of his bedroom at night. He would do this by leaving open the door to its cage. Quite an attachment grew between the two. In the evening, on entering the room, the boy would call the bat, and the animal would come.

At feeding time, the boy tossed insects into the air one at a time and watched with fascination as the agile bat scooped them up and ate them. He experimented and tried to trick the animal by throwing them at odd angles forcing the little bat to perform acrobatics. Rarely did it miss a morsel. The boy was continually amazed at the bat's ability to weave gracefully around objects and never hit one.

One hot summer evening the boy was reading in his room. The air was so warm that he could not concentrate. Unable to get relief from the open screened window, he went to the attic to bring down an old fan. Upon his return he calculated the best position to give the most circulation and turned it on "low."

Some time later the little bat came out from resting in its cage and began to fly around. The boy paid little attention at first. It didn't occur to him that the bat might be in danger, and he never gave it a thought until it was too late—the bat was on its way into the revolving blades of the fan!

That split second before the bat entered the fan, feelings of sadness and loss shot through the boy's mind. Why had he not been more responsible? How could he have been so thoughtless? The blades were whirring around at 800 revolutions per minute.

To his amazement, the bat quickly slipped through the fan without as much as touching a blade. Feelings of joy and relief came over him. He didn't lose his bat after all. But as he sat there recovering from his amazement, he wondered what might have happened had the switch been set to "high" with the blades spinning at a speed of 1200 revolutions per minute. The better part of judgment told him not to, but he turned the fan switch to "high" and the bat took on the challenge. Its high-pitched beep was barely audible over the noise of the fan.

The sounds which the bat emits are essential to its flight. As it flies, high-pitched noises are emitted at the rate of 30 per second. The comparison is approximately 30,000 cycles. As the echoes are bounced back, the bat transmits more signals until they return at the rate of 50 to 60 per second. This echo is like a messenger. It tells the bat if it is heading for an obstacle. It also defines the location, size, and shape of the obstacle and allows the bat to avoid collisions.

As the little pet bat was just about to go through the fan a second time, it suddenly made a last minute, 90-degree turn and quickly darted away from the spinning blades. The message the animal received had alerted it to danger, informing it that it could not safely pass through. The brown bat wisely and swiftly altered its course, acting quickly upon the signal of danger.

Unless an animal is incapable of taking care of itself it is never recommended to remove it from its natural habitat. Even then it should be returned when it is able to fend for itself.

SCRIPTURAL REFERENCES TO THE BAT

"And these are they which ye shall have in abomination among the fowls; they shall not be eaten, they are an abomination. . . the lapwing, and the bat." Leviticus 11:13-19

God included the bat in His list of unclean creatures among those which are "an abomination among the fowls." This may refer to their ability to transmit infectious diseases to man.

The Hebrew name for bat means "flies by night." Bats of the Holy Land lived among the many limestone caves of that area. The many varieties of bats in the land vary from the size of a mouse to the size of a rat, measuring more than twenty inches across the wing.

"In that day (of God's judgment) a man shall cast his idols of silver, and his idols of gold, which they made each one for himself to worship, to the moles and to the bats; to go into the clefts of the rocks, and into the tops of the ragged rocks, for fear of the Lord. . . ." Isaiah 2:20,21

It is significant that in the verse above God associates the final destination of man-made idols with the home of the bat. Both represent a world of darkness. The bat normally comes out at night to do its work. God points out that men of evil deeds "love darkness rather than light. . . . Neither cometh to the light, lest his deeds should be reproved." (John 3:19, 20)

The unpredictable flight pattern of a bat reminds us of the ways of a person who has turned from worshiping the living God to serve a god of his own making (Proverbs 5:6).

CHARACTERISTICS AND PHYSICAL FEATURES OF THE BROWN MYOTIS BAT

An alertness to signals of danger enabled the bat to alter its course and avoid a deadly collision. By studying the bat's unique tool to detect objects, man has unlocked the principles of sonar and produced sensitive detection instruments of his own. During World War II, the owners of this secret had a decided advantage over their enemy. Despite the sophisticated engineering that man builds into his detection units, they still lack the precision of the bat's. It is estimated that the bat's sonar system is a billion times more sensitive than anything man has yet devised. Science continues to study the bat's unique physical characteristics with the hope of unlocking further secrets. When he discovers the answers, all mankind will benefit.

WHAT UNIQUE PHYSICAL CHARACTERISTICS DOES THE BAT HAVE?

AGELESS ARTERIES - Examination of the bat indicates that there is very little difference between the arterial walls of a twenty-year-old and those of a one-year-old bat. Discovering the secret of this amazing phenomenon may help science control one of the major problems of old age.

BIRTH CONTROL - Every animal has a set number of days during which its young develop within the mother. This is called the gestation period and begins immediately after mating. The bat, however, is able to store the seed and determine, at its own convenience, when the gestation period is to begin.

Another unique aspect of the bat's reproduction is the enormous size of its young. In comparison, it is the equivalent of a woman giving birth to a thirty-pound baby.

RESISTANCE TO RABIES - The bat is the only animal that will generally survive rabies as well as resist other diseases. It can carry but will not contract the disease. Very seldom does a bat transmit rabies to man, but when this occurs, it is very difficult to cure. The normal rabies anti-toxin does not seem to be effective. It is hoped that further studies of the bat will provide man with new serum to combat rabies.

RESISTANCE TO RADIATION - Laboratory experiments have revealed that the bat is more than 300 times more resistant to the effects of atomic radiation than the rat. With the continual threat of atomic war, the secret of this characteristic could protect man from the terrible effects of radiation.

Bat colonies *are capable of producing huge amounts of waste or guano. Even these droppings have been of importance to man. Their rich nutrients make an excellent fertilizer. During the American Civil War this guano was used to produce gunpowder.*

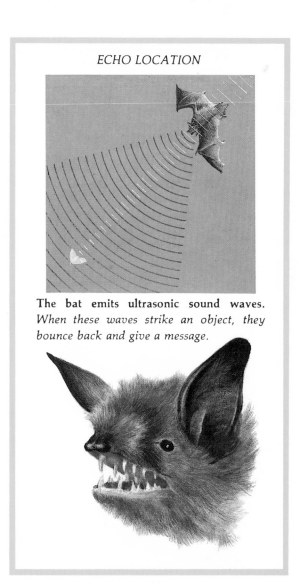

ECHO LOCATION

The bat emits ultrasonic sound waves. *When these waves strike an object, they bounce back and give a message.*

Through muscle contraction *the bat is able to close its ears as it sends the signals and open them as it receives the returning echo. This rapid muscular activity works at the astonishing rate of 50-60 sounds per second.*

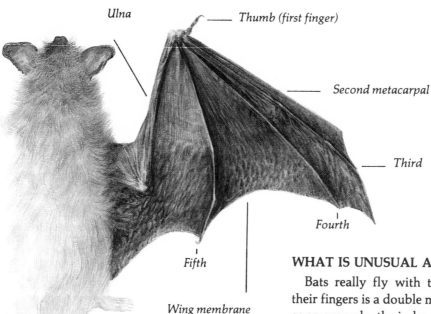

Ulna

Thumb (first finger)

Second metacarpal

Third

Fourth

Fifth

Wing membrane

Bats belong to the order Chiroptera *which means hand-winged. There are thirteen hundred species of bats which make up this order.*

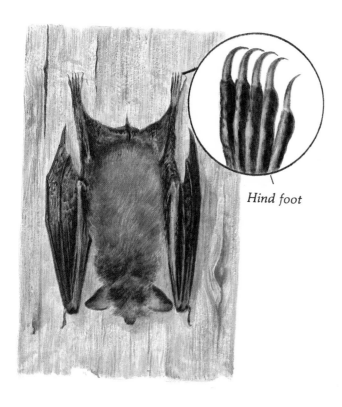

Hind foot

The hind feet of the bat *have five toes. Each toe has a well-developed, sharp claw. The bat uses its feet to move around the ground and to hang upside-down. It is very easy for the bat to hang for extended periods of time. While hanging, it will often cloak its body by draping its large wings around itself.*

WHAT IS UNUSUAL ABOUT THE BAT'S HAND?

Bats really fly with their fingers. Extended between their fingers is a double membrane. Using your own hand as an example, the index finger would be the leading edge of the wing. Both the index and middle fingers are close together. The ring and little fingers spread apart to support the main wing surface.

Because of this unusual construction, the bat has far more control in flight than most birds—even the agile hummingbird. In flight a bird's wing is rigid and can only be slightly turned. The wing of the bat, however, with its membrane of skin spread along its arms and in between its fingers, can be easily manipulated. The bat can move the whole wing or any part of it, enabling it to make right angles in a space only slightly larger than its own body length.

CAN A BAT WALK?

The bat can walk but it is slow and clumsy. Its large wings prove awkward, and its knees bend backward. On top of the wing is the bat's short thumb and sharp claw. This is the tool it uses for walking. The hook-like claw grabs the surface as it alternates from one claw to the other, pulling itself along. The feet are made up of five small toes and each is equipped with a sharp claw.

WHAT ARE THE FEET USED FOR?

Hanging. The bat's feet have tendons unusually constructed to prevent the toes from straightening out when the leg is extended. This feature allows the bat to hang with little or no effort. In fact, a bat could die and still not lose its grip.

IS THE BAT WARM-BLOODED OR COLD-BLOODED?

In a sense it is both. When the bat is active, it is warm-blooded. When it sleeps, it is cold-blooded. The bat can enter hibernation faster and more easily than any other mammal. Its breathing rate decreases from eight breaths per second to eight per minute. Its heart beat can drop from 180 to three beats per minute. During the fall the bat stores up fat and with this reserve can pass the many months of winter in hibernation.

WHAT DOES A BAT EAT?

The diet of the little myotis bat consists almost entirely of nocturnal insects, including various bugs, beetles and moths. The little animal often consumes so much food that its stomach is greatly stretched. The bat may eat as much as one-third its body weight.

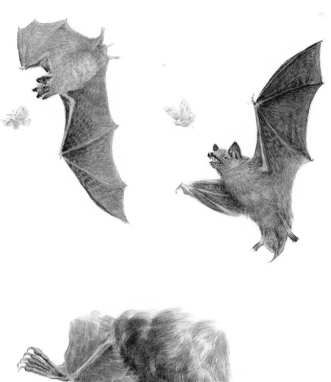

HOW DOES THE BAT HUNT?

Bats use both their mouth and tail membrane in hunting. When traveling through the air, the bat opens its mouth to gather a meal. The membrane between its hind legs is used as a net to scoop insects out of the air.

If the insect is small, the bat reaches over with its mouth and consumes it in flight. If it is larger, the bat will carry the insect to a perch to eat it. It first discards the wings by biting them off. Then it reaches over and chews up the insect while it is still in this membrane pouch. An effective insect catcher, the myotis bat consumes an average of one gram of insects for every hour it hunts.

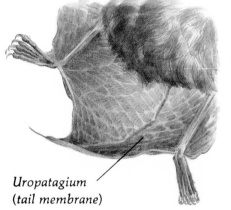

Uropatagium
(tail membrane)

IS A BAT ALWAYS SUCCESSFUL IN CAPTURING ITS PREY?

Usually, but there are a few species of moths which have learned to avoid the high-pitched squeaks of the bat. As this flying mammal emits its beeps, it is able to detect its target from three to six feet away. When the moth hears this sound, it flies wildly in a series of evasive maneuvers and loops in an effort to confuse the bat's detection system. If this doesn't work, it folds its wings and drops to the ground, motionless.

WHY DO BATS FLY AROUND YOUR HEAD AT NIGHT?

One misconception about bats is that they fly into and become entangled in women's hair. In the summertime the skillful bat may fly around a person's head but seldom, if ever, will it touch it. The bat is only interested in securing the pesky insects which the person has attracted. The bat is in effect really performing a service, reducing the population of insects.

The belief that bats are blind is another common misconception. Although the beady, black eyes of the bat are small, they do have limited vision.

The flight pattern *of the Antherea polyphemus moth as it attempts to avoid capture by the myotis bat*

Suspended by one foot, *the bat thoroughly combs its fur with the other foot. This procedure is done several times a day. The bat continually cleans and oils the skin membrane of its wings. Even during hibernation the bat wakes up from time to time to groom itself.*

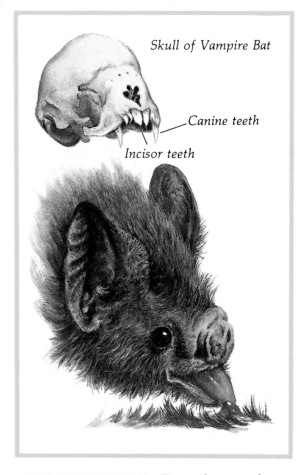

Skull of Vampire Bat

Canine teeth

Incisor teeth

THE VAMPIRE BAT *Desmodus rotundus*

DO BATS CARRY BUGS AND DISEASE?

For many years the bat has had the false reputation of transmitting bedbugs and other detrimental insects to men. Studies have shown that most of the parasites which the bat hosts appear to be unique to this animal and do not attack humans.

Another accusation against the bat is the transmission of rabies to humans and to animals. It is true that the myotis and other bats can carry rabies without showing any of the symptoms which normally accompany the disease.

IS THE BAT A FILTHY ANIMAL?

No. On the contrary, bats are exceptionally sanitary. Taking as much as a half hour, the little brown myotis bat will groom itself while it hangs upside-down. It uses its small, red tongue to wash its body. Any area which it cannot reach with its tongue is washed with the moistened hind foot.

The bat is particularly fastidious about its ears. Using the thumb of the forefoot, the animal painstakingly cleans the ears by twisting its thumb around and around. It is important that nothing block the ear, for its failure to function would result in certain death.

The hair of a bat is considered to be the finest of any animal. It also has the greatest number of hairs per unit area of skin surface. The bat's hair does not change color from season to season, and there is no apparent difference between the sexes either in size or color.

One reason the bat was thought to be a dirty animal is because of the musky odor it emits. The animal is also very oily and usually leaves a grease spot where it hangs. Another factor contributing to its reputation is the huge amount of guano that the bat colony accumulates.

HOW DANGEROUS IS THE VAMPIRE BAT?

Vampire bats very rarely bother humans. They may bite a man, but this is considered a rarity. They do feed on cattle with regularity. The bat lands on its victim and licks the area of skin which it intends to bite. The saliva of the bat is thought to have enzymes which are anti-coagulant. This allows the blood to flow freely.

The vampire has very specialized teeth. In fact, the vampire has the most specialized teeth of the bat family. It has two upper incisor teeth and four lower incisors. The bat uses its incisors to bite the victim. Although bites are only superficial, they will be sufficient to induce much bleeding. In addition, the bat has ten cheek teeth. The purpose of these is not clearly known.

Once the bat has made an incision, it extends its tongue, curling its edges to form a tube. The muscles of the tongue rapidly contract and move the blood up the tongue into the mouth. The vampire is very timid, and if its victim moves or reacts to the bite, the bat will quickly leave.

HOW DOES SCRIPTURE ILLUSTRATE ALERTNESS IN ACTING QUICKLY UPON SIGNALS OF DANGER?

Tragedies have occurred because vital information was not quickly or accurately reported to the right people. Who acted quickly with the information he learned and so saved the life of the greatest apostle to the Gentile world?

(Pause for a response—see page 20)

Clanking chains scraped along the stone floor and echoed throughout the dimly-lit prison. Well-trained guards stood at their posts. A breathless young man entered and was given permission to speak privately to a special prisoner. He quietly and carefully explained what he knew.

A deadly plot had been devised that morning. Forty men bound themselves together under an oath to kill this innocent man. They vowed neither to eat nor drink until they had accomplished their wicked scheme. Their plan was to ask the chief captain of the guard to bring this prisoner to their council the following day on the pretense that they wished to question him. But before the prisoner could reach the council, these men would murder him.

The young man had done an excellent job in securing facts and clearly explaining them to the one whose life depended on the accuracy of the report. When the prisoner realized what was planned, he called one of the guards and said, "Bring this man to the chief captain for he has something important to tell him."

The guard brought the young man to the chief captain who took him aside privately to ask what he had to say. Once again he explained, "You will receive a request to bring your prisoner to the council tomorrow. But don't do it; for forty men are lying in wait to kill him. They have bound themselves to an oath that they will neither eat nor drink until they have carried out their scheme."

When he heard this, the chief captain commanded the young man not to tell anyone else what he knew. Then he called two officers and ordered, "Make ready two hundred soldiers and seventy mounted cavalry and two hundred spearmen. Give our prisoner a horse to ride, and be ready to leave at nine o'clock tonight."

In the darkness of the night this heavily armed detachment marched and rode out of the barracks, bringing the prisoner to the safety of another province. From there he was taken to other cities. As he went, he boldly proclaimed the message God had given him.

His speaking and his letters continued to bring counsel, comfort, and warning to many people. All those who have benefited from the later ministry of the apostle Paul owe a debt of gratitude to his alert nephew who acted quickly upon signals of danger.

From Acts 23:6-35

Paul was accused of bringing a Gentile *beyond the above inscription which prohibited non-Jews from entering the sacred inner-temple courts.*

Paul was led from the rioting Jews *into the Antonia, a fortress overlooking the temple area.*

A Roman centurion carried a staff of vinewood *as his badge of office. He was in charge of one of the sixty centuries, consisting of one hundred men, of a Roman legion.*

THE QUICK RESPONSE OF PAUL'S NEPHEW BENEFITS GENERATIONS TO COME

The nephew of the apostle Paul is one of the less familiar characters of the New Testament, but his alertness and courage were used in a major way. He was used by the Lord to save his uncle Paul's life. As a result, Paul presented the Gospel to successive governors of Judea and the Jewish king, and finally reached his long-awaited destination of Rome where he strengthened the church.

DESTINATION—JERUSALEM

The whole affair began with Paul's intense burden to visit the Christians in Jerusalem (Acts 20:22). The elders of Ephesus did not believe they would ever see Paul again after this dangerous trip to a city where so many unbelieving Jews hated him (Acts 20:38). At the home of Philip, a prophet named Agabus predicted that Paul would be seized by the Jews and imprisoned by Roman authorities. The disciples begged him not to go, but Paul insisted, saying he was "ready, not to be bound only but also to die at Jerusalem for the name of the Lord Jesus." (Acts 21:13)

A RIOT IN THE TEMPLE

In Jerusalem, Paul reported to James and the church leaders. He told them of the mighty works the Lord was doing through his ministry to the Gentiles. They rejoiced in his message and gave God the glory (Acts 21:18-20). A week later when Paul was in the temple, he was recognized by some Jews from Asia Minor. They accused him of bringing a Gentile into part of the temple which was reserved only for Jews. The charge was false, but the result was a riot in the temple area.

News of the riot quickly reached Claudius Lysias, the chief captain of the Roman guard stationed in the tower of Antonia. This tower overlooked the temple area because of the frequency of such disturbances. Paul was rescued by the Romans and "bound with two chains." (Acts 21:33) Once the crowd quieted down, Paul was given permission to address the hostile mob. He gave a stirring testimony, but when he mentioned his ministry to the Gentiles, the Jews began to riot again (Acts 22:21-23).

A CONFUSED CAPTAIN—AN INQUIRING COUNCIL

The frustrated and confused Roman captain gave orders to beat a confession out of Paul; but when Paul explained that he was a Roman citizen and thereby privileged to a trial before being punished, he was sent to his cell unharmed. The next day, Paul appeared before a council of Jewish leaders which had been requested to examine him and then present some concrete charges. Paul pleaded not guilty to the charges, and another riot broke out among the council members themselves. Paul was again rescued by the Romans and sent back to prison.

FORTY MEN MAKE A MURDEROUS VOW

It was at this time that forty hate-driven Jews made a vow not to eat or drink before they killed Paul. They planned to murder him on his way to another council meeting the next morning. When Paul's nephew heard of the plot, he told Paul and then informed the chief captain. Claudius acted quickly, and by nine o'clock that night Paul was on his way to Caesarea with two hundred soldiers, seventy cavalrymen and two hundred spearmen as an escort. The escape was successful; the plot was foiled. This young man is never mentioned in the New Testament again. But because of his nephew's courageous alertness, Paul was alive and on his way to spread the Gospel at Rome.

WAS ANY RISK INVOLVED IN WHAT PAUL'S NEPHEW DID?

The fact that Paul's nephew heard of the plot indicates that he may have been associated in some way with the schemers. It has been suggested that this nephew's mother, Paul's sister, married into a high priestly family. The nephew may have overheard the plot being discussed in his own home. Paul's father was a Pharisee, and his family seems to have disinherited him after his conversion (Acts 23:6; cf. Philippians 3:8). Paul's nephew risked complete isolation from his Jewish family and friends for betraying this wicked scheme. If he had been sent to Jerusalem as a rabbinical student like his uncle (Acts 22:3), he could have faced expulsion. History records that the high priest, Ananias, was a Sadducee who often worked closely with Roman rulers. Paul's nephew had no guarantee that the chief captain, Claudius, would not eventually reveal the identity of his informant to Ananias. That could have resulted in execution at the hands of the same fanatical Jews who had vowed to kill Paul.

WHY DID THE CHIEF CAPTAIN ACT SO QUICKLY?

Before the captain would send 470 of his 1,000 soldiers on a long, night expedition, one would think he would investigate the account more thoroughly, especially when reported by only one young witness. But Claudius was only too well acquainted with the insane, irrational hatred of the Jews toward Paul. They had rioted three times against him in the last two days (Acts 21:30; 22:22; 23:10). The main reason Claudius wished to take no chances with the life of this prisoner was that he knew Paul was a Roman citizen by birth (Acts 22:3,25-29). Claudius had paid a great sum of money to became a naturalized Roman (Acts 22:28). If he allowed Paul to be assassinated without a trial, he would have jeopardized his entire career. He was thinking of himself, not Paul, when he acted so hastily.

WHY DID PAUL'S NEPHEW RESPOND TO THE DANGER FOR THE SAKE OF HIS UNCLE?

If Paul's nephew was an open and declared Christian, the reason for his intervention would be obvious. But the fact that he even knew of the plot indicates that someone thought he could be trusted with the information. The nephew, a student of the Old Testament, knew the plot of the supposed religious leaders was contrary to God's standards of justice. He may have memorized, "A true witness delivereth souls, but a deceitful witness speaketh lies." (Proverbs 14:25) His uncle had been falsely accused. There was neither concrete evidence nor reliable witness that he had brought a Gentile into the restricted temple area (Acts 21:28, 29). He also knew the Mosaic command, "And if a soul sin, and hear the voice of swearing, and is a witness, whether he hath seen or known of it; if he does not utter it, then he shall bear his iniquity." (Leviticus 5:1) Paul's alert nephew knew the truth of his uncle's innocence, and he knew the deceit of the assassins. Hence, he was responsible to avert this terrible crime lest he be guilty of being partner to the spilling of innocent blood.

"Then the soldiers, *as it was commanded them*, took Paul, and brought him by night to Antipatris."

PAUL'S NEPHEW

Alertness

IS ANTICIPATING THE ACTIONS OF THOSE WHO SEEK TO HARM US

"A prudent man forseeth the evil, and hideth himself: but the simple pass on, and are punished."
Proverbs 22:3

LIVING LESSONS ON ALERTNESS . . .

FROM THE PAGES OF SCRIPTURE

Scripture defines a simple person as one who is not aware of wrong steps of action or the consequences that follow. A wise person is one who foresees the evil and prepares himself for it, but the simple go blindly on and suffer the consequences. (Proverbs 22:3) In order to be alert to those who seek our harm, we must be aware of the predictable responses of human nature. We must also know how to apply the principles of Scripture to practical situations. Scripture provides the tragic account of a beautiful girl who was obedient but not alert. Nor did she have an understanding of spiritual truth that was required to protect herself from the treacherous scheming of a wicked young man.

ILLUSTRATED IN THE WORLD OF NATURE

RING-NECKED PHEASANT   *Phasianus colchicus*

The pheasant lives in areas where the ground is moist and fertile. Soils of high productivity which produce large amounts of grain also house or propagate large harvests of pheasant. The beautiful ring-necked pheasant is omnivorous, feeding on both animal and vegetable substance. Early in its life the young chick's diet is almost exclusively insects. Leading the list of these insects and larvae are crickets and grasshoppers. As the chick matures, it consumes more ripening grain until that becomes the mainstay of its diet. Pheasant prefer corn, wheat, oats, milo, flax, soybeans and other grains. If these are not available, it eats the less desirable berries of poison ivy, dogwood, sumac and rosewood. The pheasant attains a length of 20 to 35 inches and lives to be eight years old.

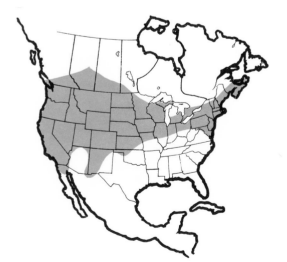

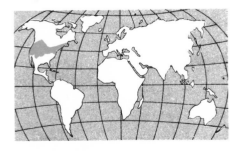

The range and habitat of the ring-necked pheasant

ALERTNESS

HOW DOES THE PHEASANT ILLUSTRATE ALERTNESS BY ANTICIPATING THE ACTIONS OF THOSE WHO SEEK TO HARM IT?

The wiliest, trickiest, most cunning, shrewd and unpredictable critter a hunter and his dog ever had to contend with—that's the pheasant! There is no trick the bird doesn't know and no limit to what it will do. It executes each elusive maneuver with finesse and ease.

Like magic, it seems, the bird can disappear. Every hunter who has pursued this crafty creature can chuckle and tell you one or more stories of how this bird eluded his most sophisticated strategy. Quick on its feet, it can easily outdistance a man.

The pheasant will elude a hunter by weaving in and out of corn rows or hedgerows, running well ahead of or doubling behind the unsuspecting hunter. With head and tail low to the ground, it sneaks inconspicuously through the low grass. If it sees an opening and an opportunity for a getaway, it lunges forward with head and tail high in the air, running like a racehorse at full gait.

At other times, when expedient, a pheasant just sits and waits for the hunter to pass by within feet of it. If for some reason, and it seldom happens, it finds itself cornered, it will explode with a burst of wings straight up into the air. It does this with such a commotion that even an experienced hunter becomes unnerved.

Waking before daybreak, two eager hunters prepared for what they hoped would be a productive day. Each year a friend of theirs made his farm available to them, and the past had always brought good hunting success. This year might be a little different, though. They hadn't been able to come on opening day and the season had begun a week ago. The birds would be skittish and hard to find due to the hunting pressure they had already experienced for a week. The hunters were hopeful, though, that this handicap would be overcome by the keen nose of their year-old dog—a German short-haired pointer.

During the summer they had occasionally taken the dog to a nearby field to develop its tracking and retrieving abilities. They had been encouraged by its progress, but it was still only a year old and would have to be watched closely.

By this time of the year the farmer had plowed all of his fields under except one. This was the field they tackled first since the brush and stalks provided likely cover for pheasant. Before they had a chance to scale the fence, their inexperienced dog slipped underneath the barbed wire and was immediately on the fresh scent of a bird.

It was a small field—no larger than a few acres—and in no time the dog had chased through the stalks to the other side where it flushed up two cock pheasants, well out of range of the eager hunters' guns. The dog stood gazing as they flew away but quickly forgot them when its keen nose caught the scent of a rabbit. Soon it was off and running again—past the field, over the hill and out of sight.

Frustrated and discouraged the hunters decided to search the field anyway hoping that a bird might still be in hiding. Systematically they strode back and forth combing every inch of the field. Finally, they gave up and decided to try another spot. After unloading their guns, one hunter gave his weapon to the other to hold while he climbed the fence. As he reached to get a good grip, an explosion of feathers shot up in front of him—a beautiful cock pheasant.

All they could do was look, laugh at their plight and admire the bird. If the hunters didn't know better, they would almost have thought that the pheasant anticipated their actions—right down to the point of waiting for them to unload their guns—before it took off.

SCRIPTURAL REFERENCES TO THE PHEASANT

The pheasant is not mentioned in Scripture, but there are several significant references to its close relative—the quail.

"And there went forth a wind from the Lord, and brought quails from the sea, and let them fall by the camp . . . and the people stood up all that day, and all that night, and all the next day, and they gathered the quails." Numbers 11:31, 32

The quail, like the pheasant, is an excellent source of food. The European quail, referred to in these verses, migrates over a wide range but has weak wings. The birds wait until the wind is with them and then fly very low. When God caused a flock of several million quail to cross the sea, the flight would have exhausted their strength and they would have been very easy to catch.

"He rained flesh also upon them (the nation of Israel) . . . they were not estranged from their lust. But while their meat was yet in their mouths, the wrath of God came upon them, and slew the fattest of them. . . ." Psalm 78:27-31

"They soon forgot his works; they waited not for his counsel, but lusted exceedingly in the wilderness, and tempted God in the desert. And he gave them their request but sent leanness into their soul." Psalm 106:13-15

Twice the Israelites murmured against God because the food was not to their liking. Their lives were built around satisfying their own desires. God's desire was to mentally and spiritually prepare them to receive His Word. Their error was in comparing their new life of freedom to the old life of slavery and flesh pots of Egypt (Exodus 16:2,3; Numbers 11:1-10).

The ring-necked pheasant *was the first bird successfully introduced to the United States. The first attempt of 1773 failed, but a subsequent try in 1881 brought the Chinese ring neck successfully to the western coast. Since that time the bird has continued to thrive with both its boundaries and numbers increasing yearly.*

Willamette Valley, Oregon

Nutten Island, New York

England

1773

1881

Shanghai, China

CHARACTERISTICS AND PHYSICAL FEATURES OF THE RING-NECKED PHEASANT

The alert ring-necked pheasant anticipated the actions of the hunters and so avoided the stinging effect of the buckshot. The pheasant has learned to survive by its wits and elusiveness. This wiliness is one of its chief assets and largely because of its ingenuity the bird continues to survive and prosper.

HAS THE RING-NECKED PHEASANT ALWAYS BEEN NATIVE TO NORTH AMERICA?

No. The colorful ring-necked pheasant's original home was Asia. It is thought that the Greeks brought the first two pheasants to Europe in the seventh or eighth century B.C. These black-marked pheasants were possibly brought to England from Europe by Julius Ceasar around the middle of the first century B.C. In 1773 a dozen pairs of English black-necked pheasants were released on Nutten Island, New York. This early attempt failed, though, and the birds died.

It was not until 1881 that the first successful transplant was made. Twenty-eight Chinese ring-necked pheasants were shipped by the U.S. Consul General at Shanghai to the Willamette Valley in Oregon. The birds adapted themselves so well that only eleven years later Oregon declared a 75-day hunting season. On the first day, an amazing harvest of 50,000 birds was taken.

Eventually a hybrid between the English pheasant and the Chinese ring neck was developed and introduced to the New England states. The bird thrived, and by the early 1900's the pheasant was abundant throughout most parts of the United States.

The Chinese ring-necked pheasant *is just one of 150 different varieties throughout the world. The American variety of the ring neck is a hybrid of the Mongolian (top), English (middle), and Chinese ring-necked pheasants (bottom).*

Female

Male

The wily ring-necked *pheasant has excellent eyesight. Its acute vision does not allow much to go unnoticed, and the bird is able to detect and avoid danger quickly.*

Occasionally sleet *storms create serious problems for pheasants if they are not adequately protected. Sleet may cover both the mouth and nostrils, freezing them shut and smothering the bird to death.*

Spur

The cock pheasant *uses its spurs when fighting to maintain territorial rights.*

WHY WAS THE RING-NECKED PHEASANT BROUGHT TO NORTH AMERICA?

The ring-necked pheasant was one of the first species of birds to be introduced to North America. It was hoped that this hardy bird would revive the sport of hunting by providing a substitute for the rapidly disappearing species of native game birds. The disappearance of these birds was particularly noticeable in the East. The turkey was near extinction and the ruffed grouse had drastically dwindled. With the introduction of this bird, sportsmen were once again given something to hunt. The pheasant was a bird that was worthy of being called a game bird—a bird that could endure hard weather, very adaptable to new terrain, and one that reproduced rapidly. In the United States alone, during an average good year, over eighteen million pheasants are harvested.

BECAUSE IT IS A HYBRID, DOES ITS APPEARANCE VARY?

Surprisingly not. The hybrid pheasant that exists in the United States today is a composite of the Mongolian, English and Chinese pheasant families. Because it is so consistent in maintaining its markings and coloration, it could almost be more correctly identified as a distinct American variety. Due to extensive crossbreeding, it is rare to find a pure Chinese ring neck roaming wild in the United States today. But the American variety is so close in appearance that it is easily confused as one.

WHAT IS THE DIFFERENCE BETWEEN A MALE AND FEMALE PHEASANT?

During hunting season many states permit hunters to shoot only male, or cock, pheasants. In the field, they may be hard to distinguish, but there are features which enable the viewer to identify each sex.

Size: The male pheasant weighs more and is larger in appearance than the female. The male weighs between two and three pounds and attains a length of thirty-five inches or more. Its tail accounts for a little less than one-third of this length. The female, on the other hand, weighs only two pounds and usually attains a length of about twenty-four inches, half of which is the tail.

Colorations: The female appears drab in comparison to the exotically colored male's ring neck. The males usually have a white ring on their neck, but this characteristic is variable. The male also has a patch of reddish, bare skin around the eyes. This is called "the bloom."

Voice: The male is more audible than the female and can be heard "singing" in the spring. This crowing establishes territorial boundaries and alerts female pheasants of its location. During the summer months the birds are seldom heard, but they resume their crowing in October.

When the bird is startled, the male emits a loud, hoarse croak as it flies away. On occasion females will also voice a cackle.

DOES THE PHEASANT TAKE TO THE AIR READILY?

The pheasant prefers the ground to the air, especially when it has dense cover. It hides and uses every evasive tactic to outmaneuver its pursuer. Only when all else has failed will it take to the air.

The bird has an unusual ability to disappear even when the cover or stubble around it is only a few inches high. It is able to squat down, lower its head and tail, and sneak through the vegetation at great speeds. Many times it holds tight to the ground, allowing the pursuer to pass within a few feet.

It flies only if cornered or if it is advantageous to do so, as in the winter when cover is reduced and the snow creates a vivid background to expose the colorful bird. When the pheasant does fly, it explodes into the air with such a flutter of wings and raucous cackle that it unnerves the pursuer, throwing him off balance just long enough to give the bird precious extra time to make a successful getaway.

IS THE PHEASANT A GOOD FLYER?

This game bird is strong in flight, but it is not capable of flying long distances. If the bird flushes when hemmed in by surrounding obstacles such as buildings or trees, it will catapult almost straight up into the air. Because its wings are broad, it can take off with great speed and quickly attain speeds of thirty-five to forty miles per hour.

This sudden burst into the air as well as its rapid flight demand great amounts of fuel. For this reason it must carefully conserve its energy or it will become exhausted and unable to fly. Therefore, pheasants fly only as fast and as long as they need to in order to avoid danger. Its wing to body ratio does not give it the ability of sustained flight and, depending on the wind, its limit is somewhat less than a mile in distance.

WHAT MAKES THE DIFFERENCE BETWEEN WHITE MEAT AND DARK MEAT?

The amount of blood vessels in it. Muscles which have many blood vessels running through them are dark meat. Those with few blood vessels are white or light meat. Migratory birds which have sustained flights and high energy requirements need many blood vessels to replace burned up fuel and oxygen. Birds that fall into this category are ducks and geese. The ring-necked pheasant is not a migratory bird and therefore does not need this elaborate vessel system. As a result, its meat is light in color.

The higher a bird flies, *the greater the amount of energy is needed to counteract gravity's pull. As the bird flies higher, air becomes cooler and thinner, providing less support for its wings. Therefore, even more energy is needed to keep warm and airborne. For this reason the pheasant tries to stay as close to the ground as possible. After it is airborne, it turns so it is flying horizontally to the ground, cruising at a height of about ten to fifteen feet.*

Silhouette of pheasant in flight

Powerful, short, broad wing

Freshly-laid eggs *can survive longer hours of exposure to cool weather than a clutch that is more developed. The female does not begin to incubate the eggs until they are all laid. Incubation requires approximately twenty-three days. The female's coloration allows her to blend in so well with her background that she is more difficult to see than her eggs. For this reason she rarely leaves the nest, even when predators are dangerously close. She doesn't flush from the nest; she just quietly slips away. Since the newly-hatched chick is sensitive to cold, the female is very careful to protect her young from exposure by nestling them beneath her wings and breast feathers.*

WHAT IS UNUSUAL ABOUT A PHEASANT EGG?

A unique characteristic of pheasants' eggs is that they all vary in shape from ovate to short ovate. Another distinctive feature is the percentage in weight of the yolk as compared to other bird eggs. The pheasant's yolk ranges from 32 to 50 percent of the content of the egg.

The female lays a clutch from eight to seventeen in number. If these unspotted, olive-brown eggs are to hatch, they must have a sufficient amount of moisture. Young pheasants are precocious; that is, they hatch with their eyes open and are able to leave the nest when only one day old.

WHAT IS A HEN TERRITORY?

The relationship of the male with its females is not a harem in the true sense of the word. The hens are not collected but each has an individual nesting sight and is not dependent upon the other females. The nesting sights form what is called a "hen territory" or a crowing territory. Both male and female make good parents. The cock is on hand to guard the broods of all its females. It is not associated with any one brood, but remains close to respond to the alarm cries of all.

Both male and female pheasants are capable of mating at one year of age. The male, or cock, is polygamous. It selects territories which it defends against other intruding males. For reproduction purposes, a ratio of one male to three females is considered the best. If a male has more than seven mates, its fertility is affected.

MAMMAL SUCKING LICE
Family Haematopinidae

These parasites feed on the blood of their hosts, and the bites they inflict are very irritating. They usually live on a particular part of the body, and on the pheasant their location is generally around the head. Eggs are attached to the pheasant's feathers. The louse spends its entire life on the host and will not survive long away from it. They are parasites of animals and birds but not of man.

Not all birds bathe in water. The pheasant is one which does not. Instead, it takes a dust bath in dry dirt. The advantages are many, and the bird may spend much time indulging in this activity. The dust helps the feathers grow straight and aids the bird in ridding its plumage of lice and other parasites. The pheasant chooses a favorite dust hole which it uses regularly. Sitting in the dust it seeks relief from the parasites by flicking the cool powder into its plumage.

HOW DOES SCRIPTURE ILLUSTRATE THE NEED FOR ALERTNESS IN ANTICIPATING THE ACTIONS OF THOSE WHO SEEK TO HARM US?

People may have hidden motives in seeking assistance. Scripture records a tragic example. A young man requested the help of a beautiful girl. She discovered too late that the one whom she tried to help was motivated by evil desires. Who was she?

(Pause for a response—see page 20)

The first signal of danger came in the form of an unusual request. It was given to a beautiful young princess by her father, the king. The request was for her to go to the home of a half brother and bake some cakes for him while he watched her. She could hardly have imagined the danger which this invitation held. Only keen alertness could protect her from the treachery she faced.

She dressed in royal apparel and followed the instructions given her by her father. He, too, was unaware of the evil motives of this son.

When she arrived at his home, she should have detected a second sign of danger. He watched her with lustful eyes as she prepared to bake the cakes for him.

The third warning signal came when he ordered all the servants to leave the room. The two were left alone. There was no righteous reason for him to require everyone to leave.

The next request was also inappropriate and should have signaled a flashing red light of danger to this attractive girl. He asked her to bring the cakes she had baked to his bedchamber. When she followed this instruction, she suddenly realized that this man was more sick in morals than in body, but it was too late. He grabbed her and demanded that she become immoral with him.

At that moment, only one thing could save her. God had provided clear instructions for what a girl should do if morally attacked. She should cry out to God. Her loud cries would have brought the servants to her rescue. And even more important, by crying out to God she would have prompted a fear of God in this wicked young man.

Instead, she tried to reason with him. To her own sorrow, she learned the futility of trying to reason with lust. She also learned what happens when lust is fulfilled—it turns to hatred. The hatred he now felt for her was greater than the lust that had prompted his vile scheme.

After morally attacking her, this wicked young man ordered her to be put out of his house. The door was bolted behind her. By doing so he rejected all further responsibility for her or for his actions. She tore her clothes, threw dust upon her head, and wept as she walked back to her home. The brother of this beautiful princess learned what her half brother had done, and he vowed revenge. Two years later he killed her attacker.

Tamar learned that it is not always possible to anticipate the actions of those who seek to harm us. It is for this reason that we must be alert to the wisdom of Scripture and the godly teaching of parents. The girl's father was King David. Years earlier he had faced treacherous enemies who planned to harm him. He escaped death by crying out to God, and then he watched his enemies retreat. David recorded the importance of crying out to God in Psalm 56:9, "When I cry unto thee, then shall my enemies turn back. This I know for God is for me."

From II Samuel 13

TAMAR'S FAILURE TO ANTICIPATE EVIL INTENTIONS BROUGHT SHAME AND DEATH TO HER FAMILY

All we know of David's beautiful daughter, Tamar, we learn from one chapter in the Bible, II Samuel 13. This chapter, so painful to read, is the beginning of the fulfillment of the prophet Nathan's strong words to David, "Thus saith the Lord, Behold, I will raise up evil against thee out of thine own house." (II Samuel 12:11) David was reaping the consequences of adultery and murder.

THE SINS OF THE FATHER ARE PASSED ON

David had had the choice of all the daughters of Israel and Judah, but he chose for himself the wife of another man. Likewise his son, Amnon, had the same opportunity but chose his half-sister, Tamar. David had murdered Uriah, the husband of Bathsheba. David's son, Absalom, murdered his half-brother, Amnon. Evil had indeed risen out of David's house, and poor Tamar was its innocent victim.

When we investigate the ancestry of Tamar, we find that her parents, David and Maacah, should never have married. Maacah's father was the ruler of the Sheikdom of Geshur, on the edge of the desert in Syria northeast of Galilee. We can only surmise the motive for this marriage, but according to the practice of the day, kings often cemented diplomatic relations with border states by various marriage relationships. In the case of David, he married "the daughter of Talmai, king of Geshur." (II Samuel 3:3) Maacah, probably very beautiful, became David's fourth wife and the mother of Absalom and Tamar.

THREE WARNINGS WERE IGNORED

Familiar as he was with the Mosaic Law, David ignored three principles of that Law. First, he married the daughter of a heathen king. Although not expressly forbidden in all cases, the principle was that these women would turn away the children from following the Lord (Deuteronomy 7:4). Second, he married for the fourth time before his other wives had died. Again, although not forbidden in the Law, the ill effect of polygamous marriages was legislated against (Deuteronomy 21:15-17). Third, David, in his position as king, completely ignored the warning that a king should not "multiply wives to himself, that his heart turn not away." (Deuteronomy 17:17)

A TRAP IS SET—A TRAP IS SPRUNG

Now it was time for David to reap what he had sown. His first-born, Amnon, lusted after his beautiful half-sister, Tamar. Amnon, the crown prince, was no doubt one of David's favored sons. When David saw this heir to his throne pining away of starvation (cf. II Samuel 13:4), he granted his unusual request to eat food at the hand of Tamar. Tamar, obeying the order of her father, proceeded into the trap that Amnon had prepared for her. In the confines of his apartment, Amnon shamed his naive sister and then threw her out of his presence.

THE PROPHECY COMES TRUE

When Absalom discovered that his beloved sister had been defiled by Amnon, he was filled with hatred and waited two years before avenging her. This may have marked the beginning of Absalom's disillusionment with his father's ability to judge the nation (cf. II Samuel 15:3,4). Absalom boldly killed his brother in full view of his other brothers (II Samuel 13:28, 29). He then fled to Geshur and remained there in exile for three years. After three years David allowed Absalom to return to Jerusalem but refused to see his face for two more years. All of these events beginning with Tamar's defilement by Amnon, led to Absalom's rebellion and further fulfilled Nathan's prophecy (cf. II Samuel 12:11,12; II Samuel 16:22). The rebellion was crushed upon the death of Absalom.

Nathan's prophecy had been bitterly fulfilled. Amnon, the crown prince, was dead as a result of his lack of moral restraint. Absalom, David's third-born, was dead as a result of his rebellion. Tamar, David's daughter, is last mentioned in Scripture remaining "desolate in her brother Absalom's house." (II Samuel 13:20)

"And she had a garment of divers colors upon her; for with such robes were the king's daughters who were virgins, apparelled."

DAVID'S WIVES AND CHILDREN

- Michal (died childless)
- Abigail (Daniel, died young)
- Ahinoam (Amnon)
- Maacah (Absalom, **Tamar**)
- Haggith (Adonijah)
- Abital (Shephatiah)
- Eglah (Ithream)
- Bathsheba (Shimea, Shobab, Nathan, Solomon)

"And she took flour, and kneaded it, and made cakes in his sight, and did bake the cakes. And she took a pan, and poured them out before him."

TAMAR CHARACTER SKETCH

WAS TAMAR RESPONSIBLE FOR AMNON'S LUSTFUL DESIRES?

There is not a shred of evidence with which to charge Tamar in tempting her half-brother to his disgraceful act. On the contrary, we read that "Amnon thought it hard for him to do anything to her." (II Samuel 13:2) The proper conduct of Tamar presented such a barrier to satisfying Amnon's lusts that only the "very subtle" Jonadab was able to devise a solution (II Samuel 13:2-5). As one of the king's daughters who wore the customary long-sleeved robe, Tamar's dress would have been impeccably modest (cf. II Samuel 13:18). Her immediate refusal to Amnon's unlawful suggestion reveals an abhorrence of such activity (II Samuel 13:12). It is no wonder that "Absalom hated Amnon, because he had forced his sister, Tamar." (II Samuel 13:22)

WHY WAS TAMAR SO GRIEVED WHEN AMNON SENT HER AWAY?

After Amnon satisfied his lust, we read that he "hated her exceedingly, so that the hatred wherewith he hated her was greater than the love wherewith he had loved her." (II Samuel 13:15) Then he told her to leave. When she protested, he had his servant put her out "and bolt the door after her." (II Samuel 13:17) By this action Amnon falsely accused her of seduction, and this disgrace was even worse than the other. Hence her protest, "This evil in sending me away is greater than the other that thou didst unto me." (II Samuel 13:16) Had she cried out, Amnon could have been tried for forcible rape as well as incest. With no witnesses, Amnon was free from prosecution and was now trying to save his name at the expense of his sister's (cf. Numbers 35:30; John 8:10).

COULD TAMAR HAVE ANTICIPATED AND AVOIDED THIS DISASTER BY BEING MORE ALERT?

When Absalom saw his weeping sister with ashes on her head and a torn dress, all symbols of great distress, he was without doubt as to the cause (II Samuel 13:19,20). Surely he had been aware of this potential danger. When her father asked her to fulfill Amnon's unusual request, Tamar could have invited her brother Absalom along for protection. When Amnon sent his servants out of the house and invited Tamar into his chamber (II Samuel 13:9, 10), she could have left Amnon's meal there and made her exit with the other men. When Amnon "would not hearken unto her voice" (II Samuel 13:14), she could have cried out for help. Since she was in the heavily populated city of Jerusalem, there is no question that she would have been heard (cf. Deuteronomy 22:24).

"**And Tamar put ashes on her head,** *and rent her garment of divers colors that was on her, and laid her hand on her head, and went on her way, crying.*"

TAMAR
tā′mĕr

113

IS VISUALIZING THE CONSEQUENCES OF SUBTLE DANGERS

"Pride goeth before destruction, and an haughty spirit before a fall."

Proverbs 16:18

"Wherefore let him that thinketh he standeth take heed lest he fall."

I Corinthians 10:12

LIVING LESSONS ON ALERTNESS . . .

FROM THE PAGES OF SCRIPTURE

Idolatry is a sin that many of us do not believe we commit because we fail to understand what it really is. If we allow a secret desire in our heart for something which God has forbidden, we begin to worship a false god. When we expect that false god to give us what only God can give, we commit idolatry. Idolatry is the illusion that lasting happiness and true fulfillment can be experienced in things which God has forbidden. A certain ruler began to lust after something which was contrary to God's Word. His deceptive heart convinced him that God's laws were designed to restrict his happiness, but their real purpose was to spare him from the destruction of unseen danger.

ILLUSTRATED IN THE WORLD OF NATURE

HOUSEFLY *Musca domestica*

Many insects which bear the name "fly"—the dragonfly, mayfly and damselfly—are not really true flies. These insects have four wings; a true fly has only two. The name of its order is *Diptera* from the Greek word which means two wings and it includes approximately 100,000 different species. The best known is probably the common housefly. The wings of the fly are so thin and transparent that its veins show through. These veins serve at least two purposes. One purpose is to carry blood to the wing, and the other is to give the wing support and stiffness. The housefly, which is about ten millimeters long, is capable of beating its wings 200 times per second and can fly an average speed of four and a half miles per hour. Faster speeds are possible for short distances in order to escape its enemies—the chiefest of which are birds and man.

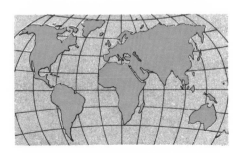

The range and habitat of the common housefly

The fly is at home anywhere in the world

ALERTNESS

HOW DOES THE HOUSEFLY ILLUSTRATE THE NEED TO RECOGNIZE SUBTLE DANGERS?

Gorged on a meal of decaying flesh and filth, the sluggish creature basked under the warm rays of the sun. An overhanging branch offered some degree of protection and seclusion, and the insect rested peacefully that beautiful mid-summer morning.

The housefly had little to fear. It is well-equipped to protect itself against enemies. For one thing, it has the ability of quick take-off. The moment its wings begin to beat it can be in the air, racing away and evading the clutches of any would-be assailant.

Another and even more remarkable defense is the housefly's keen vision. The insect has approximately 4,000 eyes! These tiny, individual eyes—each equipped with its own lens—are connected together to form one large or "compound eye." This large eye does not move but really doesn't need to because no two eyes see exactly the same thing. At each eye's strategic position the lens points in a different direction and works independently. The result is 180 degree, mosaic-type vision as each piece fits together to form the whole picture. The arrangement and structure of its eyes are of particular advantage to the fly because they enable it to detect instantly any quick movement.

The fly is alert to danger and its sensitive eyes and swift flight serve as strong allies in its struggle to survive. But this particular morning its meal and the warm sun lulled the fly into a lazy rest.

Suddenly, the fly was swept skyward. Flashing pain darted throughout its tiny body as sharp spines pierced it through. It was held tightly in a vice-like grip. The attack had come quickly and now the insect was in the unyielding claws of a praying mantis.

With long patience and cunning the mantis had stalked its prey. Its movements were almost negligible. The hunter's coloration and structure blended perfectly with the surrounding vegetation.

Slowly and deliberately, taking one step at a time, the praying mantis had approached the fly. When it came within striking range, the victim had still failed to recognize its presence. The predator had so perfectly executed its surprise attack that even the quick take-off and 4,000 eyes of the fly could not help now.

It had not seen the lightning swift movement of the outstretched claw until it was too late. Because it had failed to be alert to the subtle changes which had taken place around it, the fly lost its life.

SCRIPTURAL REFERENCES TO THE FLY

*"And there came a grievous swarm of flies into the
house of Pharaoh, and. . . the land was corrupted by
reason of the swarms of flies."*
Exodus 8:24

The "swarms of flies" could have included several species.
Among them the flies that thrive on filth and waste and
reproduce at a phenomenal rate. They breed on decay and
vermin, harbor millions of bacteria, and carry many diseases.
They would have corrupted the land in a number of
destructive ways.

This plague, as well as the other nine plagues of Egypt, was
miraculous in its intensity, violence and precise timing. God
chose to use natural phenomena for the plagues because the
Egyptians worshiped such things as the frog, the river, the fly,
etc. This was God's way of mocking their false gods and
demonstrating His supremacy over every part of His creation.
Baal-zebub, a god which the Philistines worshiped, was "god
of the flies."

*"Dead flies cause the ointment of the apothecary to
send forth a stinking savour; so doth a little folly him
that is in reputation for wisdom and honor."*
Ecclesiastes 10:1

The "ointment" which the druggist mixes is designed for
healthful purposes, but the fly breeds death and decay. A dead
fly can be removed from the ointment but its eggs will become
maggots. The spoiling mixture gives off a warning of danger
by a foul smell. A little folly is like the eggs of a fly in the
ointment. It is out of character for a wise man and causes his
good reputation to stink.

CHARACTERISTICS AND PHYSICAL FEATURES OF THE HOUSEFLY

An alertness to subtle danger was not demonstrated by the fly. As a result, its life was taken. Just as this insect needed to be aware of the gradual approach of the praying mantis, so must man be alert to the danger inherent in this seemingly harmless creature. The prolific insect has a life history of filth and disease.

WHERE DOES THE FLY'S LIFE BEGIN?

It begins in the form of an egg. The female fly lays as many as one thousand eggs. She does not lay these all at once but rather one to two hundred and fifty at a time. At the tip of the female's abdomen is an organ called an *ovipositor* through which the eggs are laid. She pushes this organ into soft masses of carrion, decay or excrement. The eggs hatch within twelve to twenty-four hours into maggots or larvae. These thrive in the filth and waste.

HOW DOES A MAGGOT BECOME A FLY?

Maggots or larvae have an appearance similar to that of worms or little caterpillars. During this stage the fly larva spends all its time eating and growing. As it grows larger, it molts or sheds its shell to grow a new one. This molting process occurs several times.

The larva then enters the pupa stage by building a strong, oval enclosure called a *puparium* around itself. Inside this enclosure the larva loses its worm-like appearance and takes on the shape of an adult fly. When the complete change has taken place, one end of the puparium splits down the back, and the adult fly crawls out. When it leaves this enclosure, its wings are moist and soft. Blood will flow into the veins of the wing and stiffen them as the air dries them. In a few hours they will have hardened, and the insect then flies away to find a mate.

HOW MANY OFFSPRING COULD A PAIR OF FLIES HAVE?

It has been theoretically calculated that if perfect conditions existed and if all the offspring of an individual pair of flies lived, their potential population during the months of April through August would reach the astounding total of 190,000,000,000,000,000,000.

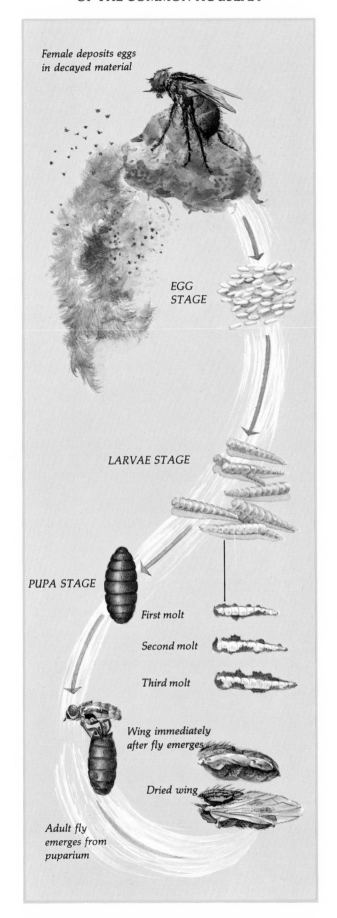

THE LIFE CYCLE
OF THE COMMON HOUSEFLY

Female deposits eggs in decayed material

EGG STAGE

LARVAE STAGE

PUPA STAGE

First molt

Second molt

Third molt

Wing immediately after fly emerges

Dried wing

Adult fly emerges from puparium

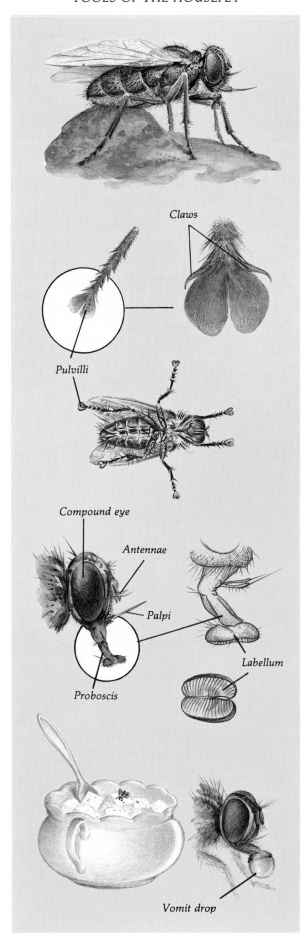

Claws

Pulvilli

Compound eye

Antennae

Palpi

Labellum

Proboscis

Vomit drop

IS THE FLY COLD-BLOODED OR WARM-BLOODED?

The fly is cold-blooded as are most other insects. Its body temperature remains just about equal to the temperature of its surroundings. As a result, body functions fluctuate depending on whether it is warm or cold. For instance, on a cool summer morning the insect will be sluggish and often unable to fly. In order for it to become airborne it vibrates its wings in an effort to raise its temperature and warm its flight muscles.

HOW MANY ENEMIES DOES THE HOUSEFLY HAVE?

Many. Spiders ensnare the unsuspecting fly in their sticky webs. Toads and frogs fire their long tongues to either snatch the insect out of the air or off of its perch. Birds prey heavily upon flies and are a major force in keeping their numbers in check. Among these birds are swifts and swallows, both skilled and agile in scooping them out of the air. Other birds which consume great quantities of both the larvae and the adult are nuthatches, chickadees, vireos, and orioles.

HOW LONG DOES A FLY LIVE?

The age of a fly is variable. A normal lifespan during the summer is about thirty days. Heat and cold influence the developing process. Flies live longer in cooler weather but are less active. Usually when the weather becomes cold, the adult fly will die. If it happens to be in the pupa stage when winter arrives it will probably live through the cold months and develop into an adult the next spring.

HOW DOES THE FLY FIND ITS FOOD?

The fly has two antennae that not only help it find its food but also warn it of danger. These antennae grow in the center of the head between the eyes. They are alert to changes of movement in the air around them and warn of an approaching enemy. They are sensitive to smell and capable of picking up the odors of chemicals in decomposing or rotting materials.

HOW COULD SUCH A SMALL INSECT BE SO DANGEROUS?

The housefly is considered to be one of the most dangerous insects to man. This creature hatches and matures in filth. Its very diet is filth. It enjoys decaying flesh, the sick room, garbage, the manure heap, and the sugar bowl on your table. It indiscriminately eats all with equal relish. To say that the fly is dangerous to man is an understatement. A single fly can harbor as many as thirty million organisms or bacteria in its internal tract and five hundred million on its body surface.

HOW DOES A FLY TRANSMIT BACTERIA?

It is not uncommon for a fly to cover an area of sixty miles in one day. This insect's body and legs are entirely covered with fine, closely-growing hair. These hairs act like brooms, sweeping up disease-ridden organisms as the fly travels from food to food. The feet are another catch-all for germs. Located on the sole of the fly's foot is a sticky substance which also accumulates many bacteria.

DOES THE HOUSEFLY BITE?

The housefly does not bite but uses its proboscis in another interesting way. Its mouthparts are a pair of soft, fleshly lobes located at the end of its proboscis. The only way a fly can eat that lump of sugar on your table is to first soften it by regurgitating a "vomit drop." Its fleshy, expandable lobes rasp the surface of the food. Then a drop of digested food from its last meal softens the material and the fly laps it back up. The only problem with this untidy method is that it leaves a residue, or fly spot, infested with bacteria.

HOW MANY DISEASES COULD A FLY CARRY AT ONCE?

The common housefly is capable of transmitting approximately forty serious diseases. Among these are typhoid fever, amebic dysentery, bacillary dysentery, cholera, anthrax, tuberculosis, yaws, conjunctivitis, cestode and nimatode worms. Listed in the box below is information about some of these diseases—their symptoms, cure, and what happens if the disease is not treated.

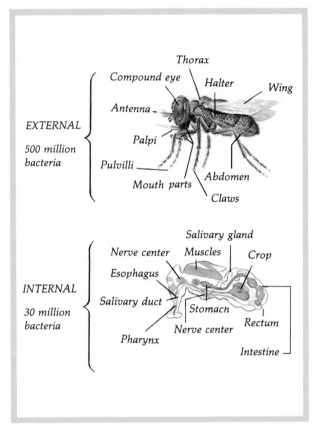

BODY STRUCTURE OF A HOUSEFLY

THE SUBTLE THREAT OF THE FLY

DISEASE	SYMPTOMS	CURES	CONSEQUENCES IF UNTREATED
TYPHOID FEVER	High fever, headache, cough, slow pulse, rose-colored spots on abdomen	Typhoid vaccine, antibiotics	Internal hemorrhage, intestinal perforation 10 percent to 30 percent death rate
AMEBIC DYSENTERY	Diarrhea with blood and pus	Bed rest, bland diet, tetracyclines	Hepatitis, abscess of liver, perforation of bowel giving rise to severe and even fatal diseases
BACILLARY DYSENTERY	Fever, drowsiness, nausea, vomiting, diarrhea, cramps	Water to prevent dehydration, tetracyclines, salt-water balance	Dehydration, colitis giving rise to severe and even fatal diseases
CHOLERA	Watery stools, dehydration, vomiting	Vaccine, salt and water replacement to prevent shock	Grave shock 60 percent death rate
TUBERCULOSIS	No early symptoms	None Chest x-ray to verify	Collapsed lung, blood when coughing, fever Always have disease

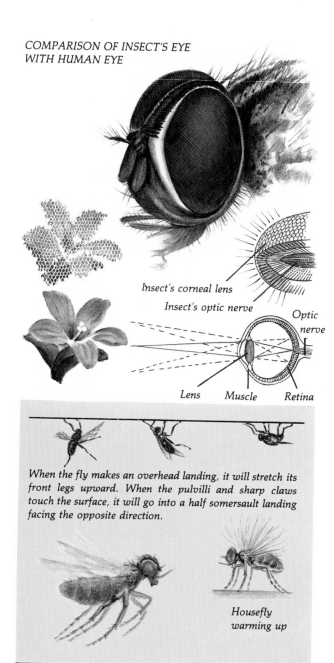

Insect's corneal lens

Insect's optic nerve

Optic nerve

Lens   Muscle   Retina

When the fly makes an overhead landing, it will stretch its front legs upward. When the pulvilli and sharp claws touch the surface, it will go into a half somersault landing facing the opposite direction.

Housefly warming up

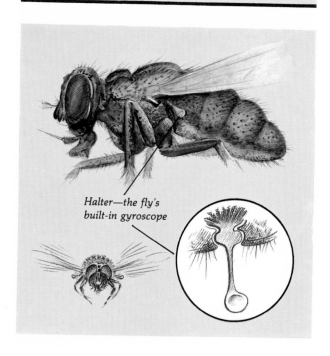

Halter—the fly's built-in gyroscope

HOW DOES THE FLY'S EYE DIFFER FROM MAN'S EYE?

This insect has many eyes; each has its own lens and all are connected to the brain with nerves. Each eye is pointed in a slightly different direction and therefore sees in a different direction. These 4,000 individual images are all gathered together into an aggregate to form a mosaic type of picture.

The human eye, on the other hand, has a single lens the shape of which can be changed by muscles which focus nearby or distant images on the retinal nerve cells. Each nerve cell transmits a small section of the total visual field to the brain. The difference in images is that the insect's mosaic-like picture appears to be broken up, whereas the human eye sees the complete continuous, unbroken image.

HOW IS THE FLY ABLE TO WALK ON A CEILING?

The fly has six legs and uses all of them when it walks. At the end of each foot is a claw. This claw helps the fly cling to any surface—even a ceiling. In addition to this, flies also have hairy pads or pulvilli on their feet. These hairs have a sticky coating. These special features enable the fly to walk on smooth, slippery surfaces whether right side up or upside down.

HOW DOES THE FLY MAINTAIN ITS BALANCE IN THE AIR?

Many insects have two sets of wings; the fly has only one. Where its second pair might be located, the fly has an organism called a halter. This halter balances or stabilizes the fly, enabling it to dart any direction. These extremely delicate sense organs are located on the metathorax.

IS THE FLY CAPABLE OF GLIDING?

No. The fly must constantly beat its wings in order to stay airborne. Its wings are continually in motion while it is in the air and do not stop until its feet have touched a surface. This can be demonstrated by simply picking up a housefly and allowing its wings and legs freedom to operate. As soon as the insect leaves the ground its wings immediately go into motion.

HOW DOES SCRIPTURE ILLUSTRATE THE NEED TO RECOGNIZE SUBTLE DANGERS?

A birthday should be the mark of growing maturity and wisdom, but for one man it was a memory of moral weakness and spiritual foolishness. Who was this man whose birthday celebration haunted him for the rest of his life?

(Pause for a response—see page 20)

History records this man as the ablest of several ruling brothers, but the security of his reign was constantly threatened. Riots and rebellions had toppled many other leaders. He recognized that there were seeds of insurrection within his own realm.

A host of aides, lords, captains, and soldiers were trained to watch for any sign of danger. He worked hard and long to maintain peace and establish his rule. Things seemed to go well, but inwardly this ruler was waging an even greater struggle. He desired to marry another man's wife.

Holding himself above the law, he did as he pleased. But his wrong action provoked sharp rebuke from one man who boldly proclaimed God's holy standard. This godly man was held in great reverence by the people. The ruler's illegal new wife wanted to kill him, but her husband knew that such action might trigger a bloody rebellion. Instead, he imprisoned him in a formidable dungeon.

Once again the political situation seemed to be in control. The day came for this ruler to celebrate his birthday. He made a great feast for his lords, high captains, and the chief leaders of his province. What was to be the highlight of this occasion became instead his moment of infamy.

This powerful ruler whose servants obeyed his every whim now sat at the feet of one who skillfully subdued him. The man who trained the eyes of many others to watch for signs of trouble, now allowed his own eyes to be dimmed to greater danger by the seductive charms of one who stood before him. Confident of his physical prowess, he was lulled into a spiritual stupor. He and his guests gaped in sensual pleasure at the lewd dancing of a young girl.

In a burst of proud revelry, he said to the girl, "Ask of me what you want and I will give it to you, even to half of my kingdom." The girl, directed by her mother, gave her answer. When the ruler heard her request, he was shocked back to reality. He had been caught in the trap of his own ways.

This girl was the daughter of his new wife, and her request was the death of that great man of God who spoke against her marriage. The ruler did not want to carry out this request and regretted that it had been made; but for the sake of his oath to the girl and to maintain the respect of his guests, he sent a messenger to the dungeon. The head of John the Baptist was brought back on a platter.

In a moment of moral weakness, Herod Antipas had added yet another scar to his seared conscience. This scar was to haunt him for the rest of his life because he failed to visualize the consequences of subtle danger. Shortly after this event, he heard of the miraculous works of Christ. His troubled conscience caused him to conclude that it was the return of this righteous man whom he had murdered.

From Matthew 14:1-14 and Mark 6:14-29

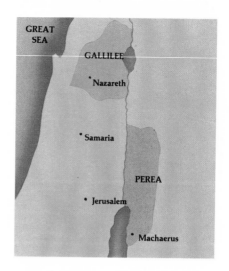

Herod Antipas was a tetrarch. *This term originally described a petty dependent prince, lower in rank and authority than a king, who ruled one fourth of a region. Herod ruled over Galilee and Perea.*

NOTABLE WIVES AND SONS OF HEROD THE GREAT

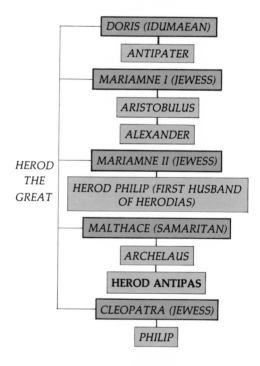

HEROD THE GREAT

- DORIS (IDUMAEAN)
  - ANTIPATER
- MARIAMNE I (JEWESS)
  - ARISTOBULUS
  - ALEXANDER
- MARIAMNE II (JEWESS)
  - HEROD PHILIP (FIRST HUSBAND OF HERODIAS)
- MALTHACE (SAMARITAN)
  - ARCHELAUS
  - **HEROD ANTIPAS**
- CLEOPATRA (JEWESS)
  - PHILIP

The site of the mountain fortress of Machaerus *where Herod Antipas beheaded John. It was located east of the Dead Sea in Herod's possession of Perea.*

CONSEQUENCES HEROD ANTIPAS SUFFERED BECAUSE HE FAILED TO BE ALERT TO SUBTLE DANGERS

Herod Antipas was raised in a family of intrigue, jealousy, greed, hatred, and murder. His father was the infamous Herod the Great who, as a diseased and deranged old man, ordered the killing of all the male children of Bethlehem who were two years old and under (Matthew 2:16). His mother, Malthace, was the fourth wife of ten whom Herod married. She bore Herod two sons, Archelaus and Antipas.

THREE SONS—ONE KINGDOM

At one time, Antipas had been designated as the sole heir of his father's kingdom. Then, just before Herod the Great died, he decided to declare the older brother, Archelaus, king. Antipas and his half-brother, Philip, were to rule over smaller localities. After the death of their father, the brothers Archelaus and Antipas went to Rome to have Caesar Augustus resolve the controversy of rule. Augustus compromised, dividing the kindgom among the three men.

ANTIPAS ATTAINS AN HONOR AT ARCHELAUS' EXPENSE

When Archelaus returned from Rome, he treated his subjects with great brutality. Thus when Joseph, Mary, and Jesus returned from their journey to Egypt and heard that Archelaus was the ruler of Judea, they withdrew to Galilee which was under the rule of the less brutal Antipas (Matthew 2:22).

In A.D. 6, Archelaus was deposed and exiled by Augustus. He had been formally charged with using excessively oppressive measures against his subjects. Antipas went to Rome with the group which pressed these charges, and it was at this time that he gained the title of Herod to attach to his name. This was of great prestige to his subjects and to the political and social circles of the Roman world.

ADULTERY DESTROYS TWO MARRIAGES

Antipas married the daughter of Aretas IV, an Arabian king. It was a marriage of the kind which Augustus especially approved because it helped solidify his empire with peaceful ties. The result of the marriage, however, was anything but peace. Around A.D. 29 on a journey to Rome, Antipas visited the home of one of his half brothers. Here he met and committed adultery with Herodias, his half brother's wife. This ambitious woman, not content to be the wife of a private citizen, secured Antipas' promise to divorce his present wife and marry her on his return from Rome. His present wife heard of the arrangement and fled to her father. The divorce was a personal insult to his father-in-law, Aretas, and severed relations between the two countries.

A CONNIVING WOMAN TRICKS HER HUSBAND

It was after this marriage that Herod Antipas became involved with John the Baptist. As a forthright prophet of God, John declared to Herod, "It is not lawful for thee to have thy brother's wife." (Mark 6:18) John's teaching was of great embarrassment to his wife, Herodias, and on her account he illegally bound him in prison. Herodias wanted to kill John because of his condemnation of their marriage, but she could not convince her husband because Antipas feared John (Mark 6:19, 20). Through scheming and deceit she tricked her husband into giving her the head of John. Antipas, like Ahab of old, has gone down in history as the dupe of his wicked wife.

HEROD ANTIPAS CHARACTER SKETCH

WHY DID HEROD IMPRISON JOHN BUT NOT WANT TO KILL HIM?

Herod Antipas was a tetrarch, not a king. He ruled under the authority of the Caesar. He had seen his brother removed by a popular appeal to Rome. His marriage to Herodias was not well-received by the powerful group of religious leaders called the Pharisees. The Mosaic Law forbad the marriage of a brother's wife (Leviticus 18:16; 20:21) with the exception of raising children of a deceased, childless brother by levirate marriage (Deuteronomy 25:5; Mark 12:19). But Herodias was not barren, and Antipas' brother was still alive. The fact that his mother was a Samaritan did not increase his acceptance with the Jews (John 4:9; 8:48). Herod could not tolerate open criticism of himself. He imprisoned John to keep him quiet. On the other hand, he feared to kill him. His conscience had not yet completely deadened, and he knew that John was a righteous and holy man. Moreover, John had made such a powerful impression on the people that he feared an unjust murder would create a riot (cf. Matthew 14:5), or even worse, cost him his career.

WHY DID CHRIST NEVER SPEAK TO HEROD?

Only three contacts between Jesus and Herod Antipas are recorded in the New Testament. First, when Herod heard of the miracles Jesus was performing, he feared that He was John raised from the dead and desired to see Him (Luke 9:7-9). Second, the Pharisees reported to Jesus that Herod wanted to kill Him. Christ knew that he was afraid to use force for fear of stirring up the people as he had done with the murder of John and so resorted to this cowardly intimidation to force Jesus to leave his domain. Jesus called him a fox—the animal which is weak and uses cunning deceit to achieve its aims—hence, a crafty coward (Luke 13:31-33). The third contact occurred when Jesus was tried before his death. Herod "questioned him in many words; but he answered him nothing." (Luke 23:9) The same Jesus who patiently talked to the despised Samaritan woman and the woman taken in adultery refused to utter a sound before Herod. Jesus knew that Herod's conscience was now completely seared and he would no longer listen to the words of truth. Jesus refused to give that which is holy unto the dogs or cast his pearls before swine, lest Herod trample them under his feet (Matthew 7:6). Humiliated by the Lord's silence, the pitiable "Herod, with his men of war, set him at nought, and mocked him, and arrayed him in a gorgeous robe, and sent him again to Pilate." (Luke 23:11)

HOW DID GOD JUDGE HEROD FOR FAILING TO VISUALIZE SUBTLE DANGERS?

In A.D. 36, the upset father of Herod's divorced wife attacked and defeated Herod's army. The Jews viewed this defeat as divine judgment for his execution of John the Baptist. In A.D. 37 the new emperor, Caligula, began his rule. He gave the brother of Herod's wife the prestigious title of king. Herodias convinced Antipas to go to Rome to request this long-coveted title. Herodias' brother, suspicious of Herod's aspirations, sent word to the emperor that Herod was planning a revolt from the empire. When Herod arrived in Rome, his wealth and tetrarchy were given to his scheming brother-in-law. Herod was banished to France where he lived out his life in obscurity with his disappointed wife.

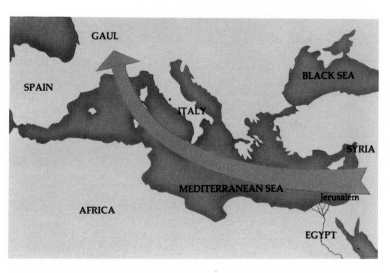

Herod's divorce and remarriage *involved him in war and murder. His unpopularity with the Jews as a result of killing John was a factor which contributed to the eventual loss of his kingdom. He was exiled to ancient Gaul northwest of Rome.*

HEROD ANTIPAS
hĕr´ŭd ăn´tĭ-pás

125

Availability

"And whosoever will be chief among you, let him
be your servant: Even as the Son of man came not to
be ministered unto, but to minister, and to give his
life a ransom for many."

Matthew 20:27-28

PART THREE

SERVING MY FAMILY FIRST BEFORE I CONSIDER OTHER NEEDS OR WANTS

REFUSING TO BE DETERRED BY DECEPTIVE DISTRACTIONS

REJECTING AMBITIONS THAT HINDER US FROM BEING WHERE WE ARE NEEDED

STANDING BY A TASK UNTIL IT IS FULLY COMPLETED

Availability

IS SERVING MY FAMILY FIRST BEFORE I CONSIDER OTHER NEEDS OR WANTS

"But if any provide not for his own, and specially for those of his own house, he hath denied the faith, and is worse than an infidel."

I Timothy 5:8

LIVING LESSONS ON AVAILABILITY . . .

FROM THE PAGES OF SCRIPTURE

The most discerning audience we will ever have is our own family. They know precisely whether or not our life matches our message. Only when we pass the test of consistent living at home are we qualified to expand our ministry. Our family responsibilities are not barriers to a future ministry; they are basic training for it. For example, the skills David learned in order to protect and feed the family flock were later used to conquer a giant and feed a nation. The skills a church leader learns in order to meet the needs of his own family will be used to understand and meet the needs of the church. This explains why Christ told a certain man to go home to his family and first demonstrate his faith to them.

ILLUSTRATED IN THE WORLD OF NATURE

BROWN-HEADED COWBIRD   *Molothrus ater*

In the Greek language, *molothrus* refers to a tramp, vagabond, parasite, or greedy person. The cowbird's name characterizes the species well. The bird entered North America from Mexico. Then it spread through the prairie states and expanded its range to the east and west coasts as civilization cleared forests and cultivated the land. The cowbird prefers the habitat of farm lands, groves, and the edge of forests. The adult is six to eight inches in length and undergoes a complete molt in September, but the plumage change is inconspicuous. The male is black except for a brown head and neck; the female is a dull, slate gray. This bird is described as a parasite because of the manner in which it allows its young to be raised.

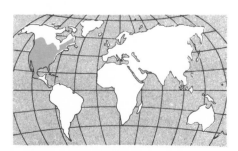

The range and habitat of the brown-headed cowbird

AVAILABILITY

HOW DOES THE COWBIRD ILLUSTRATE THE NEED TO SERVE ITS FAMILY FIRST?

The bird appeared to be excited and anxious as it flittered from bush to bush in the hedgerow. There seemed to be an urgency in its activity. In fact, it appeared to have lost its nest. The events which followed were typical for this particular bird but very unusual in the avian world.

Finally, it found the nest low on a branch. Slipping inside, it reached down, stretched its beak wide open, picked up one of the four eggs and then darted away. Finding a perch, she cracked and ate the egg—the contents as well as part of the shell. Once she had destroyed the egg she stayed away from the nest until the following day. Why would she destroy one of her own eggs?

Late the next morning when it did fly back to the hedgerow, the bird did not go directly in. It seemed very hesitant and anxious as it waited. After a delay of several minutes, it made a nervous and cautious approach to the nest and perched on its rim.

Quickly the female entered the nest, staying only a few seconds before flying rapidly away. But when she left, there was something different in the nest—a new egg, a different color than the others.

The cowbird is referred to as a parasite. This bird does not build its own nest but instead relies on the construction of others.

In the spring, the cowbird watches for birds building their nests and waits as they complete their busy construction work. Or it may find an already completed nest and make plans to use that.

One day before the cowbird lays its egg it waits until the owner of the marked nest is gone. Once the parent bird leaves, this interloper slips in and steals an egg from the nest of the rightful occupant. This it destroys.

The next day it cautiously returns, lays its own egg in a period of less than one minute and quickly leaves again. It is very careful not to disturb the nest for it will not return but will rely on the owner of the nest to care for the young cowbird.

But in this particular case, the female cowbird made a wrong choice. She had chosen the home of a robin. Upon returning to the nest, the robin immediately recognized the foreign object. By using its bill, the robin worked the egg up to the rim of the nest and rolled it over the edge. The egg tumbled to the ground, smashing the shell and spilling its liquid contents.

The cowbird succeeded in shirking its responsibility and in the process failed its young. While the negligent parent abandoned its egg to enjoy a carefree life with others of its kind, the embryonic life of the one she was supposed to be serving was destroyed.

SCRIPTURAL REFERENCES TO THE COWBIRD

There is no direct reference to the cowbird in Scripture, but an unusual trait of the cowbird is also a trait of the cuckoo. The cuckoo was a bird of Palestine and is mentioned twice in Scripture. It does not maintain a storehouse of provision for the future but is totally dependent on the food at hand for its survival. Like the cowbird, the cuckoo goes one step further in freedom from worry—it lays its eggs in the nest of another bird, then leaves. This apparently irresponsible action does not negate the lesson taught by Christ.

"Therefore I say unto you, take no thought for your life, what ye shall eat, or what ye shall drink: nor yet for your body, what ye shall put on, is not the life more than meat and the body more than raiment? Behold the fowls of the air, for they sow not, neither do they reap, nor gather into barns, yet your heavenly father feedeth them. Are ye not much better than they?"
Matthew 6:25,26

Man stores provision for times of scarcity, but his storehouse tends to become his source of security rather than God. Hence the command, "Behold the fowls of the air." If God takes care of birds that don't even take care of their own young, how much more will He take care of the needs of His own children?

*Typical egg
of the cowbird*

CHARACTERISTICS AND PHYSICAL FEATURES OF THE BROWN-HEADED COWBIRD

By failing to serve its own family first, the unavailable cowbird destroyed the life of the one it was to serve. During the summer when it should have been concentrating on its nest and rearing its offspring, the cowbird lived a carefree life, free from the burden of responsibility. This freedom has an expensive price tag, for not only are her eggs jeopardized but the eggs of her host as well. Many birds needlessly die—some species' survival is a actually being threatened—because the brown-headed cowbird is not responsible or available to anyone.

IS THERE ANY SPECIES OF BIRD THAT WILL ACCEPT A COWBIRD'S EGG?

It is estimated that there are approximately one hundred ninety-five species of birds which the cowbird victimizes. It is surprising that ninety-one of these do not seem to mind the intrusion, or at least they accept it, because they do incubate and hatch the egg.

Some of the smallest birds which are affected by this parasite are gnatcatchers and kinglets. Other nests which the cowbird regularly uses belong to the wood thrush and other thrushes, song sparrows, redstarts, oven-birds, towhees, scarlet tanagers, and vireos. Both the redstart and the vireo have been known to reject the egg by putting a nest floor over all the eggs and starting over again.

WHAT IS DIFFERENT ABOUT THE COWBIRD'S EGG?

The semi-glossy and granulated shell of this egg is stronger than the eggs of other songbirds. The background color varies from almost pure white to a gray color. It occasionally takes on a pale blue cast. Over this background the surface is covered with blotches and specks. These also vary in color from shades of light brown to dark brown and cinnamon. The markings or specks are heaviest at the larger end of the egg and occasionally form an irregular wreath. The eggs are also irregular in their shape and vary from elongate ovate, round, to short ovate.

COMMON SPECIES THAT HOST THE COWBIRD'S EGG

Song sparrow

Wood thrush

Red-eyed vireo

Redstart

Among the birds most often victimized *is the vireo. The cowbird regularly invades nine of the twelve species of vireos found in North America.*

133

Parasitic cowbird egg

Young cowbird monopolizing food

Oversized cowbird squeezing out nestmates

Even after the cowbird leaves the nest it will still be necessary for the foster parent to continue feeding it.

Young cowbird joins its own kind.

DOES IT MATTER WHEN THE COWBIRD LAYS ITS EGG?

Yes. The cowbird must wait for the host bird to lay its eggs first. If the cowbird becomes impatient and lays its egg first, the other bird may desert the nest and begin a new one somewhere else.

WHAT IS DIFFERENT ABOUT THE INCUBATION PERIOD OF THE COWBIRD?

The cowbird's incubation period is the shortest of any songbird. Depending on the host bird, it takes approximately ten to thirteen days to incubate and hatch the cowbird egg. As a general rule it hatches one day earlier than the eggs of the host. For instance, a song sparrow may hatch the invader a day before its own brood, giving the cowbird a head start and a distinct advantage over its nestmates.

HOW DO PARENT BIRDS KNOW WHICH OF THE YOUNG TO FEED FIRST?

The parent bird does not have a rotation system but simply feeds the hungriest one first. It continues to feed the young bird until one of its nestmates becomes hungrier, cries louder, and is able to stretch its neck up farther.

A young bird has built-in regulators, and when it is full, the muscles in its throat do not work. Even after the bird is full it will keep its mouth open as long as the parent is near. The parent may look down the throat of its squawking young. If there is any unswallowed food, it reaches down to pull it out and feeds it to the next one.

This procedure works well in a normal nest, but if a baby cowbird is present, it monopolizes the food with its larger appetite, bigger mouth, and longer neck. The cowbird usually receives a large percentage of the food, if not all of it.

WILL THE COWBIRD TRY TO ELIMINATE ITS NESTMATES?

The cowbird does not normally try to push the others out of the nest. It is rarely necessary. Because it has up to a day's head start over the others and often has a monopoly on the food supply, it grows quite rapidly. Many times a cowbird chooses a host much smaller than itself. Its mere size as it grows could push one or more of the other birds out.

HOW MANY EGGS WILL A COWBIRD LAY?

The cowbird normally lays from one to five eggs per season. She lays one a day, if possible, and chooses a different nest each time. Incidents have been recorded though, of the bird laying two to four eggs in one nest if there is a shortage of nest sites available. Sometimes more than one female cowbird uses a host nest, so there might be three to four cowbird eggs in competition with the original brood.

ARE THERE ANY SPECIES THAT THE COWBIRD DOES NOT MOLEST?

Woodpeckers, wrens, chickadees, bluebirds, and nuthatches are rarely, if ever, bothered by the cowbird. These birds make their nests in holes of trees or similar places, making it rather difficult for the cowbird to invade the nest. Others free from the cowbird's visits are kingbirds and shrikes. It appears that the cowbird does not want to risk confrontation with the shrike. If caught molesting its nest, the cowbird's attempt could prove fatal.

ARE THE EGGS OF ALL COWBIRDS REJECTED IN THE SAME WAY?

Various species react to the intrusion of the cowbird in different ways. Although there is a general pattern of response within a species, it is not always absolute. The vireo, for example, occasionally covers up the intruder's eggs and starts over, but in general the cowbird eggs are incubated and the young reared. Listed below are the typical responses of various species.

HOUSE WREN - It is rare for a cowbird to lay its egg in a wren's nest for this little bird normally makes its nest in a small house or cavity. But if it should happen, the wren almost always tries to dispose of the egg one way or another. The wren will either try to toss it out or, if the egg is too large, it destroys it by breaking it with its sharp bill.

ROBIN - The robin is very intolerant of the presence of the cowbird's egg and, like a catbird, will throw it out by rolling it up the side and then out of the nest.

YELLOW WARBLER - The yellow warbler will not accept the cowbird's egg and builds another nest over it. If the cowbird should successfully try again, the yellow warbler repeats the process. There have been cases when the yellow warbler has made three or four nests on top of one another to free itself of the cowbird's intrusion. Other birds that have been known to do this are the chestnut-sided warbler, redstart, meadowlark, white-crowned sparrow, cardinal, red-eyed vireo, yellow-throated vireo, warbling vireo, blue-headed vireo, and the indigo bunting.

YELLOW CHAT - This bird will neither dispose of the egg nor build a nest on top of it. It simply leaves. Extremely shy and nervous, it has an unusual ability to distinguish its eggs from foreign ones. It is very rare that the chat would ever be fooled into accepting the cowbird's egg.

MOURNING DOVE - This bird might be able to accept the cowbird's egg, but the chances of it successfully raising it are remote. The dove regurgitates to feed its young "pigeon" milk. With this type of nourishment it is questionable that the cowbird would survive.

Another bird which would spell disaster for the cowbird is the killdeer. This bird builds its nest on the ground and leaves the nest soon after hatching its brood. The young cowbird, too weak to follow, would probably die.

Wren

Robin

Yellow warbler

Three-story nest

Yellow chat

Mourning dove

TRAVELING COMPANIONS
OF THE BROWN-HEADED COWBIRD

Purple grackle

Red-winged blackbird

The cowbird enjoys dining on the insects that cattle kick up as they move through the grass.

IS THE YOUNG COWBIRD ABLE TO CARE FOR ITSELF WHEN IT LEAVES THE NEST?

At seven days of age the young cowbird has grown so much that it will have outgrown the nest. It may climb out and perch nearby on a branch. Soon it begins to follow the foster parents, still depending on them for food. It makes its need know to them by begging. It is a peculiar sight to see parents straining to feed this immature bird almost twice their size. When the young cowbird has grown sufficiently to take care of itself, it looks for and returns to flocks of its own kind.

DOES THE COWBIRD MIGRATE?

Yes. It is one of the earliest migrators to leave its southern winter range and one of the last to leave its northern summer range, leaving as late as November. It travels by day early in the morning and late in the afternoon. These birds may fly in flocks of thousands, but the usual number is from fifty to two hundred. The mature males arrive first, followed by mature females. Last to arrive are the immature males and females.

HOW DID THE COWBIRD GET ITS NAME?

Because of its association with cattle. The cowbird discovered that where there were cattle there was food. As these grazing animals feed on grass they kick up many insects such as grasshoppers and crickets. The cowbirds roam freely between the hooves of cattle, catching insects as they stir. In fact, it is not unusual for a number of these birds to perch right on the back of a cow, searching through the hair of these animals for food such as parasites and flies. In earlier times the bird was also known as the buffalo bird, for the bison was another animal it associated with. It is interesting that the cowbird seems to limit itself to these two animals and rarely has the same relationship with pigs, sheep, or horses.

DOES THE COWBIRD JUST EAT INSECTS?

No. In fact, only a small percentage of its diet is made up of this food. About twenty-two percent is animal matter; the remaining seventy-eight percent is vegetable matter. The vegetables it does eat are basically waste grains. The bird also eats fruits and berries such as cedar berries, blackberries, huckleberries, wild cherries, and grapes.

IS THE COWBIRD BENEFICIAL TO MAN?

If one were to evaluate only its food habits, the cowbird would be rated positively. It aids the farmer by eating and destroying many destructive insects such as the alfalfa and cotton boll weevils. But if one regards the bird from a full perspective, its bad nesting habits far outweigh the limited benefits that this bird might claim. The cowbird is responsible for the destruction of multitudes of small birds which, had they lived, would have consumed large numbers of injurious insects.

HOW DOES SCRIPTURE ILLUSTRATE THE NEED TO CONSIDER OUR FAMILY FIRST BEFORE OTHER NEEDS OR WANTS?

Sometimes it is easier and more glamorous to serve the Lord in a faraway country than to be a faithful witness in front of our own family. Who in Scripture could have given a sensational testimony of his own conversion but instead was told by the Lord to go home and first demonstrate his new-found faith to his family?

(Pause for a response—see page 20)

The silence of the night was pierced by blood-curdling screams from a distant cemetery. Wide-eyed children ran to their parents. Their parents explained what they had heard and firmly warned them never to go near those graves. A wild man was slashing himself with sharp stones and crying out as he ran among the tombs.

The incidents at that cemetery were frightening enough when this man was contained, but it became even more terrifying when he broke his chains and ran unrestrained. Whenever this occurred, a large group of men from the village gathered to search for the maniac. They would capture him and bind him to the tombs. But again and again he broke the chains that held him.

Curious villagers would approach the tombs to look at him from a distance, then they returned to eager listeners and reported what they had seen. This man was an embarrassment and threat to his family as well as to the villagers who were linked to the terrifying stories of this behavior.

Then one day an incredible event took place. This wild man watched a boat edging toward his shore and ran toward it. As the men stepped out of the boat, he knelt before one of them. Bystanders watched in amazement as the unclean spirit and legion of demons were commanded to leave him. After coming out of him, they entered a huge herd of swine which immediately ran down a steep hill and drowned in the sea.

Those who saw what had happened rushed back to the city and returned with a great crowd of frightened and curious citizens. They saw the wild man clothed and being taught by Jesus Christ. They saw that the herd of swine had been destroyed. They were filled with fear. Rather than rejoicing over what had happened to the man possessed of devils, they begged Jesus to leave their countryside.

As He returned to the boat with His disciples, the man who had been possessed of the devils begged to follow Jesus. Wisely Jesus commanded, "Return to your own house and show how great things God hath done unto you." So the Gadarene went as Jesus had commanded to the most difficult people he would ever reach—his own family, relatives, and neighbors—and proclaimed throughout the whole city the great things Jesus had done unto him.

From Mark 5:1-20 and Luke 8:26-39

Pigs were not eaten by orthodox Jews *but were eaten freely by the large number of Gentiles living throughout the predominantly Greek Decapolis.*

The east side of the lake of Galilee *where the swine rushed down a steep shore into the water*

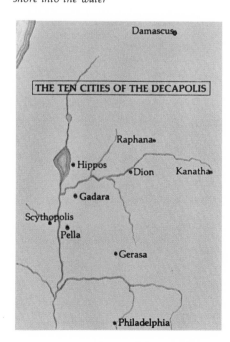

THE GADARENE WAS TO GO HOME FIRST AND SHARE THE GOOD NEWS

Jesus had probably risen early in the morning to meet with His Heavenly Father before beginning an unusually busy and active day (cf. Mark 1:35). He was touring the cities and villages of Galilee,"preaching and showing the glad tidings of the kingdom of God." (Luke 8:1)

HE HEALED THE BLIND MAN

Because of His increased fame in the area, a great multitude of people gathered together in the morning to hear Jesus preach and see Him perform miracles. When He healed a blind and dumb man who was possessed with a devil, some Jewish religious leaders accused Him of being empowered by the prince of the devils (Matthew 12:22-24). Others demanded a sign from Him to demonstrate that He was the Messiah (Matthew 12:38). Finally, His mother and brothers tried to carry Him away, thinking that He may have become insane (Mark 3:21, 31).

HE CALMED THE WATERS

After this emotionally tense encounter, Jesus spent the afternoon teaching "a great multitude, so that he entered into a ship, and sat on the sea; and the whole multitude was by the sea on the land. And he taught them many things by parables." (Mark 4:1,2) After a long afternoon of teaching and answering questions, He sent the crowds home and decided to cross over to the other side of the sea of Galilee to spend the night. He was so tired and worn out that He slept soundly during a severe storm. His disciples had to wake Him for fear that they would perish. "And he arose, and rebuked the wind, and said unto the sea, Peace, be still. And the wind ceased, and there was a great calm." (Mark 4:39)

HE EXORCISED THE DEMONS

When they reached the other side of the sea in safety, they no doubt looked forward to a peaceful night of rest on the eastern shore. But their long day was not yet over. They were immediately met by a raving lunatic who wore no clothes. Most men would not even pass near the area where this man lived for fear of bodily harm, but when he addressed the Lord, Jesus boldly said unto him, "Come out of the man, thou unclean spirit." When Jesus asked his name he answered, saying, "My name is Legion; for we are many." (Mark 5:8, 9)

The disciples were shocked by this response. They knew that a Roman legion consisted of 6,000 soldiers. Mary Magdalene had been delivered of seven demons (Luke 8:2), but this was an altogether extreme case of possession. The Lord had just shown His disciples that He had authority over the physical elements; now He was to demonstrate His absolute authority over all the forces of evil. He permitted the demons to enter 2,000 pigs feeding nearby which "ran violently down a steep place into the sea . . . and were choked in the sea." (Mark 5:13)

HE WAS ASKED TO LEAVE

The next morning, the men of the area came to investigate the unusual story told them by the pig herder. When they saw the previously demon-ravaged man "sitting, and clothed, and in his right mind...they were afraid." (Mark 5:15). They begged Him to return to Galilee, but the healed man pleaded that he be allowed to accompany them. Jesus left without him, instructing him to go home and tell his friends and family "what great things the Lord hath done." (Mark 5:19) Jesus crossed over the sea, left the man whole, and began another very busy day.

GADARENE CHARACTER SKETCH

WHY WAS EVERYONE ALARMED WHEN THEY SAW THAT THE GADARENE HAD BEEN HEALED?

It was probably early the next morning when the men who had heard the startling news came to investigate. By this time, the Gadarene had dressed, cleaned his bruised body, and was quietly sitting with Jesus and the disciples "in his right mind." (Mark 5:15) The men were struck with awe and fear and begged Him to leave. It is doubtful that their request was prompted only by the loss of the swine. There was no doubt in their minds that One possessing supreme and unlimited power was in their midst. Gadara was one of ten cities in the Greek federation known as the Decapolis (cf. Mark 5:20). The predominantly non-Jewish population was ignorant of spiritual truth and steeped in pagan superstition. The loss of their pigs indicated to them that this supreme Power was hostile. They were not seeking the truth and begged the man with such awesome power to leave.

WHY DID THE GADARENE ASK TO REMAIN WITH JESUS?

There is a striking contrast between the attitude of the men in the area and the attitude of the healed demoniac. The men begged Jesus to leave, and he agreed; the healed man begged to stay in the company of Jesus, and his request was refused. There are at least two reasons why he wanted to remain with the Lord. Jesus was going to leave immediately. The Gadarene had many questions to ask and many things to learn about his new Master. He had been with the Lord only a few, short hours—the happiest of his life. He could not bear the thought of leaving the One who had freed him from his bonds of men and the devil. Second, he had found calm, safety, and happiness only in His presence. Would he remain free from the demons that had possessed him, or would he be returned to the tombs and chains? He had been an outcast from his fellow men for such a long time; it was difficult for him to be denied further fellowship with the One who had made him whole.

WHY DID CHRIST FIRST SEND THE GADARENE HOME TO HIS FAMILY?

The reason is given in the Lord's directive, "Go home to thy friends, and tell them what great things the Lord hath done for thee, and hath had compassion on thee." (Mark 5:19) In Capernaum, Jesus had strictly forbidden the leper he had cleansed to let anyone but the priest know (Mark 1:43,44). But this healed man, the Gadarene, was commanded to spread the news. There are good reasons for this apparent inconsistency. First, the area in which the Gadarene lived was predominantly Greek. Christ had been called to deliver His message first to the house of Israel (cf. Matthew 10:5, 6). Second, the people had not welcomed His presence. These men needed evidence that the Lord would not only perform great miracles but that He could permanently transform a life. By sending the man home, Christ was ensured a witness in a needy area. The man "began to publish in Decapolis what great things Jesus had done for him; and all men did marvel." (Mark 5:20) He may have been the very first apostle to the Gentiles. When the Lord returned to that area later, He was much better received. The Gadarene had prepared the way, and Jesus was now able to work in their midst (cf. Mark 7:31-37).

"Then they went out to see what was done; *and came to Jesus, and found the man, out of whom the demons were departed, sitting at the feet of Jesus, clothed, and in his right mind; and they were afraid."*

THE GADARENE
găd-à-rēn

Availability

IS REFUSING TO BE DETERRED BY DECEPTIVE DISTRACTIONS

"No man that warreth entangleth himself with the affairs of this life; that he may please him who hath chosen him to be a soldier."

II Timothy 2:4

LIVING LESSONS ON AVAILABILITY . . .

FROM THE PAGES OF SCRIPTURE

A wise trial lawyer takes special notice of which point his opponent emphasizes the most; often that is the weakest argument. Every leader must have the skill of a lawyer when dealing with the many appeals which come to him, especially appeals which would deter him from accomplishing his basic objective. God illustrates this principle in an account of one of history's most important military campaigns. The commanding general led an army of hundreds of thousands of men. They conquered powerful enemies and great walled cities, but one small group of clever men outwitted this general and his leaders. If the general and his men had not been deterred by an appeal, they would have avoided a dangerous and deceptive distraction.

ILLUSTRATED IN THE WORLD OF NATURE

TIMBER WOLF   *Canis lupus*

As early as 1630, just ten short years after the Pilgrims arrived in America, a reward was offered for killing the wolf. This first bounty was offered in Massachusetts, and the conflict between man and wolf has continued even to this day. Many methods have been used to exterminate this animal. Trapping was one attempt, but it was only moderately effective. Trappers consider this animal to be the smartest in America. Another effort was strychnine poisoning—effective only until the wolf learned to recognize and avoid the smell. But the more man understood the intelligence and habits of the wolf, the more he wanted to protect it. The wolf was placed on the endangered species list. Of twenty-four subspecies of the North American gray wolf, six are believed to be extinct. The male timber wolf is considerably larger than the female, measuring approximately three feet high at the shoulders and six feet long. It weighs from 60 to 175 pounds and lives to be fourteen to sixteen years of age.

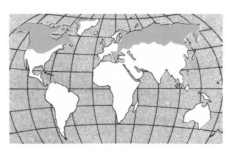

The range and habitat of the timber wolf

AVAILABILITY

HOW DOES THE WOLF ILLUSTRATE AVAILABILITY BY REFUSING TO BE DETERRED BY DECEPTIVE DISTRACTIONS?

A promising scent in the air made the animals eager with excitement. An aroma had drawn the group together and they were all wagging their tails excitedly. The animals were alert and expectant; it had been quite a while since they last smelled this fragrance . This was the beginning of a very important mission.

Conditions were hard and food was scarce. The cold winter had sent many of their food sources to sheltered places to wait out the bitter weather. The white-tailed deer was always a favorite food, but over the years its population had dwindled. These animals were now few and far between, and the chances of the pack finding and overtaking a deer were remote.

Another animal in the area was more plentiful, but it was a creature the wolf preferred to avoid. This mighty beast was not an easy target and should the wolf become careless or over-confident, an attempt to attack might prove fatal.

The massive moose is almost twelve times the wolf's weight. It is surprisingly agile. Its senses are almost as keen as those of the wolf, and its hooves and antlers are lethal weapons.

The head male wolf had returned to the pack that day bringing the good news that its acute sense of smell had picked up the fresh aroma of a nearby moose. Their empty stomachs and the scarcity of the winter made them all eager to accept even this formidable challenge. If they were to be successful, however, they would have to rely on strategy to hunt this mighty beast.

This pack was a family composed of eight wolves. Each worked in harmony with the others and because of this teamwork the animals were usually successful in capturing their prey. One by one each wolf moved toward their quarry. Soon they caught a glimpse of the mighty bull. The animal had a magnificent set of horns and appeared healthy. The wolves set their plan into operation.

Each animal quickly took its position. Soon all eight had encircled it. The alert bull angrily snorted and braced itself for the onslaught of these intruders. The lead female wolf positioned herself in front of the moose. It began rushing at the moose in an effort to force it to run. But it refused to move. Alternately others lunged at it, trying to excite the beast, but to no avail. It continued to stand its ground. The enraged moose defied them, bellowing and raking the ground with its hooves, daring them to try again.

Unexpectedly, the wolves turned and left. They did not bother to try again. They knew it was fruitless. This animal was too healthy. They would only be wasting their precious strength to persist any further.

The wolves would not be detained by this distraction. The hope of bringing it down was a deception. They knew that if they couldn't get the animal to panic and run within the first few minutes, they would not be able to conquer it. The pack moved on to find a weaker or more inexperienced animal—one that they could overtake.

Severt Andrewson

SCRIPTURAL REFERENCES TO THE WOLF

"Beware of false prophets, who come to you in sheep's clothing, but inwardly they are ravening wolves." Matthew 7:15

A wolf is ordinarily shy and would prefer to avoid a man rather than confront him. But, a pack of wolves is an entirely different matter. Each wolf of a pack becomes one of the most dangerous animals alive. Relentless in pursuit, wolves maintain their chase for hours at a time. The wolf usually singles out the weakest member of the herd, bypassing other prey until it has tracked down and devoured its victim.

The comparison of a wolf to a false prophet is revealing. A false prophet seems harmless when alone; but once inside the church he singles out the weaker Christians and, with other false prophets with whom he associates, makes easy prey of them. Their goal is to satisfy their ever-growing greed for money and sensual fulfillment (I Timothy 6:5; II Timothy 3:1-8; II Peter 2:10-22).

"Her princes in her midst are like wolves ravening the prey, to shed blood, and to destroy souls, to get dishonest gain."
Ezekiel 22:27

"Behold, I send you forth as sheep in the midst of wolves; be ye, therefore, wise as serpents, and harmless as doves." Matthew 10:16

"But he that is an hireling . . . seeth a wolf coming, and leaveth the sheep, and fleeth; and the wolf catcheth them, and scattereth the sheep."
John 10:12

JAW AND TOOTH STRUCTURE
OF THE TIMBER WOLF

CHARACTERISTICS AND PHYSICAL FEATURES OF THE TIMBER WOLF

The timber wolf pack was not distracted by the deceptive attraction of possible meat. They knew that that moose would not be theirs. On an average, the wolf harasses twelve moose for every one it is able to excite into running. When the moose does run, the wolves begin their attack from the rear. With powerful jaws they tear at the legs and hindquarters, weakening the animal by crippling and loss of blood. The wolves then play a waiting game, resting for a while waiting for the moose to become weaker and weaker. The wolves are experienced enough to know not to rush the kill, for the moose has the extremely dangerous capability to kill them easily with a powerful thrust of its legs. When the wolves sense the end is coming, they move in, aim for the muzzle and throat, and finish the kill.

HOW POWERFUL ARE THE JAWS OF A WOLF?

The teeth of the wolf are designed to kill its prey as well as to tear and cut flesh. Its jaws are so powerful that they easily crush bones. It is not unusual for the wolf to sever a deer's spine or leg with one bite.

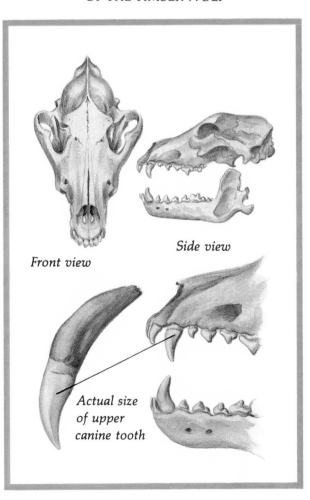

Front view

Side view

Actual size
of upper
canine tooth

The parents sometimes prepare *for the arrival of young by storing caches of food in the nearby vicinity of the den. This supply will be used to feed the female and her young.*

The wolf will scratch out a shallow hole with its forefeet and bury its food

It covers the hole by pushing the dirt with its nose

The wolf normally eats *almost all the meat of a kill, leaving behind the bones, patches of the hide and the head.*

DO WOLVES MAKE GOOD PARENTS?

The wolf is a loyal and affectionate parent. Both parents share the responsibilities of caring for their young. This responsibility is not limited exclusively to the parents but is shared among all the other members of the pack as well. They will babysit, feed, and play with the pups while their parents are hunting. Unless it is hunting, the father guards the young. Should danger approach, it will try to lure the enemy away. If some disaster befalls the mother, the father will assume the responsibilities of taking care of the pups himself or, if the young have not been weaned, will bring in another female to nurse them.

WHERE DOES THE FEMALE HAVE HER YOUNG?

The female selects a site for its den. There are a variety of locations which it could choose such as among rocks, large hollow logs, or in an underground den. When the animal makes the den, it will dig a tunnel between six and thirty feet in length. At the end of the tunnel is the natal chamber. Freshly excavated dirt mounded out in front betrays the entrance. She normally makes the den near water.

The animal does not usually make a bed but rather has her young on the hard, dry ground. She has from four to fourteen pups between April and early June. For two weeks, the mother will not allow any other wolf to enter the chamber. During this period she spends most of her time in the den, leaving only to feed. She eats the meat that either her mate or another member of the pack provides, or she eats from the stored food supply previously cached in the vicinity.

HOW DOES THE PARENT PROVIDE FOOD FOR ITS YOUNG?

The male feeds the female while she is in the den. He may travel great distances to secure this food. He carries back bony pieces in his jaw or gorges himself by swallowing large chunks of meat. He then returns to the den and regurgitates the meat for his mate. As the young grow older and are weaned, they crowd around the parent and nuzzle its mouth. By so doing, they stimulate the parent into regurgitating the contents of its stomach. The parent either spills this on the ground or allows the pup to thrust its head into its mouth to eat the partially-digested contents.

WHERE DID THE TERM "LONE WOLF" ORIGINATE?

This term refers to a male or female that has lost its mate. Wolves mate for life and are very devoted and loyal to each other. When either one loses its partner, it generally does not mate again nor does it participate with the group, but it stays to itself. It becomes a "loner."

HOW FAST IS THE WOLF?

The wolf does not have exceptional speed. In fact, if the wolf was pitted against its prey in a straight race, it would probably lose. The wolf's speed is approximately twenty to twenty-four miles per hour. It can maintain this speed for about two miles after which it reduces to about ten to fifteen miles per hour.

WHAT ADVANTAGE DOES THE WOLF HAVE OVER SWIFTER ANIMALS?

Because the wolf is slower than its prey, it must rely on cunning and strategy to catch its quarry. Wolves work as a team to subdue their prey. They maintain top speed by running in relays, each animal taking its turn to chase the victim. Another commonly-used tactic is to divide the pack as one group circles the animal and drives it to the others which lie in wait. One of the greatest advantages the wolf is considered to have is its endurance. It employs this great endurance to tire and run its prey down. It can maintain a loping gait for long periods of time, and it is not uncommon for this persistent animal to run all night if necessary. The animal seldom runs at full speed—reserving that for the occasions when it is in range and can leap upon its prey.

HOW IMPORTANT ARE "BIG GAME" ANIMALS TO THE WOLF?

Ninety percent of the wolf's diet is meat. Although the animal consumes many mice, rabbits, and squirrels, these do not usually provide enough meat to support an entire pack. For this reason the wolf is very dependent upon big game animals such as deer, caribou, and moose. One of these large animals is capable of feeding the whole pack. The wolf preys primarily upon the sick, injured, or young of the species. Healthy, mature animals are usually able to elude or stand off these predators. The wolf is not above eating carrion, some of which is quite rank.

IS THE WOLF A WASTEFUL ANIMAL?

It depends on whether there is an abundance or a shortage of food. When there is an abundance, the wolf may be a little more fussy in its eating habits and concentrate on the most desirable parts—the internal organs, the tongue, and thigh regions. But this selectivity is not really common, and the animal usually eats a good portion of what it kills. An adult wolf will eat up to one-fifth its own weight.

What it does not eat it will cache, carefully burying the food under debris or in the ground. When it is hungry again, it returns to the spot to continue feeding. Trappers who know this habit use it to their advantage by setting traps around the carcass of a kill.

Stimulating regurgitation

Young pup feeding

The parents chew hard bones into bits and leave them for the young to eat.

The coloration of the wolf has no geographical uniformity but varies from snow white to coal black with varying shades in between.

The wolf can produce a ventriloquial effect which confuses the listener as to the number of wolves present.

DOES THE HOWL OF THE WOLF MEAN ANYTHING?

Yes. It may communicate a mournful loneliness or it may call the pack together for a chase. At sunset and daybreak the wolf generally makes its lonesome call.

DOES THE WOLF HAVE ANY ENEMIES?

Wolves have relatively few enemies. Man is the greatest. Others are the grizzly bear or mountain lion—superior in size and strength to the wolf. Particularly the bear with its weight, thick hide, and long claws makes a formidable opponent. These animals usually back down and retreat, though, when faced with a pack of wolves.

WHAT'S AN "ALPHA MALE"?

The wolf population is comprised of packs. Each pack has its own territory and operates as a separate unit. Packs vary in number. Each member has a different standing within the pack. None are equal. This social order is known as a "dominance hierarchy" or "pecking order."

The leader of the pack is usually a male known as the "alpha male." This top male and its mate are responsible for patrolling the boundaries of the pack's territory. They control the movement of the pack and settle disputes among the members. At the bottom of the social scale is the outcast. This animal lives on the outskirts of the pack, feeding on the scraps of meat left over from the group.

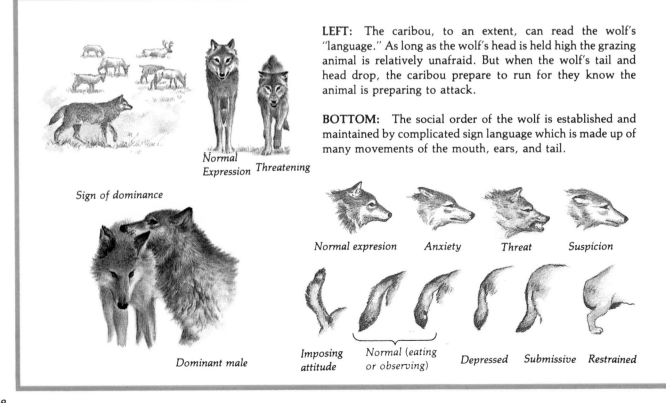

LEFT: The caribou, to an extent, can read the wolf's "language." As long as the wolf's head is held high the grazing animal is relatively unafraid. But when the wolf's tail and head drop, the caribou prepare to run for they know the animal is preparing to attack.

BOTTOM: The social order of the wolf is established and maintained by complicated sign language which is made up of many movements of the mouth, ears, and tail.

Normal Expression   Threatening

Sign of dominance

Dominant male

Normal expresion   Anxiety   Threat   Suspicion

Imposing attitude   Normal (eating or observing)   Depressed   Submissive   Restrained

HOW DOES SCRIPTURE ILLUSTRATE THE NEED TO REFUSE TO BE DETERRED BY DECEPTIVE DISTRACTIONS?

Scripture warns that anyone who flatters his neighbor spreads a net for his feet. What leader was flattered by a group of neighbors and stumbled into their net?

(Pause for a response—see page 20)

Weary men in tattered clothes hobbled toward a distant army camp. Dusty sacks covered their donkeys. The men clutched worn out wineskins and dry, moldy bread. As they neared the camp, soldiers resting from battle stared at these curious visitors. The general and his army leaders listened as they explained their mission. "We are ambassadors from a far country. Now, therefore, make a league with us."

This was hardly the time to think about a league with a distant country. Surrounded by hostile enemies in nearby cities, this army had been commanded to conquer and destroy. Strict instructions had been given to the general not to make an alliance with any of those cities. Several army leaders voiced their hesitation. "What if we find out that you actually live in this country? How could we then make a league with you?"

The matter was almost dropped. The leaders nearly escaped deception, but the general grew curious. He asked a few more questions. "Who are you? From where did you come?" The clever visitors had carefully prepared their answers. They told the general and his army that the fame of their previous battles had spread to their country. When their nation, which was very far away, had heard the news, they wanted to become their allies.

This proposal appealed to the pride of the general and his men. Then they took their moldy bread and their worn-out wineskins and passed them around to the general and his leaders. "This bread was fresh from the oven when we began our journey," they said, "and these wineskins were new; but we have traveled a long distance to come to you."

Through these arguments and evidence they appealed to human reason. At this point the general and his leaders should have asked counsel of the Lord. Instead, they relied upon their own reasoning and entered into the league.

Their military campaign continued. Every army they fought was conquered and destroyed. After their battles they returned to the camp for what should have been a joyous celebration. Instead, the army and their families wept. An angel of the Lord brought them a message from God. "You were commanded to make no league with the inhabitants of this land but to destroy them totally and to throw down their altars. But you have not obeyed. Therefore, they shall be thorns in your sides and their gods a snare unto you."

Among other things God was referring to the small group of travelers who had deceived them. Three days after the league was made, the general and his men discovered that their visitors actually represented a neighboring city which God had marked for destruction. But they were bound to honor the alliance which they had made. If only Joshua had refused to be deterred by the deception of flattery, he would have avoided a major obstacle in reaching his goal. He would have also removed from future generations the conflict and temptations which came as a result of this league.

From Joshua 9:1-10:14

A DECEPTIVE DISTRACTION DIVERTED JOSHUA FROM GOD'S SPECIAL PLAN

A wine jar handle found in 1956 inscribed with the name "Gibeon" followed by "gdr." This and many other inscribed handles provide evidence which identifies the present-day site of el-Jib as the old city of the Gibeonites.

In preparation for the conquest of Canaan, Joshua was solemnly reminded by the "captain of the host of the Lord" that this was the Lord's battle and he was to be second, not first in command (Joshua 5:13-15). Moses had already clearly instructed Joshua that when a major or difficult decision was to be made, he was to "stand before Eleazar, the priest, who shall ask counsel for him after the judgment of Urim before the Lord; at his word shall they go out, and at his word they shall come in, both he, and all the children of Israel with him, even all the congregation." (Numbers 27:21)

HE FAILED TO TAKE A BATTLE SERIOUSLY

After their overwhelming victory over Jericho, Joshua did not bother to consider his attack on the small city of Ai seriously. Without consulting the Lord through Eleazar, he sent a mere three thousand men to take Ai. The men were repelled, and thirty-six of them were killed. This failure should have been a caution to him, but in the very next major decision Joshua faced, he committed the same error.

HE FAILED TO TAKE A SIMPLE REQUEST SERIOUSLY

A group of Hivite ambassadors, representing Gibeon and three allied cities, approached Joshua in Gilgal. Having disguised themselves with torn clothing and aged provisions, they claimed to be from a far country. When they asked for a peace treaty, the strangeness of the request prompted the men of Israel to reply, "Peradventure ye dwell among us; and how shall we make a league with you?" (Joshua 9:7)

Their cautious hesitation was well-grounded. The Lord had commanded that they were not to make any league with the inhabitants of Canaan (Exodus 23:32; 34:12; Numbers 33:55; Deuteronomy 7:2). The men of Gibeon reiterated their claim of being from a far country and cleverly omitted any reference to the recent victories at Jericho and Ai (cf. Joshua 9:9,10).

HE BELIEVED AND WAS DECEIVED

And the men took their food, "and asked not counsel at the mouth of the Lord. And Joshua made peace with them, and made a league with them, to let them live; and the princes of the congregation swore unto them." (Joshua 9:14,15) Rather than questioning the Lord, they questioned the Gibeonites only. Confident of their ability to weigh the outward evidence and testimony, they thought it unnecessary to pursue the matter. They believed the report and, in supposed accord with Deuteronomy 20:11, ratified the treaty.

Three days later, when they realized that they had been deceived, they made another hasty decision. As punishment for this deception the princes suggested, "Let them be hewers of wood and drawers of water unto all the congregation." (Joshua 9:21) Joshua concurred and said to the Gibeonites, "Now, therefore, ye are cursed, and there shall none of you be freed from being bondmen, and hewers of wood and drawers of water for the house of my God." (Joshua 9:23)

When the Canaanite kings of the area discovered the peace pact, they grouped for a united attack upon their traitorous neighbors. Joshua responded to the call for help by the men of Gibeon. The long day of battle ended with the Israelites in firm control of all of southern Canaan. The Gibeonites were put to forced labor throughout the lifetime of Joshua and for years afterward.

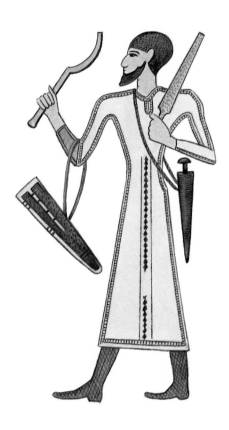

An ancient sketch of a Canaanite warrior shows how the Gibeonites would have appeared to Joshua if they had decided to fight rather than resort to deception and disguise.

JOSHUA CHARACTER SKETCH

WHY WAS JOSHUA FORBIDDEN TO MAKE PEACE WITH THE CANAANITES?

The primary reason was that the Lord purposed to destroy utterly the Canaanites because of their wickedness. "And the land is defiled; therefore I do visit the iniquity thereof upon it, and the land itself vomiteth out her inhabitants." (Leviticus 18:25)

A second reason is that the Lord knew that involvement with these wicked people would cause the Israelites to imitate their ways (cf. Exodus 23:33). This proved to be painfully true throughout the history of Israel. A recurring theme in the book of Judges is: "And the children of Israel did evil in the sight of the Lord, and served Baalim . . . and followed other gods, of the gods of the people who were round about them, and bowed themselves unto them, and provoked the Lord to anger." (Judges 2:11,12)

WHY DIDN'T JOSHUA LET THE CANAANITE KINGS DESTROY THE GIBEONITES?

When Joshua made the original league with the Gibeonites, there was no mention of a protection clause in regard to third party invaders. Such an agreement was impractical. Joshua would never have consented to lead his army to a distant land in order to defend these strangers, nor was there any offer by the Gibeonites to help fight Joshua's enemies.

The responsibility of protection was added three days later when they made the Gibeonites their slaves. The Mosaic Law was clear in its exhortation to the master of a slave. If he cruelly punished him so that he happened to die, the master himself was to be punished (Exodus 21:20). Having made the Gibeonites their bond slaves, the Israelites were bound by honor to protect them.

WHAT DID THIS DECEPTIVE DISTRACTION COST THE ISRAELITES?

After the conquest of Canaan, the city of Gibeon was allotted to the tribe of Benjamin (Joshua 18:25; 21:17). It may be significant that this tribe became so corrupt that it was almost annihilated soon after Joshua's death (cf. Judges 20:12, 28; 21:6). Saul, the first Israelite king, was from the tribe of Benjamin and felt that the nation would be better off without the Gibeonites, treaty or no treaty (II Samuel 21:1). The unfortunate precedent that Joshua established with the Gibeonites was repeated again and again with other Canaanites. These people were put to forced labor rather than being driven out of the land (cf. Judges 1:28,30,33,35). As a result of these disobedient leagues with the Canaanites, the Lord made them to be a thorn in their side and their gods became a snare unto the Israelites (Judges 2:2,3).

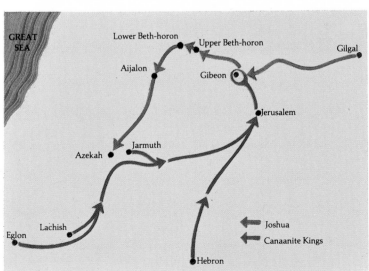

"**And the men of Gibeon** *sent unto Joshua to the camp to Gilgal, saying, Slack not thy hand from thy servants; come up to us quickly, and save us, and help us; for all the kings of the Amorites that dwell in the mountains are gathered together against us. So Joshua ascended from Gilgal, he and all the people of war with him, and all the mighty men of valor.*"

JOSHUA
jŏsh'u̇-ȧ

Availability

IS REJECTING AMBITIONS THAT HINDER US FROM BEING WHERE WE ARE NEEDED

"No man can serve two masters: for either he will hate the one, and love the other; or else he will hold to the one, and despise the other."

Matthew 6:24

LIVING LESSONS ON AVAILABILITY . . .

FROM THE PAGES OF SCRIPTURE

Being available is a practical evidence that we are under the authority of the one we serve. Availability requires us to be where we are needed, when we are needed. It means that the one we are serving can count on us. Scripture provides an important illustration of a servant who was not available when he was needed. The one whom he served suspected that personal ambitions were involved. Personal ambition is the enemy of availability. That is why it is vital to reject any ambitions that might hinder us from being where we are needed.

ILLUSTRATED IN THE WORLD OF NATURE

EASTERN TURKEY   *Meleagris gallopavo*

The first white men to see the wild turkey of North America were sixteenth-century Spanish explorers. They brought the bird back to their homeland about 1519 and domesticated it. The turkey spread rapidly, was carried throughout Europe, and reached Germany by 1530. Shortly afterwards it came to England. It is interesting to note that nearly a century later Englishmen brought this domesticated relative of the wild turkey back to America to provide food for the early settlers. The wild turkey is almost identical in appearance to its domesticated counterpart except that it is much slimmer. The wild turkey is the largest game bird found in North America. It can weigh as much as twenty to twenty-five pounds and lives nine years or more, reaching full maturity at the age of two.

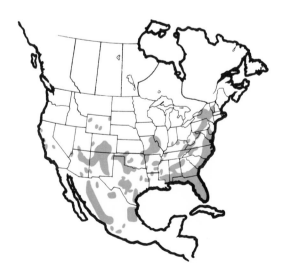

The range and habitat of the eastern turkey

AVAILABILITY

HOW DOES THE TURKEY ILLUSTRATE AVAILABILITY BY BEING WHERE IT IS NEEDED?

As it scratched through the leaves the bird ate every bit of food it could find. It was preparing for a very special responsibility—one which would affect many others. It was never in better condition than now, and the more it ate the more it ensured this strength.

One day it was put to the test. Early in the morning, before it left its roost in the tree, it began to gobble. It was proclaiming to the males that this was its territory. The call also notified the females that it was available.

A young tom in the area was aroused by the proclamation and came to contest the gobbler's domain. It is through combat that the position of dominancy is established in the community. The

victorious bird has the responsibility of servicing the females. Healthy offspring are assured by having strong, healthy parents.

If this young male won, it would unseat the older gobbler which for the last two years had had the prestige of maintaining the number one position in the pecking order.

The gobbler jumped down from the roost and faced the young opponent. The birds positioned themselves, and with a flurry of feathers and wings the two collided. The fight was spirited, but the older gobbler soon overpowered its younger opponent. Its size and long experience in using its wings and spurs had made the crucial difference. The younger bird acknowledged defeat by retreating.

Combat was not the major reason for its preparation, though. During the next month—the mating season—the gobbler would have extra demands on its time. It was important that nothing hinder it from being available when needed. At the yelp or cluck of an approaching female, the male jumps off its roost to respond. At the end of three or four weeks, the females have finished laying all their eggs, after which time they begin incubation and no longer seek out the male. Only when no longer needed will it find some secluded place to take care of its own personal needs.

To ensure its availability, the gobbler had taken steps to prepare for this time. Weeks before the mating season began, the male concentrated on feeding. The more it fed, the more its chest expanded. Soon it was bulging and formed what is known as a breast sponge. The sponge is made up of a mass of thick, cellular tissue. Because of this stored food, the gobbler was not concerned with its own feeding needs but rather could concentrate on being where it was needed to ensure strong, healthy offspring for future generations.

SCRIPTURAL REFERENCES TO THE TURKEY

The turkey is not mentioned in Scripture, but its close relative, the peacock, is.

"Once in three years came the navy of
Tarshish, bringing gold, and silver, ivory, and apes,
and peacocks. So King Solomon exceeded all the kings
of the earth in riches and for wisdom."
I Kings 10:22,23

There is evidence that King Solomon devised extensive classifications of animals and wildlife. In connection with this interest, he brought unknown animals to Israel to teach his people about them. One such animal was the peacock which he imported from India. The bird spread throughout the region of the Mediterranean.

"Gavest thou the goodly wings unto the
peacocks. . . ."
Job 39:13

The iridescent splendor of the peacock's wings distinguishes it as one of the most colorful of birds. During the time of the early church the peacock was a symbol of everlasting life. Its image was painted on catacomb ceilings and on the tombs of early martyrs. Over the years, however, its "goodly wings" and strutting posture have become a symbol of pride and vanity. Thus the expression, "proud as a peacock."

Another family member, the turkey, is also given to a strutting walk and a full display of the colorful feathers with which it is endowed.

The streamlined appearance of this male and female wild turkey distinguishes them from their domesticated cousin.

Female   *Male*

CHARACTERISTICS AND PHYSICAL FEATURES OF THE EASTERN TURKEY

Because the gobbler made preparation to be where it was needed, its availability ensured a healthy strain of turkeys. When the dominant male's presence is no longer necessary, it leaves to replenish its strength. If disaster befalls the female's nest and destroys the eggs, the female may want to renest and go through the mating process again. Tests have shown that when a female remates with another bird other than the dominant gobbler, there will be a large proportion of infertile eggs. By mating only with the dominant male a greater number of eggs are laid and very few are infertile. When these eggs hatch, the poults grow strong and will have greater resistance to disease and harsh weather conditions.

HOW CAN YOU TELL THE AGE OF A TURKEY?

By studying the plumage of the turkey it is possible to approximate its age.

At the age of fifteen weeks, the turkey replaces its two central tail feathers. These new feathers are considerably longer than the rest. The uneven arrangement exposes a yearling turkey.

A group of long flight feathers at the end of the wings are called primary wing feathers. If a bird is less than a year old the tips of these feathers are generally sharply pointed. An older turkey's feather tips are worn and rounded.

Another distinguishing feature of the feathers of older birds is alternating light and dark bars which extend all the way to the tip of the primary wing feathers.

Male breast feather

Female breast feather

Central feathers

Adult

Immature

157

Female

Male

Waddle

Caruncle

Frontal caruncle

Strutting

Frightened

MOODS OF THE TURKEY

HOW DO A MALE AND FEMALE TURKEY DIFFER IN APPEARANCE?

Not until the chick is twelve to fourteen weeks old and has had a partial molt is it easy to distinguish the male from the female. The most obvious difference is the size of the birds. The male, or gobbler, is generally larger than the female. Another distinction is that of coloration. The male's head has a lighter color while its body is darker. The female takes on a lighter body appearance because the tips of her body feathers are buff or white in color. The female's head has more feathers and less exposed skin than the male's. One of the most characteristic differences is the male's ability to strut by fanning its tail, puffing its feathers, and gobbling.

WHAT IS A CARUNCLE?

The caruncle is the smooth skin that is located on the head, side and back of the neck. This skin area is large and prominent in the male. The frontal caruncle is the large growth which appears from the base of its bill. On a female the frontal caruncle appears almost wart-like, whereas on the male it is quite extended. The male is able to expand or contract this skin-like growth. Thus, it may hang down from its bill several inches or it may contract, creating a horn-like appearance.

The growth that hangs underneath the chin is called a throat waddle—conspicuous and easily identified on the male. In females it is absent in one-year-old birds but may be present in older birds.

HOW CAN YOU TELL THE MOOD OF A TURKEY?

By its color. The frontal caruncle and the waddle are capable of changing color—especially in the male. These colors vary in vividness. Skin areas of the head are also richly pigmented. The color changes from blue to light blue to white to light red to dark red. As the emotions of the bird change, so does its color.

When the bird struts, blood pressure increases and the caruncles and waddle become a brilliant red; the top of the head takes on a whitish appearance. When the bird is frightened, the blood leaves the sinuses, and the head takes on a pale blue appearance. This blue color is probably the most common for us to see because when we observe the bird it is usually frightened. When the bird is butchered, the color in the head quickly changes to an almost whitish blue.

During the mid-winter months color variations are more stabilized. When spring approaches and the mating season arrives, these changes are once again noticeable as the fleshy areas take on brighter colors.

WHY DOES A TURKEY FEATHER SEEM TO CHANGE COLOR?

The color change or the iridescent effect is due to the structure of the feather. The barbules in iridescent feathers have a flattened appearance and are twisted at a ninety-degree angle. The surface is covered with air-filled platelets of various sizes. They act like tiny prisms producing a rainbow of colors. As light strikes these barbules, it is refracted at a certain angle and separates into beautiful colors. Different parts of the plumage of an adult turkey reflect different colors. The iridescent upper back and breast feathers reflect shades of brown, bronze, green, blue, purple and red. The tail coverts reflect copper or bronze. The rectrices or long tail feathers reflect black and brown shades.

WHAT KINDS OF FEATHERS DOES THE TURKEY HAVE?

The feathers of a turkey are basically of three types: down, vein, and filoplume.

DOWN FEATHERS   These are the feathers that are close to the body surface. They give a fluffy appearance and are particularly evident in the young poult stage. These feathers insulate the bird and allow it to conserve heat.

VEIN FEATHERS   These contour feathers provide a shield for the down feathers and cover most of the bird's body. They also help conserve heat and give the bird its sleek, trim appearance.

FILOPLUME FEATHERS   These are the small feathers located on the turkey's head.

IS THE TURKEY SUITED FOR COLD WEATHER?

The turkey is quite capable of adjusting to cold weather. With its down feathers it is able to keep warm and well-insulated. There have been recorded incidents of the bird weathering a heavy snowstorm with only a thin coat of snow clinging to its back. If there is a strong wind, the bird is careful to face into it. Doing so prevents the wind from getting underneath and lifting up its feathers which would cause them to lose their insulating qualities.

The turkey can handle most of the elements of winter except for large amounts of snow for extended periods of time. During the winter the bird needs food to give it energy in order to produce heat. The majority of its food is either on the ground or close to the ground. The turkey can scratch through snow as deep as a foot; however, should the snow become deeper than this or if there is a thaw and refreezing which forms a crust, it will be very difficult for the turkey to find food. These conditions would have a severe effect on the bird.

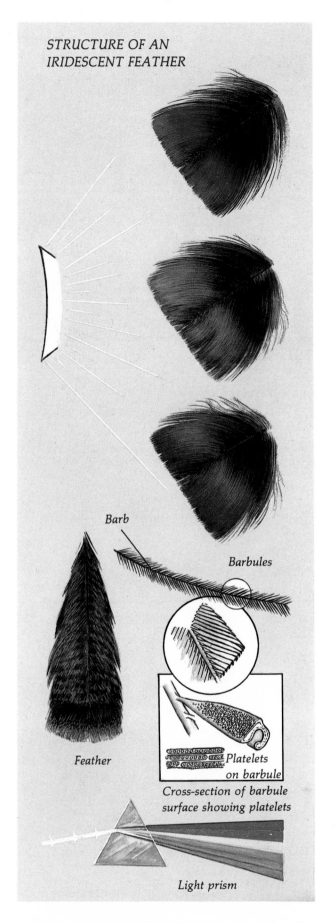

STRUCTURE OF AN IRIDESCENT FEATHER

Barb

Barbules

Feather

Platelets on barbule

Cross-section of barbule surface showing platelets

Light prism

As iridescent feathers reflect *the sun's rays, many tiny transparent platelets on the barbule surface mirror the light's wavelengths and give the appearance of changing colors.*

Pectoral tuft or beard

It is not unusual *for a turkey to have more than one beard. The bird may have as many as five.*

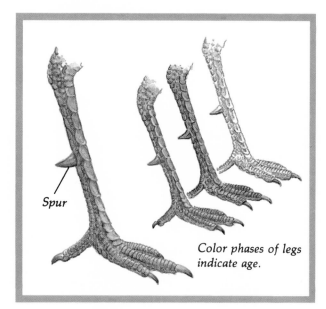

Spur

Color phases of legs indicate age.

DOES THE TURKEY REALLY HAVE A BEARD?

The turkey does not have a beard, but it does have a bunch of feathers with a horsetail-like appearance growing at the middle of its breast. Another name for this beard is the "pectoral tuft." The growth is characteristically found in the male; however, it is not uncommon for a female to grow one, too. When she does, she tends to be more aggressive, and the other females regard her with respect.

DOES THE TURKEY LOSE ITS BEARD WHEN IT MOLTS?

These "beard" feathers are not shed; they grow continuously. When a young gobbler reaches its first winter, the feathers are just beginning their growth. By April they reach a length of three to four inches. In adulthood, the turkey's beard is approximately eight to nine inches in length. One of the longest beards on record was thirteen inches. These beards contain as many as six to seven hundred feathers or bristles.

HOW DO THE SPURS AND LEGS TELL A BIRD'S AGE?

The spur is a horny protrusion on the turkey's leg. It can grow from an inch to an inch and a half in length. These spurs do not come to a sharp point until the gobbler is at least three to four years of age, after which time they take on a slight curve.

The color of the legs also indicates age, but this is not as reliable a method as the spur. A young bird has a reddish leg which turns gray and finally silver as it grows older.

A source of writing equipment

A source of tools

What the great seal of the United States might have looked like

A TRIBUTE TO THE TURKEY

A source of food

The turkey was a major factor in helping the Pilgrims and Puritans survive the long, lean winters. The bird was abundant and its meat was very delicious. Indians, too, ate the meat, and utilized the feathers for ornaments and the hard, pointed spurs for arrowheads.

When a national emblem for the United States was being chosen, Benjamin Franklin recommended the turkey in view of the contribution it had made during the settlement of the country.

HOW DOES SCRIPTURE ILLUSTRATE THE NEED TO REJECT AMBITIONS THAT HINDER US FROM BEING WHERE WE ARE NEEDED?

The service we give is often measured by the degree of sacrifice required to give it. Who was given a treasure when he expected death but lost half of it when he failed to give service in the right place at the right time?

(Pause for a response—see page 20)

His clothes were dirty and worn, and his feet stank. His hair and beard were matted and unkempt. Clothes, feet, hair, and beard would actually be evidence in an approaching trial. He was sure that his future wealth—possibly even his life—depended on this evidence.

Jerking the reins of his donkey, he nervously approached the royal procession. The king stared at him. There was an awkward silence before the king asked, "Where were you when I needed you?" This was the grave question that he must answer.

Months earlier, he had not been available for service when this king was in desperate need. The king's own son had led an organized rebellion, and the king had been forced to flee for his life. He expected this servant to accompany him with his other faithful men. This servant's support and encouragement would have been a special comfort on that day of humiliation when so many of his trusted friends turned against him.

It was especially important that this servant declare his loyalty to the king at that time. His grandfather had been the previous king, and the people were still divided in their loyalties to the leadership. By remaining in the royal city, this servant had really failed to declare his loyalty during the civil war.

An assistant of this servant brought food to the king when he was forced to leave the city and at that time accused his master of having personal ambitions to become the king himself. The king rewarded the assistant by turning over to him the lands he had previously given the servant. Now that servant must explain why he failed to be where he was needed.

The man made his defense. He claimed that he had intended to come to the king but that his assistant had deceived him and then slandered his intentions. In order to prove that he was innocent of the charge, he had not bathed his feet, washed his clothes, or cut his hair or beard since the day the king left.

Well acquainted with signs of disloyalty, the king weighed both sides. He was familiar with the actions of those who make extra efforts to give service when it is needed.

Everyone waited for the king's decision. In firm, final tones he spoke. The servant and his assistant were to divide the land equally between themselves and, for the sake of a covenant made with the servant's father, the man was invited to return to the king's table. The fact that all the land was not returned to him was a personal rebuke from the king.

The servant had not overcome personal obstacles to render service when and where it was needed. This servant was lame in both feet, and his name was Mephibosheth.

From II Samuel 9:1-13; 16:1-4; 19:24-30

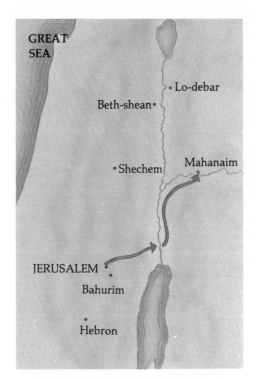

When David left Jerusalem *he crossed the Jordan River and made his camp at Mahanaim. Mephibosheth met David at the Jordan on his return.*

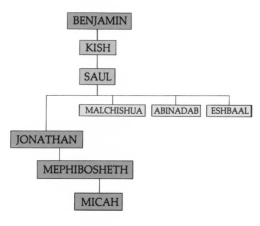

Ziba, the servant who betrayed Mephibosheth, *brought David one hundred bunches of summer fruit—probably fig cakes. Figs ripen during the summer in Israel.*

```
BENJAMIN
   |
  KISH
   |
  SAUL
   |
   +-------------------+-----------+
   |        MALCHISHUA  ABINADAB  ESHBAAL
JONATHAN
   |
MEPHIBOSHETH
   |
  MICAH
```

PERSONAL AMBITION HINDERED MEPHIBOSHETH FROM BEING WHERE HE WAS NEEDED

Mephibosheth's grandfather, King Saul, and father, Prince Jonathan, had been killed by the Philistine army on the slopes of Mount Gilboa. When the tragic news reached the palace where the five-year-old Mephibosheth was playing, "his nurse took him up, and fled; and it came to pass, as she made haste to flee, that he fell, and became lame." (II Samuel 4:4)

THE KING REMEMBERS A PROMISE

For his protection, Mephibosheth was brought to the house of Machir in Lo-debar on the east side of the Jordan River. Here he grew up in complete dependence on strangers who kindly took him into their household. There may have been a relationship between those people and the men of Jabesh-gilead, who gave the remains of Saul and Jonathan an honorable burial after a daring night-long raid (I Samuel 31:11-13).

Years later, when David had brought peace to the nation of Israel and was sitting on his throne in Jerusalem, he remembered that he had made a covenant with his beloved friend, Jonathan. Jonathan caused David to swear that when the Lord would "cut off the enemies of David, every one from the face of the earth" David would not cut off his kindness from Jonathan's house (I Samuel 20:15). Now that David's enemies had been conquered, David inquired about the house of Saul (II Samuel 9:1). A servant of Saul by the name of Ziba was found who knew the whereabouts of Mephibosheth, Jonathan's only surviving heir. David sent for him immediately.

AN INVITATION TO THE KING'S TABLE

Fearful that David had summoned him in order to remove him as a threat to the throne, Mephibosheth "fell on his face and did reverence" upon being presented to David (II Samuel 9:6). When David offered to restore to him his father's inheritance and invited him to eat regularly at his table, Mephibosheth was overwhelmed with humility and gratefulness. "And he bowed himself, and said, What is thy servant, that thou shouldest look upon such a dead dog as I am?" (II Samuel 9:8)

THE SERVANT CAME BUT THE MASTER STAYED HOME

For years Mephibosheth lived with David in the palace at Jerusalem. Then one day "there came a messenger to David, saying, The hearts of the men of Israel are after Absalom. And David said unto all his servants that were with him at Jerusalem, Arise, and let us flee . . ." (II Samuel 15:13, 14) Just outside the city, David was met by Ziba, the servant of Mephibosheth, who had two asses loaded with provisions for David's men. When questioned about Mephibosheth, Ziba said, "Behold, he abideth at Jerusalem; for he said, Today shall the house of Israel restore to me the kingdom of my father." (II Samuel 16:3) Having no opportunity to investigate this serious charge, David hastily gave Ziba the land and possessions which he had formerly given Mephibosheth.

THE CONSEQUENCES OF PERSONAL AMBITION

Absalom's rebellion was short-lived, and upon David's return to Jerusalem he was met first by Ziba and then by Mephibosheth. David inquired, "Wherefore wentest not thou with me, Mephibosheth?" (II Samuel 19:25) Mephibosheth answered by saying that Ziba had refused to help him and that he was unable to go alone because of his infirmity. He charged Ziba with slander. Who was David to believe? Apparently there were no witnessses to confirm either account. Being an experienced judge, David must have felt that neither Ziba nor Mephibosheth was telling the complete truth. Hence, he reversed his former decision and gave half of the possessions back to Mephibosheth.

Since David did not rescind his offer to allow Mephibosheth to eat at the king's table (II Samuel 9:7), we can only assume that he was allowed to continue this privilege. Later we learn that David spared Mephibosheth's life from the vengeance of the Gibeonites because of his covenant with Jonathan (II Samuel 21:7). After this incident, both Ziba and Mephibosheth fade from the pages of Scripture into obscurity.

MEPHIBOSHETH CHARACTER SKETCH

WHY DID DAVID WANT MEPHIBOSHETH TO ACCOMPANY HIM OUT OF JERUSALEM?

It is clear that Mephibosheth would be of no military help to David since he was lame in both feet (II Samuel 9:13). On the contrary, Mephibosheth would have been a burden to care for under the circumstances. There was, however, a very good reason why David wanted Mephibosheth to accompany him. Many in Israel were still loyal to the family of King Saul and wanted his heir to regain the throne. Support for Saul's family would come from the neighboring tribes of Benjamin and probably from Jabesh-gilead on the east of the Jordan (cf. II Samuel 16:5; I Samuel 31:11-13). By leaving Jerusalem with David, Mephibosheth would have declared his loyalty and signalled this contingent to support David rather than Absalom.

DID MEPHIBOSHETH REALLY HAVE AMBITIONS TO BECOME THE KING OF ISRAEL?

Although Mephibosheth was the sole heir of Jonathan, the natural successor of Saul, it is hard to believe that he felt he could ascend the throne—even with the remote possibility that Absalom and David would kill each other off. The powerful tribe of Judah would never rally behind a crippled member of the small tribe of Benjamin. David's sons remained to contend with for the kingship. One of the main reasons that Israel desired a king in the first place was for him to go out before them and fight their battles (I Samuel 8:20). In addition, everything we know about Mephibosheth indicates that he was a timid person with no aspirations whatsoever. When he first appeared before David he cowered in fear, comparing himself to a dead dog (II Samuel 9:8). No semblance of a rebellion is recorded either during or after the war on the part of Mephibosheth or the Benjamites. When David restored to him half of his father's land, Mephibosheth was willing to let Ziba keep it all (II Samuel 19:30). It seems that he was more interested in preserving his life than his property or his grandfather's throne.

WHO WAS TELLING THE TRUTH, MEPHIBOSHETH OR ZIBA?

What new evidence did David discover that caused him to reconsider his original decision made when Ziba accused Mephibosheth of treason? Certainly the personal testimony of Mephibosheth was not an adequate defense in the case of a man accused of treason. We learn not from the mouth of Ziba nor from the mouth of Mephibosheth the following fact: "And Mephibosheth, the son of Saul, came down to meet the king, and had neither dressed his feet, nor trimmed his beard, nor washed his clothes, from the day the king departed until the day he came again in peace." (II Samuel 19:24) David's apparent conclusion was that Mephibosheth was a coward. He chose no sides, so that if Absalom was to win the battle, his life might be spared. He had just demonstrated his ability to travel without Ziba's help. Ziba had also deceived David in order to obtain possession of the land which he had controlled after the death of Saul and then had to return to Mephibosheth. Neither men had told the complete truth, and as a result David divided the land in half.

"And **Mephibosheth, the son of Saul,** *came down to meet the king, and had neither dressed his feet, nor trimmed his beard, nor washed his clothes, from the day the king departed until the day he came again in peace."*

MEPHIBOSHETH
mē-fĭb'ŏ-shĕth

163

Availability

IS STANDING BY A TASK UNTIL IT IS FULLY COMPLETED

"Therefore, my beloved brethren, be ye steadfast, unmovable, always abounding in the work of the Lord, forasmuch as ye know that your labor is not in vain in the Lord."

I Corinthians 15:58

LIVING LESSONS ON AVAILABILITY . . .

FROM THE PAGES OF SCRIPTURE

An employee's natural inclination is to decide if his employer has been fair. Usually such a worker does not limit his evaluation to the promises his employer has made to him. He also evaluates what other employees receive. The result of such comparison is often resentment, ungratefulness, and discontent. Scripture describes a conflict which arose from such a comparison. Certain workers mentally divided a job and decided they had done more work than the others. They resented their employer for giving equal pay to those who had worked less, but they did not understand the principle or value of availability.

ILLUSTRATED IN THE WORLD OF NATURE

OPOSSUM *Didelphis marsupialus*

There are three things the opossum needs in order for it to be happy—woods, food, and water. The opossum will den up in a hole anywhere, whether it be on the ground or up in a tree. It is particular, though, that the lodge be warm, dry, and near woods. The wandering habits of this nocturnal animal usually force it to seek out a new lodging every day. An omnivorous feeder, the opossum's diet is unlimited—from plants to small animals. It is not above eating carrion; in fact, that is a major portion of its diet. The opossum is very easygoing and can tolerate almost any environment and all types of weather. Because this animal is so congenial and adaptable, its range and its population are increasing.

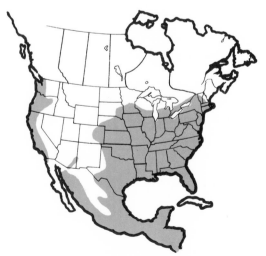

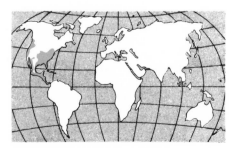

The range and habitat of the opossum

AVAILABILITY

HOW DOES THE OPOSSUM ILLUSTRATE AVAILABILITY BY STANDING BY A TASK UNTIL IT IS COMPLETED?

Frightened, two boys scrambled for garden rakes in order to defend themselves against the intruder. The biggest rat they had ever seen had wandered into the garage and stowed itself behind some tall boxes.

The animal had a long, hairless tail. The shape of its body and head also closely resembled a rat's. One of the boys had seen some rats at the town dump a few years ago. He was sure they were up against a giant rat.

As the boys approached, the hissing creature turned and ran for the corner of the garage. Dodging through the jungle of tools, boxes, and stacks of wood, the animal was able to outmaneuver the boys, slip through the open door, and quickly scale the large oak tree outside the garage.

As it climbed farther and farther out of reach, the boys stared up in surprise. They had never known a rat to be able to climb a tree. Then they noticed that the colors of the animal's fur were black, gray, and white. The boy remembered that the rats he had seen were brown in color.

Determined to identify the animal, they went to the library. There they were interested to discover that this was not a rat but an opossum. As they read further, they learned that the opossum is marsupial. Like the kangaroos, this animal has a pouch in which the mother feeds and carries her young as they develop. After an incredibly short gestation period of twelve days and eighteen hours, her tiny young are born.

Because her young are so minute and require such special care, the opossum is provided with a protective pouch on its abdomen. This pouch frees the mother from having to coax or herd the young to safety. This is a particular advantage because confronted with danger and having the young secure in her pouch, she needs to concentrate only on her own escape.

This built-in pouch also enables the mother to give her young the warmth and special protection they so vitally need. Until able to fend for themselves they cling to her, enabling her to stand by and complete the task of bringing them through the critical development period.

It was only a few weeks later that the boys saw the animal again when the family car pulled into the driveway. Its headlights illuminated the beady eyes of the opossum as it stopped and stared into the bright lights. As the boys looked again, they noticed something different. Little babies clung to the fur of this mother's back. The boys realized that when the opossum was in the garage her pouch must have contained these young. They relaxed back in their seats thankful that they had been unable to catch the animal and that no harm had befallen either the mother or her young.

SCRIPTURAL REFERENCES TO THE OPOSSUM

The opossum is not named in Scripture. A distinctive characteristic of this animal is its ability to feign death in order to deceive its attackers. A variation of this concept of "playing opossum" was used by David when he found himself in the hands of his enemies.

"And he changed his behaviour before them,
and feigned himself mad in their hands, and
scrabbled on the doors of the gate, and let his
spittle fall down upon his beard."
I Samuel 21:13

CHARACTERISTICS AND PHYSICAL FEATURES OF THE OPOSSUM

Because the opossum is available and faithful in the task of raising its young, it makes an exceptionally good parent. The mother is patient, careful and methodical in preparing and caring for them. While she waits for her young to be born, she carefully readies her pouch, frequently washing it with her tongue to ensure that this built-in nest is clean and comfortable for the new occupants. As the time approaches for her to give birth, she helps her young reach the pouch through a special procedure.

HAS MAN ALWAYS UNDERSTOOD THE BIRTH OF THE OPOSSUM?

No. Man has been familiar with the opossum since about 1500 A.D., but it was not until 1847 that its birth process was understood. It was recognized from eyewitness observation that the opossum's birth was marsupial, but men failed to understand how the young opossum entered the pouch. Many theories were proposed—that the young were conveyed into the pouch by the mother's mouth, licked into the pouch, even the idea of being sneezed into the pouch was entertained.

HOW DOES THE BABY OPOSSUM GET TO THE POUCH?

It "swims." The baby is completely on its own. The mother assists the young opossum only by washing the chorionic fluid from her thirteen-day-old embryos. She also licks the three inch path from the vulva to the pouch. By so doing, she eliminates the possibility of the infant embryo sticking to the fur as it crawls up the belly.

HOW BIG IS AN OPOSSUM AT BIRTH?

At birth the opossum is approximately four-tenths of an inch long and about one tenth of an inch in diameter, or two-thirds the size of a honeybee. It is so small that a litter of twenty babies could be placed into a teaspoon. It weighs approximately 0.13 grams or 0.0046 ounce. By the time it is an adult, the animal weighs approximately 28,000 times its weight at birth. Man on the other hand weighs, on the average, twenty times his weight at birth.

Actual size of opossum embryo

Baby opossums "swimming" to pouch

Young attached and concealed in pouch

Size of nipple before opossum attaches to it

Before

After

"Swimming" motion of its crawl to pouch

Before and after three-inch trip

Undeveloped center teeth

HOW DOES THE BABY OPOSSUM KNOW WHICH WAY TO GO TO THE POUCH?

By a process called negative geotropism—movement away from the earth against the force of gravity. For many years the baby opossum's ability to navigate was referred to as a "mysterious" force. As scientists studied further, they realized that there was nothing mysterious about it. The answer lay in the construction of the embryo. The front legs of the baby opossum are fairly well-developed, and the tips of the front feet are equipped with strong claws. The body tapers toward the tail, and the hind legs are developed only to the point of having five lobed pads.

The front legs are the only means by which the baby opossum is able to move itself. It is with these strong legs that it pulls itself upwards in an overhand stroke, dragging its body along as it goes. This climbing motion permits it to move only straight ahead. If the mother were to lie down horizontally, her young would crawl aimlessly. But by positioning herself upright on her haunches, her babies crawl accurately upward to her pouch.

HOW DOES THE BABY OPOSSUM KNOW WHEN TO STOP?

As the baby opossum moves toward the pouch, it touches its mother's skin with its snout. With each stroke of its forearm it sways its head, stretching as far as possible in an attempt to find one of its mother's nipples—no larger than the head of a pin.

When it does find one, it immediately stops crawling and clamps its small mouth around the nipple. Once the baby fastens onto the mammary gland, the gland swells. It becomes so swollen inside the baby's mouth that it cannot be shaken off. The baby opossum maintains this grip for nearly 60 to 70 days until it is almost completely grown.

DOES THE MOTHER HAVE AN ADEQUATE FOOD SUPPLY?

The mother is capable of producing enough milk for her young, but she does not always have enough nipples to go around. She is normally equipped with 11 to 17 nipples. However, she may have as many as twenty young. Because these nipples are distributed on a first-come first-serve basis, any who do not find a nipple will perish.

DO THE BABY'S TEETH HURT THE MOTHER?

As the baby opossum gains nourishment from the mother, its body grows and its teeth develop. But there is something unusual about the development of these milk teeth; that is, the side teeth grow and develop, but the center teeth do not. This feature benefits both the baby and its mother during their long, literal attachment. It protects the teeth from damage and prevents the mother from being injured or bitten.

WHAT IS UNIQUE ABOUT THE DEVELOPMENT OF THE OPOSSUM'S CLAWS?

Once the infant has reached the pouch, is securely attached to one of the mammary glands, and no longer has any need to propel itself, an unusual thing happens to the claws. They drop off in a manner similar to that of the baby wood duck's egg tooth. There is a good reason for this. In such confined quarters the long, sharp claws would be a hazard to the opossum and to the others in the pouch. By losing their claws the risk of injuring one another is much less.

HOW DOES THE BABY OPOSSUM EAT AND BREATHE AT THE SAME TIME?

The lid to the larynx, or epiglottis, opens and closes the opening to the air passage. The construction of the opossum's epiglottis is tubular, and extends up into the nasal chamber. This arrangement allows the milk to run down into the stomach without obstructing the air passage or causing the animal to choke.

WHEN DOES THE OPOSSUM LEAVE THE POUCH?

After 60 to 70 days. Toward the end of this period the mammary glands will have stretched so much that the young are able to crawl outside of the pouch and remain attached. At 70 days the opossum are approximately the same size as full-grown mice. They are ready to detach themselves from the mammary gland and leave the pouch. When hungry, they return to feed. During the next 30 days the young continue to stay with the mother. Holding tightly to her hair with their feet and wrapping their tails around her tail, they spend most of their time outside the pouch riding on her back.

WHAT IS UNUSUAL ABOUT THE OPOSSUM'S TEETH?

The opossum is equipped with more teeth than any other land animal in America. Foxes and coyotes have 42; the weasel, 34; the bobcat, 28; and man, incidentally, 32. But the opossum outdoes them all with an average grand total of 50—26 in the upper jaw and 24 in the lower. Of these, 18 are incisors. Their teeth resemble those of carnivorous animals and are used basically for the same purpose—for tearing, cutting, and grinding meat. Even with all these teeth, the opossum is slow to use them as a weapon against man. It rather shows them off and hisses in a threatening manner. If forced, however, it will not hesitate to bite its pursuer.

IS THE OPOSSUM NOCTURNAL OR DIURNAL?

Nocturnal. This animal is most commonly seen at night when in search of food. It is well-suited for activity in darkness with its keen sense of smell and acute night vision. When fully grown the opossum ranges from 24 to 34 inches in length. It weighs from 4 to 15 pounds. The male is normally larger than the female.

17th day

Development of hind quarters

36th day

Young still attached to
mammary gland but
outside of pouch

A warning hiss
to its enemies

Tooth and jaw structure of the opossum

Prehensile tail

*Typical way of
opossum carrying tail*

Front foot

Hind foot

The opossum's hind feet produce an unusual and distinctive footprint. *The print of the front foot is much smaller than that of the hind, and the track is further distinguished by the mark of its dragging tail.*

DOES THE OPOSSUM REALLY HANG BY ITS TAIL?

The opossum's tail is very strong and flexible. It is referred to as prehensile which means grasping. The opossum can hang by its tail, especially early in its life. As it grows older it becomes increasingly hard for it to do so.

When walking, a healthy animal carries the end of its tail in a downward curl, the tip touching the ground. It is said that only near death will the opossum curl its tail upward.

HOW CLEAN IS THE OPOSSUM?

This creature is extremely clean. It spends many hours grooming its fur. When scientists studied the food content of an opossum's stomach they were surprised to find large quantities of its own hair—the result of heavy grooming and cleaning.

The value of its fur is negligible because of its poor wearing quality. Its fur value is compared to other animals on the following chart.

FUR VALUES
(Rating scale from 1-100)

Rabbit 5
Opossum 37
Muskrat . . . . .35 to 60
Striped skunk . . . . .50 to 75
Mink 75
Raccoon 80
Beaver 85
Otter 100

THE DEFENSE OF THE OPOSSUM

How the opossum will react to danger is unpredictable. It may choose to run, stand its ground, flash its teeth and hiss, or—most remarkable of all—play dead . . . from which the term "playing possum" originated. The animal lies on its side, mouth open, tongue protruding, and legs partially extended. The heart beat as well as the respiratory system decrease to the point that movement cannot be detected. Increased salivation foams from the mouth. During this state the opossum will not respond to rough treatment. Even touching the cornea of the eye does not arouse it. It is believed that the opossum is not acting but is rather responding to stimulus which is triggered internally—a response that the animal is unable to control.

HOW DOES SCRIPTURE ILLUSTRATE THE NEED TO STAND BY A TASK UNTIL IT IS FULLY COMPLETED?

King David resolved a conflict among his soldiers by establishing the standard that those who "stayed by the stuff" would share equally with those who went out into battle. Where in Scripture was this same principle applied in a business situation?

(Pause for a response—see page 20)

A scorching sun beat down on men working in a vineyard. The owner of this vineyard had hired them early that morning. They had all agreed on a wage for the day's work.

At mid-morning the owner of the vineyard observed the progress of his workers and realized that more laborers would be needed. So he went to the market place and hired more men. He assured them that he would pay a fair wage for the hours they worked. Then he sent them into his vineyard.

At noon and at three o'clock in the afternoon he did the same thing. Each time he employed more workers, he told them he would pay them a fair wage.

About five o'clock the owner realized that still more laborers were needed to finish the job. Again he went into town and engaged more men. An hour later the foreman was told to call the workers together so that they could be given their pay.

The first ones to be paid were those who had worked only one hour. They were given a full day's wage! When they received their pay, they were delighted and grateful. Those who had worked only three hours were paid next. They also received a whole day's pay! So did those who worked only half a day and three quarters of a day.

Those laborers who had worked since the early morning hours saw what the owner paid the others. They assumed that he would give them more money than what had been agreed upon. But when they were paid it was exactly the same amount that the other men had received. They began to murmur against the owner of the vineyard. "These who have worked only one hour you have made equal to us who have worked through all the heat of the day."

The owner replied to one of them, "My friend, I am not being unjust to you. Didn't you agree to work for the money I have paid you? Take your money and go your way. I have purposed to give those who worked only one hour as much as I have given you. Is it not lawful for me to do what I want with what belongs to me? Must you be jealous because I am doing right?"

The owner of that vineyard was just in his dealings because he paid his workers according to the agreement. Scripture states that when he hired the final group of laborers, he asked them, "Why stand ye here all day idle?" They replied, "Because no man has hired us."

The men who had worked only one hour were waiting and available to be called all day long. Even though they had not been hired, they stayed and stood by the task until it was completed. Their example and their reward emphasize the value of those who are available—whether they are called to work or not—and stand by a task until it is fully completed.

From Matthew 20:1-16

LABORERS WHO DIDN'T REALIZE WHAT IT MEANT TO STAND BY A TASK

Grapes and viticulture have been symbols of the land of Israel ever since the twelve spies brought back a cluster of grapes so heavy that two men had to bear it between them on a staff (Numbers 13:23). The climate of the country is particularly well-suited to this industry with its bright sunshine and the heavy dew of late summer nights.

A DEMANDING FORM OF AGRICULTURE

A vineyard requires more regular labor than any other form of agriculture. Because of their usual location on a hillside, vineyards must be terraced to keep the soil in place. This necessitates the laborious job of constructing a series of stone walls. The walls run parallel to the side of the hill and form a series of steps. Next, large boulders which might hinder the growing vines are removed. A hedge or wall is usually built around the vineyard, too. This may be accomplished by digging a ditch and using the sod to form a wall. A fence of posts, branches, and twigs is constructed on top of the sod wall and topped with thorn branches to discourage foxes, jackals, and other animals from entering. Because of its protective wall and rocky terraces, the vineyard must be tilled by hand. Constant pruning of the vines is necessary if the clusters of grapes are to reach full maturity.

Although the grapes begin to ripen in July and continue to bear fruit until October, the main harvest usually takes place in September. At that time a majority of the grapes are sweet and ripe. Often the whole family is drafted to help pick the mature grapes. If it is a large vineyard, the owner will need to hire workmen to assist him. The season ends with the tasks of pressing the grapes into juice and making raisins or a sweet product known as grape honey.

A GENEROUS CONTRACT

The Lord Jesus used the familiar scene of a vineyard to teach his disciples an important spiritual principle. He told how the foreman of a vineyard needed to hire some laborers. His specific purpose is not stated. The laborers may have been employed to clear another section of land or stones, to build another terrace, to help with the spring pruning, or, most likely, to help harvest ripe grapes.

The owner of the vineyard left early in the morning for the market place where men were waiting to be hired. He offered them one denarius for one day's work. This was a generous contract. It was the pay of a Roman soldier per day and was considered a very liberal recompense, if not extravagant pay, for an agricultural laborer.

MANY MEN WERE NEEDED

We are not told why the foreman returned to the market place at the third, sixth, ninth, and eleventh hours. We can only assume that he had an urgent need for more laborers. He made no contract with those men but merely promised them a fair wage. The Jewish workday was divided into twelve equal parts. It ended when the stars were first seen, at the twelfth hour. Because the laborers were relatively poor men who had no permanent job, they were to be paid at the end of the day. This practice was, in fact, commanded by the Law of Moses (Leviticus 19:13; Deuteronomy 24:15).

PAYMENT PRODUCED CONTROVERSY AND COMPLAINT

When those who were hired last were paid exactly the same as the first hired, the men under a fixed contract protested and murmured against the foreman. It was not that they felt underpaid, but they resented the fact that the other men had, in their opinion, been overpaid. The foreman accused them of having an "evil eye", a Jewish expression for a greedy and covetous spirit (cf. Deuteronomy 15:9; Proverbs 28:22). The foreman refused to alter their wages and quickly dismissed them to their homes.

A wall and watchtower *in a terraced vineyard*

For good grapes *it is important to prune the vines each spring.*

Grapes have been a symbol *of the Hebrew nation ever since two of the spies carried a cluster back to Moses on a pole.*

THE LABORERS CHARACTER SKETCH

HOW DOES THE OLD TESTAMENT ILLUSTRATE THE PRINCIPLE OF RECOMPENSE?

In battle against the Midianites, one thousand men from each of the twelve tribes were chosen to represent the nation. When the Israelite soldiers returned with a huge spoil, the Lord commanded Moses to divide it equally among those who were chosen to go to war and those who remained at home—an illustration of tribal solidarity (Numbers 31:27).

After Joshua dismissed the fighting men of the two and one-half tribes to return to the east side of the Jordan, he commanded them to divide the spoil of cattle, silver, gold, bronze, and raiment with the non-fighting men who were not chosen to go to war (Joshua 22:8).

When David returned from battle against the Amalekites, some of his men did not want to share the spoil with those who were so physically exhausted that they were unable to keep up with the rest and fight. David rebuked them for their greedy attitude, commanding them to divide the spoil with the others equally. "And it was so from that day forward, that he made it a statute and an ordinance for Israel to this day." (I Samuel 30:25)

The Old Testament commands, "Thou shalt love thy neighbor as thyself." (Leviticus 19:18) It nowhere encourages greed or stinginess, rather it encourages love and generosity.

WHY WAS IT IMPORTANT TO THE FOREMAN THAT THE LABORERS STAND BY THEIR TASK?

It seems almost foolish for the foreman to hire men at the eleventh hour if they weren't really needed. Why hadn't he hired those men earlier since he knew that they had been standing idle all day? (cf. Matthew 20:6) A simple explanation is that he didn't think he needed them. Had he underestimated the work, or overestimated the workers? In light of the attitude revealed in the men first hired, the latter is a more probable explanation. He had a task to complete before nightfall, and he needed extra help. Although the last group of men worked only an hour, they were just as vital to the completion of his goal as the others. Since they remained available when he needed them to finish his task, he gave them a full day's pay.

WHAT IS THE SPIRITUAL REWARD FOR STANDING BY A TASK UNTIL IT IS COMPLETED?

The parable of the laborers was a response to Peter's question, "Behold, we have forsaken all, and followed thee. What shall we have, therefore?" (Matthew 19:27) Peter wanted to know what was in this for him. Jesus told him that there was much in it for him, but the parable was a gentle rebuke that he had the wrong focus. Only the very first group of laborers had a contract. They received just what they had bargained for, and they were the only ones who were not satisfied. The others had no contract and were delighted and grateful with the foreman's generosity. Jesus wanted followers who asked for no reward and whose concern was not for what they would gain. The greater rewards are for those who seek none. He is looking for those who ask only the opportunity to work in His vineyard. The parable teaches that service for Christ will be faithfully rewarded and that faithfulness to one's opportunities will be rewarded. The amount will depend more on motive and availability than on ambition and activity.

"**But he answered one of them,** *and said, Friend, I do thee no wrong. Didst not thou agree with me for a denarius? Take what is thine, and go thy way; I will give unto this last, even as unto thee.*"

THE LABORERS

Endurance

"For consider him that endured such contradiction of sinners against himself, lest ye be wearied and faint in your minds."

Hebrews 12:3

PART FOUR

Endurance

IS SETTING ASIDE PRIVILEGES WHICH WEAKEN ME OR OTHERS

"It is good neither to eat flesh, nor to drink wine, nor any thing whereby thy brother stumbleth, or is offended, or is made weak."

Romans 14:21

LIVING LESSONS ON ENDURANCE . . .

FROM THE PAGES OF SCRIPTURE

True love will always show deference. Deference is limiting our freedom in order not to offend the convictions of other Christians. The alternative to deference is defending our right to engage in a questionable activity. This defense usually involves trying to prove that the activity is acceptable, but the real question does not concern the activity at all. The real question is whether we are willing to cause a weaker Christian to stumble. In every period of church history there have been questionable activities which have caused Christians to be divided. When this matter was discussed in the very first church council, clear principles were given which required Christians to set aside any activity which would spiritually weaken themselves or others.

ILLUSTRATED IN THE WORLD OF NATURE

EASTERN BOX TURTLE   *Terrapene carolina*

The box turtle is referred to as a terrestrial turtle because it has a tendency to spend more time on land than in water. Though it is not as agile as other turtles and has difficulty propelling itself in water, it still is very fond of it and prefers to inhabit open woodlands and fields which have brooks, streams, or ponds. Like most other turtles, it is not active at night. It is a cold-blooded animal and is most comfortable when the temperature is between 55 and 60 degrees. The box turtle avoids the heat of the day by seeking shelter in underground burrows or under logs and leaves. In extremely hot weather it heads for shaded waters and remains there to cool off. Its gentle temperament makes it an excellent pet.

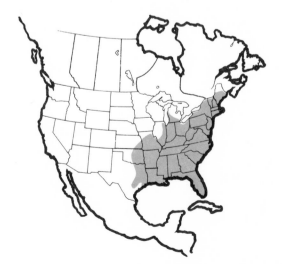

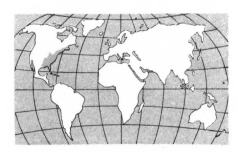

The range and habitat of the eastern box turtle

ENDURANCE

HOW DOES THE TURTLE ILLUSTRATE THE NEED TO SET ASIDE PRIVILEGES WHICH WEAKEN IT?

Lumbering through the tall grass, the hard-shelled creature forged ahead in search of food. It was a laborious and cumbersome task to transport its bulky, bone-like covering from one place to another. The inconvenience of the large, heavy shell often created extra hazards and obstacles which were of no significance to other animals.

For example, a fallen log in the path often required a long trek around instead of over the obstacle. Turning over on its back could be a major problem—it might even prove fatal—if it were not able to right itself. Lack of speed was another disadvantage, especially when it came to moving out of the path of an oncoming car. This apparently misfortunate creature was the box turtle—more precisely the eastern box turtle.

The ground over which it crawled was still damp from a heavy, mid-summer rain. It was the peak of the berry season now, and it had been a good year for wild fruits. Dark stains around the turtle's jaw betrayed the fact that it had been eating one of its favorite foods—sweet, succulent blackberries.

Without a care in the world the turtle leisurely ambled from plant to plant. Its home, 250 yards in diameter, contained an abundance of food and a convenient pond.

As the berry feast continued, the turtle's tranquility was broken by an unwelcome sight. The perceptive eyes of a racoon had detected the feeding turtle and the masked bandit quickly scampered over to investigate. The box turtle viewed this intruder as an inconvenience but not as a real danger. For although the shell did have its drawbacks at times, it also had advantages. And at times like this, these advantages were very much appreciated.

The turtle's tough, bony covering protected it from the teeth and claws of potential predators. The box turtle's shell in particular provides an advantage even greater than that of other turtles. The bottom of its shell is hinged in such a way as to allow the animal to pull itself completely inside, leaving no part of its soft skin exposed. It can hold this position for hours if necessary.

Today it was more difficult to retreat into the shell. The turtle had overeaten. It had all it could do to hold the shell tightly closed. As the raccoon determinedly gnawed on the outside of the shell, the pressure on the turtle to hold the shell together became more and more intense. It waited and waited until finally it could hold no longer. The turtle had to relieve the pressure. The privilege of the morning's over-indulgence and now a moment's respite from the pressure didn't seem too crucial.

Just slightly, it released the hinged bottom to relieve the pressure for a moment. But that slight opening was all that the raccoon needed. With its strong jaws and nimble paws it pried the shell open and exposed the soft skin of the little creature.

Had the turtle just waited a little longer, the raccoon would have given up and moved on—the turtle would have been safe. But because the turtle weakened its endurance by overindulgence, it forfeited its life.

Scriptural references to the turtle

"These also shall be unclean unto you among the creeping things that creep upon the earth; the weasel, and the mouse, and the tortoise after its kind."
Leviticus 11:29

Scriptural background

The Hebrew word means lizard, although it may refer to several species of tortoise. The Moorish tortoise is common throughout Palestine. Although the Israelites were forbidden to eat it, the flesh of this tortoise is highly esteemed by a Palestinian bird, the ossifrage. In order to reach the flesh, these birds carry the tortoise high into the air and drop it to the ground until the tortoise's shell shatters.

Also included in this category of tortoise was the Arabic dabb which lives in the rocky terrain of Palestine.

CHARACTERISTICS AND PHYSICAL FEATURES OF THE EASTERN BOX TURTLE

CARAPACE
(upper shell)

The endurance that the eastern box turtle lacked to resist the privilege of over-indulgence is not a common occurence. This situation only occurs when there is an abundance of food which the turtle greatly favors. At the slightest indication of danger it withdraws into its shell and remains there as long as necessary—even hours—in order to avoid harm. So perfectly can the box turtle clamp the lobes of the lower shell, or plastorm, to the upper shell, or carapace, that it is difficult to insert even a blade of grass between the shells. It is aided by extremely strong muscles and can normally thwart any predator's effort to gain enough leverage to pry it open. Because of this defense the box turtle has few living enemies with the exception of man.

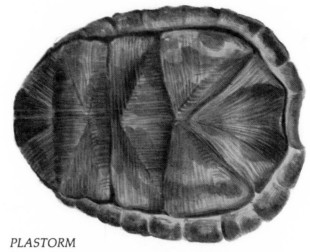

PLASTORM
(lower shell)

DOES A BOX TURTLE HAVE TEETH?

The box turtle, like others of its kind, lacks teeth. Its jaws, though, are covered with a horny sheath equipped with a sharp cutting edge. The turtle is very gentle and will not usually bite an individual when picked up. Instead, it retreats into its shell. The length of time which the turtle remains in the shell varies. There have been instances when a turtle taken for a pet remained in its shell for days after capture.

WHY DOES THE TURTLE LIKE TO SUN ITSELF?

The box turtle is a cold-blooded animal. On cold days its life processes slow down. By warming itself in the sun's rays, it can become active again to carry on its daily activities.

Another motivation for sunning are the leeches and other parasites which attach to the turtle and lodge themselves in inaccessible spots, making it impossible to scratch or relieve the irritation. The hot sun brings relief to the turtle by helping to kill or dislodge these pests.

A third reason for this practice is that light from the sun is a great healer for any cut, infection, or fungus which may have developed on the skin of the animal. When the sun becomes too hot, the turtle resorts to water or burrows into moist soil or leaves. There it remains until sufficiently cooled. This adjustment process is called thermoregulation, and by this means the turtle maintains a temperature around 60 degrees Fahrenheit.

THE BOX TURTLE'S DEFENSE

The box turtle is able to draw back *into its shell by flexing its muscles and the eight vertebrae of its neck to form a tight, "S" shape.*

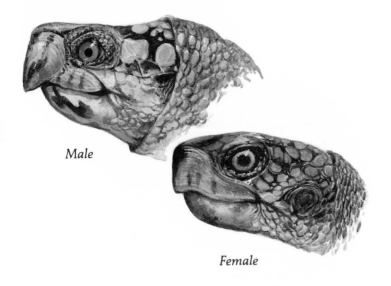

Male

Female

PLASTORM

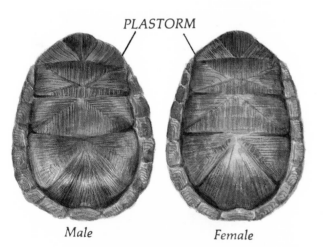

Male   *Female*

Male

Female

DOES THE SHELL HAVE ANY FUNCTION OTHER THAN PROTECTION?

Yes. The box turtle controls its body temperature by the color and texture of its shell. Years ago it was a popular practice to paint pictures or shellac the shells of turtles and then sell them in stores. It was later discovered that the airtight, waterproof covering prevented circulation and resulted in a slow, painful death or deformity of the turtle. This practice has since been outlawed.

IS IT POSSIBLE TO IDENTIFY THE SEX OF THE TURTLE?

When determining the sex of a turtle there are no concrete rules short of dissection to establish whether it is a male or female. There are basic guidelines which are fairly accurate when applied to a full grown box turtle.

IDENTIFICATION OF THE MALE AND FEMALE BOX TURTLE:

SIZE: The male is usually larger than the female.

EYES: The eyes of the male are often red in color. The female's eyes tend to be brown or gray-brown.

SHELL: The carapace, or upper shell, of the male turtle is more flattened than that of the female. The female's carapace is higher and wider.

The lower shell, or plastorm, is flat and curved inward in the male. The plastorm of the female is also flat, but it curves outward.

FEET AND CLAWS: The claws of the male are short and stocky and have a curved appearance. The claws of the female are slender, longer, and straighter.

TAIL: The tail of the male is longer and thicker than that of the female.

MOUTH: The male's hooked beak is more prominent than that of the female.

EGGS: Only the female lays eggs.

WHAT HAPPENS WHEN A FEMALE CAN'T FIND A PARTNER?

It is not necessary for a female turtle to mate every year. There have been cases when a female had the remarkable ability to lay fertile eggs each year for three to four years after mating only once.

WHY DO SO MANY MALES LOSE THEIR LIVES DURING MATING SEASON?

Spring marks the beginning of the box turtle's breeding season, and the season may continue throughout the summer into autumn. During the courtship and mating process it is not uncommon for males to lose their balance and roll over on their backs. If they are unable to right themselves by securing sufficient leverage and footing, they will die.

WHAT KIND OF A NEST DOES THE BOX TURTLE MAKE?

The female carefully and painstakingly goes about the task of nest making. She usually begins around twilight and finishes after dark, taking as long as five hours to ensure that it is done to her satisfaction. An open, elevated site in sandy soil is her normal choice.

The female digs a three-inch hole in the ground in a flask-like shape. Using her forelegs as a brace, she places them in a fixed position and then digs the entire nest with her hind feet. The length of the nest corresponds to the reach of these hind legs—usually three inches. The feet dig alternately, scraping and shovelling soil and removing obstructions such as small pebbles which are stacked at the rear of the hole. As these accumulate they are pushed out of the way.

Once the hole is complete, the female begins laying her eggs at intervals of one to six minutes. The eggs are arranged in the nest with the assistance of her hind feet.

When the last of the eggs is laid, the hole is filled by using one or both hind feet to scoop the loosened soil forward. When she has carefully smoothed out the surface by tramping the soil down and smoothing it with her toes, knees, feet, and plastorm, she leaves the nest never to return.

HOW LONG DOES IT TAKE FOR THE BOX TURTLE'S EGGS TO INCUBATE?

The time required to incubate turtle eggs depends on the temperature of the soil. The warmer the soil, the quicker the incubation. The soil's temperature is regulated by such factors as air temperature, rain, availability of sun rays, and characteristics of the soil. The incubation period may be as short as 70 days or as long as 136.

The two to seven creamy-white, elliptical eggs have thin, flexible shells. They measure 1 to 1½ inches long and about ¾ inch wide and weigh from six to eleven grams. The eggs hatch from early September until October. Young turtles either remain in the nest throughout winter or leave the nest to enter hibernation.

Young box turtle *emerging from egg in its underground nest*

Digging the nest

Depositing the eggs

Box turtle egg

Burying the eggs

CARAPACE

SCUTE

Growth rings

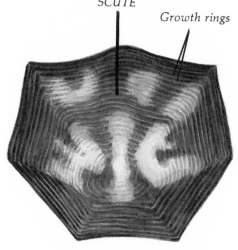

In the early stages *of the turtle's life the growth rate is much more rapid averaging approximately one-half to three-quarters inch per year. As it gets older this growth rate diminishes. The coloration is also very vivid in early years but with age becomes faded and less distinct.*

WHAT ARE THE CHANCES OF THE NEST AND ITS CONTENTS SURVIVING?

Actually, its prospects for survival are very good. Although it is not completely free of predators that would try to destroy it—raccoons, skunks, crows, and even cottonmouth or copperhead snakes—studies indicate that the survival rate of the eggs is approximately 78.6 percent.

IS IT POSSIBLE TO TELL THE AGE OF A BOX TURTLE BY ITS SHELL?

The horny shields or scutes on the turtle's carapace add a ring of growth each year. After five years, though, the accuracy of counting shields to determine age decreases.

At four to five years, the turtle is sexually mature. At twenty years it has achieved full growth. The average life expectancy of a turtle is about forty years, but some have lived to be 138!

DOES THE DIET OF THE BOX TURTLE CHANGE AS IT GROWS OLDER?

A young box turtle is largely carnivorous, feeding on a varied diet of slugs, crayfish, snails, earthworms, insects, butterflies, beetles, even mice and small snakes. As the turtle matures, its diet changes to vegetation—leaves, buds, fruits, berries, mushrooms, grains, grasses, and mosses. Turtles drink water, sometimes consuming great quantities at a time by submerging their head as they drink.

HOW DOES THE ADULT TURTLE SPEND ITS WINTER?

It hibernates. The turtle prepares for hibernation by burrowing about three to four feet beneath the surface of soft soil. The turtle may dig deeper depending on the depth where the soil freezes. At that level it constructs a nest of hay around itself.

In the spring, the turtle must be careful not to leave its winter quarters too early or it will die of exposure. Pets kept in captivity and not allowed to hibernate often die during the winter months.

THE BOX TURTLE AND THE MUSHROOM

Although the meat of the box turtle can be eaten, it is not generally used for that purpose. Years ago, miners in need of food caught and ate these turtles. Many of them became sick. It is believed that the flesh of the reptiles may have become temporarily poisonous because of the turtle's diet of poisonous toadstools. The turtle is very fond of the toadstools and their poison does not seem to affect it.

HOW DOES SCRIPTURE ILLUSTRATE ENDURANCE BY SETTING ASIDE PRIVILEGES WHICH WEAKEN OTHERS?

One measure of a mature Christian is his willingness to refrain from activities which some Christians think are right and others believe are wrong. Who clarified God's will on questionable activities in an early church council?

(Pause for a response—see page 20)

A man carefully chose the best lamb of his flock and made his way to the heathen temple. There he sacrificed it according to the temple ritual. A pagan priest took the lamb, slipped out of that temple and went directly to the meat market. In order to get money quickly for the lamb, the priest sold it at a low price.

Many Christians shopped in this village meat market. They knew that the meat available at a bargain price came from a heathen temple. They also knew that it was the best meat available. It was easy to find reasons why it was perfectly proper to purchase this meat. Some thought it was right; others felt strongly that it was wrong. The controversy grew.

Soon it threatened to divide Christians, and a church council was held. The leaders of the early church gathered together. Several questions were presented and vigorously discussed.

One man waited until everyone else had expressed their thoughts. Then he spoke. Everyone had great respect for him and listened attentively to his suggestion. When he finished speaking, they all agreed that his conclusion was in harmony with the principles of Scripture and the leading of the Holy Spirit.

His conclusion was written in a letter and sent to Christians in the early churches who were waiting for it. That letter explained that the unanimous decision of the church as confirmed by the Holy Spirit was that all Christians abstain from meats that were offered to idols.

This decision established a precedent for all future questionable activities. The speaker of that council was the apostle James.

From Acts 15:1-35

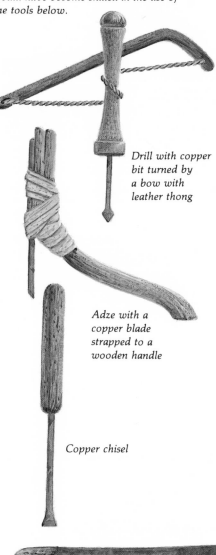

As carpenter's sons, *Jesus and James would have become skilled in the use of the tools below.*

Drill with copper bit turned by a bow with leather thong

Adze with a copper blade strapped to a wooden handle

Copper chisel

Saw

Some of the newly converted Pharisees, *still retaining their prayer shawls and phylacteries, wanted believing Gentiles to be circumcised and obey the entire Mosaic Law. James settled the dispute with his wise counsel.*

BY SETTING ASIDE PRIVILEGES, JAMES STRENGTHENED THE CHURCH AS WELL AS HIMSELF

James, the bishop of Jerusalem, had the rare privilege of growing up in the same family as his older brother, Jesus. He is listed first among the three brothers and at least two sisters of Jesus, suggesting that he was the second-born of the family (Matthew 13:55; Mark 6:3). If this was the case, he would have spent more time with Jesus during His youth than any other person. He would have eaten, slept, played, worked, and gone to school with his older brother.

A BROTHER WHO EMBARRASSED THE FAMILY

We know nothing specific of James' relationship with Jesus, however, until they were both grown men. In one incident, James was certainly among the brothers who wanted to talk to Jesus and discourage him from his strenuous ministry. They evidently thought Jesus had become so exhausted that he was losing control of his mind (cf. Mark 3:20, 21, 31). James did not understand that his own brother was the promised Messiah he had learned of in the synagogue who was now beginning His ministry among men. James and his brothers later tried to persuade Jesus to leave Galilee and go to Judea with them for the Feast of Tabernacles. After they chided Him we read, "For neither did his brethren believe in him." (John 7:5) His spectacular claims of being the Son of God must have embarrassed and puzzled James and his brothers.

DISBELIEF TURNS INTO ARDENT SUPPORT

The next we hear of James is after the crucifixion and death of Jesus. We do not know the details, but he had become a staunch believer and the leader of the infant church of Jerusalem. His conversion must have been a surprising and unexpected event to the disciples who had known his previous attitude toward Jesus.

James' chief contribution to the early church seems to have been his handling of the first church council which was held in Jerusalem. A crisis had arisen as a result of Paul's first missionary journey. The great influx of Gentile believers had led to a separation between believing Gentiles and believing Jews who still obeyed the Law of Moses. Some Jewish Christians wanted the Gentiles to be circumcised and promise to keep the Mosaic Law; others merely avoided eating and having fellowship with them. The church in Antioch felt the brunt of this controversy and referred the problem to the church in Jerusalem headed by James.

A MAN WHO LIVED BY HIS CONVICTIONS

After hearing all the arguments, the wise and respected James decided upon a compromise. He clearly favored freedom from the Mosaic Law for Gentile believers, but he urged Gentiles to avoid practices which would unnecessarily offend Jews. Because James himself had been such an example of setting aside privileges which would weaken or offend others, his decision was accepted without controversy.

EVEN UNBELIEVERS MOURNED HIS DEATH

Josephus, the contemporary historian, relates the death of James. During a transition of governors, the high priest, Ananias, charged James and others of breaking the law. As a result, he was stoned to death. Josephus reports that this unjust act was protested by pious non-Christian Jews who respected him so highly. As a result, the high priest was relieved of his office. James died a Christian martyr about A.D. 62.

WHAT WAS THE REASON FOR JAMES' UNEXPECTED CONVERSION?

While Jesus was ministering on earth, James and his brothers were not in agreement with His claims. When Christ was rejected at Nazareth, He implied that opposition was ever "among his own kin" and "in his own house." (Mark 6:4) But when James wrote his epistle, he began, "James, a servant of God and of the Lord Jesus Christ." (James 1:1) He didn't refer to himself as the Lord's brother or even as His apostle. The word used literally means slave.

The details of his conversion are not given, but it appears that his skepticism was completely removed by a special appearance of the risen Christ. "After that, he was seen by James; then of all the apostles." (I Corinthians 15:7) Like Paul after him who saw the risen Lord on his way to persecute Christians in Damascus, James' life was completely turned around. The fact that he believed that his brother was the Son of God is very significant. One of the main tenets of Christianity is that Christ was without sin in His own life in order that He might die for the sins of others (cf. John 1:29; II Corinthians 5:21). The fact that James believed this truth proves that not once during the many hours they had spent together as children, teen-agers, and young men could James recall a single incident when Jesus committed a sin.

WHY DID JAMES RISE TO LEADERSHIP SO QUICKLY AFTER HIS CONVERSION?

It is true that his human relationship to the Lord as brother would have made James an important and credible witness to the claims of Christ. But the fact that he was elected to such a significant and key position in the mother church of Jerusalem indicates the respect he held. Non-biblical writings and traditions support the New Testament picture of James as a man of impressive character and intense piety. One historian says that James was known as "the Just" and as "the bulwark of the people." His knees were said to be as hard as a camel's because he was so constant in prayer for his people. Even non-believing Jews respected him for his exemplary life.

WHAT WAS THE RESULT OF JAMES' DECISION TO SET ASIDE PRIVILEGES WHICH WOULD WEAKEN OTHERS?

With remarkable tact and equity, James announced his conclusion to the council at Jerusalem that Gentiles should not be troubled with circumcision and the Mosaic Law. He suggested certain restrictions which would enable Jewish Christians to be able to live with their Gentile brothers. The Gentiles would be expected to abstain from meat offered to idols and meat which contained large quantities of blood, a Gentile delicacy. These foods were objectionable to strict Jews and would hinder Jews and Gentiles from eating together, thus preventing an important form of fellowship. He also warned against participating in the sexual immorality so common to the Greek and Roman world. Such practices were offensive to Jews and harmful to the Gentiles (cf. I Corinthians 5:1). When James finished, his decision pleased the "apostles and elders, with the whole church." (Acts 15:22) After the news reached Antioch, the church "rejoiced for the consolation." (Acts 15:31) James had averted a disastrous split and corrected false teaching in the early church. As a result, the young church continued to grow among Gentiles and Jews alike.

Because James forbad the believing Gentiles *to participate in four things which were offensive to the believing Jews, he helped heal a major cause of division. The two groups were now able to fellowship freely, even at meals.*

JAMES
jāmz

Endurance

IS MAINTAINING COMMITMENT TO A GOAL DURING TIMES OF PRESSURE

". . . Let us lay aside every weight, and the sin which doth so easily beset us, and let us run with patience the race that is set before us."

Hebrews 12:1

LIVING LESSONS ON ENDURANCE . . .

FROM THE PAGES OF SCRIPTURE

Familiarity often breeds contempt. We may begin by placing other people on pedestals, assuming that they live above the daily struggles we experience. We may even believe that by being around them we, too, will achieve freedom from the distressing pressures of the world. This may have been the motivation of a young man who volunteered to serve the apostle Paul. Before long, though, the disciplines and distresses of Paul's circumstances caused this man to become disillusioned. His commitment was further weakened by a secret love for the pleasures of this world. To his own shame, his name has gone down in Scripture as one who gave up when pressure increased.

ILLUSTRATED IN THE WORLD OF NATURE

NORTHERN FLYING SQUIRREL *Glaucomys sabrinus*

This gentle little creature, a member of the order *Rodentia,* is easily tamed and fascinating in its unique habits. England's King James I was so intrigued by the flying squirrel that he requested one of the members of the Virginia Company's counsel to bring him one for a pet. The flying squirrel is not quite so docile in its dealings with the downy woodpecker, often confiscating the woodpecker's dwellings for its own. The transition is effected simply. The squirrel merely throws out the woodpecker's bedding and makes itself a new nest of finely shredded bark and lichen. Once it finds a satisfactory home, it may remain there for the rest of its life. The squirrel lives to a ripe old age of five years, achieving a length of 8 to 11 inches and a weight of 2 to 5 ounces.

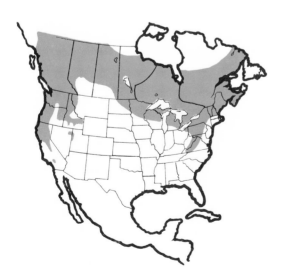

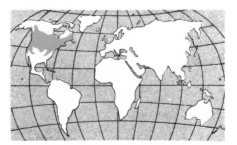

The range and habitat of the northern flying squirrel

ENDURANCE

HOW DOES THE FLYING SQUIRREL ILLUSTRATE THE NEED TO WITHSTAND PRESSURE?

With raised axe, he prepared to give a mighty swing. The boys were happy and excited about gathering firewood. For weeks they had looked forward to this time. Their father had promised them that as soon as the school year was over, he would take them camping. Now their dream was a reality.

They had neatly packed their canoe with all the food, clothing, and equipment necessary to make their camping trip a success. They portaged deep beyond the Canadian border. They had paddled their canoe most of the day and finally decided to turn into shore and set up camp.

Each of the adventurers had his own assignment. Once the tent was erected the two boys left to look for firewood. They were careful not to damage a growing tree, but selected a dead cedar to chop.

With a vigorous swing of the axe, the young camper's sharp blade sliced into the trunk. As his partner stood back to watch he noticed, to his surprise and delight, a furry little animal poke its head out of a hole in the trunk. They had not noticed the hole before, nor had they considered that the cedar could possibly be a home for anything living.

The animal was frightened and leaped from the tree. As it jumped they recognized it to be a flying squirrel. It tried to glide to a distant branch. Its jump was hasty because it didn't have sufficient time to make its pre-flight calculations. It missed its mark and hit the ground with a jolt. The animal was shaken and momentarily stunned.

One boy ran over and with a sweep of his hand, grasped the animal. Fearful that it might bite him, he held on to it tightly. Excited, he rushed over and showed his friend. Together they studied the soft, terrified little animal.

As he maintained his tight grip on the helpless creature, he suddenly felt the animal go limp. He opened his hand; the squirrel was still. He tried to coax it back to life, but the creature was lifeless. He couldn't understand what had happened.

Could the furry little squirrel have hurt itself in its jump? Might the boy have done something to hurt it when he grabbed it? Why was this little animal, so alive just minutes ago, lifeless now?

What the boy did not realize was that the flying squirrel is a very gentle, friendly creature. Even if given the opportunity, it probably will not bite. Because it is so fragile and shy, excessive pressure or fright causes the animal to become terror-stricken and paralyzed with fear.

The flying squirrel does not have the ability to withstand great pressure. Rather than make a forceful attempt to escape, the gentle creature will give up. Its paralyzing fear causes it to go into shock and die.

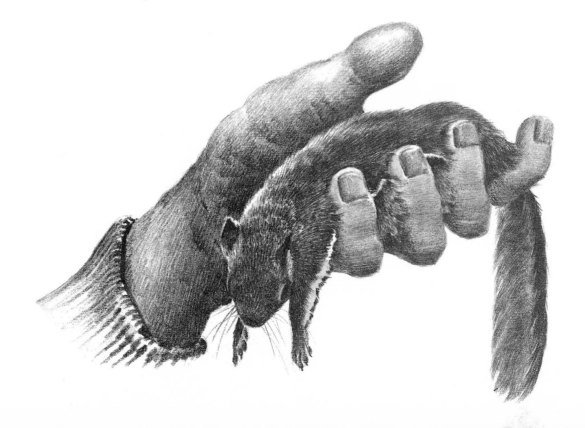

192

SCRIPTURAL REFERENCES TO THE SQUIRREL

The squirrel is a member of the rodentia class of animals and, as such, falls within the list strictly forbidden for human consumption (Leviticus 11). The flying squirrel's vulnerability to pressure and its characteristic of experiencing paralyzing fear provide important spiritual applications for us.

"If thou faint in the day of adversity, thy strength is small." Proverbs 24:10

The Christian has been called to endure many kinds of pressures. There is the pressure of a Heavenly Father's correction. "My son, despise not thou the chastening of the Lord, nor faint when thou art rebuked of him." (Hebrews 12:5)

There is also the pressure of outside temptations. The Christian is to flee from the presence of temptation and into the presence of the Lord through prayer. "Flee also youthful lusts." (II Timothy 2:22) "Men ought always to pray, and not to faint." (Luke 18:1)

Communion with the Lord through prayer is a control to the area of fear. He often calmed the fears of His saints when they were walking within His will. When God does not remove fear, it may be a signal that we are involving ourselves in pressures which He did not intend us to experience. "God has not given us a spirit of fear...." (II Timothy 1:7)

CHARACTERISTICS AND PHYSICAL FEATURES OF THE FLYING SQUIRREL

The limited endurance of the flying squirrel did not allow it to withstand the pressures of the boys' surprise and capture. As a result, the little creature died. Even though it is easily frightened, the flying squirrel can be tamed. By placing food each night near the area where one is known to live, a patient observer can lure the squirrel from its home. In a few weeks time it will become very tame, unalarmed by a person's presence. With time and patience the squirrel can even be trained to come when called.

IS THE FLYING SQUIRREL REALLY A SQUIRREL?

Yes. It is a true squirrel and belongs to the family *Sciuridae* along with the non-tree squirrels and ground squirrels of the *Rodentia* order. There are approximately thirty-seven species of flying squirrels.

The majority of flying squirrels live in the tropical forests of southeastern Asia. One species lives in temperate Eurasia and two in North America. They range in size from the pygmy flying squirrel's three inch length to the giant flying squirrel which is about the size of a cat.

The two North American species are the northern flying squirrel—*Glaucomys sabrinue*—and the southern flying squirrel—*Glaucomys volans*. The latter means "flying gray mouse," a name given to the animal by Captain John Smith.

WHAT DISTINGUISHES THE NORTHERN FLYING SQUIRREL FROM THE SOUTHERN?

At first glance it is difficult to distinguish between the northern flying squirrel and the southern. One difference is their size and shape. The northern is slightly longer—approximately 10¼ inches to the southern's 8½ inches. The southern has a more rounded head and a pert little nose.

Another difference is appearance. The underside of the northern species is a dark gray; the southern's underside fur is white to the roots. This squirrel's coat is brownish gray with a black trim along the putagium—the flap of loose skin connecting the front and back legs which permits the animal to "fly." Its eyes are rimmed with black.

The species differ in their range and habitat, too. The northern lives in the old growth of coniferous and hardwood forests covering territory from the western and extreme northeastern United States to Nova Scotia and across much of Canada to central Alaska. Its southern cousin prefers the hardwood trees such as beech and maple. It lives primarily in the eastern United States and in parts of Mexico. There is even a small population of these squirrels in Honduras.

COMPARISON OF THE TWO NORTH AMERICAN SPECIES

Southern Flying Squirrel
Smaller, with lighter underparts, darker back fur, and dark ring around the eyes

Northern Flying Squirrel
Larger, with gray underparts and head not quite as round. Putagium edge lacks distinctive black trim.

RANGE AND HABITAT OF THE TWO NORTH AMERICAN FLYING SQUIRRELS

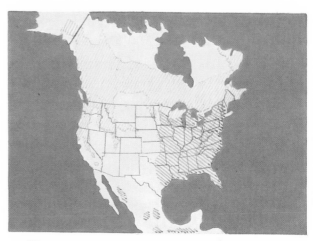

☐ *Northern Flying Squirrel*
▨ *Southern Flying Squirrel*

IS THE FLYING SQUIRREL AN ENDANGERED SPECIES?

No. The flying squirrel is as abundant as the fox squirrel and the red squirrel. It is rarely seen because it is nocturnal, active at night when it forages for food.

Rarely, if ever, will it leave its sleeping quarters during the day. It will do so only if disturbed or very curious. The loud thump which it makes when it lands on the side of a building or roof will indicate its presence. The flying squirrel remains active almost all winter long and will come out every night unless the weather is extremely cold, wet or windy.

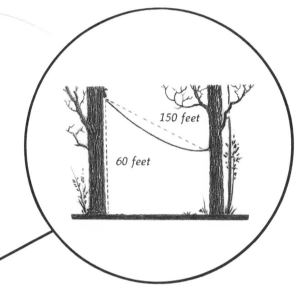

The greater the height from which it jumps, the farther it is able to go.

The large eyes of the flying squirrel enable it to gather enough light for excellent night-time vision.

Calculates distance and direction before leaping

Controls flight with flat tail and spurs

Breaks impact with an upward sweep

WHY IS THIS SQUIRREL ABLE TO FLY?

The flying squirrel does not actually fly—it glides. The little squirrel is equipped with folds of skin which stretch from its wrists to its ankles. When its arms and legs are spread out, these folds of skin act much like a sail. The air pressure from underneath forces the skin and the animal upward similar to the way a shallow parachute works.

WHAT DETERMINES HOW FAR THE SQUIRREL CAN TRAVEL IN A SINGLE JUMP?

Three factors are involved. The first is the height of the tree from which the squirrel jumps. The higher the takeoff point, naturally, the farther it will travel. Factors two and three are the angle of the glide and the slope of the ground. On a normal jump from 60 feet high, the squirrel can glide directly downward for about 20 or 30 feet. But on a more gradual, horizontal angle it is capable of a 150 foot glide. And if the ground slopes downward, the squirrel may travel as far as 300 feet.

The flying squirrel is very fastidious about grooming. It washes and combs its fur with its tongue. The squirrel likes to give particular attention to its flattened, specialized tail.

IS THE FLYING SQUIRREL ABLE TO JUDGE DISTANCES ACCURATELY?

Yes. It is able to judge distance by using a form of triangulation—finding a position by bearings from two fixed points a known distance apart. It prepares for take-off by gathering its tiny feet together. Then it bobs its head from one side to the other and up and down to fix its position, flight and goal. By this simple form of geometric triangulation it is able to land accurately on any chosen spot. When the squirrel is forced to take off hurriedly without assessing where it is going, it usually lands off course.

ONCE IT JUMPS CAN IT EVER TURN BACK?

When the squirrel is ready to jump, it leans forward, pushes with its hind legs, and spreads all four legs outward at right angles from its body. The membrane between the legs is stretched out giving the appearance of a square. It uses its tail as a balancing mechanism and as a rudder for steering. The little growth, or spur, on each wrist is also used to control flight. The squirrel can further alter its flight by varying the slack in either "wing."

Should the squirrel change its mind in mid-flight it is capable of turning completely around with these steering and control devices, landing on the same spot from which it took off.

DOES A FLYING SQUIRREL EVER HURT ITSELF WHEN IT LANDS?

If it doesn't have enough time to accurately assess where it is going, the squirrel may hurt itself on landing. Normally, the aviator can reduce the impact by flicking its tail upward just before it lands. This has a braking effect and allows the animal to position its body so that its feet land flat against the surface. The bottom of the squirrel's feet have pads which help absorb the shock of landing.

The flat tail *is normally equal in length to the head and body of the squirrel. The hairs of the tail grow out like the veins of a feather. It is never recommended to pick up this little flyer by the tail. The delicate tail is so loosely attached that with very little pressure the skin can be slipped off the bony structure just like removing a glove from a hand.*

STEERING DEVICES

Spur

Flattened tail

By altering the plane of the spur and the tail, a squirrel is able to steer its body as it glides through the air with remarkable accuracy and agility.

In order to grasp a pecan nut in its mouth, *the squirrel tries to cut a slight groove and notch in the two depressed areas on either side. It then grips the notch and groove in its teeth and carries the nut by its small end.*

Hanging upside down seems to be a favorite feeding position of the flying squirrel.

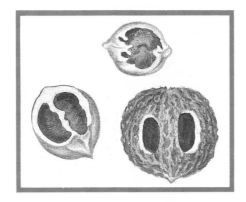

Typical gnawings made by the flying squirrel

DOES THE FLYING SQUIRREL HAVE ANY NATURAL ENEMIES?

Because the little squirrel is not a suspicious creature it makes an easy target for predators. Some enemies which take their toll are weasels, martins, bobcats, raccoons, ravens, hawks, and the most feared— owls. Squirrels have even been found in the mouth of large trout. One safety precaution which the squirrel does take is to run quickly around to the back of the tree after landing in order to avoid any predator which it might have attracted while gliding through the air. In the past, trappers used to be upset with the curious squirrel because it would often inadvertantly trap itself, preventing them from capturing a more prized animal.

WHAT DOES THE SQUIRREL EAT?

This hearty little eater lives largely on vegetation. It particularly likes the buds of pussy willows. Staple foods are nuts and seeds from the hickory, oak, pine, fir and beech trees. It also eats insects and meat when available.

Squirrels especially enjoy dripping sap which may drain from the borings of woodpeckers. When farmers tap their maple trees and hang open buckets on them, these little thieves, in an attempt to reach the sap, many times fall into the bucket and drown.

Their large energy output also requires huge quantities of water. Their daily intake is equivalent to a man drinking twenty gallons. For this reason the squirrel likes to live near a good supply of drinking water. Their gliding folds, or "wings", make it difficult for them to swim so they must be careful when near water for they can easily drown.

WHAT IS THE HARDEST NUT FOR THE FLYING SQUIRREL TO CRACK?

Pecans. These hard-shelled nuts require so much work to open that the animal has to be very hungry to even bother with them. When a squirrel tackles one, it does so in intervals, working on one for days.

One can always distinguish the gnawings of a flying squirrel because it has a special way of cutting open its nuts. A fox squirrel or chipmunk cuts the shell apart, shattering it into many pieces. The cutting of the deer mouse, too, can be distinguished from those of the flying squirrel because the deer mouse makes two openings in the shell opposite each other. With fine tooth marks along the edge, the flying squirrel makes an oval hole on one side. Once accomplished, it removes bite-size pieces using its teeth and tongue.

HOW DOES SCRIPTURE ILLUSTRATE THE NEED TO MAINTAIN A COMMITMENT EVEN DURING PRESSURE?

Who admired a great man of God so much that he was willing to follow him to prison but was unable to maintain this commitment because of a secret desire?

(Pause for a response—see page 20)

A man whose name meant "popular one" sat in a closely guarded prison. He was there by his own choice. The man who was actually imprisoned was the one he served—a mighty man of God whose rugged discipline and spiritual perception had conquered many pagan cities with the Gospel.

Their prison was actually more like a headquarters. Dedicated companions came and went. They even had their own personal physician. A steady stream of visitors also came and listened to the Gospel as it was skillfully proclaimed by this prisoner in chains.

It was exciting to be on a winning team! During those busy days important letters were written and different men among this trusted group were chosen to carry them to faithful believers in distant cities. This man whose name meant "popular one" requested that his personal greeting be added to two of the letters which were written.

As more and more men were sent away, the years wore on, and pressures increased. One day the prisoner dictated a letter to a young man in a distant city, but its message spoke to a hidden need in the life of this servant. "For we brought nothing into this world, and it is certain we can carry nothing out. And having food and raiment let us be therewith content. But they that will be rich fall into temptation and a snare, and into many foolish and hurtful lusts, which drown men in destruction and perdition."

With these words the perceptive prisoner spoke powerfully to that secret struggle raging in the heart of this servant. The days and months slowly passed. Opposition increased against the prisoner. Rather than being released as this man had hoped, the prisoner felt that he had only a short time before he would be executed. The last drops of his life were being poured out for God.

One day this servant slipped out the prison door not to return. Now only two remained—the prisoner and his personal physician. One picked up a pen and began to write. The words he wrote concerned the man who had left—the one whose name meant "popular one." "Demas hath forsaken me having loved this present world."

Thereafter his name would be associated by millions of readers with a man who gave up when the pressures increased.

From Colossians 4:14, Philemon 24, II Timothy 4:10

DEMAS' COMMITMENT WEAKENED AS PRESSURES INCREASED

When we think of Peter, we recall his impetuosity; when we think of Judas Iscariot we remember a traitor; when we think of Paul, we call to mind his boldness; when we think of Luke, we envision a loyal friend; but when we hear the name Demas, we think of a deserter.

FEW WORDS SPEAK VOLUMES

There are only three references to Demas in the New Testament, but those three speak volumes about him. The first two are found in letters to the Colossians and to Philemon. These two epistles were almost certainly written during Paul's first imprisonment in Rome. Paul was Caesar's prisoner awaiting trial. Although he was chained to a Roman soldier, he was free to receive visitors and carried on his ministry through faithful and committed co-laborers (Acts 28:16, 20, 30, 31).

A FRIEND UNWORTHY OF SPECIAL RECOGNITION

In Paul's letter to Philemon he ends, "There salute thee Epaphras, my fellow prisoner in Christ Jesus, Mark, Aristarchus, Demas, Luke, my fellow-labourers." (Philemon 23, 24) From this we gather that Demas was an accepted and beloved member of the intimate circle which helped Paul carry out his ministry in Rome. The expression my "fellow labourers" indicates that Demas was actively engaged in the service of Christ with Paul.

In the letter to Colosse, written at about the same time, Demas sent his greeting. In this passage we learn that Demas is a Gentile believer since only Aristarchus, Mark and Justus are included among those "who are of the circumcision" (Colossians 4:10-14). It is interesting that in this list of Paul's six friends, only Demas has no special word of commendation attached to his name. Aristarchus, Mark, and Justus were a comfort to Paul; Epaphras was a servant of Christ who always labored fervently; Luke was called the beloved physician. But Demas' name stands alone.

WHEN PRESSURE INCREASED, HIS FRIENDSHIP CEASED

Paul was confined at Rome for two full years—the maximum time a prisoner might be held after appealing to Caesar should no charges be pressed. Since Luke's account in Acts ends at this point, we cannot be positive of what happened after Paul's first imprisonment. The evidence points to the fact that Paul was released as he expected (Philippians 2:24; Philemon 22).

For three years we are not informed of Paul's ministry, but somehow he returned to Rome and was imprisoned again. The atmosphere of Paul's second epistle to Timothy is much different from that of his previous letters. This time Paul is in prison expecting execution rather than freedom (II Timothy 2:9; 4:6, 7). It is here that we have our final glimpse of Demas. Paul requested Timothy to come to him, explaining the reason for the request, "For Demas hath forsaken me, having loved this present world, and is departed unto Thessalonica; Crescens to Galatia, Titus unto Dalmatia. Only Luke is with me." (II Timothy 4:10, 11)

A LASTING REMEMBRANCE OF AN UNFAITHFUL FRIEND

The known story of Demas closes with this dismal blemish on his name. We do not know if he later overcame his weakness for the things of this world. Tradition states that Demas completely abandoned his faith and became apostate. This is uncertain, but what is certain is that Demas forsook the apostle Paul in what was probably his greatest hour of need. How striking is the contrast between Demas and Luke who alone remained at Paul's side in those dark, final hours. Demas is doomed to be remembered as a deserter until the memory of sin shall be no more.

Paul may have stayed in an apartment building of this type *while awaiting trial the first time in Rome. Paul was only under house arrest then.*

Sculpture of the emperor, Nero, *who made the Christians in Rome his scapegoats*

According to tradition, *Paul was imprisoned in Rome's Mamertine Prison prior to his execution. The lightless cell was twelve feet underground, originally designed to be reached only through a hole in the ceiling.*

DEMAS CHARACTER SKETCH

WHAT PRESSURE CAUSED DEMAS TO FORSAKE HIS COMMITMENT TO PAUL?

The situation surrounding Paul in Rome was grave. In July of A.D. 64, a fire had broken out in a slum area and destroyed half the city. A rumor was circulated that the emperor Nero had set the fire to free space for his own building plans. His scapegoat became the Christians of Rome, and an active persecution of believers followed. In this hostile climate, many of Paul's associates were forsaking him (cf. II Timothy 1:15; 4:16). Paul was a prisoner and could not leave. But Demas was not chained to Rome and decided to leave before he was arrested and condemned as well. Concerned for his own safety and lacking the courage of Luke, Demas decided to leave Paul and Rome for the safer climate of Thessalonica. His concern for safety and security in this present world caused him to lose sight of the future kingdom which Paul so eagerly awaited (cf. II Timothy 4:6-8).

WHAT DID PAUL MEAN BY SAYING THAT DEMAS LOVED THIS PRESENT WORLD?

When Paul referred to being in love with this world, he referred to the world system with its opportunities for pleasure, profit, and fame. To Demas, life was too precious, too full of delightful possibilities to be thrown to Nero's lions for the amusement of thousands of bloodthirsty spectators. He remembered all of the friends and ambitions he had left behind when he became a Christian. The excitement of missionary work with Paul had then offered even more opportunities for him, but now the glamour had completely faded. And so he "departed to Thessalonica," (II Timothy 4:10) probably the place where he had been born and raised. Demas was like the seeds in the Lord's parable "which fell among thorns," and "when they have heard, go forth, and are choked with cares and riches and pleasures of this life, and bring no fruit to perfection." (Luke 8:14) Demas had not heeded Paul's advice to set his "affection on things above, not on things on the earth" (Colossians 3:2) and had slowly become more and more "conformed to this world" (Romans 12:2). As a result, he was unwilling to maintain his commitment to Paul and the Lord during a time of intense pressure and persecution.

WHAT WERE THE CONSEQUENCES OF DEMAS' LACK OF COMMITMENT?

Demas was a member of the body of Christ. Scripture says, "And whether one member suffer, all the members suffer with it." (I Corinthians 12:26) Demas' desertion caused the body of Christ to suffer. Not only did he greatly disappoint Paul, but he failed the faithful Christians of Rome. Paul was constantly exhorting the believers to be brave in persecution and pointed to himself as an example (II Timothy 1:8; 2:3; Philippians 3:17). The young believers looked to Paul and the courageous commitment of his close associates to help them through those difficult days of trial. To witness one of Paul's inner circle leaving Rome in fear would have been a blow to the entire church and may have caused other weaker members to stumble. Demas also caused Timothy's work outside of Rome to be interrupted. Because he left Paul alone except for Luke, a replacement had to be called in. Timothy had to leave his work and face possible persecution. Finally, Demas forfeited the great privilege of being able to say at the end of his days the words of Paul, "I have fought a good fight, I have finished my course, I have kept the faith; henceforth there is laid up for me a crown of righteousness, which the Lord, the righteous judge, shall give me at that day; and not to me only, but unto all them also that love his appearing." (II Timothy 4:7,8)

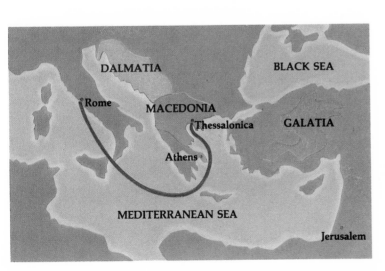

"Do thy diligence to come shortly unto me; *for Demas hath forsaken me, having loved this present world, and is departed unto Thessalonica; Crescens to Galacia, Titus unto Dalmacia. Only Luke is with me.*"

DEMAS
dē'mȧs

Endurance

IS UNITING WITH THOSE OF LIKE MIND TO WITHSTAND DESTRUCTIVE INFLUENCES

". . . Follow righteousness, faith, charity, peace, with them that call on the Lord out of a pure heart."
II Timothy 2:22

"Two are better than one . . . and a threefold cord is not quickly broken."

Ecclesiastes 4:9a, 12b

LIVING LESSONS ON ENDURANCE . . .

FROM THE PAGES OF SCRIPTURE

Scripture states that two are better than one and a three-fold cord is not easily broken (Ecclesiastes 4:9,12). It may be easy for one person to become discouraged and give up, but it is not so easy for two or three to surrender a purpose to which they are committed. The survival of a family depends upon the ability of its members to unite quickly with harmony of conviction when anything threatens to diminish their purpose or potential. One time a treacherous plan was designed by a proud, godless ruler to destroy every family that put God's laws above his laws. The plan would have succeeded had it not been for the effectiveness of a counterproposal which allowed families of like-mind to unite together.

ILLUSTRATED IN THE WORLD OF NATURE

AMERICAN COOT   *Fulica americana*

The coot's antics, constant calling, and general behavior often earn it the title "clown of the pond." Other names attached to the coot are "mud hen" and "rice hen." It's an interesting bird which, except during breeding season, is very sociable, mixes well, and enjoys the company of other waterfowl. As a rule, it spends most of its time in the water. It even sleeps in the water. The coot prefers a habitat of marshes or the reed-grown shores of ponds, lakes, rivers, creeks, saltwater estuaries, and bays. It achieves an average wingspan of 28 inches and attains a weight of 22 ounces. The bird's lifespan is between seven and eight years.

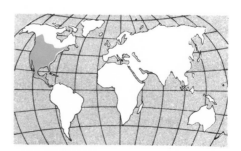

The range and habitat of the American coot

ENDURANCE

HOW DOES THE COOT ILLUSTRATE ENDURANCE BY UNITING TOGETHER?

A clamoring chorus of high, cackling notes could be heard for half a mile. The alarm alerted the birds in the water and everything else within hearing range. These wary birds were alert to possible danger and quick to notify the rest of the flock.

It was mid-August. Their breeding season was over, and the coots had begun to regroup after being separated in various individual territories to raise their young. By this time the fledglings were mature enough to join the flock with their parents. The coot is a sociable and tolerant bird which enjoys the company of its own kind and mingles well with ducks and other waterfowl.

The loud, clamoring noise made by these raucous birds was precipitated by a large goshawk which flew overhead. When a hungry hawk such as this is on the prowl, there is only one thing the coot can do to protect itself.

There are other alternatives which might seem more feasible but each of these end in destruction. For example, the coot could take to wing and try to escape by flying away, but the hawk could quickly and without much difficulty snatch it in mid-air.

The coot could also dive under the water to elude its predator. But this, too, is a futile tactic for the hawk would watch the coot's underwater course. When the bird surfaced for air, the hawk would drive it beneath the water again. It will continue to do so until the coot is exhausted. Finally it will be forced to surface, and when it does, the hawk will pluck it from the water.

The most effective defense against the hawk, the one which will afford the greatest protection for the coot, is the one that seems least likely to succeed. When the danger alarm is given, the coots immediately swim together to form a solid mass in the middle of the water.

As the hawk circles above, it begins to work its strategy of intimidation and fear on the congregated birds. It fixes its wings and dives toward the group making sweep after sweep in an effort to dislodge and single out one of the members of the flock. If it is successful in doing this, it will have no difficulty capturing that bird. But the wily coot seems to know this and rather than flee, the flock unites together to withstand the destructive attack.

It is very difficult to coax one of these birds away from the flock. As long as they remain together, huddled in this tight mass, they will thwart the enemy. For the hawk appears to have a fear that if it attacked the group, the whole flock would respond in a united counter-attack against it. As long as the birds stay together they are safe, and the hawk will be forced to move on and look for a more accessible meal.

SCRIPTURAL REFERENCES TO THE COOT

The coot, not directly identified in Scripture, has the unique characteristic of banding together for protection. This is an important concept which we are encouraged to practice.

"Two are better than one...and if one prevail against him, two shall withstand him; and a threefold cord is not quickly broken."
Ecclesiastes 4:9, 12

"In the multitude of counsellors there is safety."
Proverbs 11:14

Like many other birds, the coot is equipped to protect itself from most of its natural enemies—except man. It is for this reason that God gives instruction in Scripture to spare the female so that she can maintain the balance in nature.

"If a bird's nest chance to be before thee in the way in any tree, or on the ground, whether they be young ones, or eggs, and the dam sitting upon the young, or upon the eggs, thou shalt not take the dam with the young; but thou shalt in any wise let the dam go, and take the young to thee, that it may be well with thee, and that thou mayest prolong thy days."
Deuteronomy 22:6, 7

CHARACTERISTICS AND PHYSICAL FEATURES OF THE AMERICAN COOT

The ability of the coots to unite together is their most effective defense against the destructive force of a hawk's attack. This ability to endure is evidenced in other areas as well. The coot is an efficient feeder. It adjusts well to winter conditions and in addition to this, is a very successful breeder. The coots have survived well, and their population is on the increase today.

WHAT DISTINGUISHES THE COOT FROM OTHER NORTH AMERICAN BIRDS?

The coot is the only slate-colored bird in the United States with a white bill and a frontal shield. Other characteristics, although not entirely unique to this bird, are unusual. The eyes of the coot are bright red. Another distinction is its lobed toes—designed to enable the bird to walk without sinking on floating vegetation or the soft mud of marshes and shorelines.

The coot's lobed toes enable the bird to walk easily without sinking on soft mud and floating vegetation.

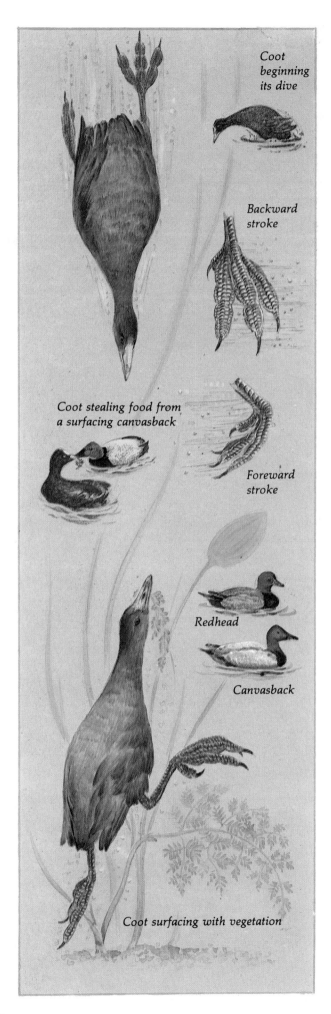

Coot
beginning
its dive

Backward
stroke

Coot stealing food from
a surfacing canvasback

Foreward
stroke

Redhead

Canvasback

Coot surfacing with vegetation

WHAT DO THE COOT'S LEGS TELL YOU ABOUT THE BIRD?

Their length—the bird's sex; their color—its age. The leg length distinguishes the male from the female. The metatarsus is the unfeathered portion of the leg which extends to the toe, excluding the claw. On a female this distance measures five inches or 127 mm or less. If the metatarsus is longer than five inches, the bird is probably a male.

The leg color indicates the age of the bird. An immature bird has blue or grayish-green legs. A two-year old's legs are yellow-green. The following year they turn a clear yellow. An older coot's legs are reddish-orange in appearance.

HOW DOES A COOT SECURE ITS FOOD?

Coots employ a variety of methods to secure their food. They look for it on land along the reeds and grasses of shorelines. They may dive to the bottom of a lake or river, bringing up material and then examining it to determine whether or not anything edible is to be found.

The coot is not known to be a deep diver nor does it stay beneath the surface for long periods of time. In order to dive, the coot must enter head first. It propels itself with its lobed feet by spreading its toes wide and making a backward stroke. On the forward stroke the toes come together and reduce resisting friction. After each dive the coot pauses and rests for a moment before resuming its search.

WHAT DOES THE COOT EAT?

The coot's diet consists largely of vegetation. Much of this food is secured by repeatedly diving to the bottom. The bird's migration route and winter range are limited to areas which contain plenty of submerged vegetation. During the summer months, the coot supplements its diet with insects and aquatic animal life.

The duck hunter has little patience with the coot for it competes with ducks and depletes their natural food. Coots occasionally kill and eat small ducklings.

ARE THE COOT AND THE CANVASBACK DUCK THE BEST OF FRIENDS?

The canvasback, as well as the redhead duck, are two species that have little appreciation for the clever antics of the coot. When these two ducks dive to the bottom of the lake for vegetation, the coot may wait close by for them to surface, grab the material out of their bill, and make off with the contents.

The coot has its own problem with thieves, though. Two ducks, the gadwall and the widgeon, employ the same stealing techniques against the coot.

IS THE COOT CAPABLE OF DEFENDING ITSELF?

Yes. The coot has weapons and its own repertoire of strategies. Its weapons are a sharp bill, long, strong legs and sharp claws. When cornered on land, it rears on its back, thrusts out its legs and violently scratches to ward off the attacker. It also plunges its sharp, pointed bill toward its enemy. When in the water, the bird uses its legs in a noisy, splashing manner to churn and kick water into the air. With this tactic, the coot disorients and frightens away its would-be attacker.

WHY IS THE COOT CALLED "BLUE PETER"?

Like Jesus' disciple Peter, the slate blue coot is able to "walk" on water. It actually runs across the surface of the water for several yards, flapping its wings until it is airborne. The bird has difficulty getting into the air and this running leap helps. Once in the air it draws its hanging legs up below the tail. The bird can maintain a steady wing beat and continue this pace for considerable distances.

The coot's wings do not begin to grow until it is six weeks old, and it cannot fly until it is 60 days old. When the coot flies it normally hovers five or six feet above the surface of the water. During its migration the birds fly at a considerably higher altitude.

The coot can be identified in flight by the white tail and white trailing edge of its secondary wing feathers contrasted against dark gray body feathers.

IS THE COOT A TERRITORIAL BIRD?

Yes, the coot is territorial, particularly during its mating season. The bird's life and social activities revolve around boundaries. The male coot's ability to attain a mate depends upon acquiring and holding its territory. By patrolling the borders it keeps a constant vigil to make sure no rival enters and will aggressively attack any trespasser.

When two birds engage in combat they charge each other with necks extended low to the water. They jab and rake one another with sharp bills and claws. Finally, one admits defeat and leaves the area. Occasionally the battle may be so intense that one bird is killed.

Once the male has successfully defended its territory, the female chooses whether or not she will join him. If she does, their union will probably be a lifelong partnership.

Spraying water in the air to ward off enemy

Using legs to claw victim

Coots "run" on the water for long distances before they are airborne.

Silhouette of coot in flight

The coot doesn't like to fly and uses this form of escape only as a last resort.

Floating nest anchored to reeds *is similar to the nest of the pied-billed grebe.*

Parent coot feeding young

Young coot

WHAT KIND OF NEST DOES THE COOT MAKE?

Coots build a nest of reeds, rushes and other plant material. Both parents take part in constructing the nest and take great care to make sure the material they use is dry. They are very diligent in its construction, returning with building supplies as often as fourteen times in ten minutes. The lining of the nest is made of fine plant material. They do not use down, as many other birds do.

When completed, the nest is a large structure from twelve to eighteen inches in diameter mounded seven to eight inches above the water level. The nest is situated near the water's edge, well-hidden from sight. Its close proximity to the water makes it easier for the tiny coots to return to it for rest as they learn to swim.

The nest is fastened securely to the tall reeds and marsh plants of the area to keep it from drifting. If a storm should cause the nest to be torn away from its anchoring, it is still capable of floating. In fact, there have been cases reported of the coot continuing to incubate its eggs even though its nest was adrift.

BROODING THE YOUNG—A COOPERATIVE EFFORT

Once the nest is constructed, the female begins to lay the eggs—eight to twelve in number. She does not wait for the entire clutch to be laid but rather begins incubation as each is laid. As a result, the young hatch at different times.

The male stands by ready to guard the nest and drive off any intruder which approaches. It is very aggressive in this protection—so much so that the coot's nests are far more successful than those of nesting ducks in the same marsh.

After 21 to 22 days of incubation, the eggs begin to hatch. On the chick's first day, it remains in the nest to be brooded by the mother while the father brings food. Soon one of the parents leads it into the water and begins to teach and feed it while the other parent remains at the nest. The coot chick will learn to swim during its very first day in the water.

After a week or two all the young have hatched, and the family is united. They grow quickly—their feet faster than the rest of the body. Very soon the young coots are able to care for themselves.

HOW DOES SCRIPTURE ILLUSTRATE ENDURANCE IN UNITING WITH THOSE OF LIKE MIND?

A wise government will not design programs for "the good of the community" but rather for the good of the family. Who in Scripture thwarted an attempt to sacrifice godly families for the supposed benefit of the government and the economic welfare of the community?

(Pause for a response—see page 20)

An ambitious official of one of history's greatest empires stared scornfully at a man who refused to bow down to him. The official learned that this man was committed to following God's laws rather than the laws of government when the two conflicted. He also learned that the law of the empire gave this man and his people the right to do just that.

The official realized that as long as these families remained in the empire, he would not have the worship and power he desired. He carefully composed a government program and presented it to the ruler. The king was told that certain families who were a threat to his kingdom could be eliminated if this measure was signed into law. The king was assured that the program would be politically sound and economically beneficial. He agreed to authorize it.

The new law was translated into all the languages of that great empire and carried by swift messengers to all parts of the kingdom. Those who were marked for destruction looked at each other in disbelief, then cried out to God in prayer and fasting.

The man who had refused to bow to that official rent his clothes and humbled himself in sackcloth and ashes before God. Then he sent a message to his cousin, the beautiful queen, whom the king favored. That message informed her of what was to happen and urged her to appeal to the king. The king had no idea that she was a member of one of those families that he had marked for destruction. This was a time of crisis, she was told, and "who knows whether you are come to the kingdom for such a time as this."

The queen fasted and prayed for three days and then prepared a wise and gracious appeal to the king. He was shocked to learn the implications of the law he had signed and the wicked motives of the one who designed it. He ordered that that ambitious officer be killed, but he was unable to change the decree which had been made. The people would be destroyed and their possessions stolen. The king gave Queen Esther the authority to do what she could to save her people, but she had to move swiftly.

A new law was quickly written and translated into the languages of all one hundred twenty-seven provinces. Then it was hastily delivered by horses, mules, camels, and young dromedaries. Families that were marked for death listened eagerly to the proclamation. Their weeping turned to hope. They now had a chance to survive. The king was allowing them to gather their families and unite against their enemies. They were given the authority to defend themselves against all who would assault them.

As the day of their planned destruction approached, families united together throughout the empire. God gave them favor among all the people, and they were greatly helped. Those who had purposed to kill them were destroyed. Millions of families celebrate the memory of this event each year in a feast called Purim. It is a tribute to brave Queen Esther and to the power of families uniting to withstand destructive influences.

From Esther 3-9

QUEEN ESTHER HELPED HER PEOPLE WITHSTAND DESTRUCTION THROUGH UNITY

Scripture introduces us to Esther as the ward of her cousin, Mordecai, "for she had neither father nor mother, and the maid was fair and beautiful, whom Mordecai, when her father and mother were dead, took for his own daughter." (Esther 2:7) Esther lived with Mordecai in the summer palace of the Persian empire. The story of Esther begins soon after the demotion of Queen Vashti. Vashti was deposed after refusing to display her acclaimed beauty before a crowd of drunken diplomats attending a state function.

A QUEEN CHOSEN FOR HER BEAUTY—NOT HER HERITAGE

The sudden lack of a queen occasioned an intense search for a new one. Beautiful young girls from the 127 provinces under Persian control were brought to Shushan. Esther, who lived in the city of Shushan itself and whose exceptional beauty was certainly known, was unable to avoid being included in the contest. Esther was brought to the king's house to begin a twelve month period of preparation for her meeting with Ahasuerus. Just as "God had brought Daniel into favor and tender love with the prince of the eunuchs" (Daniel 1:9), so He brought Esther into favor with the keeper of the women. "And the maiden pleased him, and she obtained kindness from him. . . and he preferred her and her maids unto the best place of the house of the women." (Esther 2:9)

When it was Esther's turn to meet the king, the result was "the king loved Esther above all the women, and she obtained grace and favor in his sight more than all the virgins, so that he set the royal crown upon her head, and made her queen instead of Vashti." (Esther 2:17)

AN EVIL SCHEME THREATENS THE NATION

Three years and three months later, Esther discovered why the Lord had made her the queen. Her cousin, Mordecai, refused to pay homage to Haman, the king's second-in-command. Haman was unable to punish him legally for this lack of worship (cf. Esther 3:2, 6). He was so enraged with Mordecai and his privileged people that he fabricated an evil charge against the Jews and talked the king into destroying the entire Jewish population of the Persian empire (Esther 3:8, 9). Ahasuerus unknowingly signed a decree which doomed the Jews to annihilation. The day of the slaughter was set for "the thirteenth day of the twelfth month, which is the month Adar." (Esther 2:13)

THE DINNER WHICH EXPOSED A PLOT

Mordecai requested that Esther appeal to her husband, the cruel and capricious King Ahasuerus. Esther agreed under the condition that all the Jews in Shushan remember her before the Lord and courageously replied, "If I perish, I perish." (Esther 4:16) Unannounced, Esther boldly appeared in the throne room of Ahasuerus whom she had not seen for thirty days. The Lord caused the king to respond to Esther with favor. Concerning her request he said, "Even to the half of the kingdom it shall be performed." (Esther 5:6)

Strangely, Esther passed by this seemingly ideal opportunity to plead for the life of her people. She merely invited the king and Haman to a banquet the following day. It was on the second day of feasting that Esther announced to the king that she was a Jewess and accused Haman of plotting the murder of her and her people. The outraged king had Haman executed that very day on the same gallows Haman had prepared for Mordecai.

A QUEEN'S FAITHFULNESS IS REMEMBERED

But the Jews were not as yet out of danger. The king did not have power to change the destructive decree, even though he himself had signed it into effect. Ahasuerus gave Esther permission to write any other legislation she desired; he agreed to approve it. Mordecai thought of the perfect solution—merely permit the Jews to gather together and defend themselves. The letters were signed and distributed. On the appointed day, the Jews defended themselves and destroyed their enemies.

Mordecai replaced Haman in the position of first assistant to the king. Largely because of his influence, the Jewish people gained respect throughout the empire. Because of her willingness to identify with her people, Esther has become one of the true heroines of Israeli history. Her great character is remembered annually to this day by Jewish families during the feast of Purim.

This relief of an archer-spearman *from the Persian royal guard was found at Shushan where Esther reigned as queen.*

A supporting column *from Ahasuerus' palace at Shushan*

ESTHER CHARACTER SKETCH

WHY DIDN'T ESTHER SEIZE THE FIRST OPPORTUNITY TO MAKE HER REQUEST?

When Esther went to appeal to her husband, she knew that if Ahasuerus did not raise his sceptre, she would be put to death according to Persian law. She also knew that "the king's heart is in the hand of the Lord, like the rivers of water; he turneth it whithersoever he will." (Proverbs 21:1) This was why she requested that Mordecai and all the Jews in Shushan fast for three days before she even dared approach her capricious and unpredictable husband. When "she obtained favor in his sight," he said unto her, "What wilt thou, Queen Esther? And what is thy request? It shall be even given thee to the half of the kingdom." (Esther 5:2,3) Why didn't Esther reveal her Jewish identity and plead for the cause of her people then? Esther, sensitive to the promptings of God's Spirit, knew that this was not the best time. That very night the king would have insomnia and be reminded of the time that Mordecai had saved his life. The next day Haman, having prepared a gallows for Mordecai's execution, would be commanded by the king to honor him instead. The Lord was still turning the heart of Ahasuerus, and Esther was sensitive and patient to wait for an even more ideal opportunity two days later.

WHAT WAS THE SECRET OF ESTHER'S ENDURING FAITH?

Esther was born a Jew without a nation. The land of her fathers had been taken captive and her people sold into slavery. As a young girl she was orphaned. Even her rare beauty seemed to work against her, for one day she was seized from her loving cousin to become the possession of the cruel king, Ahasuerus. Torn from the only family she had, she could have cried out in bitterness and cursed her lot. But Esther had been taught by her righteous cousin that there is a God who controls the universe and orders our lives. She had been instructed in the great promises given to the Jewish nation through Abraham, Isaac, Jacob, David, and Daniel (Genesis 28:13,14; II Samuel 7:12,13; Daniel 9:24-27). She knew that God was not finished with Israel, and she identified with her nation in its hour of crisis (Esther 7:4). Like Moses, she chose "rather to suffer affliction with the people of God than to enjoy the pleasures of sin for a season." (Hebrews 11:25)

HOW DID ESTHER'S EXAMPLE HELP HER PEOPLE WITHSTAND DESTRUCTION?

Even though the king was inclined to spare the Jews, he was limited by Persian law. The permission he had granted the enemies of the Jews to rise up and kill them on the thirteenth day of the month Adar could not be revoked. The only solution was for the Jews to be allowed to gather together in various cities throughout the 127 provinces. Since many were probably still in slavery, they needed permission to leave their assigned tasks (cf. Esther 2:6). Others, like Esther, were able to conceal their Jewish identity and might have been able to escape harm (cf. Esther 2:10). It was those Jews who needed to identify themselves with their brothers in order to make the solution work. If they refused to unite to help defend their people, the known Jews would be slaughtered without defense. But Esther provided the example. She dramatically risked her life by revealing her identity. As a result, the Jews rallied together on the appointed day and were able to defeat their enemies.

HEBREW CALENDAR

No.	Name	Modern Equivalent
1	Nisan	March - April
2	Iyyar	April - May
3	Sivan	May - June
4	Tammuz	June - July
5	Ab	July - August
6	Elul	August - September
7	Tishri	September - October
8	Heshvan	October - November
9	Kislev	November - December
10	Tebeth	December - January
11	Shebat	January - February
12	Adar	February - March

"**Now in the twelfth month,** that is, the month Adar, on the thirteenth day of the same...the Jews gathered themselves together in their cities throughout all the provinces of the king, Ahasuerus, to lay hand on such as sought their hurt. And no man could withstand them."

ESTHER
ĕs'tĕr

Endurance

IS KNOWING HOW AND WHEN TO USE THE RESOURCES AVAILABLE TO ME

"Trust in the Lord with all thine heart; and lean not unto thine own understanding. In all thy ways acknowledge him, and he shall direct thy paths. Be not wise in thine own eyes: fear the Lord, and depart from evil. It shall be health to thy navel, and marrow to thy bones."

Proverbs 3:5-8

LIVING LESSONS ON ENDURANCE . . .

FROM THE PAGES OF SCRIPTURE

If we think we are suffering for our faith, we must be very sure that we are not really suffering because of our own failures. All too often we violate God's principles, fail to display the fruit of Christ-like character, and in so doing attract reaction. God promises that when our ways please Him, He will make this kind of enemy to be at peace with us (Proverbs 16:7). But there are also enemies of God who may oppose us the more they see godliness in us (II Timothy 3:12). A certain king who sought the Lord won a great victory over God's enemies, but then his desire for the Lord decreased. The experiences he had in further battles warn us of the importance of discerning whose battles we are really fighting—God's or ours.

ILLUSTRATED IN THE WORLD OF NATURE

MOSQUITO *Family Culicidae*

There are over two thousand species of mosquitoes in the world today. Each one of these species has its own breeding and flight habits, food, and climate. They are found almost everywhere—from the Arctic to the Antarctic, in the plain and in the forest. Mosquitoes breed in water, and individual species have their own preference—freshwater, saltwater, clear water, polluted water, large bodies of ocean water, or puddles in treeholes. Mosquitoes do not usually travel very far from their birthplace; the average distance is one thousand feet. A few though, may fly as far as fifty or seventy-five miles. Man has helped increase the range of the mosquito. In 1828 a sailing vessel introduced the mosquito to the Hawaiian Islands for the first time—the result of a stagnant pool in the hull of the ship. It appears that few civilizations in the world are free from the irritation of this little insect.

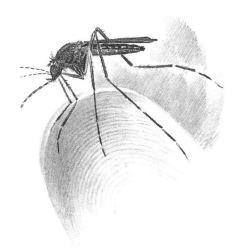

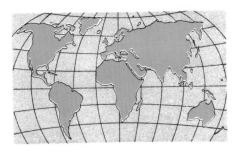

The range and habitat of the mosquito

ENDURANCE

HOW DOES THE MOSQUITO ILLUSTRATE ENDURANCE BY KNOWING HOW AND WHEN TO USE ITS RESOURCES?

The irritation was so annoying that it was hard for him to concentrate on anything else. The more he scratched, the worse it became. He had rubbed so much that now the area was an open sore. He was a strong, burly man toughened by constant exposure to harsh weather and the rigorous life of a lumberjack. His skin was like leather. It was a wonder that anything could have penetrated it. But something had, and the large, itching welt on his arm was an exasperating reminder of a tiny insect.

It was early June, and the mosquitoes were just hatching. Within a few weeks a profusion of these little creatures would fill the woods, giving no rest to the occupants. This was the lumberjack's first bite of the season. Each year he noticed that the first was always the worst. It would take a while for his body to build up an immunity to the irritating stings, but by the end of the season the bites would have very little effect and he would be able to overlook and ignore these pesky, little things.

The mosquito is a remarkable creature. It actually has no teeth, so it is not accurate to say that it bites. It would be more correct to say that it pierces the skin with its long, slender beak. During its seventeen to thirty-day lifespan, the female engages in a "biting" spree every two or three days.

How is it possible for this tiny insect to penetrate tough skin? The secret lies in its proboscis. It is difficult to fully appreciate this insect without the use of a magnifying glass or microscope. When studying the insect under a microscope, one is astonished to see the intricate and complex way in which the mosquito is constructed. What appears to the naked eye as a simple piercing instrument is actually a sheath-like case formed by the mosquito's lower lip. Like a surgeon's black bag, it contains a set of specialized tools neatly arranged and ready for the mosquito's use.

These minute instruments include a pair of lances, two saws—each with a different cutting edge, one fine and one coarse—and two syringes. One syringe is for the purpose of injecting saliva; the other draws out the victim's blood. On either side of the mosquito's head is another set of instruments—long feelers which the mosquito skillfully uses to perform its operations. To overcome a difficult object such as the lumberjack's tough skin, the mosquito explores the surface with these long feelers attached to the sides of its head. The feelers assist it in finding the softest spot to attack.

Once the spot has been found the mosquito skillfully goes to work using the tip of its beak as a guide. It forces the cover back around the tools and begins operating, first penetrating the skin with sharp lances and saws. The mosquito uses whichever tool is necessary to make a cut through the surface of the skin. It then inserts the syringes into the cut and injects saliva with an anticoagulant quality. This allows the blood to be freely siphoned up through the other syringe.

Its array of precision tools, the skill with which it uses them and great persistence in obtaining the blood necessary for its offspring, enables the mosquito not only to endure but abound in vast quantities.

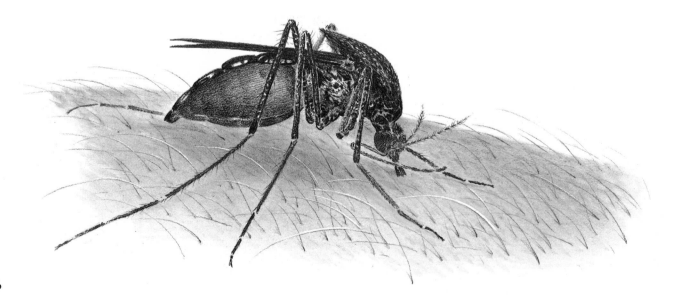

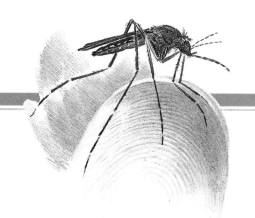

SCRIPTURAL REFERENCES TO THE MOSQUITO

"Behold, I will send swarms of flies upon thee . . . and thy people, and into thy houses . . . shall be full of swarms of flies, and also the ground whereon they are."
Exodus 8:21

The mosquito may have been found in the swarms of flies which God sent against the land of Egypt as a rebuke to Pharaoh. The Hebrew word for "fly" can be translated "mosquito, gnat, midge, or fly." The persistent nuisance and irritation of the mosquito would have increased the destructiveness of God's judgment, especially since the insect transmits serious diseases such as malaria, yellow fever, and worms to both people and animals.

The attack of a mosquito has several parallels to Satan's attack upon a Christian. At first sight the insect appears to be quite harmless, more a nuisance than a danger. If not resisted immediately, it finds an unprotected area in which to do its work. It first deadens the victim's feelings in that area by injecting a fluid. Then it reaches into the very life stream of the victim. "The life of the flesh is in the blood...." (Leviticus 17:11) After it takes what it wants, it leaves behind two reminders—one is an immediate irritation, and the other is a delayed reaction which may manifest itself much later.

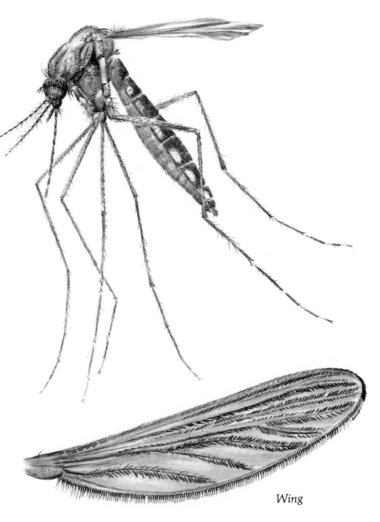

The double membrane of a mosquito's wing is reinforced and strengthened by veins. The hairs on the wings are sensitive to temperature, humidity, and air currents.

CHARACTERISTICS AND PHYSICAL FEATURES OF THE MOSQUITO

The endurance of the mosquito and knowing when and how to use its tools enabled the insect to overcome the leathery obstacle of the lumberjack's skin. Although the mosquito's quest is little more than an annoyance to us, its bloody business is a matter of life or death for the insect. It is vital for the female to obtain either human or animal blood because this liquid contains an essential vitamin which acts as a stimulus for egg production as well as a nourishment for developing eggs. If the vitamin is unavailable, the strain of the species will weaken and eventually die. The male and female mosquito must mate before the eggs become fertile. The female stores the reproductive cells from mating in a special receptacle or sac within her body. At a future date she is able to draw upon these receptacles and fertilize the eggs herself.

Wing

WHAT IS THE LIFE EXPECTANCY OF A MOSQUITO?

The mosquito's lifespan varies. The male lives only eight or nine days. Soon after birth it scouts the area for a female. Once mating is accomplished, its purpose for living is over, and the male dies shortly thereafter.

The female lives approximately thirty days. If unable to deposit her eggs before winter, she may enter hibernation for three to five months. When weather conditions are more favorable, she completes her task and then dies.

HOW DOES THE MOSQUITO MAKE THAT SINGING SOUND?

The humming noise is produced by the vibration of wings. As the female flies, her beating wings produce a whining noise. The pitch of this hum varies within species from C to E flat.

The antennae of the male are very sensitive to these vibrations. A male, equipped with "whirls" of long hair at the base of which are sensory cells, can perceive the sound from a distance of approximately ten inches. The intensity of the female's humming moves the individual whirls of hair and the male's antennae, stimulating the sense organ. The male's wings also give off a vibrating hum but this pitch is considerably lower—almost inaudible to the human ear.

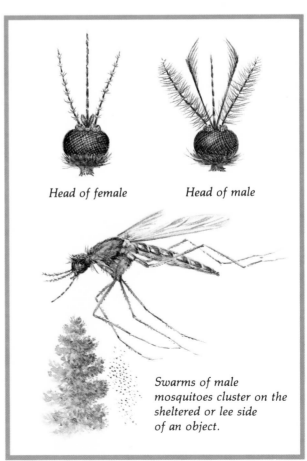

Head of female   *Head of male*

Swarms of male mosquitoes cluster on the sheltered or lee side of an object.

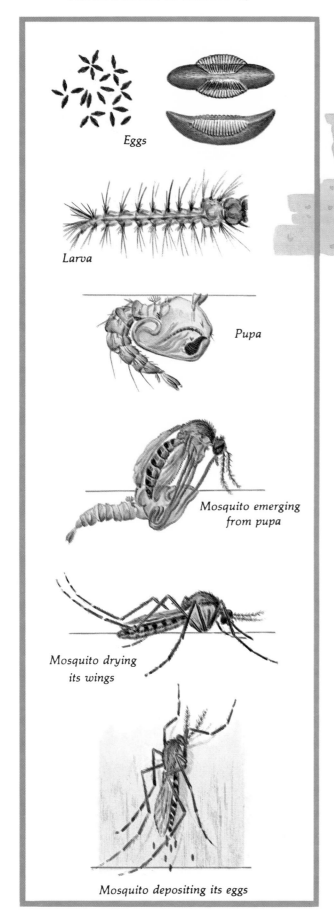

Eggs

Larva

Pupa

Mosquito emerging from pupa

Mosquito drying its wings

Mosquito depositing its eggs

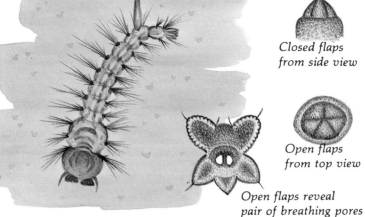

Wriggler breathing surface air

Closed flaps from side view

Open flaps from top view

Open flaps reveal pair of breathing pores

STAGES OF DEVELOPMENT IN THE MOSQUITO'S LIFE

The mosquito's life is divided into four stages: egg, larva, pupa, and adult. The insect usually completes the life cycle from egg to adult in ten days.

EGG STAGE: The female lays the eggs, which may number up to one hundred, on the surface of the water. Some species lay their eggs in clusters; others lay them singly.

LARVA STAGE: When the larva or wriggler hatches from the egg, it continues to live in the water, but is able to breathe air. The larva is equipped with a tube-like structure on the tip of its abdomen. At the end of this tube are five flaps which open and allow air to come in; they close when the larva submerges. With regularity the active wrigglers work their way to the surface and breathe the air they need.

PUPA STAGE: The pupa is also very active. It, too, comes to the surface for air, breathing through a trumpet-like structure on its head. When the pupa is ready to leave the shell, it splits open the casing and emerges as a full-grown mosquito. It leaves the water, crawls to an object, and rests. When its wings have dried it flies away.

ADULT STAGE: Males usually hatch before the females. They hover in the air and scout for a potential mate. When the female emerges from the water, its humming wings attract waiting males. The two mate in the air. Afterward the male feeds and wanders aimlessly, waiting to complete its life span. The female looks for a meal of blood and then lays her eggs.

WHAT IS UNUSUAL ABOUT THE FEMALE'S FEET?

Her feet are equipped with non-skid, friction pads on the bottom. This equipment enables her to hold on very tightly to the victim's skin. It also gives the little insect important leverage in order to penetrate thick skin and continue probing until it finds a capillary which will yield blood.

WHY DON'T WE ALWAYS KNOW WHEN WE ARE BEING BITTEN?

Sometimes a mosquito lands on a spot on our skin which is not sensitive to touch. We may not feel the puncture because she first deadens the victim's feelings by injecting a fluid called allergen. There are two reactions to this fluid. One reaction is immediate itching. The other reaction is delayed and can start from one to five days later.

Once the mosquito has penetrated the skin, she gluttonously draws blood from her victim. She does this with a built-in syringe connected to a palpitating pump located in her head. Medical researchers have been unable to duplicate this achievement of the mosquito. The diameter of a doctor's syringe must be many times larger to accomplish the same thing.

IS IT WISE TO AVOID A SWARM OF MOSQUITOES?

Not necessarily. A swarm of mosquitoes is usually composed entirely of males which do not have the equipment for piercing. Usually only the female bites. These swarms vary in size from a few to thousands of insects. They usually gather on summer nights and tend to favor the lee side of a structure such as a tree, church steeple, etc.

DOES THE FEMALE FEED ON ANYTHING OTHER THAN BLOOD?

Both the male and the female derive their main source of nourishment not from blood but from nectar and other solutions. They eat by dipping the tip of their proboscis into the sweet substance and sucking. This material does not go directly into the stomach but is siphoned into a large sac at the base of the abdomen beneath the stomach. This sac, or ventral diverticulum, is as large as the stomach itself and stores the food. As it is needed, small quantities of this sugar are drawn into the stomach to be digested.

When the female takes blood it is for the purpose of producing eggs. Each meal of blood that she secures produces a batch of eggs. Some females can make their first deposit of eggs without blood because of reserves built up during their larva stage.

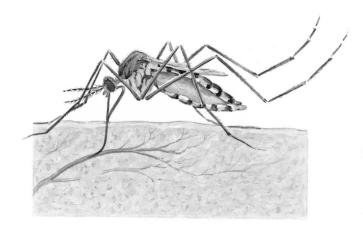

The female mosquito probes with her proboscis *until she finds a capillary from which she can draw blood. She sucks large quantities into her body until it becomes greatly distended and takes on a red appearance. She can extract as much as three to four times her own body weight.*

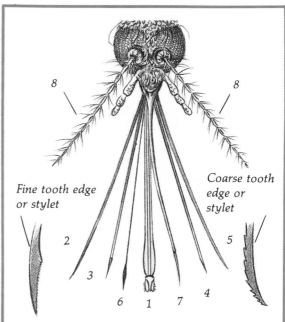

Fine tooth edge or stylet

Coarse tooth edge or stylet

The female mosquito is equipped with a very elaborate snout, or proboscis. It consists of:

1 - *a protective sheath encasing six very delicate instruments*

2, 3, 4, 5 - *the cutting stylets*

6 - *the saliva duct or syringe through which the mosquito injects her anti-coagulant juices*

7 - *a tube which allows the mosquito to draw blood when the saliva duct presses against the canal*

8 - *antennae used to sense the condition of the skin surface*

Cross-section of proboscis

Saliva duct

Tube

221

Avoid heavy breathing and overheating.

Wear light colored clothes.

Break up male swarms by disruptive noises in the range of the note C.

Eliminate breeding areas.

WHY IS IT HARD TO KILL A MOSQUITO WHEN IT LANDS ON YOU?

When we prepare to swat a mosquito which has landed on us, our muscles tense and our nerves send off a rippling motion which is a very distinct signal and warning of danger to the mosquito. If the mosquito has gorged itself on blood, however, it will be sluggish and less apt to make a quick getaway. At this time you may be able to crush its tiny body, leaving behind a pool of your blood.

HOW CAN YOU AVOID THE IRRITATION OF THE MOSQUITO?

It has recently been discovered that our breathing, more particularly the exhaling of large amounts of carbon dioxide, may be a major attraction to this piercing insect. This would explain why the mosquito tends to "bite" around our head area. To stop breathing is not a practical solution, but there are things one can do to reduce the irritation.

The lighter the color of clothing worn, the less mosquitoes are attracted. White, yellow, and light green are suggested colors which have little appeal for the insect.

Humming or banging on a pan is another means, again not too practical, of ridding oneself of mosquitoes. Creating a noise around the note C scatters the male swarms and disrupts the reproductive processes.

A more logical approach to the mosquito problem is to remove stagnant bodies of water in and around your area during the spring of the year. Another possible solution is to float a coating of oil on the surface of the water; although it is effective, it has its disadvantages. Since the larva and pupa need air, they will drown in the sealed pond. It is also possible to drown them at night by placing a waterproof flashlight at the bottom of a stagnant pond containing mosquito larvae. Wrigglers are attracted to light and will go to the source of it for oxygen. In the process, they will suffocate.

MOSQUITOES HAVE THEIR IRRITATIONS, TOO!

You may be interested to know that the mosquito has its own problems and irritations. Tiny midges and mites cause this insect considerable annoyance and discomfort. The mosquito itself is a major source of food to others in all its stages of life. The larva and pupa are food for small fish and aquatic life. The adult mosquito provides nourishment for many birds. One bird in particular, the purple martin, is capable of eating 300 mosquitoes per day!

The mosquito is extremely prolific, though, and there is little likelihood of it becoming extinct. It is estimated that in six generations, if the mosquito were unmolested, it would produce 31 billion descendants.

HOW DOES SCRIPTURE ILLUSTRATE THE NEED TO KNOW HOW AND WHEN TO USE THE RESOURCES AVAILABLE TO US?

What king conquered an army of a million men because he relied upon the Lord but when faced with a much smaller army depended upon his own wisdom?

(Pause for a response —see page 20)

A young king heard reports of an approaching army. At first he was confident. He had spent ten years preparing his nation for battle. Tearing down all the heathen altars, images, high places, and groves, he had commanded the people to seek the Lord and follow His commandments. He built fortified cities and established a standing army of over half a million mighty men of valor. But when he approached the battlefield, he was dismayed to face an army of a million men with hundreds of chariots.

He realized that his resources were insufficient and cried out to God, "It is nothing with Thee to help, whether with many, or with them that have no power: help us, O Lord our God; for we rest on Thee, and in Thy name we go against this multitude. O Lord, Thou art our God; Let not man prevail against Thee."

He recognized that this was God's battle, and God fought for him. The invading army was completely destroyed. Vast amounts of gold, silver, precious things, cattle, sheep, and camels were carried away by this victorious king and his men.

News of the victory spread throughout the land, and many came to live in the kingdom when they saw that the Lord God was with him. All the people renewed their covenant to seek the Lord. The king even removed his grandmother from being queen because she had made an idol. But the high places—altars of improper worship—began to reappear.

Another enemy came against the king. This time he took money from the house of God and hired a neighboring army to fight against his enemy. This strategy was successful militarily, but a prophet warned, "Was not the first army huge but because you relied on the Lord He delivered them into your hand? But now because you have relied on a neighboring army you have done foolishly. It was God's intention that you conquer that neighboring army also. From this time forth you will have wars."

Three years later the king faced another test when he became diseased in his feet. Once again he failed to rely upon the Lord. Instead he sought only the help of physicians. Two years later he died.

It is inconceivable that a king would fail to use the resources which had already proven so effective, but those resources required in him a perfect heart. To this king, Asa, these words were spoken, "The eyes of the Lord run to and fro throughout the whole earth, to show Himself strong in the behalf of those whose hearts are perfect toward Him."

From I Kings 15:9-24 and II Chronicles 14-16

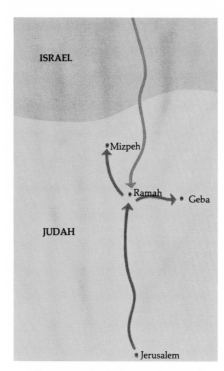

ISRAEL

•Mizpeh

•Ramah → •Geba

JUDAH

•Jerusalem

By paying the Syrians to distract the army of Israel, *Asa was able to recapture Ramah and push the border between Judah and Israel north. Asa fortified Mizpeh and Geba with materials from Ramah.*

Though their technique was crude by present standards, *physicians of Asa's day were able to remove a section of bone from the skull to relieve pressure on the brain. If the operation was successful, the bone was replaced.*

It is possible that Asa consulted a physician *who had been trained in the pagan schools of the surrounding nations. The clay image of a sheep's liver, marked with magical omens, was often used to peg a patient's future.*

ASA KNEW HOW TO USE A SPECIAL RESOURCE, BUT HE DIDN'T ALWAYS EMPLOY IT

It is somewhat difficult to piece together a biography of King Asa of Judah from the brief smatterings of his life found in Scripture. The effort, though, is well-rewarded. His good and admirable beginning followed by his tragic end provide a valuable warning for us all.

A KING WHO BROKE WITH TRADITION

When we consider Asa's heritage, we are surprised by his zeal for the Lord as a young man. His father, Abijah, "walked in all the sins of his father, which he had done before him; and his heart was not perfect with the Lord his God, as the heart of David, his father." (I Kings 15:3) When Asa became king after Abijah's death, there were "high places, and images, and groves, on every high hill, and under every green tree. And there were also sodomites in the land; and they did according to all the abominations of the nations which the Lord cast out before the children of Israel." (I Kings 14:23,24)

Asa's father, Abijah, had claimed to worship the Lord. As a matter of fact, he was very proud of the way the worship of the Lord was prospering (cf. II Chronicles 13:10-12). His sin lay in not ridding his nation of wicked religious practices as he was commanded to do in the Mosaic Law (Deuteronomy 17:2-5). Had it not been for the Lord's promise to David that his dynasty would never end (II Samuel 7:16), Asa would not have been permitted to succeed his father (I Kings 15:4).

TEN YEARS OF REFORM

Since Asa reigned for 41 years, he was still a young man when he ascended to the throne (I Kings 15:10). In fact, he may have been so young that his idolatrous grandmother, Maacah, ruled as queen while he was still a boy (cf. I Kings 15:2, 10, 13). During his first ten years as king (cf. II Chronicles 14:1), Asa "did that which was good and right in the eyes of the Lord his God; for he took away the altars of the strange gods, and the high places, and broke down the images, and cut down the groves, and commanded Judah to seek the Lord God of their fathers, and to do the law and the commandment. Also, he took away out of all the cities of Judah the high places and the images." (II Chronicles 14:2-5)

GOD FIGHTS THE KING'S BATTLE

After ten years signs of outside aggression must have appeared, for Asa turned his attentions to building up his army (II Chronicles 14:6-8). In any case, his energies were well-directed, for an army numbering one million men came up from North Africa against them. Asa had no choice but to gather his forces, only half as large, and meet them in battle. Asa cried unto the Lord for help, rested in His strength, and cooperated with the Lord in a decisive victory.

This victory won the respect and confidence of the people for Asa's leadership. His strengthened position and encouragement from a prophet of the Lord caused Asa to take courage and continue his work of religious reform (II Chronicles 15:8). He expanded his reform outside of Judah into the possessions of Benjamin and Ephraim. He then gathered the people to celebrate the renovations of the altar in Jerusalem and caused them to enter "into a covenant to seek the Lord God of their fathers with all their heart and with all their soul." (II Chronicles 15:12) He even removed his grandmother from her position as queen and destroyed the idol she had made (II Chronicles 15:16).

THE KING FORGETS THE SOURCE OF HIS STRENGTH

Unfortunately, Asa reached his zenith early in his reign and, for some unknown reason, drifted away from the Lord thereafter. He paid the Syrians out of the Lord's sanctuary to fight against his brothers in Israel and became enraged when rebuked for this action. Asa threw the prophet who spoke against him into prison. As punishment, the Lord brought a disease to his feet. The king refused to seek the Lord for help. Asa seems to have died in his foolishness.

ASA CHARACTER SKETCH

WHY WAS YOUNG ASA SO ZEALOUS FOR THE LORD?

When a son does not follow the wicked example of his father, it is natural to look for another influence. Sometimes a wise, godly mother can compensate for the damaging effects of a godless father, especially in the polygamous households of the Hebrew kings (cf. Proverbs 31:1). Asa's father had fourteen wives (II Chronicles 13:21); the child rearing responsibilities were delegated to the respective mothers. There is evidence, though, that Asa's mother died when young. His idolatrous grandmother, Maacah, (cf. I Kings 15:2, 10) retained the post of queen-mother after he became king, rather than his mother whose name is not mentioned. If she had died, Asa would most likely have been raised under the supervision of the priests and Levites and taught the Law of Moses. His father, Abijah, who hypocritically boasted of his conformity to the Law (cf. II Chronicles 13:10, 11), would have permitted this training. Priests would have encouraged the crown prince to write out his own copy of the Law and read it continually (Deuteronomy 17:18, 19). Although this is only a supposition, it follows very closely the pattern of godly king Joash whose father was also wicked (cf. II Kings 11:2-3; 12:2).

WHY DID ASA IMPRISON ONE OF HIS VALUABLE RESOURCES?

King Baasha of Israel had invaded northern Judah and set up a blockade at Ramah. He evidently was concerned about the large number of people migrating to Judah because of the religious reforms which Asa had instituted (II Chronicles 15:9). In an effort to thin Baasha's forces at Ramah, Asa paid the king of Syria from the temple treasury to invade Israel from the north. From a military perspective, Asa's strategy was very clever. When Baasha withdrew, Asa invaded from the south and successfully conquered the city.

When Hanani rebuked Asa for making this league with Syria, he was imprisoned. Asa probably justified his action by his success. If he was wrong, he reasoned, his plan would have failed. He belligerently refused to consider the long-range effects of his actions and labeled Hanani a false prophet. His receptivity to the prophet Azariah (II Chronicles 15:1-8) had been destroyed by the pride which so often accompanies success.

WHY DID ASA ONCE AGAIN OVERLOOK A PROVEN RESOURCE?

Two years before Asa died, his feet became diseased. The disease is not described other than it continued to worsen "until his disease was exceeding great." (II Chronicles 16:12) Perhaps he had dropsy or a sclerosis which narrows the arteries of the legs, creates lameness, and may result in gangrene. In any case, Asa should have sought the Lord for the cause of the disease. The Law which he once so enthusiastically upheld contains a curse for those who disobey. "The Lord shall smite thee in the knees, and in the legs, with a sore botch that cannot be healed, from the sole of thy foot unto the top of thy head." (Deuteronomy 28:35) Asa's heart had been lifted up in pride. He had not sought the Lord in regard to the military decision concerning Ramah and had been successful. Now he felt he could control his health by turning to physicians (II Chronicles 16:12). It was not the mere inquiring of the physician that is condemned but rather the godless manner in which Asa trusted in the physicians rather than God—his best resource who was constantly available to him.

This Canaanite altar at Megiddo *is over 26 feet wide and 4½ feet high. Early in his reign, Asa completely destroyed these high places in his kingdom of Judah. He did not remove them, however, from the portion of Israel he later conquered. His zeal for the Lord diminished with age.*

ASA
ā-sa

Joyfulness

"*Looking unto Jesus the author and finisher of our faith; who for the joy that was set before him endured the cross, despising the shame . . .*"

Hebrews 12:2

PART FIVE

PROVIDING BRIGHTNESS IN THE LIVES OF OTHERS REGARDLESS OF OUTWARD CONDITIONS

Illustrated in the World of Nature.......Black-capped Chickadee
From the Pages of Scripture......................Paul and Silas

REFUSING TO ENJOY ANYTHING WHICH HARMS THE PERSON OR REPUTATION OF ANOTHER

Illustrated in the World of Nature..............Northern Shrike
From the Pages of Scripture...........................Jezebel

MAINTAINING A SPIRIT OF CHEERFULNESS DESPITE PHYSICAL LIMITATIONS

Illustrated in the World of Nature.............American Dipper
From the Pages of Scripture...........................David

KNOWING AND BEING WHERE GOD INTENDED ME TO BE

Illustrated in the World of Nature.....................Bobcat
From the Pages of Scripture......................Four Lepers

Joyfulness

IS PROVIDING BRIGHTNESS IN THE LIVES OF OTHERS REGARDLESS OF OUTWARD CONDITIONS

"Blessed be God . . . who comforteth us in all our tribulation, that we may be able to comfort them which are in any trouble, by the comfort wherewith we ourselves are comforted of God."

II Corinthians 1:3, 4

LIVING LESSONS ON JOYFULNESS . . .

FROM THE PAGES OF SCRIPTURE

The only effective way to eliminate darkness is to let the light in. God explains in Scripture that Christians are the light of the world.Many Christians fail to visualize the dark circumstances through which they must shine, but Christ actually experienced them for us. He was falsely accused, rejected, despised, forsaken, misunderstood, challenged, beaten, slandered, and threatened. We are called to believe on Jesus and also to suffer for His sake. Power of the right kind of response to suffering was demonstrated by two men who were subjected to cruel outward conditions. Because of their right response, eternal brightness was brought into the lives of many around them.

ILLUSTRATED IN THE WORLD OF NATURE

BLACK-CAPPED CHICKADEE *Parus articapillus*

The migration of the black-capped chickadee is one of the shortest of any bird. In fact, many do not migrate from their birthplace at all, and if they do, they travel only a short distance. These cheerful birds commonly inhabit deciduous and mixed forests and are often seen near homes in residential areas. This little bird has an amazing longevity of up to nine years. The male and female are similar in appearance, growing to a length of five inches. The chickadee is gray all year long and undergoes a post-nuptial molt during which its plumage takes on a rich color to replace worn, faded feathers. When they leave the nest the young birds closely resemble their parents.

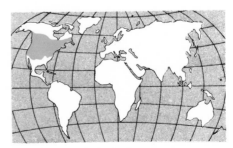

The range and habitat of the black-capped chickadee

JOYFULNESS

HOW DOES THE CHICKADEE ILLUSTRATE JOYFULNESS BY PROVIDING BRIGHTNESS IN THE LIVES OF OTHERS?

The woods were deathly quiet with a foreboding silence in the air. Only a few days before, the countryside had bustled with activity and the songs of excited birds preparing for their southern migration. Then a sense deep within triggered their inner timeclock and they were gone. Many of the animals, too, had retreated to various chambers and underground dens not to return for many months.

The temperature had dropped and biting, brisk winds ripped away what few leaves remained on the trees. Winter was fast approaching. Lakes had already frozen over, and it would not be long before heavy snows would blanket the northern forest. It was not unusual for the snow to accumulate six feet in depth. The winter would be cold and hard. The mercury would drop well below zero during many of the days ahead.

In preparation for the cold months birds, animals, and reptiles had made special provision and had either left the area or fortified themselves to ensure survival. It appeared as though the forest was stripped of all life. Even the trees had taken on a stark appearance—a look of death.

As strong, northern winds continued to blow, gray clouds, filled with snow, began to gather. The skies grew darker and the temperature plummeted.

Then, faintly in the distance above the whistle of the wind came a soft, chattering noise. The noise grew louder. It was a bird. Not just one bird, but a flock of them were flitting from tree to tree. Could these birds have lost their way? Could it possibly be that they did not realize a blizzard would soon form and snow would cover the countryside?

The birds did not appear concerned as they sang their cheerful songs to one another. Even as the snow began to fall, they actively moved about in a confident search for dormant insects hidden in the crevices of tree bark.

The large snowflakes fell throughout the night. By morning the storm had passed; everything was still. Snow covered the forest. It was a beautiful sight to behold the bright sunlight sparkling on the glistening white.

Once again the air was filled with melody. The chickadees had not gone. They appeared happier than ever, seeming almost to welcome the snow. Some dipped into the powdery flakes to bathe. These hardy little birds would not leave as the others had, but would continue to make this their year-round home.

The countryside could look forward to their bright, cheerful song and joyful activities even though outward conditions tended to discourage such a spirit. It is for this reason that one well-known naturalist referred to the chickadee as the "bird of the merry heart."

Scriptural references to the raven

"The eye that mocketh at his father, and despiseth to obey his mother, the ravens of the valley shall pick it out . . ."
Proverbs 30:17

"And he sent forth a raven, which went forth to and fro until the waters were dried up from off the earth."
Genesis 8:7

Scriptural background

The raven and the chickadee belong to the same order of perching birds. A scavenger, the raven feeds on dead or dying animals. When approaching a carcass, it first pecks at the animal's eye. This indicates whether the animal is dead or alive. If an animal allows its eye to be pecked, it is probably dead.

It is interesting to note that Noah chose to release a raven from the ark. With its scavenging habits the raven could feed on the carcasses of the dead.

CHARACTERISTICS AND PHYSICAL FEATURES OF THE BLACK-CAPPED CHICKADEE

Even in the grim conditions of deepest winter, the joyful spirit of the chickadee persists. Regardless of weather, the chickadee sings its cheerful song, serenading the countryside with a variety of melodies. The chickadee is a small bird so its body cools quite rapidly. Yet this hearty little creature is able to withstand sub-zero weather because it has a highly effective layer of insulating feathers. With these feathers the bird is protected from the cold and maintains optimum warmth by ruffling and puffing them up. By so doing it traps airspace for better insulation. This ruffling also gives the effect of a much larger appearance. During the winter the little chickadee has many more feathers than it does in the summer.

WHY IS THE SONG OF THE CHICKADEE SO IMPORTANT TO THE BIRD?

The chickadee is quite sociable and usually travels in flocks which range in size from four birds to one hundred. They spend the winter searching the woodlands for food. These birds scatter to such an extent as they search that they often lose sight of each other. By continually calling, the chickadees are able to keep track of one another and stay together. This also makes it easy for bird watchers to locate the birds and determine the direction in which the flock is moving.

The chickadee's song has another purpose. When one member of the flock finds a new source of food, it communicates this message to the rest and they, too, are able to share in the find.

DOES THE SONG OF THE CHICKADEE CHANGE?

This bird is named after the melody which it most commonly sings—*chickadee-dee-dee*. When the days begin to warm and the first signs of spring appear, the chickadees change their song to *phee-bee*. During courtship they serenade their mate with this whistle. In spring and fall, another call is heard which involves three notes. These latter calls are whistles, and the quality and sound are distinctly different from their characteristic *chickadee-dee-dee*.

The plumage of the male and female black-capped chickadee is the same.

CHICAKDEE'S TRAVELING COMPANIONS

Tufted titmouse

Nuthatch

Kinglet

Brown creeper

Downy woodpecker

*Prying open bark
to secure insects*

*Chickadee holding
sunflower seed and
hammering with its bill
to open
shell*

The chickadee is adept *at feeding with its sharp
bill. It searches every nook and cranny, prying
open bark that might possibly house some insect
eggs, larva or bug.*

IS THERE A PATTERN OR ORDER WITHIN A FLOCK OF CHICKADEES?

There is a definite hierarchy in the chickadee flock. The dominant bird, usually a male, is referred to as the alpha bird. Its mate is second in command. The dominant bird and its mate are the first to feed. Once these birds have had their fill, other members of the flock are then permitted to eat. Dominancy is determined by the bird's age, size, sex, and learning ability.

IS THE CHICKADEE A TERRITORIAL BIRD?

Yes. During spring breeding the chickadee spends as much as forty percent of its day trying to protect its territory from intruders of its own species. During nesting, the bird spends about thirty percent of its day in defense. The average territory of the male is three or four acres.

DOES THE CHICKADEE ASSOCIATE WITH OTHER BIRDS?

It is safe to assume that if chickadees are in the area, there are other birds traveling with them. Some of the common companion birds are the tufted titmouse, nuthatch, kinglet, brown creeper, and the downy woodpecker.

HOW IS A CHICKADEE SIMILAR TO A WOODPECKER?

Like a woodpecker, the chickadee often lands on the side of a tree trunk or perpendicular limb and clings to it while feeding. It is very adept in finding insects and insect eggs between crevices in the bark. It differs from the woodpecker, however, in that it does not climb up and down the tree. It seems to enjoy even hanging upside down by its relatively long, thin legs and feet.

HOW CAN THE CHICKADEE CRACK A NUT WITH SUCH A SMALL BILL?

Its bill may be small, but it has a long, sharp point. The chickadee places the seed between its toes, and with a series of quick, hammerlike thrusts punctures the shell and continues to hammer until the hole is large enough for it to extract the nutmeat.

WHAT COMPRISES THE CHICKADEE'S DIET?

After the stomachs of many chickadees were examined, it was found that sixty-eight percent of its food was insect material such as caterpillars, moths and their eggs, bees, ants, etc. It is interesting to note that this is true even in winter. Another thirty-two percent was vegetable matter. Two-thirds of this second figure consisted of buds, berries, and nuts. The chickadee is also very fond of sunflower seeds.

DOES THE CHICKADEE HAVE ANY ENEMIES?

Small hawks and shrikes are enemies, but this little bird has two effective defenses. The first is that it is always watchful for danger. The second is its ability to move quickly. Like magic, the chickadee disappears by launching into flight with both its wings and legs. This little bird is so quick that if it becomes frightened in flight, it can change its course of travel in three-tenths of a second.

WHAT IS UNUSUAL ABOUT THE EYES OF A CHICKADEE?

The chickadee, like a man, is able to use both eyes together to focus on a single object. It can also use each eye independently. By using its eyes separately, it can actually be both nearsighted and farsighted at the same time. Like other birds, the chickadee protects itself with this ability. By cocking its head, it is able to sit on a branch, search for insects and focus up close while the other eye watches the sky for distant objects such as circling hawks. This ability helps the chickadee to be a predator rather than a prey.

IS THE BEE DANGEROUS TO THE CHICKADEE?

The chickadee seems to have no fear of bee stings and is quick, if opportunity permits, to eat the insect. It has a simple and effective means to catch them. It perches itself at the entrance of a hive. When a bee comes out, it snatches it up and flies away to a perch. Holding it in its foot, the bird tears the bee apart with its bill and eats it. It continues this procedure many times until it is full. It has been known to eat other potentially harmful creatures, such as spiders, without any apparent ill effect.

The tent caterpillar is a favorite meal of the chickadee. When it sees a nest it tears open the web and then rapidly devours the worms as they are exposed.

Bees make an easy meal for the chickadee as they leave their hive.

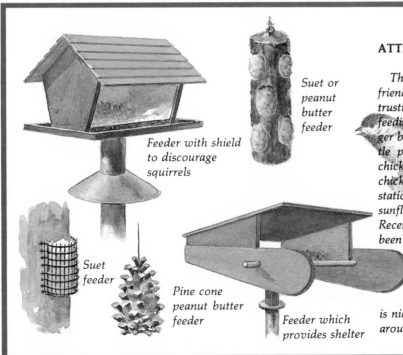

Feeder with shield to discourage squirrels

Suet or peanut butter feeder

Suet feeder

Pine cone peanut butter feeder

Feeder which provides shelter

ATTRACTING THE CHICKADEE

The chickadee is considered one of the friendliest creatures in the wild. It is very trusting and the least aggressive bird at a feeding station. It will quietly wait for the bigger birds to have their fill and leave. With a little patience and stillness, one can have the chickadee feed out of his hand. In the winter the chickadee is particularly attracted to feeding stations. Many things can be offered, such as sunflower seeds, suet, and even peanut butter. Recently, the advisability of feeding birds has been questioned. The opinion is that this convenient food discourages chickadees from preying on destructive insects. The degree to which this is true is not known. What is certain is that it is nice to have these cheery little birds singing around the house during bleak, winter days.

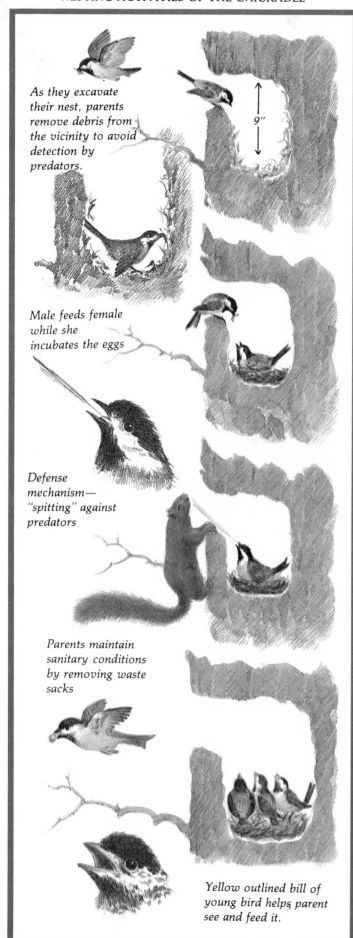

As they excavate their nest, parents remove debris from the vicinity to avoid detection by predators.

Male feeds female while she incubates the eggs

Defense mechanism— "spitting" against predators

Parents maintain sanitary conditions by removing waste sacks

Yellow outlined bill of young bird helps parent see and feed it.

HOW DOES THE WOODPECKER BENEFIT THE CHICKADEE?

The chickadee often uses the deserted hole of a woodpecker for its home. It may excavate its own nest by removing the soft, rotten material from a tree such as a white birch. It must choose trees with rotten centers because its small bill cannot chip away sound wood as a woodpecker's does.

When constructing the nest, both parents actively dig, enlarging the cavity to nine or more inches in depth. The entrance hole itself is rarely larger than two inches. They visit the nest alternately, waiting for the other to leave before entering. Rather than throwing wood chips outside the hole, and leaving telltale evidence for predators, they carry the chips away and scatter them. The nest at the bottom of the cavity is made of moss, feathers, and grasses.

DO BOTH PARENTS PARTICIPATE IN RAISING THE YOUNG?

Yes. It is believed that chickadees mate for life. The female lays five to eight white eggs which are finely spotted with brown. Once the eggs are all laid, the female sits on them. Incubation usually lasts from twelve to fifteen days. While the female sits on her eggs, the male feeds its mate with the choicest bits of food it can find. After the young have hatched, both parents feed them. The young have ravenous appetites and keep the parents continuously busy gathering food. One observer noted parent chickadees making as many as forty-two trips in two hours in order to satisfy the appetites of their young. The young are fed insects almost exclusively.

HOW DOES A CHICKADEE DEFEND HER NEST?

While incubating her eggs, the female uses a unique strategy to discourage intruders. When an animal such as a squirrel pokes its head in the entrance, the little bird quickly sucks in its breath. Then, with a quick, explosive sound, it causes the air to escape. When the jet stream hits its mark, this amusing tactic is often all that is needed to turn away the intruder.

HOW DO CHICKADEES KEEP THEIR NEST CLEAN?

The parent chickadee is even joyful and enthusiastic when it comes to keeping the surroundings of its nest clean. Darting back and forth the little bird will carry a small sack away from the nest in its bill. These sacks are the result of the young depositing their waste in a membranous package. Rather than allowing these to remain in the nest or to be thrown out the entrance, the parents cart these miniature diapers some distance away from the nest.

HOW DOES SCRIPTURE ILLUSTRATE JOYFULNESS IN PROVIDING BRIGHTNESS IN THE LIVES OF OTHERS?

It is understandable that people who need the Gospel will expect those who bring it to pass their most rigid test—the ability to rejoice when everyone else would become discouraged. Who in Scripture brought a cynical bystander to salvation because they passed this kind of test?

(Pause for a response—see page 20)

Several men sprang out of their hiding places and rushed upon two surprised travelers. They caught hold of them and dragged them into the town court. First, the two men were falsely accused. Then they were brought before the village rulers and magistrates. Again, false statements and accusations were hurled against them.

The magistrates were easily swayed. The coats and shirts of the two men were ripped off. Guards were commanded to beat them. The two men knew that these magistrates were violating the law, because it was unlawful for any Roman citizen to be whipped before he was found guilty by trial.

The muscles tightened in the backs and arms of the guards as they lifted the leather thongs with their metal balls high into the air and then brought them down with great force upon the backs of these two men. The crowd grew. Shouting increased as the mob urged on the guards in their bloody ordeal. First the metal balls produced large welts. Then the strips of leather cut into the skin and tore the flesh away.

When the guards saw that the prisoners were nearing death, they stopped the whipping. Then the men were cast into prison. A startled jailer was given strict instructions not to let them escape. Having received such a charge, he thrust them into the inner prison and locked their feet into heavy, wooden stocks.

The two men had been falsely accused, denied a fair trial, illegally beaten, and unlawfully imprisoned. Their backs were bleeding; their ankles were in pain. They were tired and hungry, separated from their friends, and suffered the sting of public humiliation.

What did they do next? They rejoiced in the Lord with singing and prayer. The other prisoners marveled at what they heard. Such a response deeply impressed the jailer. He found himself considering the possibility of becoming a Christian himself. Obviously these men had something he and his family needed.

Later that night an earthquake rocked the prison, springing open the doors and chains. The jailer thought his prisoners had escaped, and he was going to kill himself. But they cried out in a loud voice, "Do yourself no harm. We are all here." The jailer called for a light, ran in and fell down before these two prisoners. He brought them out of their cell and asked, "What must I do to be saved?"

They replied, "Believe on the Lord Jesus Christ and thou shalt be saved and thy house." That very night the jailer and his family believed and were baptized. They washed the wounds of the prisoners, set food before them, and rejoiced together at their new fellowship in Christ. Paul and Silas produced joy in the lives of others because they were able to rejoice in the cruelest possible circumstances.

From Acts 16:11-34

PAUL AND SILAS' JOYFUL SPIRITS
BROUGHT BRIGHTNESS TO A DARKENED PRISON CELL

Paul and Silas walked many miles *on paved Roman roads throughout the empire.*

The stream near Philippi *where Paul and Silas met Lydia and other women at a prayer meeting*

The ruins of an early Christian church *built near the jail in which Paul and Silas were imprisoned at Philippi*

The council of Jerusalem had made its decision concerning the Gentile believers' obligation to the Mosaic Law. Judas and Silas were chosen to be Paul and Barnabas' companions when delivering the decision to the church at Antioch. Silas, a Greek-speaking Jew, was a leading member of the church at Jerusalem (Acts 15:22).

A MISSIONARY CHOOSES A FELLOW CITIZEN

Silas was also a prophet through whom the Lord gave fresh communications of His will for Christians of the early church. In Antioch, he impressed Paul with his God-given abilities to preach and exhort (cf. Acts 15:32). After an unfortunate dispute betwen Paul and Barnabas concerning Mark, Paul chose Silas to accompany him and visit the churches he founded during his first missionary journey. The fact that Silas was a Roman citizen, as was Paul, may have had some bearing on his decision. Roman citizens were offered better protection under the law, an advantage which Paul realized could be most helpful.

A VISION TO MINISTER TO THE MACEDONIANS

When Paul and Silas reached Troas, a harbor town on the northwestern coast of Asia Minor, Paul received his famous vision of the Macedonian man beckoning them to come over and help (Acts 16:9). Paul responded to the call. He sailed with Silas to Neapolis and then went directly to Philippi. Philippi was a Roman colony and, as such, enjoyed special privileges (cf. Acts 16:12). It was part of Paul's missionary plan to go straight to strategic centers.

Paul's first convert was Lydia. He met her at a prayer meeting by the river among some women "who worshipped God." (Acts 16:14) Next Paul encountered a poor slave girl who possessed "a spirit of Python." She was being exploited by her owners. Devotees of the Python were ventriloquists whose words were controlled by demons. Evidently the girl could throw her voice into the mouth of an object used for telling fortunes. They charged great sums of money for their services (cf. Acts 16:16). When Paul cast out the demon from the girl, her masters trumped up false charges against Paul and Silas who were then beaten and thrown into prison without a trial.

PUNISHED AND IMPRISONED—BUT JOYFUL

As Roman citizens, this represented a grave miscarriage of justice. Wounds untreated, Paul and Silas were thrown into the dark, inner prison and bound in stocks as though they were dangerous criminals. Their only companions were hungry rats and fellow prisoners who bitterly cursed their fates. But instead of filling the midnight hour with groans and justifiable complaints, "Paul and Silas prayed, and sang praises unto God." (Acts 16:25)

God answered their prayers and honored their praises by sending a great earthquake to free them. The doors were opened, and chains and stocks became detached from the wall. The awakened jailer, helpless to prevent an escape, decided to commit suicide at once. He knew that after he lost his prisoners, he would face disgrace and execution (cf. Acts 16:23, 27). When Paul assured him that no one had left, the jailer came in and fell down before these unusual men. He no doubt was familiar with the nature of their charges and cried out for an explanation of their message of salvation.

GOD REWARDS A RIGHT SPIRIT

The jailer became a believer in Jesus Christ, and his whole attitude was transformed. Instead of thinking of himself, he thought of the pain and hunger of Paul and Silas. He took them home, dressed their wounds, and fed them a good meal (Acts 16:33, 34). The following day the charges against Paul and Silas were dropped. The two men made one last visit to the home of Lydia to comfort and encourage the new believers and then departed from the city. Their example of joy in adversity remained to encourage the small band of believers in their newly found faith.

HOW COULD PAUL AND SILAS SING WHEN THEIR OUTWARD CONDITION WAS SO BLEAK?

Music in Scripture is not always associated with merriment and happiness. One purpose of music in the Old Testament was to calm a troubled heart. David played on his harp to refresh the heart of Saul (I Samuel 16:23). When Elisha saw the wicked king Jehoram, he was so disturbed that he called for the minstrel to calm him down. "And it came to pass, when the minstrel played, that the hand of the Lord came upon him." (II Kings 3:15) Paul and Silas may have sung to prepare themselves for prayer. When they prayed and were assured of their deliverance, their singing would have changed to praise. "Then sang Moses and the children of Israel this song unto the Lord, and spake, saying, I will sing unto the Lord, for he hath triumphed gloriously: the horse and his rider hath he thrown into the sea." (Exodus 15:1; cf. Judges 5:1,2) Paul later told all Christians to make singing an important part of their worship (Ephesians 5:19,20; Colossians 3:16).

WHY DIDN'T PAUL AND SILAS ESCAPE WHEN THEY HAD THE OPPORTUNITY?

It would have been simple for Paul and Silas to justify their escape. They could have easily slipped out of Philippi at night and headed on their way. Had not God miraculously opened the jail door, loosed their chains, and provided this opportunity for that purpose? But Paul and Silas were more concerned about the reputation of the Gospel than their own safety. They were both Roman citizens (cf. Acts 16:37) and were entitled to the protection of the law. If they ran, they would have been considered guilty. As a result, the believers who remained in Philippi would have been condemned as associates of criminals. Even after they were given official permission to leave the next morning, they demanded an honorable release in public view. This was not to pamper their hurt pride but rather to demonstrate the legitimacy of their message and to encourage these new believers to be bold in their faith. Paul and Silas assured the integrity of the Gospel before they departed.

HOW DID GOD BLESS PAUL AND SILAS' JOYFUL SPIRIT?

Before Paul and Silas left Philippi, they visited the home of Lydia, the first convert. Her home had become a meeting place for the small church which now included the household of the jailer. Whether or not the slave girl became a believer we are not told, but it is reasonable to suppose that she did. There is some indication that Luke, the physician, was also a member of this new fellowship. In spite of his brief time spent there, Philippi became one of Paul's most loved churches. It brought him more joy than any other (cf. Philippians 1:3, 8). He used the Philippians as an example of generosity to the church of Corinth (II Corinthians 8:1-6). His epistle to the Philippians was written to a firmly established church which included "bishops and deacons." (Philippians 1:1). It is a tender letter to mature believers, and comparatively little is said about doctrinal error. The joy of the Lord which Paul and Silas demonstrated to the first believers in Philippi may have been a major reason for their quick growth and maturity.

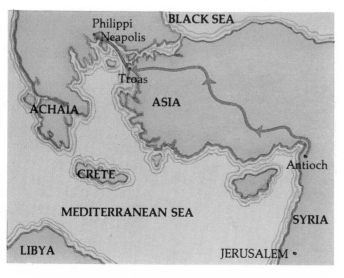

"And after he had seen the vision, *immediately we endeavored to go into Macedonia, assuredly gathering that the Lord had called us to preach the gospel unto them. Therefore, loosing from Troas, we came with a straight course to Samothracia, and the next day to Neapolis; and from there to Philippi, which is the chief city of that part of Macedonia, and a colony; and we were in that city abiding certain days."*

PAUL AND SILAS
pôl and si-las

Joyfulness

IS REFUSING TO ENJOY ANYTHING WHICH HARMS THE PERSON OR REPUTATION OF ANOTHER

"For our rejoicing is this, the testimony of our conscience, that in simplicity and godly sincerity, not with fleshly wisdom, but by the grace of God, we have had our conversation in the world. . ."

II Corinthians 1:12

LIVING LESSONS ON JOYFULNESS . . .

FROM THE PAGES OF SCRIPTURE

Everything we have loses its value to us when we desire something we cannot have. This is one of the penalties of envy and covetousness. It is a serious matter to set our affections on something we shouldn't have because those around us will often do what they can to get it for us. To assist us in learning this lesson, Scripture includes a vivid account of envy which resulted in murder, destruction and death. A king had great riches but was unable to enjoy them because he wanted something he could not have. The wicked scheme devised by his wife gave him his wish, but neither of them considered the final price of what they had done.

ILLUSTRATED IN THE WORLD OF NATURE

NORTHERN SHRIKE   *Lanius excubitor*

The northern shrike's Latin name, *Lanius excubitor*, means "watchman" or "sentinel." A literal translation of its name is "the watchful butcher." This is an appropriate title for the alert predator. Perched high atop the tallest trees, it is constantly on the lookout for prey and is equally aware of its own possible attackers such as the hawk. When it spots a hawk flying overhead, the shrike utters a shrill whistle and then drops into the densest foliage of the trees to hide. It will reappear only after the predator has passed. The northern shrike is one of the largest shrikes measuring from nine to ten and one-half inches in length.

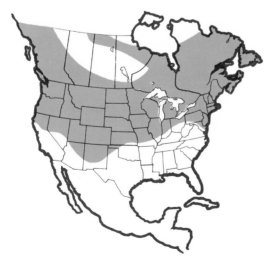

The range and habitat of the northern shrike

JOYFULNESS

HOW DOES THE SHRIKE ILLUSTRATE THE NEED TO REFUSE PLEASURES WHICH HARM OTHERS?

The trap was set. High in the western forests a naturalist performed his study and research, recording the unusually high bird population of the area.

He had placed wire mesh traps for the purpose of catching various birds. These large traps were made of screen material allowing the birds to enter freely. But the construction of the door prevented the birds from flying back out. A door at the top of the trap permitted the naturalist to reach in, catch the specimens and study them. He measured and weighed the bird, determined the gender, banded it by placing a little metal tag around its leg, recorded the data, and then released the bird, unharmed.

He had been having a high degree of success with these traps and was very encouraged with his progress thus far. The bait of seeds and bits of food had lured many different species such as chickadees, red-polls, and various sparrows. The traps varied in size; some were capable of holding more birds than others. The naturalist regularly made his rounds, checking the traps as many times during the day as possible.

One day while he was checking his sets, he came upon one of the larger traps and heard a loud commotion. As he drew closer he could see that the trap contained four or five birds frantically trying to escape. When he looked inside, he noticed a different bird—one he had not caught before. Its actions were astounding. Rather than trying to escape from this trap, this bird was attacking the others! It would jump on another bird's back and strike the victim with its beak—shaking, twisting, and choking it until it was finally dead. Instead of eating its kill, it then flew after another bird.

The naturalist stood and stared at the spectacle. One by one the captive birds were savagely attacked by this blood-thirsty killer. The presence of the naturalist did not seem to bother this crazed villain. It was fearless, bold, and relentless as it went about its gruesome business, appearing almost to enjoy and delight in snuffing out the lives of the helpless birds.

Its natural tendency to caution and alertness was deadened. It seemed totally unaware of its own dangerous captivity. The joy and pleasure which this butcher seemed to derive at harming the others disturbed the naturalist. Reaching inside the trap he captured the bird and destroyed it, ending the wanton slaughter.

SCRIPTURAL REFERENCES TO THE SHRIKE

The shrike and the raven are both members of the passeriformes order. The shrike is not mentioned in Scripture, but references to the raven are of significance.

"The eye that mocketh at his father, and despiseth to obey his mother, the ravens of the valley shall pick it out, and the young eagles shall eat it."
Proverbs 30:17

The raven, a scavenger bird, is usually the first to arrive at the scene of death. It has exceptionally keen eyesight to detect dead or dying prey.

First a raven determines if its prey is dead by picking at the eye of the victim. If its victim does not defend its own eye, it is assumed to be dead. After the raven has begun to satisfy its appetite, the eagles arrive. They are larger and more powerful scavengers which finish the work which the ravens began.

These facts from the world of nature add astonishing depth to the warning of Proverbs 30:17. When a son or daughter despises or rejects the authority of his parents, he or she begins to show signs of spiritual death. Those that feed upon destruction can see it by looking in their eyes. "The light of the body is the eye...." (Matthew 6:22) Paul warned that one who lives in pleasure is dead while he lives (I Timothy 5:6). Rebellion to authority invites destructive temptation, and after smaller "scavengers" have begun their work, larger ones will come and finish the job.

CHARACTERISTICS AND PHYSICAL FEATURES OF THE NORTHERN SHRIKE

Tooth

The beak and hook-like claws assist the shrike in its savage business of killing.

The bite of the shrike *is so strong and its grip is so persistent that it seldom releases its prey unless pressure is applied to its neck.*

The pleasure which the shrike seemed to derive at the expense of the captive birds is typical of this small marauder. The songbird appears to gain such delight from killing that when it turns "butcher" and goes on the rampage, it loses all its inner cautions and does bizarre things that jeopardize its own life. Many accounts have been given of its fierce cruelty and savage boldness.

One such account given years ago occurred when a naturalist shot a robin for study purposes. The wounded bird flew a short distance and then landed on the ground. A shrike swooped down and grasped the bird. The hunter went over to take it away, but the determined shrike was not willing to relinquish it and did so only when it, too, was shot.

Another account attesting to the boldness of the shrike involved two caged canaries placed in a building near an open window. The sight of the butcher bird created such fear and commotion that the frightened canaries rushed to the side of the cage in an attempt to get as far from the villain as possible. One of the birds accidentally thrust its head through the bars of the cage on the opposite side. The butcher immediately seized this opportunity and tore off its head, leaving only the lifeless body on the bottom of the cage.

DOES THE NORTHERN SHRIKE HAVE MANY RELATIVES?

There are at least sixty-four species of shrikes. They inhabit most of the world with the exception of Australia and South America. Two species of shrike are found in North America—the loggerhead and the northern shrike.

WHAT IS THE DIFFERENCE BETWEEN THE LOGGERHEAD AND THE NORTHERN SHRIKE?

The northern shrike is approximately one inch longer than the loggerhead. Its breast is faintly barred and its lower mandible is light. The loggerhead's bill is all black, and the mask on its face meets over the bill.

The habits and characteristics of the two birds are very similar, although the northern seems to be more savage. Their ranges differ. The northern shrike inhabits the northern United States, Canada and Alaska. The loggerhead is found from southern British Columbia to New Brunswick and south to southern Mexico.

Loggerhead Shrike

Adult Northern Shrike

Immature Northern Shrike

Shrike hovers over well-used rodent trail in search of food.

Through mimicry the shrike coaxes a songbird within range.

Perched high in a tree the shrike can see grasshoppers as far as 70 yards away

Grasshopper

Diversionary flight of songbird

Shrike kills prey by delivering repeated blows to the head and neck.

WHY IS THE SHRIKE SO SAVAGE?

One reason the shrike is so savage and bloodthirsty is because it is really not well-equipped for the business of killing. The shrike belongs to the order *Passeriformes*, or songbirds, which includes robins and thrushes and lacks the specialized tools of the predatory hawk or owl.

The northern shrike does have a strong beak which is well-constructed for tearing. Its maxillia, or upper beak, has a sharp, hooked tip. Side cutting edges are equipped with a tooth-like growth, a feature similar to that of the hawk. Although its beak is strong, it is not always sufficient in itself to kill, and the shrike therefore must incorporate what appear to be fierce and cruel means to accomplish its task.

DOES THE SHRIKE JUST EAT BIRDS?

No. The shrike preys upon many birds but they do not exclusively make up its diet. Some of the species it kills are snow buntings, vireos, kinglets, downy woodpeckers, chickadees, mourning doves, cardinals, longspurs, siskins, goldfinches and horned larks. The shrike is carnivorous and eats a wide range of meat including mice, voles, and lemmings. It also consumes insects such as grasshoppers, spiders, beetles, and caterpillars. Mice and birds account for approximately sixty percent of its diet; the other forty percent is made up of insects.

HOW DOES THE SHRIKE USE ITS VOICE TO ITS ADVANTAGE?

Because it belongs to and looks like a member of the Passeriformes order, the shrike can conceal its murderous character beneath the "disguise" of an innocent songbird. The butcher bird hides in a clump of bushes or high in the leafy branches of a tree and from this vantage point sings and imitates various birds of the area. The shrike uses this tactic to gain an advantage over its would-be victims since it is clumsy and not very swift in the air. With a variety of calls it tries to deceive a songbird into coming within close range. From behind its cover it suddenly darts out and begins a deadly pursuit.

DOES THE SHRIKE'S IMITATION CALL WORK?

It is surprising how effective the shrike's mimicry is. Many times a shrike even resorts to feigning the calls or cries of another songbird in pain. It plays this act in the hope of inducing a bird to fly to the aid of a fellow member of its species. Even when it employs this mimicry, because of its ill-equipped wings it may be difficult for the shrike to draw its quarry into a close enough range to attack.

On the other hand, the victimized songbird has tactics of its own. If the shrike pursues it, the fleeing bird will fly higher and higher into the sky so that the shrike is prevented from flying above it. It then drops out of the sky and disappears into a thick cover, foiling the attack.

ARE THE FEET OF THE BUTCHER BIRD EQUIPPED FOR KILLING?

Not really. The feet of the shrike are comparatively less powerful than those of the hawk; however, they are not as ineffective as those of the common songbird. As weapons, they are in a unique category all their own.

The butcher bird's feet are weak and small; the shrike has a difficult time grasping its prey. Its claws, on the other hand, are very sharp and capable of inflicting severe wounds. They contribute significantly to the capture and death of its prey. The shrike's claws and its strong, hook-like beak are its two basic tools of attack. Both appear inferior and unsuited for their task, but with its skill and will, the shrike is able to succeed.

HOW DOES THE BUTCHER BIRD KILL ITS VICTIMS?

The shrike has two basic strategies in hunting. One is to wait patiently and be alert to any unsuspecting quarry that comes near. The other tactic, the one more commonly used, is to pursue its prey. It attacks mammals and small birds from a distance of approximately two hundred yards and insects from a distance of one hundred yards.

Its procedure of attack varies. If its victim is a bird, the shrike will try to fly above it, dive down upon its back with a powerful impact from its feet, and break its neck or back with a blow from its beak. This stunning blow will often prove fatal, and the bird either falls or is carried to the ground. If the original blow failed to kill the bird, the shrike quickly follows it to the ground and strikes the base of its skull or attacks the vertebrae of the neck, causing great internal injuries which result in death.

If the victim is an insect, the shrike snaps it up with its beak and crushes it by repeated bites in the thorax region.

The shrike appears to be the most vicious with mice and other rodents because it has such difficulty killing them. Rather than striking the animal with its feet, it first attacks the rodent with its beak, viciously shaking its victim from side to side, biting hard on the neck in an attempt to crush and damage the vertebrae. It will not pick up the rodent in its feet until it is dead.

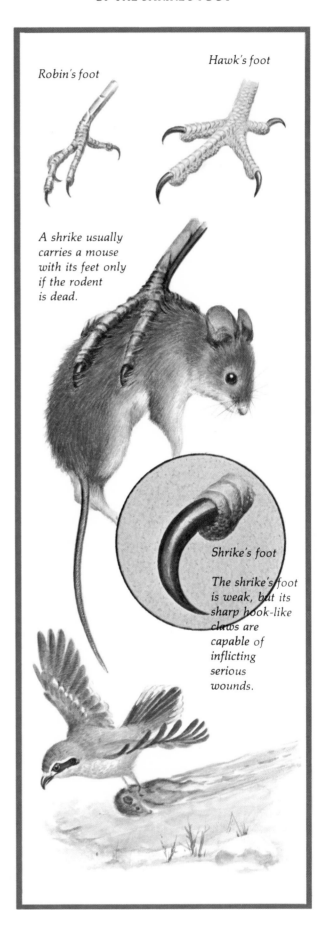

Robin's foot

Hawk's foot

A shrike usually carries a mouse with its feet only if the rodent is dead.

Shrike's foot

The shrike's foot is weak, but its sharp hook-like claws are capable of inflicting serious wounds.

Open-air larder
of the shrike

Shrikes depend
on the assistance
of a thorn or
fork in the tree.

Pellet or
casting

The northern shrike attacks *birds much larger than itself. The Germans call this bird the "nine killer" because it was said to kill nine songbirds each day.*

When the shrike kills more than *it can eat, it stores this excess using a variety of devices such as the thorns of a thorn tree or the fork or crotch of a tree or bush. It even uses barbed-wire fences to accomplish this purpose. It doesn't usually leave until its victim is securely fastened in this open-air larder. Whether or not the butcher bird returns is subject to its needs and food supply.*

HOW DOES THE SHRIKE STORE ITS FOOD?

The shrike caches its food in an unusual way. It makes a larder in the open air. Choosing a tree, the butcher bird lands on one of the lower branches. It then works its way up, hopping from branch to branch until it has selected a suitable place. If it has chosen a thorn tree, it will try to impale the corpse of its kill on one of the thorns, dashing it many times against the spike. Or it may wedge the victim's head in a fork of the tree.

The shrike employs this gory procedure for feeding as well as for storage. Because its feet are weak, the bird wedges its meal securely and then tugs at it with its bill in order to dismember it so that it can be eaten. Everything is eaten—meat, feathers, fur, and all, and indigestible parts are disgorged in the form of pellets or castings.

The shrike has a very good memory and will return to its storehouse to feed. But if food is plentiful, or if the morsels on the tree should become dry, the shrike may abandon its larder.

During nesting season the parent shrikes often maintain one of these storehouses near their nest since their young are ravenous eaters. By having such a supply the parents are better able to meet their offspring's needs.

HOW DOES SCRIPTURE ILLUSTRATE THE NEED TO REFUSE TO ENJOY ANYTHING THAT HARMS OTHERS?

God created a wife to be an helpmeet for her husband (Genesis 2:18). It is tremendously important for a wife that her husband's goals are honorable and just. What wife in Scripture used evil ingenuity to help her husband reach a wicked goal and lived to see God judge both of them for doing so?

(Pause for a response—see page 20)

The cold eyes of a wicked queen stared at her sulking husband. It was in her interest to keep everyone around her happy, but the king was greatly displeased and dejected. She played the part of a doting wife. "Why aren't you eating? What has made you so upset?"

The king answered as though he was a little boy telling his mother who hurt him. "I asked our neighbor if he would trade me his vineyard for a better one or accept money for it, but he refused." "Why would he refuse?" she probed. "Because he claims that the law of God prohibits such a sale." With irritation she demanded, "Are you the king or aren't you?" Then with a cunning gleam in her eye, she assured her husband, "Don't worry about it. I'll see that you get that vineyard."

The evil queen despised God's prophets and delighted in destroying them. Why should she allow a neighbor who kept God's laws to interfere with her husband's happiness? So she went about her deadly scheme against the vineyard owner.

Letters were sent in the king's name to the leaders of the city. "Call the citizens together, proclaim a time of fasting and prayer. Then put the vineyard owner on trial. Hire two men to falsely accuse him of cursing God and the king. Then execute him."

The leaders of the city followed her instructions.

When the report of the man's death reached the queen, she proudly announced to her husband, "Do you remember the vineyard your neighbor wouldn't sell you? You can have it now. He is no longer living."

The king grinned like a spoiled child used to having his own way, but when he left the palace to claim the vineyard he was met by a prophet of God. The king was startled and deeply convicted by the prophet's words.

"God has a message for you, O king. Isn't it bad enough to kill your neighbor and his family? Must you steal his vineyard, too? Because you have done this, dogs will lick your blood outside the city just like they licked the blood of your neighbor's. None of your sons will survive, and the dead body of your wife will be ripped apart by the dogs."

Several years later that king was killed in battle. As men washed his blood out of the chariot, dogs came and licked it. Later still, the general of the army entered the royal city. The wicked queen was waiting for him. She had painted her eyelids, fixed her hair, and was sitting in an upper window of her palace. The general shouted, "Throw her down."

The servants who surrounded her obeyed and threw her out the window. Her blood splattered against the wall. The general trampled her body beneath his horses. Later, soldiers were sent to bury her, but they found only the skull, feet and hands of that wicked queen Jezebel. The dogs had eaten her just as the prophet said they would. But even the dogs refused her bloodstained hands, her feet that were swift in running to mischief, and her corrupted mind that found joy at the expense of others when they stood in the way of her evil plans.

From I Kings 21 and II Kings 9:30-37

This ivory carving traces back to the general time and place of Jezebel. Her husband Ahab was a lover of ivory and built an ivory house. The woman may reflect the hair and eye styles that Jezebel was so concerned about.

This gold covered statuette of Baal is similar to the many that Jezebel introduced into the nation of Israel. Even after Elijah exposed Baal on Mt. Carmel, she continued to pursue her foolish worship of this man-made object.

These signet rings may be similar to the one Jezebel used to seal her wicked letter to the unjust elders of Jezreel. One stamps the impression while the other rolls it on the intended paper.

JEZEBEL SOUGHT HAPPINESS AT THE EXPENSE OF OTHERS

The life of infamous Jezebel illustrates a thorough fulfillment of the Mosaic command, "Thou shalt make no covenant with them, nor shew mercy unto them. Neither shalt thou make marriages with them; thy daughter thou shalt not give unto his son, nor his daughter shalt thou take unto thy son. For they will turn away thy son from following me, that they may serve other gods; so will the anger of the Lord be kindled against you, and destroy thee suddenly." (Deuteronomy 7:2-4)

TWO WICKED RULERS WHO DESERVED EACH OTHER

Jezebel was born into royalty. She was the daughter of Ethbaal, king of the Sidonians (I Kings 16:31). As a child she was taught to fear Baal, the god of Phoenicia. Baal was believed to control the fertility of the earth, beasts, and men. In a land with little water and uncertain rainfall, most people were zealous to procur his favor. The connection of Baal with fertility led to vile and abominable practices associated with his worship. Her husband, Ahab, was also born of a royal family. He was the son of wicked Omri, king of Israel. It is likely that the marriage of Ahab and Jezebel sealed a trade agreement between Israel and Phoenicia.

SHE LEFT HER HOMELAND BUT BROUGHT HER FALSE GODS

When Jezebel married Ahab she left her country, but she refused to abandon her religion. She became a self-appointed ambassador to spread the worship of Baal in the capital city of Samaria. She either imported or trained 850 men to assist in the worship of Baal (I Kings 18:19). She also initiated the slaughter of the prophets of the Lord (I Kings 18:4,13). When Elijah killed her prophets on Mount Carmel, Jezebel's hardened heart determined to kill him. Even this bold and courageous man of God who had stood alone against 850 prophets of Baal was unable to face the fury of Jezebel (I Kings 19:2,3).

AN INNOCENT DEATH TO SATISFY A SELFISH WHIM

The murder of Naboth reveals the worst side of Ahab's weak character and also displays the clever, scheming, even ingenious mind of Jezebel at its ruthless worst. When she discovered that Ahab was unable to obtain the field of Naboth which adjoined the summer palace in Jezreel, she confidently declared that it would soon be his.

Naboth refused to sell his inherited land on the basis of the Mosaic Law which was higher than Ahab's desires (Leviticus 25:23). Jezebel would not be thwarted by Naboth's righteous refusal, and so she arranged that two worthless witnesses be bribed to accuse him of blasphemy. The unjust jurors convicted him and sentenced him to death (cf. Deuteronomy 17:5-7). Jezebel caused the death of an innocent man. It was she, not Naboth, who deserved the death penalty for idolatry and blasphemy.

A REPUTATION THAT STILL LIVES

Although Jezebel outlived her husband by ten years, she did not escape a violent and humiliating death (II Kings 9:33). In Revelation 2:20, the name Jezebel is used for a false prophetess within the church of Thyatira who encouraged idolatry and immorality. Her name is synonymous today with wickedness and treachery. Jezebel's tragic epithet is given in conjunction with her husband's, "But there was none like unto Ahab, which did sell himself to work wickedness in the sight of the Lord, whom Jezebel, his wife, stirred up." (I Kings 21:25)

JEZEBEL CHARACTER SKETCH

WAS JEZEBEL GENUINELY CONCERNED ABOUT BRINGING JOY TO HER HUSBAND?

Jezebel was motivated more by a contempt for the Lord and righteous Naboth than by a noble desire to please her husband. Jezebel had seen Ahab "heavy and displeased" ever since the prophet of the Lord rebuked him for sparing the life of the king of Syria and made the bitter announcement that Ahab was to be killed for this sin (I Kings 20:42,43). Now Ahab "laid him down upon his bed, and turned away his face, and would eat no bread." (I Kings 21:4) To Jezebel, familiar with the despotic and ruthless rule of heathen kings, this action of her husband was weak and cowardly. Such behavior would not inspire the respect and fear she thought he deserved. She was furious with Ahab's fear over the Lord's prophetic word and his submissiveness to Naboth's refusal. If her husband was overthrown because of his weakness, she would lose her power and life of luxury as well.

WAS JEZEBEL'S INFLUENCE CONFINED TO THE COUNTRY OF ISRAEL?

Unfortunately, it was not. Jezebel's daughter, Athaliah, was given in marriage to the son of Jehoshaphat, king of Judah (II Kings 8:16-18). The marriage was designed to strengthen the military and economic relations between Israel and Judah, but the spiritual consequences were disastrous. Athaliah inherited her mother Jezebel's unscrupulous nature and influenced both her husband and son for evil. She exhibited her mother's zeal for Baal shortly after her husband took over the throne. Athaliah usurped the Davidic throne for six years after her son's death. To eliminate rivalry she murdered her own grandchildren. During her reign the worship of Baal was zealously promoted (II Chronicles 24:7). Athaliah was finally overthrown and replaced by her sole surviving grandson, Joash, who had been rescued from her slaughter (II Kings 11:1,2).

DID JEZEBEL'S ACTIONS BRING JOY TO ANYONE?

Jezebel did succeed in giving Ahab the vineyard he desired, but it did not bring him happiness. He was met at the field by the prophet Elijah who proclaimed to Ahab the Word of the Lord. "Behold, I will bring evil upon thee, and will take away thy posterity . . . The dogs shall eat Jezebel by the wall of Jezreel." (I Kings 21:21,23) His elation changed to depression, and "he rent his clothes, and put sackcloth upon his flesh, and fasted, and lay in sackcloth, and went softly." (I Kings 21:27)

The prophecy was fulfilled. Ahab was wounded in battle and died; the dogs licked up his blood (I Kings 22:35,38). His two sons who succeeded him on the throne both died violent deaths. One son, Ahaziah, was killed by a fall in the palace (II Kings 1:2,17). Another, Jehoram, was killed in his chariot by his successor, Jehu, and his body was cast into Naboth's plot of ground (II Kings 9:24,26). Jezebel was thrown down from her window and eaten by dogs (II Kings 9:33-36).

"And they went to bury her; *but they found no more of her than the skull, and the feet, and the palms of her hands."*

JEZEBEL
jĕz´ĕ-bĕl

251

Joyfulness

IS MAINTAINING A SPIRIT OF CHEERFULNESS DESPITE PHYSICAL LIMITATIONS

"My grace is sufficient for thee: for my strength is made perfect in weakness. Most gladly therefore will I rather glory in my infirmities, that the power of Christ may rest upon me . . . for when I am weak, then am I strong."

II Corinthians 12:9, 10

LIVING LESSONS ON JOYFULNESS . . .

FROM THE PAGES OF SCRIPTURE

Every person must be prepared for calamities. They are the truest test of character and motive. Under the strain of a disaster, some will turn to God; some will turn to human wisdom; others will give up and become bitter against God. The most important skill to be learned and used at such a time was demonstrated by a godly young man who experienced many catastrophes. This young man was greatly loved by God and is mentioned more often than any other person in Scripture. His name is recorded over 1,100 times. The skill which he learned and demonstrated through calamities enabled him to maintain a spirit of brightness despite physical limitations.

ILLUSTRATED IN THE WORLD OF NATURE

AMERICAN DIPPER *Cinclus mexicanus*

The dipper bird is also known as the water ouzel. It belongs to the genus *Cinclus* which consists of only five species. Four of these species are found in Europe, Asia, Africa, and South America. The other, the American dipper, inhabits the mountain ranges of western North America spreading south from Alaska to southern California and New Mexico. It seeks the clear, cool rushing waters of mountain streams and is especially attracted to waterfalls and rapids. Generally, the bird inhabits the shorelines of mountain lakes. Although it is not confined to any particular elevation, the dipper moves to lower levels when winter cold freezes the high streams. The ouzel is approximately eight inches long but appears much smaller because of its short, stubby tail.

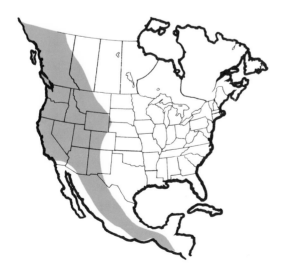

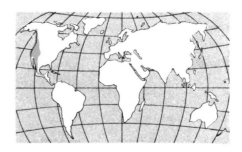

The range and habitat of the American dipper

JOYFULNESS

HOW DOES THE DIPPER ILLUSTRATE JOYFULNESS BY MAINTAINING A SPIRIT OF CHEERFULNESS?

It was a cold and dreary November day in the mountainous Northwest. The pouring rain was thick and slushy but not quite cold enough to form snowflakes. Over the past few weeks, heavy rainfall had swollen the rivers and streams. When the foaming torrents raced downstream, many new falls, rapids and cascades were created as the water rushed over and around huge boulders and stones.

A penetrating wind caused one to feel colder than the temperature actually was. The monotony of the chilling rain and the lifeless appearance of naked vegetation created a gloomy, depressing atmosphere.

Most birds of the area had already migrated south. Those that remained behind sat silent and numb near any protected shelter, huddled with their feathers fluffed out for maximum warmth. The area's reptiles and amphibians had entered their homes deep in mud and rocks to rest for the winter. Many other animals had sought shelter—some for the winter, others just until the rain came to an end.

Except for the sound of falling rain and rushing water, it seemed as though all activity had ceased.

Everything was silent and motionless. Everything, that is, except for one small bird which fluttered from rock to rock, surveying the turbulent waterway. Suddenly the bird disappeared. It had actually walked into the icy water! A few minutes later it reappeared on the opposite shore apparently undaunted and unhurt by its frigid plunge.

The amazing thing was that this bird did not seem suited for aquatic life. Its appearance resembled that of an overgrown wren, and yet it maintained its exuberant immersing activity in and along the stream. The more turbulent the water, the more it seemed to enjoy it. Repeatedly, the little bird entered the water and searched among the rocks for food.

This bird, the size of a robin, appears to have no special features to equip it for this activity. To the casual observer it would appear to be more at home in the forest than in a turbulent stream. Yet it moves in and around the water, easily and effectively navigating the streams despite its physical limitations.

Even more significant than this unusual activity is the fact that the dipper constantly has a song. Adverse weather seems not to affect it in the least. Even on the harshest day of winter the beautiful, cheery song of the little ouzel can be heard breaking the chilling silence of the landscape. Despite the dipper's physical limitations, it joyfully and energetically goes about its business with a song.

SCRIPTURAL REFERENCES TO THE DIPPER

The dipper, not mentioned in Scripture, belongs to the same family of perching birds as the sparrow. Both the dipper and sparrow have a reputation for making nests in unusual places. The dipper nests under stumps, beside rocks and roots, and even behind waterfalls.

"Yea, the sparrow hath found an house, and the swallow a nest for herself, where she may lay her young, even thine altars. . . ."
Psalm 84:3

The sparrow's ability to make its nest in almost any place is necessitated by the fact that it is such a prolific bird. It thrives best in man's environment and is found in practically every part of the world.

Sacrifices and fire would prevent the sparrow from nesting on the altar itself, but these small birds undoubtedly found a haven nearby.

The sparrow was abundant in Palestine during the time of Christ. He used the bird to illustrate and assure us of our Heavenly Father's care.

"Are not two sparrows sold for a farthing? And one of them shall not fall on the ground without your Father. Fear not, therefore; ye are of more value than many sparrows." Matthew 10:29,31

CHARACTERISTICS AND PHYSICAL FEATURES OF THE AMERICAN DIPPER

The dipper's joy was apparent as it delighted in the frigid, turbulent waters. Hardly a day passes that the ouzel does not serenade the countryside. Its cheery song begins in August and September. This melodious song, piercing even the roar of rushing water, continues to mount in tempo until it reaches its peak in spring.

Appearing always to be in motion, the ouzel busily dashes in and out of the icy waters in search of food. It scurries among rocks on the river's floor looking for aquatic life and knows exactly how to overcome the turbulence of the swirling, frigid waters.

HOW CAN THE DIPPER WITHSTAND SUCH COLD WATER TEMPERATURES?

The plumage of the ouzel is very dense. Its protective covering of feathers is thicker than either of its relatives the wren or the thrush. The ends of its feathers are also more loosely formed—a characteristic of other true water birds. This feature prevents the feathers from soaking up water.

The dipper is also aided by uropygial oil glands. These glands, located at the base of the tail, are approximately ten times larger than those of other Passerines. The dipper waterproofs its feathers with this oil. Because of its thick, warm, waterproof coat the dipper can stay warm and dry and remain unaffected by the icy waters.

The dipper's feathers afford another kind of protection as well. Their dull, slate color enables the bird to blend perfectly with the rocks and logs of rivers and streams.

HOW MANY EYELIDS DOES THE DIPPER HAVE?

The dipper's rather small eyes have three eyelids each. The upper eyelid and part of the lower eyelid are covered with a narrow border of short, white feathers. When the bird blinks its eyes these border feathers create a white flash.

Underneath these lids is a third eyelid or nictitating membrane. This membrane moves across the cornea in a semi-horizontal direction; the two true lids move straight up and down. The purpose of the third lid is to clean and wipe the cornea free of watery mist created by the spray and splashes of rapids and falls. The reflex of the nictitating lid is much quicker than the other two lids, and it is used more often. With all these eyelids, it appears as though the dipper is always winking.

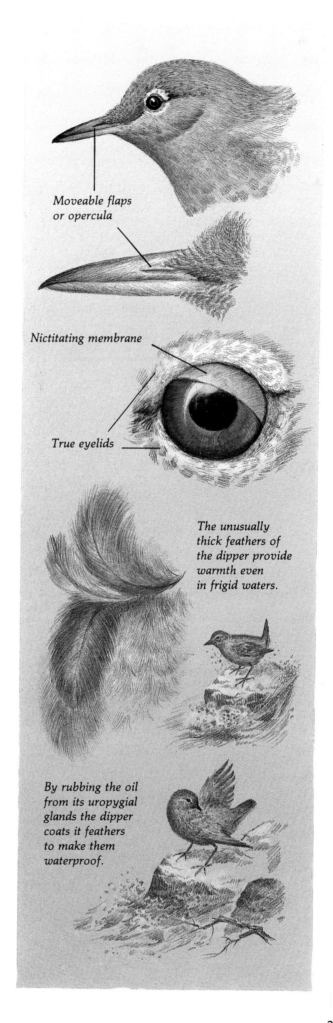

Moveable flaps or opercula

Nictitating membrane

True eyelids

The unusually thick feathers of the dipper provide warmth even in frigid waters.

By rubbing the oil from its uropygial glands the dipper coats it feathers to make them waterproof.

Foot of the
water ouzel

Using strong legs and feet, the dipper
walks on the bed of a stream.

The dipper can swim
but its progress is slow.

Ouzel uses current to its advantage.

CAN THE DIPPER BREATHE UNDER WATER?

No. Like other aquatic birds such as ducks, the dipper cannot breathe under water. It can hold its breath and remain beneath the surface up to ten minutes, but it must then return to the surface for oxygen.

The dipper does have some specialized equipment that even the duck lacks. On its nose are two flaps or seals which close off each nostril and prevent water from entering when the bird submerges. Two other interesting physiological features are its abilities to decrease its heartbeat from fifty-five to sixty-nine percent and to increase the amount of oxygen stored in its blood. The ouzel is North America's only perching bird that is purely aquatic.

WHY IS THE BIRD CALLED A DIPPER?

This bird has a characteristic habit very obvious to an observer. It is constantly engaged in a dipping or bobbing motion. Because of this action it has also been referred to as the "teeter bird", although the movement is not really a teeter such as that which characterizes the spotted sandpiper.

The dipper's is not an up and downward movement of the tail nor a downward movement of the head. Rather the bird's whole body moves as it bends its legs, first crouching and then standing up again. This up and down movement of approximately one inch is a constant motion which occurs approximately forty to sixty times per minute.

ARE THE DIPPER'S FEET EQUIPPED FOR WATER?

Yes—in their own way. The dipper's feet are not webbed like those of a duck or goose, but its legs are normal in length and strong. Its toes are large, long, and very strong. The first toe is much stronger than the rest, and the third is substantially longer than the first, second, or fourth—all approximately the same length. With its feet the bird can maintain a toehold and firmly grip slippery rocks and stones as it pushes against the strong current to walk along the bed of the stream.

The dipper can also swim on the surface of the water. It propels itself by using its feet. Because they are not webbed, its progress on the surface is slow, and the dipper does not usually swim more than a few yards at a time.

CAN THE DIPPER USE THE WATER CURRENT TO ITS ADVANTAGE?

Yes, but it does so in a way you would not expect. The dipper points its body headlong into the current and by spreading its wings, skillfully positions itself in such a way that the force of the current holds its otherwise buoyant little body under the water.

DOES THE DIPPER REALLY FLY IN OR BENEATH THE WATER?

By using its wings in an unorthodox way, the dipper can actually "fly" through the water. The manner in which the bird uses its wings in water is quite different from its technique in the air.

Its submerging dive is accomplished when the bird places its head beneath the surface and elevates the posterior part of its body, including its legs. Then with one or two strokes of its wings, the bird is propelled beneath the water.

To overcome gravity and sustain flight in the air, wings must provide lift and forward motion. Underneath the water, wings must overcome a different obstacle. Because the dipper's body is less dense than the water, its outstretched wings must overcome this natural buoyancy. The thrust of the wing's anterior edge moves the bird downward toward the bottom, and the return posterior movement propels it forward. When it wants to return to the surface, it changes the pitch of its wing.

It does not appear that the bird's legs assist its wings at this point. They are drawn close to the body. When the bird reaches the bottom it then uses its legs to help it move forward, particularly if the current is swift. They are also used in a paddling motion when the bird returns to the surface.

The dipper is not perfectly suited for water travel, for its feathers do not form an effective rigid surface to cope with the resistance of the water. This does not seem to bother the bird, however, for it simply works harder to reach its destination.

IS THE DIPPER AS COMFORTABLE IN THE AIR AS IT IS IN THE WATER?

The ouzel usually flies following the course of a stream or river. The bird is rather reluctant to take to the air, but if it must it glides just above the surface of the water, avoiding any obstacles or obstructions such as rocks, overhanging branches, or logs. Its wingbeat in flight is steady and rapid.

The bird does not normally dive from the air into the water, but rather walks into the water and then immerses. Or it may land on the water's surface and then dive in.

The dipper does not have a long southern migration flight as do many other songbirds. Its migration is limited to moving to lower elevations of the mountains when the higher stream and river surfaces freeze. The birds stay as long as possible, flying about in the snow to find air holes and diving beneath the ice. In the spring the dipper returns to higher altitudes to raise its young.

As the dipper travels up and down streams it flies close to the surface of the water.

10-1/2 inch wingspan

Sequential study of the wing movement under water

With open mouths chicks hungrily wait at the doorway of their unusual nest.

It is common for the ouzel to build its nest behind a waterfall for added protection.

Dipper bird "watering" its nest.

WHAT'S UNUSUAL ABOUT THE DIPPER'S NEST?

Both the structure of the nest and its location are unique. The nest is built almost entirely by the female. It resembles a large ball about a foot in diameter and is constructed with a neatly arched opening near the bottom. The female uses mosses, hypnum, and grasses to build it. These materials are neatly woven together. The floor of the nest is thinly lined with a layer of grass.

Many pieces of moss on the outer surface are green and living. Observations indicate that the dipper periodically "waters" these live plants by drying its feathers. It does so by standing on top of the nest and shaking its feathers free of the beaded water on its plumage.

The other unique feature is the nest's location. The female constructs its home near water, utilizing the protective cover of stumps, roots, and rocks along shore or midstream. It has even built its nest behind waterfalls. In order to reach its home it must fly through the waterfall which it accomplishes with ease.

The female dipper lays from four to five eggs. The dipper is extremely clean in its habits. If excrement is found in the interior of the nest, it is removed, and any soiled grass is carefully picked out and replaced. The young continue to use the nest for approximately eighteen days after hatching.

A favorite feeding place *of the ouzel is the waterfall. Here it finds small fish fry, larva, and insects and it also catches insects which have dropped into the stream, such as mayflies and caddisflies.*

HOW DOES SCRIPTURE ILLUSTRATE JOYFULNESS IN MAINTAINING A SPIRIT OF CHEERFULNESS DESPITE LIMITATIONS?

Joyfulness is maintaining a spirit of brightness despite physical limitations. When we expend our physical energies we become exhausted. When we drain our emotional energies we become depressed. Who experienced a personal calamity that should have destroyed his family, future, position, and possessions but by drawing on a special skill turned defeat into victory?

(Pause for a response—see page 20)

Our true self is revealed when all the things important to us are stripped away. God wanted to reveal the true self of a certain young leader. He and his six hundred men were just returning home from a battle in which they were not required to fight.

As they neared their city several shouted, "Look! Our city has been burned!" They ran toward the smoldering ruins of what had been their home and stared in shock and disbelief. Everything had been burned or taken away. A plundering band of soldiers had attacked while they were gone, taken their wives and children as captives, stolen their possessions, and burned their homes.

He and his men sat down and wept until they had no more strength. Then the anger and frustration of the men began to mount. Who was to blame? Their attention turned to their leader. Bitter words were heard. "Let's stone him. He is responsible for this."

This young man had known the praise and acceptance of an entire nation. He had had power and authority, riches, and reputation. Then he was rejected by the very one he faithfully served. Falsely accused, he was forced to flee. All he had were his family and a few faithful companions. Now he had lost his family, and those companions wanted to kill him. In that helpless moment of despair, he called upon a skill he had learned in the past and put it to its ultimate test.

His men watched and grew silent. The mood began to change, and soon there was a different spirit. Fresh courage and new hope was given. The real victory had just been won and a precedent had been set for all who would experience calamity in the future.

What happened next is exciting, but it is incidental. This leader and his six hundred men pursued the plundering enemy. They overtook and surprised their attackers while they were in wild celebration, destroying them through fierce fighting. They rescued those who had been taken captive and recovered all their possessions and more.

The secret of this young man's success was not his courage in battle, the might of his weapons, or his persuasiveness with people; but it was a skill he applied whenever he experienced personal sorrow or despair—the skill of encouraging his own heart in the Lord. He had learned to use the loss of temporal things to see more clearly the reality of eternal things.

Thus, in the depths of a calamity, David was able to experience the joy of spiritual reality through the motivation of physical limitations.

From I Samuel 30:1-20

Ziklag was located in the Negev wilderness. *This area is mountainous, has a scarcity of rainfall and few sources of underground water. The few people who lived there were easy targets for bandits from the south.*

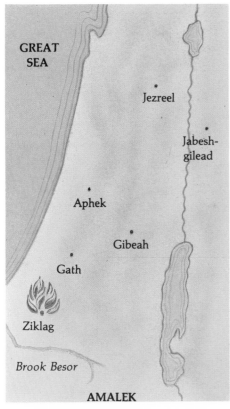

When David and his men returned *from Aphek to their home at Ziklag, they found it burned to the ground. They pursued the Amalekites over the brook Besor where they overcame and defeated them.*

DESPITE THE REJECTION OF THOSE AROUND HIM, DAVID MAINTAINED A CHEERFUL SPIRIT

David was not unfamiliar with danger, difficult decisions, and misunderstandings. As a shepherd boy, he faced the peril of wild animals preying on his flock. As a young man, he faced the dangerous Goliath in hand-to-hand combat. He had been misunderstood by his oldest brother, Eliab, who accused him of pride and naughtiness of heart (I Samuel 17:28). His great military triumphs in behalf of his country were interpreted as a threat by King Saul, and his motive was misunderstood (I Samuel 18:5-9).

A MISUNDERSTOOD LEADER WITHOUT A HOME

He had made the difficult decision of fleeing from Saul to the enemy stronghold of King Achish where he was once again misunderstood (I Samuel 21:10-12). He chose to return to his own country as a fugitive. In an attempt to prove his loyalty to Israel, he rescued the inhabitants of Keilah from slaughter at the hands of the Philistines. He was rewarded by being betrayed by the men he had just saved (I Samuel 23:5, 12). Realizing that Saul's heart was hardened against him, he returned to King Achish in hope of securing protection for his growing family and the families of his six hundred men (I Samuel 27:1-4).

AN ENEMY WELCOMES HIM AND GRANTS HIM A CITY

Achish, now convinced that David was not an agent of Saul, welcomed him and his band into Philistine territory. He even granted David his request of a city. He gave him Ziklag, a city which had been allotted to the tribe of Simeon but was now controlled by the Philistines.

From Ziklag, David launched raiding parties against the nomadic invaders who terrorized southern Judah. This established favor among the elders of Judah but risked the wrath of King Achish. David was then faced with another difficult decision. Achish wanted David to accompany him in a major invasion of Israel. David agreed to go as Achish's bodyguard, but he must have been relieved when he was dismissed from battle by the four other Philistine generals (I Samuel 28:1,2; 29:9).

HIS HOME DESTROYED, HIS FAMILY CAPTURED, HIS MEN REBEL

When David returned home, he discovered that "the Amalekites had invaded the south, and Ziklag, and smitten Ziklag, and burned it with fire, and had taken the women captives that were in it; they slew not any, either great or small, but carried them away, and went on their way." (I Samuel 30:1,2) It was now, after years of pressure and anxiety, that David's world began to close in on him. Not only had his home been destroyed and his family taken captive, but the band of six hundred men who had supported him through the worst conditions now spoke of stoning him. "And David was greatly distressed." (I Samuel 30:6)

BUT HE "ENCOURAGED HIMSELF IN THE LORD"

In a situation like this Job's wife would have cursed God and died (Job 2:9). Elijah would have sat down under a juniper and requested death (I Kings 19:4), and Jonah would have said, "It is better for me to die than to live." (Jonah 4:8) "But David encouraged himself in the Lord his God." (I Samuel 30:6) After this time of renewal, he inquired of the Lord for direction. The Lord told David to pursue the Amalekites and promised complete victory. David and his men recovered their wives, children, and all their possessions.

Only a few days later Saul was killed in battle, and David was anointed king over the house of Judah (II Samuel 2:4). It was with true insight and understanding that David wrote, "It is God who avengeth me, and subdueth the peoples under me. He delivereth me from mine enemies: yea, thou liftest me up above those who rise against me. Thou hast delivered me from the violent man. Therefore will I give thanks unto thee, O Lord, among the heathen, and sing praises unto thy name." (Psalm 18:47-49)

DAVID CHARACTER SKETCH

HOW DID DAVID MAINTAIN A CHEERFUL SPIRIT DESPITE HIS PHYSICAL LIMITATIONS?

A previous event in his life gives us a clue to what David did. When he was so hurtfully wronged by the men of Keilah, Jonathan went to him "and strengthened his hand in God." (I Samuel 23:16) He strengthened David by reminding him of the Lord's promise that he was to be king over Israel. This was not merely an optimistic goal; the prophet Samuel had already anointed him for this purpose (I Samuel 16:13). In this moment of great distress, David must have again called to mind the promise that one day he would be the king of Israel. If he was to be king, then the Lord would not allow him to be stoned to death. He may have also reflected on the promise in the Law, "The eternal God is thy refuge, and underneath are the everlasting arms; and he shall thrust out the enemy from before thee; and shall say, Destroy them." (Deuteronomy 33:27) At this time David did not know how the Lord was going to deliver him, but he did know that he would be delivered.

WHAT WOULD HAVE BEEN THE RESPONSE OF A LESSER MAN?

It is significant that King Saul—whom David was going to replace—was in a similar state of distress at almost the exact moment. The Philistine army which had just dismissed David was camped in Gilboa. "And when Saul saw the host of the Philistines, he was afraid, and his heart greatly trembled." (I Samuel 28:5) Unlike David, Saul went to the priest for counsel without encouraging his heart in the Lord. There was no answer (I Samuel 28:6). In desperation to know the outcome of the battle, Saul violated his own decree and the Law of God by consulting a fortune teller (Deuteronomy 18:10-12). When he discovered that he was to die in battle, "Saul fell straightway all along on the earth, and was sore afraid." (I Samuel 28:20) With their leader in such a confused state of mind, it is little wonder that the Israelites were so soundly defeated. What a contrast to the outcome of David's battle with the Amalekites.

WHY WAS IT SO IMPORTANT FOR DAVID TO RENEW HIS JOY BY ENCOURAGING HIMSELF IN THE LORD?

The situation was very grave. "David and the people who were with him lifted up their voice and wept, until they had no more power to weep." (I Samuel 30:4) The Lord's solution for this situation was that the men pursue the Amalekites and battle against them. He had already prepared an Egyptian slave to point out the way (I Samuel 30:11-15). But in their present state of mind, neither David nor his men were in any condition to attack a group of professional fighters who greatly outnumbered them. Regarding warfare the Mosaic Law stated, "What man is there who is fearful and fainthearted? Let him go and return unto his house, lest his brethren's heart faint as well as his heart." (Deuteronomy 20:8) If this applied to a private, it applied doubly to the general. When the men observed David's renewed hope and strength, their strength and confidence were renewed; and they followed him on to a great victory.

"And David was greatly distressed; for the people spoke of stoning him, because the soul of all the people was grieved, every man for his sons and for his daughters. But David encouraged himself in the Lord his God."

DAVID
dā'vĭd

IS KNOWING AND BEING WHERE GOD INTENDED ME TO BE

"If ye keep my commandments, ye shall abide in my love . . . these things have I spoken unto you, that my joy might remain in you, and that your joy might be full."

John 15:10, 11

LIVING LESSONS ON JOYFULNESS . . .

FROM THE PAGES OF SCRIPTURE

A sense of purpose and a sense of belonging are basic to joyfulness. We must know that we are needed and that what we have to contribute is of value to others. Based on these ideas, what could four lepers know about joyfulness? Shunned by family and friends, their lives held no purpose. The lepers had nothing to give. They were aware that they were going to die, and they realized that in them were no resources for life. This is the basis for being "poor in spirit." God allowed these men in their pitiable condition to be in the right place at the right time to discover an important aspect of joyfulness.

ILLUSTRATED IN THE WORLD OF NATURE

BOBCAT *Lynx rufus*

Bay lynx or wildcat are two other names by which this carnivore is known. The bobcat is secretive and stealthy. Few see it or are aware that it is North America's most numerous wildcat. Until recently it coped very well with civilization, actually increasing its number and extending its range. Its coat color indicates its territory. A bobcat from the desert regions takes on a sandy, buff color; those from northern forest ranges are grayer with more distinctive markings. The color of the animal does not change as it matures nor differ between the male and female. The male is approximately ten percent larger and weighs thirty percent more than the female. In captivity the bobcat has lived from fifteen to twenty-five years.

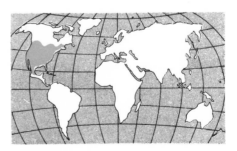

The range and habitat of the bobcat

JOYFULNESS

HOW DOES THE BOBCAT ILLUSTRATE JOYFULNESS IN BEING WHERE GOD INTENDED IT TO BE?

A blood-curdling scream pierced the silence of the night. Each time the father and son heard the cry they worked even faster to complete their task.

Their family was spending the summer in the Northwoods. Together they were building a small cottage on lakefront property which the father had acquired the year before. This was their family project, something they had all saved their money for and looked forward to—a place where they could retreat from pressures and interruptions in order to know one another better and meet each other's needs.

The father and son had gone into town to pick up supplies. On their way back one of the car's tires went flat because of a sharp stone on the unpaved surface. Even though they knew what the eerie sounds were, chills still crept up and down their spines. Hurriedly they completed the repair job and then continued on their way.

The sounds were those of a bobcat calling to its mate. In the weeks and months to come, this family would become very familiar with that wild animal.

Several days later as they once again returned home along the dirt road, they spotted an object rolling around in the dust. When they drove beside it, they stopped. It was a little kitten playing in the road.

The children excitedly jumped out of the car, but when they reached down to pick it up, they realized it was not a domestic house cat. Long tufts of hair on its

ears and its short stubby tail identified it as a young wildcat of the Northwoods. Since no parent cat was in sight, they concluded that it must have been abandoned. Despite its warning snarls and hisses, they picked it up. Feeling sorry for the orphan, the parents agreed to allow their children to care for it until it was old enough to take care of itself.

The children were diligent in their new task and spent much time trying to win its friendship. The kitten was a male bobcat and had a fierce disposition even at its young age. They hoped that with love and a little time they could win its confidence and affection.

For a while their attempts worked; it seemed to respond to their love and warmth. But despite all their efforts, the cat never appeared to be really happy. When they first picked it up it snarled and showed its teeth, but with each stroke it quieted down and gradually purred like a house cat.

The kitten seemed to love the outdoors and enjoyed going outside. When the children went to the lake to swim they tied a leash around its neck and brought it along. Although it was never too fond of the water, it romped up and down the shore looking for food and anything else that aroused its lively curiosity.

As time passed the animal grew from a little kitten to a mature cat and its disposition changed, reverting back to the wild. One minute it was gentle; the next it was savage and fierce, lashing out with its sharp claws if someone came too close.

The situation worsened. The cat's temperament simply wasn't suited for confinement. One day when the children were playing with a neighbor friend by the water, their guest teased the cat. In anger it leaped on the child's leg; its claws making deep cuts. The family was forced to face the fact that it was no longer safe to keep the cat confined. They decided to release it to its natural home. They freed their cat to return to the wild.

In subsequent years when members of that family heard the lonely call of the bobcat, they were reminded of their kitten and the fact that, although it looks like its domestic cousin, its personality and disposition are very different. One cat is tameable; the other is not. Their bobcat kitten did not really belong with them and would never truly be happy until it was released to return where its Creator intended it to be.

SCRIPTURAL REFERENCES TO THE BOBCAT

The bobcat is a close relative of the lion and demonstrates many of the same characteristics. The lion, mentioned over one hundred fifty times in over thirty books in the Bible, is an important symbol with much spiritual application.

"Be sober, be vigilant, because your adversary, the devil, like a roaring lion, walketh about, seeking whom he may devour." I Peter 5:8

A hungry lion in its own realm is cause for great caution and alertness. No other animal is so invisible in the darkness of night. Hunters report their inability to see a lion even though one may be so close he can hear its breathing.

The comparison made in Scripture between a lion and the devil is a warning which takes on added meaning when we consider the power, stealth and ferocity of the beast. Generally, a lion secures its prey in silence. It crouches close to the ground near its prey, watches, and in a moment strikes down a careless straggler.

"Will a lion roar in the forest, when he hath no prey?" Amos 3:4

"The fear of a king is like the roaring of a lion; whoso provoketh him to anger sinneth against his own soul." Proverbs 20:2

CHARACTERISTICS AND PHYSICAL FEATURES OF THE BOBCAT

The bobcat can be truly happy and joyful only when allowed to roam freely in the country where God intended it to be. It is never recommended to take an animal from the wild unless one knows for certain that its parents are dead. Many times they are just waiting behind cover until the intruder leaves so that they can retrieve and care for their young. Because a person can never administer the same kind of care natural parents can, it is almost always harmful to "adopt" the animal.

Many fruitless attempts have been made to tame the bobcat. In a few instances there has been limited success, but in the majority of cases cats retain their wild disposition and their owners are forced to release them or turn them over to a zoo.

One such account of a bobcat raised in captivity concerned the feeding of the pet. When the owner gave it raw meat, the bobcat became so wild that he had to throw the meat into the bathroom and slam the door behind the cat while it ate. If he opened the door too soon and did not allow sufficient time for the cat to finish, the cat would turn on its owner and attack him.

The bobcat distorts its face in rage with the slightest provocation. With hair ruffed and eyes flashing it bares its teeth, growls, and hisses in true fighting-cat fashion. The bobcat appears to do so more often and more readily than other members of the cat family.

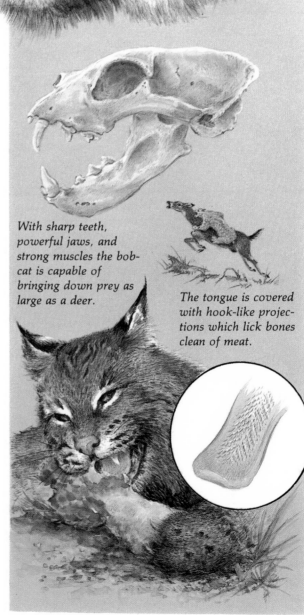

With sharp teeth, powerful jaws, and strong muscles the bobcat is capable of bringing down prey as large as a deer.

The tongue is covered with hook-like projections which lick bones clean of meat.

The bobcat eats a variety of food— *mice, squirrels, birds, even deer and antelope weighing ten times as much as the cat. The cottontail rabbit and varying hare make up about half of its diet.*

Ear tufts aid the bobcat in hearing.

Night vision

Day vision

When hunting, the bobcat pounces on unsuspecting victims from a high overhang.

WHAT'S SPECIAL ABOUT THE BOBCAT'S MOUTH?

Its sharp teeth and tongue projections. The bobcat is equipped with a total of twenty-eight teeth designed for tearing, piercing, and crushing. They are not exceptionally long, but they are sharp. In addition to its powerful mouth and muscles it has another special feature—hook-like projections on its tongue which point inward toward the throat. These sharp projections enable the bobcat to strip a bone of its meat and lick it clean in just a few minutes.

DO THE TUFTS ON THE BOBCAT'S EARS HAVE ANY PURPOSE?

Yes. The black hair tufts at the tips of the bobcat's ears collect sound waves and improve its hearing. Experiments involving captive bobcats show that when the tufts are cut off, the animal is not as alert to sound.

Besides its acute hearing, the cat also relies on its sight when hunting. The vision of the bobcat is sharper than most carnivores. The rods in its eyes are able to pick up much lower intensities of light than the cones. This gives the animal the ability to see at night. Although the eyes function well in dim light, the cat cannot see in total darkness.

The bobcat does not rely on its sense of smell to the same degree that a wolf does.

DO RODENTS HAVE A CHANCE AGAINST A HUNGRY BOBCAT?

Surprisingly, yes. If the cat is to be successful it must use its full concentration and skill to capture a rodent.

The bobcat cannot hurry but must patiently wait for the right opportunity. It seldom tracks its prey by following a scent with its nose. Instead, it locates the potential victim with its eyes and ears and then stalks, trying to get within as close a range as possible. Then the cat will spring.

If the animal catches a glimpse of it or if the cat miscalculates so the prey escapes the first pounce, it is unlikely that it will pursue the swifter rodent for more than a short distance. In order for the cat to capture a

The bobcat's claws are a major hunting tool. *When it overtakes a rabbit, it knocks it off balance by flipping it into the air with these hooked weapons. The claws are short but very sharp.*

To keep its claws sharp, the bobcat retracts them, protecting them from needless wear.

The bobcat sharpens its claws by scraping them against a tree.

Tree used to sharpen claws

The porcupine is sticky business for the bobcat.

snowshoe rabbit, it needs to be within forty feet before attacking.

HOW CAN A BOBCAT BRING DOWN A LARGE DEER?

First, the bobcat hides in a strategic position and quietly waits for a deer to pass by. Or if the cat happens to see a deer roaming the forest, it will stalk the animal. When it is within several feet of its prey, it makes a tremendous leap, trying to grab the deer's head with its front legs and foreclaws.

The cat tries to clamp its teeth around the victim's neck and throat at the base of the skull. With quick, strong bites the predator pierces the skin with its foreteeth; the victim bleeds to death.

The bobcat's skill usually prevents the victim from running more than thirty yards, but there have been records of the combatants traveling a considerable distance before the cat is shaken off or its victim is killed.

Bobcats attack antelope as well as deer. Big game animals killed by the bobcat are usually weak, lame, very old, or very young. A healthy deer is too quick for the bobcat and can generally elude it.

If the kill is successful, the cat begins voraciously eating its victim at the top of the hindquarters, turning the skin inside out. It eats anywhere from one to five pounds before it has had its fill.

The cat buries for future use that part of the carcass which it does not eat. Tainted meat does not seem to bother the animal. Like other cats, it washes itself after each meal.

WILL A BOBCAT EAT A PORCUPINE?

Studies indicate that porcupines constitute a major part of the cat's diet in certain localities. Even the quills are swallowed, and they do not seem to cause injury to the cat, although they can work their way through the walls of the intestines.

If the cat fights with a porcupine and its quills lodge in its mouth and paws, infection may set in. Then it would be impossible for the predator to eat, and it would subsequently die of starvation.

WHAT CAUSES A BOBCAT THE MOST TROUBLE?

Its own curiosity. Like a domestic cat the bobcat is very curious and explores and investigates anything that attracts its attention. Trappers who seek this animal for its soft fur exploit the cat's curious nature to their advantage. With a number two trap and catnip oil as bait, the bobcat can be easily caught.

IN A FIGHT BETWEEN A DOG AND A BOBCAT, WHICH WOULD WIN?

Even a dog three times the size of the cat is no match for the little scrapper. The snarling and ferocious bobcat either holds the dog at bay or defeats it. Even against three or four dogs it will put up an admirable fight, viciously striking with its claws and teeth.

WHERE DID THE TERM "WILDCAT BANK" COME FROM?

It is believed to have originated in a midwestern bank during the early part of the nineteenth century. Notes were issued bearing a picture of a bobcat. They had no financial backing and were very risky to deal with. Other banks issued the same kind of note, and they soon became known as wildcat banks. This term caught on and was later applied to any unsound commerical enterprise involving high risks.

"Wildcat" can refer to an oil field where the drilling is haphazard and there is no certainty that oil lies beneath. The term is also used to describe unexpected labor strikes within industries.

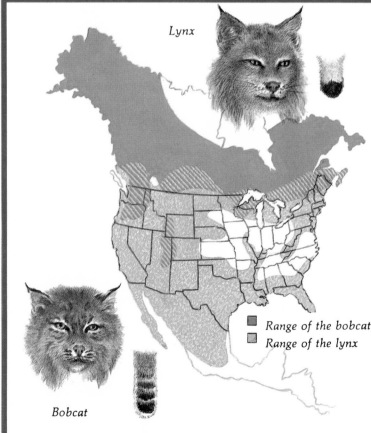

Lynx

Bobcat

Range of the bobcat
Range of the lynx

HOW DOES THE BOBCAT DIFFER FROM THE LYNX?

The bobcat is not as shy as the lynx, and it does not inhabit areas where snow is deep for several months at a time. The lynx lives in primitive forests and retreats farther and farther within them as timber is cut down. The bobcat, on the other hand, enjoys open country and has been able to avoid men and survive despite civilization. The animals differ in appearance, too. Tufts of fur on the lynx's ears are approximately one and a half inches long; the bobcat's are an inch or less in length. The markings on the tails also vary. The tip of the bobcat's has black bars whereas just the tip of the lynx's tail is black.

HOW DOES SCRIPTURE ILLUSTRATE JOYFULNESS IN BEING WHERE GOD INTENDED?

Jesus taught that unless we are prepared to lose our life for His sake we will never find it, and if we try to save our life for our sake we will lose it. Where in Scripture did four men save their lives and bring a message of joy to others because they were prepared to lose them?

(Pause for a response—see page 20)

Four ragged, starving men slumped against the city wall. They stared blankly into the distance. Death stared back at them. They could see a huge army waiting for their beseiged, starving city to surrender. Within the walls a frantic woman cried out to the king. When he gave her permission to speak, she poured out a shocking story.

"This woman said to me, 'Give your son that we may eat him today and we will eat my son tomorrow.' So we boiled my son and ate him: and I said to her on the next day, 'Give your son that we may eat him.' But she has hidden her son."

The horrified king rent his clothes. News of what had happened reached the ears of those four starving men. It stirred them to action, but what could they possibly do? If they entered the city, they would die of starvation. If they remained where they were they would also perish from hunger. If they retreated to the camp of the enemy, they would probably be killed.

Actually, these men were in exactly the place that God wanted them to be. The very law of God prescribed that they should remain outside the city. Each of them was afflicted with the dreaded disease of leprosy. They were forbidden to be with other people.

The lepers began to reason among themselves. "Let us go over to the camp of the Syrians. If they spare us, we shall live; and if they kill us, we shall but die."

When the four men reached their camp, they found it empty. God had caused the enemy to hear the pounding of hoofbeats, the sound of chariots, and the shouts of a great army. The troops had fled in terror, leaving everything behind, in the belief that they were being attacked. Tents, horses, food, and their possessions all remained for the taking. With delight the lepers went from tent to tent, satisfying their hunger and scooping up silver, gold, and clothes. They took it out to hide it and then came back for more.

Suddenly they stopped and realized what they were doing. For years they had survived by the generosity of their neighbors. They were always receiving and never able to give. They knew how it felt to be hungry and watch well-fed people pass by without caring. Now they were in a position to give, and their city was full of people who were starving to death.

They said to each other, "We are not doing right. This day is a day of good tidings. If we hold our peace—if we wait until the morning light, some mischief will overcome us: now therefore come and let us go and tell the king's household."

Because the four lepers of Samaria were where God wanted them to be, they experienced the joy of reporting a life-giving message.

From II Kings 6:24-7:20

THE LEPERS HAD A JOYFUL MESSAGE BECAUSE THEY WERE WHERE GOD INTENDED THEM TO BE

Benhadad, the king of Syria, had been frustrated in his plans to conquer Israel. He had attempted to weaken the nation with bands of terrorist raiders, but the prophet Elisha always revealed their target to the king of Israel and foiled the attack. Benhadad even tried to assassinate the prophet and was humiliated in the attempt. Now he decided to mobilize the entire Syrian army and besiege Samaria, the capital city of Israel.

CONQUERING A CITY BY STARVATION

Samaria was the most strongly fortified and protected city in the country, and its booty included King Jehoram and the enemy, Elisha. The Syrians' strategy was not to break into the city by force but rather to starve the people into submission. Samaria was ideally located on a three hundred foot hill, but the city spring was a mile away. Water had to be stored in cisterns inside the wall. As a result, the supply was limited—a severe defensive weakness during a prolonged siege.

Benhadad's new strategy was working as planned, and it appeared as if his patience was soon to be rewarded. The occupants of Samaria were starving. Soon they must open the gate and surrender, or die. Elisha, in consultation with the elders of the city (II Kings 6:32), was evidently counseling not to surrender but rather to wait upon the Lord for a miraculous deliverance. King Jehoram was willing to wait until one day when a woman cried to him for help. She described how she had boiled her own son and shared him with her neighbor. Now her neighbor refused to share her son, and the woman appealed to the king for justice. This atrocious act of cannibalism caused Jehoram to tear his clothes in grief.

THE KING TRIES TO PIN HIS PLIGHT ON THE PROPHET

The king blamed the prophet Elisha for his poor counsel, but the real cause of the situation was the king and his people's disobedience to the Word of the Lord. Moses had accurately predicted that, "The tender and delicate woman among you, who would not adventure to set the sole of her foot upon the ground for delicateness and tenderness, her eye shall be evil toward the husband of her bosom, and toward her son, and toward her daughter, and toward her young one who cometh out from between her feet, and toward her children whom she shall bear; for she shall eat them for want of all things secretly in the siege and straitness, wherewith thine enemy shall distress thee in thy gates." (Deuteronomy 28:56, 57)

THE ENEMY HAD FLED, BUT NO ONE KNEW

The king, believing that the situation was unjustly caused by the Lord, angrily vowed to kill the prophet of the Lord that very day. But Elisha predicted that the famine would end within twenty-four hours (II Kings 7:1). That very evening the Lord worked the predicted miracle. The Syrians imagined that they heard the sound of chariots, horses, and a great army coming from the north and the south. They suspected the powerful Hittites and Egyptians (II Kings 7:6). The Syrian army left their tents, animals, and provisions and fled east across the Jordan River in a desperate attempt to reach safety. The starving occupants of Samaria were at liberty to come out from behind their walls to eat and drink freely, but no one inside the city knew what had happened.

THEY TRIED TO HOARD THE TREASURES, BUT THEIR CONSCIENCES WOULDN'T LET THEM

The good news of their freedom from the Syrians came from a most unlikely source. Four lepers who lived outside the walls of Samaria were also starving. They finally decided to risk death and enter the Syrian camp in hope of finding some food and water. The surprised lepers arrived only minutes after the Syrian army had fled (cf. II Kings 7:5,7). They ate and drank until they were satisfied. Then the lepers began to hoard the silver, gold, and clothing which remained.

In a short time they experienced guilt about withholding the great news of freedom from the people. They announced their good tidings to a skeptical city which decided to investigate the report. When the investigators returned with a confirmation, the people of Samaria stampeded to the food and water. The city was saved. Of the four lepers we read nothing more. It is certain, however, that they would not have been able to enjoy their spoil had they refused to share their good news with others.

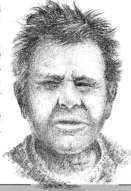

The person who had leprosy or was suspected of having the disease *was to be "shut up" outside the city gate. There that person would remain, an unclean outcast, for the rest of his life or until he was pronounced cured by the priest.*

"And the priest shall look on the plague *in the skin of the flesh: and when the hair in the plague is turned white, and the plague in sight is deeper than the skin of his flesh, it is a plague of leprosy: and the priest shall look on him, and pronounce him unclean."*

SYMPTOMS

1. Intermittent fever accompanied by aching bones and headache. There may be periods of several weeks or months between attacks.
2. Hoarseness due to lesions in the larynx and pharynx.
3. Generalized itching.
4. The first lesion that is noticed is most often a depigmented patch of skin.
5. The later eruptions tend to be localized and become nodular, tubercular, or ulcerated.
6. Acute periodic outbreaks of skin lesions characterize the course of the disease. These attacks are preceded by vague pains and followed by fever.
7. Hair falls out in the affected areas. Loss of the eyebrows is an early and characteristic symptom.

MODERN TREATMENT

Complete recovery is the exception rather than the rule. Treatment is most effective in early cases in young, strong individuals. A change of climate, good food, and proper hygiene exert a beneficial influence.

FOUR LEPERS CHARACTER SKETCH

HOW DID GOD BRING THE LEPERS TO THE PLACE WHERE THEY COULD BE USED?

The lepers knew that if they took no action, they would soon die. They had nothing to lose by asking the Syrians for food. "If they save us alive, we shall live; and if they kill us, we shall but die." (II Kings 7:4) Death held no sting for these men. In fact, it might have been viewed as a welcome release from their difficult and at times painful existence. Because of the contagious nature of their disease, strict isolation laws were imposed which made the lepers feel like feared outcasts. The disease could flare up for hours, days, or weeks during which time the victim would suffer fever, pain, and prostration. A leper could live as long as ten to twenty years, but death by tuberculosis or some other invasion of the weakened body was probable. The only hope a leper had was that his leprosy was of the less severe tuberculoid type which, even if untreated, can heal in one to three years. These men lived in the presence of death constantly; they were free from its fear.

HOW DID THE LEPERS DEMONSTRATE HUMAN NATURE WHEN THEY DISCOVERED THEIR FREEDOM?

"And when these lepers came to the uttermost part of the camp, they went into one tent, and did eat and drink, and carried thence silver, and gold, and raiment, and went and hid it; and came again, and entered into another tent, and carried thence also, and went and hid it." (II Kings 7:8) They acted like self-centered men with a strong tendency toward materialistic greed. They knew that once the city realized what had happened, there would be a stampede to the camp. As lepers, they were prohibited by law from coming near a non-leper. This meant that they would have to get their spoil before the crowds came. They also must have been tired of begging for food and clothing from the Samaritans. If they had enough silver, gold, and clothing they would never have to beg again. Knowing that this was an opportunity that would never be repeated, they were storing up for the rest of their lives. The only problem with their plan was that their consciences would not cooperate in their self-centered endeavor.

HOW DID GOD REWARD THE LEPERS FOR BEING WHERE HE INTENDED THEM TO BE?

Godliness is the opposite of self-centeredness. The Mosaic Law was clear in its command: "Thou shalt not avenge, nor bear any grudge against the children of thy people, but thou shalt love thy neighbor as thyself: I am the Lord." (Leviticus 19:18) When a certain legal expert summarized the main duty of the Law he said, "Thou shalt love the Lord thy God with all thy heart, and with all thy soul, and with all thy strength, and with all thy mind; and thy neighbor as thyself." (Luke 10:27) These lepers, so dependent on the charity of the citizens of Samaria in the past, could not withhold this new-found fortune from them. Possibly that very night another child would be boiled and eaten. Possibly that very night another weak man or woman would die of starvation. They realized that their self concern was not right. They were not treating their neighbors in the city as they were treating themselves until they came to their senses and proclaimed the good news to the men of the city. Soon everyone was comfortably fed. The lepers were heroes and experienced the satisfying joy of knowing that they had played a part in saving an entire city from death.

"Then they said one to another, *We do not well. This day is a day of good tidings, and we hold our peace. If we tarry till the morning light, some mischief will come upon us; now, therefore, come, that we may go and tell the king's household. So they came and called unto the porter of the city."*

FOUR LEPERS

275

Hospitality

"In my Father's house are many mansions: if it were not so, I would have told you. I go to prepare a place for you. And if I go and prepare a place for you, I will come again, and receive you unto myself; that where I am, there ye may be also."

John 14:2, 3

PART SIX

IS MAKING SURE THE ENVIRONMENT IS SUITABLE FOR THOSE WE SERVE

"Let brotherly love continue. Be not forgetful to entertain strangers: for thereby some have entertained angels unawares."

Hebrews 13:1, 2

LIVING LESSONS ON HOSPITALITY . . .

FROM THE PAGES OF SCRIPTURE

In the days when Scripture was being written, individual citizens were expected to welcome a traveler into the safety and comfort of their own home. Today the traveler simply stays at a local motel. But hospitality does not just comprise caring for the needs of a traveler. Hospitality also involves benefits and blessing for the host's home and family. Scripture urges us not to neglect hospitality. Through it some have even entertained angels unaware (Hebrews 13:2). There are many illustrations of genuine hospitality in Scripture. One example shows how a gracious hostess who provided a suitable environment for a traveler was greatly rewarded by her guest. The Scriptural account demonstrates the truth that in the same way we give to others, God gives to us.

ILLUSTRATED IN THE WORLD OF NATURE

DEER MOUSE   *Peromyscus maniculatus*

The deer mouse is a sociable little creature with a communication system all its own. Mice communicate with one another through a series of rapid taps against a hard surface. This sound can be imitated by drawing one's fingernail over screen wire. The tone and volume of sound vary depending on the object on which they drum. It is an accomplished soloist, too. At its best it is able to buzz or sing for a period of five to ten seconds. These little animals have long, bi-colored tails which are at least one-third their total length. The mouse molts once a year in August. There are some color variations among the animals, and the male is slightly larger than the female.

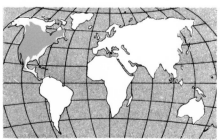

The range and habitat of the deer mouse

HOSPITALITY

HOW DOES THE MOUSE ILLUSTRATE THE NEED TO MAKE SURE ITS ENVIRONMENT IS SUITABLE?

It did not take them long to decide to stay. There was plenty of food and an array of assorted materials which could be used to build a warm, comfortable nest.

The spot the mice had chosen was a summer home located on the Atlantic coast's oceanfront. Unoccupied for the past few years, the beach house had only recently acquired new owners. For the next few weeks the owners would visit only on weekends, but when school was over they planned to stay for the whole summer. They were not aware that two mice had chosen their cottage as headquarters. They carelessly left food out on the counter, and each night the little deer mice had a feast.

But something even more important than food was on the female's mind now. She needed to begin building a nest for her family. Searching in every nook and cranny, she looked for a suitable place. The nest should be close to the food supply and yet her young must be protected from possible danger.

After looking for quite awhile, she found what seemed to be an ideal location. She climbed inside a box-like structure for a final look of confirmation. Then she began to make many trips bringing soft material with which to form a warm, snug home for her expected family.

Her mate came to join her. At first she fought his advances. Then the tables were turned, and the disinterested male played "hard to get." After much coaxing, she finally won his cooperation, and he joined her in the nest. But the reversals weren't over yet. When the time came for her to have her young, she again chased the male away. Not long afterwards five hairless little mice lay in the soft material.

Until now, it seemed to be an ideal home. Then the owners returned to spend another weekend in preparation for their summer stay. The little deer mouse was extremely cautious not to expose her family or reveal the nest's location. She would wait until everything was quiet before slipping out of the nest to feed that night.

But despite her intentions of good hospitality, the mouse family was in danger. As she sat on the nest waiting for the commotion in the room to subside, she grew warmer and warmer. It became uncomfortably hot. At first she did not sense anything unusual, but as the heat became more intense, she knew something was wrong. Because she was a good mother, she stayed with her helpless young. She hoped this would pass, but instead it grew hotter and hotter.

Soon an awful aroma permeated the beach house. The owners had cooked their meal for the evening, and they had cooked the visiting family of mice as well.

The structure had provided a protected and secluded environment, but the oven made an unsuitable home for the infant family.

SCRIPTURAL REFERENCES TO THE MOUSE

"Wherefore ye shall make images of your . . . mice that mar the land." I Samuel 6:5

Even though the Philistines were a heathen nation they understood that the destruction of their livelihood from the forces of nature or wildlife was in the control of God. They examined their ways and removed the cause of God's anger by returning the sacred Ark of the Covenant which they had previously captured in battle.

"These also shall be unclean unto you among the creeping things that creep upon the earth . . . the mouse . . . after its kind." Leviticus 11:29

The Hebrew word for mice comes from two words which signify destruction of corn. The word referred to several different species of the rodent. One species will devour every kernel of corn and any sapling that is planted. It even burrows under the ground to dig out the seed before it sprouts. In spring it eats the green blades; in harvest it climbs the stalks to plunder the ripe ears. Later, the mouse invades the barn and continues to feast.

CHARACTERISTICS AND PHYSICAL FEATURES OF THE DEER MOUSE

The place which the deer mouse selected and prepared was not a suitable home for her young. As a result, they perished in the heat. Such an incident is not uncommon, for the mouse is quick to make its home in any convenient location. The female is loving and available to her young, but she does not always choose an appropriate environment in which to raise them.

HOW AND WHERE DOES A DEER MOUSE MAKE ITS NEST?

One likely nest site is a tree. The mouse chooses either the interior—an abandoned squirrel's or woodpecker's home—or an exterior site—a bird's deserted nest. If it chooses the latter, it adds to the top of the structure to form a woven ball. It constructs two entrances, holes barely large enough for the mouse to fit through. The parent may build the nest on the ground underneath an old stump or log, in stone walls, cliffs or caves. Another favorite location is buildings, abandoned or occupied.

Mice have infuriated and frustrated many with their choice of nest-making items. It does not show particular preferences and is just as quick to use the fabric from a favorite sweater as the cotton from an old, worn-out sweatshirt.

These little rodents are very creative in gathering material. An observer once watched a deer mouse strip off the paper covering on plasterboard. It grabbed the paper at the top of the wall, jumped off and scaled down the steep side tearing strips as long as two feet. Over a period of time the little mice stripped the board down to the bare plaster all along the top of the wall.

Equally resourceful are some of its nest locations—sealed boxes, closed drawers, mattresses, and even shoes! One incident is recorded of a man who took off his boots at seven o'clock in the evening, and found a nest containing young inside one boot when he returned at ten!

HOW CAN YOU DETERMINE WHO THE HEAD MOUSE IS?

Mice group together for warmth during the winter. There is a class structure within the group itself. If they form a circle, the dominant mouse will be at its center taking the warmest spot, and the lesser ones on the outskirts. Any interloper or intruder to the group is chased away.

Dominant mouse

Using grasses and other soft material the mouse weaves a dome over an abandoned bird nest to form a ball-like structure.

The deer mouse frequently uses an abandoned squirrel or woodpecker nest for its home.

A female may have her first family *when she is only 35 days old. It will be small in number but with successive breedings she begins to average from three to six young per brood. The normal litter is four offspring. She begins breeding in February or early March and has a gestation period from twenty-one to thirty-seven days. She may have as many as four broods from February until November.*

At birth their toes are stuck together. The tips of the ears appear to be fastened down over the openings.

Mother dragging its young.

Post juvenile

THREE COLOR STAGES

HOW MANY YOUNG CAN THE FEMALE RAISE?

Although a normal litter averages from three to six, the female mouse can handle more young than the six mammary glands she has for feeding. Unlike young opossums which permanently attach themselves to the nipples, baby mice share. They take turns feeding and thus allow the mother to care for all if the litter is larger.

HOW DEVELOPED ARE THE YOUNG AT BIRTH?

Baby mice are blind, and their ears flop down over the ear openings giving the appearance of lumps. Their toes are stuck together except at the tips. Mice are pink and hairless except for their tiny whiskers and eyebrows. The mother is careful to lick them thoroughly clean and eat the afterbirth. The young weigh 1.5 to 2 grams at birth and measure approximately an inch and a half long.

DEVELOPMENT SEQUENCE OF YOUNG MICE:
FOUR DAYS

At four days of age their ears pop up, although the opening is still sealed. Their front toes separate. Mice begin to show a few gray hairs on their upper parts and white hairs on their underside. Their skin is still very loose. The young continue to nurse and sometimes hold on so tightly that, when the mother leaves the nest, she drags them out with her.

SEVEN DAYS

At seven days of age mice are nearly covered with fur and are approximately three inches in length from nose tip to the end of their tail.

NINE DAYS

At nine days mice are still blind but their ears are open. They are now four inches long and very active.

FOURTEEN DAYS

At fourteen days their eyes open.

TWENTY-FOUR DAYS

At twenty-four days mice are weaned and accompany the mother outside the nest. They have excellent hearing and are very sensitive to touch. Though their night vision is very good, the young appear almost blind in sunlight.

WHAT DOES FUR COLOR TELL YOU ABOUT A MOUSE?

Its age. Mice undergo three pelages. The first, or juvenile, is gray in color. The fur changes later during its post-juvenile stage and becomes richer, taking on a slightly brown appearance. When the mouse reaches adulthood, its fur is a rich brown shade.

Once the mouse has adult pelage, it usually undergoes one molt each year. Extreme wear and bleaching from saline soils may give the appearance of an additional molt.

Mice are very careful about their personal grooming. After each meal they thoroughly wash themselves with their tongues, cleaning from tip of tail to nose. They are careless, though, about maintaining cleanliness in the nest. As a result, within a short period of time unpleasant odors actually force them to move.

WHAT DOES THE DEER MOUSE EAT?

This mouse is carnivorous. It eats insects, insect larvae and eggs, and the flesh from carcasses of small dead animals and birds, although it prefers seeds, berries and nuts.

When tackling hard acorns, the mouse uses a special procedure. First it removes the cap and cuts the acorn in half around the middle. Then the mouse removes the meat from each half of the shell. The bitterness of some acorns such as the red, does not seem to bother the deer mouse, for it eats this fruit as readily as any other.

When feeding on hickory nuts, the mouse applies a different procedure. First it gnaws two holes on opposite sides of the nut, usually a quarter of the surface of each side. The mouse then carefully removes and eats the meat within. When it is through, it has usually removed every bit of food. The hardness of the shell does not seem to deter the mouse at all.

Other substances on which the mouse periodically feeds are antlers and the bones of dead animals. It is thought that the rodent eats these prior to breeding in order to offset a calcium and phosphorous deficiency. When these are not available, it eats certain plant roots and stems containing these nutrients.

The mouse is very tidy in its grooming.

Mouse pounces on insects to catch them.

Acorn

Hickory nut

Mouse has a set procedure to open nuts and acorns.

The mouse can store as much as two spoonfuls of seeds in its jowls at one time.

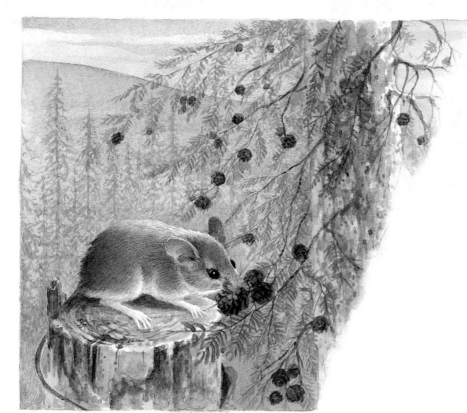

OFFSPRING

	10,000
	9,000
	8,000
	7,000
	6,000
	5,000
	4,000
	3,000
	2,000
	1,000
	2

← ONE YEAR →

The reproductive potential of one pair of mice

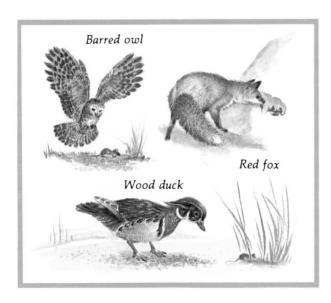

ENEMIES OF THE DEER MOUSE

The deer mouse is a menace and threat *to the conifer or pine tree forests. These rodents devour vast quantities of seeds both in natural and reforestation projects. It is estimated that they consume between three to four hundred Douglas fir seeds daily. They also invade corn fields and do similar damage there. They do benefit man by eating many harmful insects, usually in their larva and egg forms.*

HOW COMMON IS THE DEER MOUSE?

It is the most common of all North American rodents. The deer mouse is found almost everywhere south of the Arctic circle. Wherever mammalian life is possible, this mouse can be found. It lives as high as 16,000 feet above sea level and as low as 270 feet below sea level.

At approximately thirty-five days the females are sexually mature to reproduce; the male is capable at forty-five days of age. Their reproductive capacities are phenomenal; mice are capable of producing four generations in one year. If every member of every litter survived, one pair of mice could theoretically produce 10,000 offspring in one year! Because the mouse is a main food source for many predators, it must readily reproduce itself in order to maintain its species.

WHAT ENEMIES DOES THE DEER MOUSE HAVE?

Many. The deer mouse is a major source of food for nocturnal predators which range from the tiny shrew to the large bear. Both the red and gray fox take a large share of the mouse population. Snakes, too, are able to enter their dwellings and capture many of these rodents. There are even occasions when the wood duck preys on the lowly mouse. Probably the greatest threat is the owl—the horned, saw-whet, screech, and barred.

Because it is heavily preyed upon by such a wide variety of predators, it does not engage in play and is extremely alert to quick movement and sounds. The average life expectancy of the deer mouse can be as long as eight years in captivity, but because of the heavy pressure on it in the wild, it rarely lives to four years of age.

HOW DOES SCRIPTURE ILLUSTRATE HOSPITALITY IN PROVIDING A SUITABLE ENVIRONMENT?

One person in Scripture received a reward which meant joy, then sorrow, then great joy. It demonstrated the principle of birth, death, and fulfillment of a vision. Who provided hospitality that was not sought and received a reward that was not requested?

(Pause for a response—see page 20)

Those who knew her might have assumed that she and her husband lived in two different worlds. He was old. She was younger and very vivacious. He spent his energy in the field with his hired men. She spent long hours at home. Perhaps their close friends wondered what held them together. There were no children to bridge the gap of their age difference and to provide common concerns and interests.

But the fact was that she knew how to build fellowship with her husband and strengthen their happiness and security. Scripture calls her a "great woman." She was alert to the needs of those around her and discussed with her husband which needs they could meet with the resources God had given them.

One day she invited a servant of the Lord to share a meal with them. They invited him to return to their home whenever he passed through their village. He accepted their invitation and ate many meals with them.

She and her husband discussed how they could make their home more suitable for the needs of that servant of the Lord. They constructed an addition to their home—an extra room—and furnished it for their guests. God rewarded them for their care of His servant by giving them a child.

But the joy that was brought into their home by that child was turned to sorrow years later when their son died. The servant of the Lord was summoned, and he raised the child back to life.

After her husband died and a great famine spread throughout the land, the widow and her son were advised by the servant of the Lord to leave and live in a neighboring country for seven years. When she returned, she found that others had moved into her house and claimed possession of her fields. She went to the king to request the return of her house and land and was granted a hearing.

As she and her son entered the room a man who was talking to the king exclaimed, "Why this is the very woman I was telling you about and this is her son." This woman was then asked to explain in more detail how the servant of the Lord had raised her son to life. The king recognized that God had rewarded her and he purposed to add a further reward. He appointed an officer of the court saying, "Restore all that was hers, and all the fruits of the field since the day she left the land, even until now."

She gave fellowship, food, and lodging to the servant of the Lord. God returned to the Shunammite woman a son, a home, and fruitful fields. With these provisions she could continue to demonstrate the hospitality that made her a "great woman."

From II Kings 4:8-37; 8:1-6

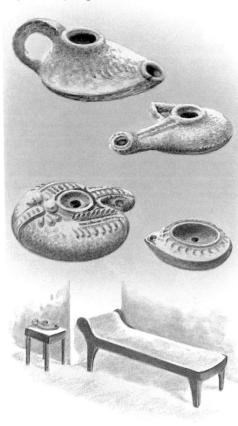

The lamps below are typical *of those used in ancient Israel. They burned oil by means of a lighted wick.*

The Shunammite provided Elisha *with a lamp by which he was able to read in the quiet of his room.*

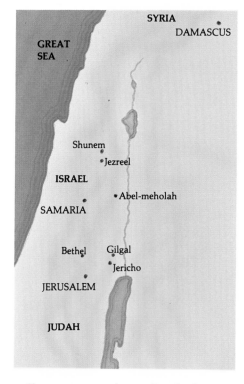

SYRIA
DAMASCUS
GREAT SEA
Shunem
Jezreel
ISRAEL
Abel-meholah
SAMARIA
Bethel   Gilgal
Jericho
JERUSALEM
JUDAH

Shunem was on the regular circuit **Elisha traveled** *which included Mt. Carmel, Gilgal, Jericho, and Bethel. He may also have visited his native town of Abel-meholah from time to time.*

288

THE SHUNAMMITE WOMAN PROVIDED A SUITABLE HOME FOR AN UNPOPULAR PROPHET

The town of Shunem is known primarily because of two women mentioned in Scripture who lived there. One was beautiful Abishag, David's nurse, who cared for him shortly before his death. The other woman is known as the Shunammite, the feminine form of Shunem in Hebrew. The former lived in a time of peace when the Lord was honored throughout the land. The latter lived in a time of religious apostasy.

A NEW KING MORE TOLERANT OF THE PROPHETS

Most of the priests and Levites, whose responsibility it was to teach the Mosaic Law, had been forced to migrate to Judah during the reign of Jeroboam. Elijah had tried to compensate for this loss with various schools for prophets, but Jezebel declared war against the prophets and killed many of them. Although Jezebel was still alive, she had lost some of her influence after the death of her husband.

Her son, Jehoram, was king of Israel. Although "he wrought evil in the sight of the Lord," he was "not like his father, and like his mother; for he put away the image of Baal that his father had made." (II Kings 3:2) King Jehoram feared Elisha and allowed him to travel about as he pleased in his ministry of teaching younger prophets and the people.

UNEXPECTED HOSPITALITY

Shunem was one of the towns on Elisha's regular circuit. Because of the deeply ingrained laws of hospitality among the Hebrew people, inns were not necessary at that time. Travel was difficult and dangerous; people considered it a sacred duty to offer any traveler a place to sleep in their own home (cf. Leviticus 19:34; Deuteronomy 10:18). Only the wicked dared close their doors to travelers (cf. Judges 19:15).

The prophets, however, were often looked upon with contempt in a land where only seven thousand had not bowed down and kissed the images of Baal (I Kings 19:18). In the religious center of Bethel, even the children had mocked Elisha "and said unto him, Go up, thou bald head; go up, thou bald head." (II Kings 2:23)

Elisha, familiar with scorn and mocking, was now being treated kindly by this hospitable woman of Shunem; he was overwhelmed with gratefulness. He must have joyfully anticipated the times he could spend in fellowship with her and her husband who had provided him with such a comfortable room. It was a place to restore his spirit before he had to leave and again endure the scorn of the Baal worshipers in Israel.

THEIR KINDNESS REPAID BY THE GIFT OF A SON

Because of her kindness to Elisha, the Lord removed her barrenness and gave her and her husband a son. Years later, when her young son suddenly became ill and died, she was grief-stricken. She knew, however, where to turn for help. Elisha was almost twenty miles away at Mount Carmel, and she said to her servant "slack not in riding for me, except I bid thee." (II Kings 4:24) The prophet responded immediately to her request. He went to the boy who had been placed upon a bed and "prayed unto the Lord." (II Kings 4:33) The boy sneezed, opened his eyes, and was returned to his mother who was henceforth referred to in Scripture as "the woman, whose son he had restored to life." (II Kings 8:1,5)

GOD CONTINUED TO REWARD

Years later, this woman was forced to appeal to the king for justice. When she entered his presence, he had just been told of the miracle of the resurrection of her son. He also had been informed of how she so graciously provided a room for Elisha. The king was so impressed that he granted her request and even more (II Kings 8:6).

The Shunammite lives on today as an example of hospitality demonstrated by her provision of a "prophet's chamber." Her idea has become an institution which has brought blessing to countless families—especially to the children of those families who have been exposed to the committed lives of men and women in the Lord's service.

SHUNAMMITE WOMAN CHARACTER SKETCH

HOW DID THE SHUNAMMITE WOMAN PROVIDE A GODLY ATMOSPHERE IN HER HOME?

Aside from the common laws of hospitality, which her neighbors were ignoring, the Shunammite gives evidence of other noble motives. At first she "constrained him to eat bread" and later "she said unto her husband, Behold now, I perceive that this is an holy man of God, which passeth by us continually." (II Kings 4:8, 9) How had she developed such a keen sense of spiritual discernment in a land of abject apostasy? The clue is given in a later reply by her husband, "Wherefore wilt thou go to him today? It is neither new moon, nor sabbath." (II Kings 4:23) This indicates that it had been her practice to meet at the prophet's house for worship and teaching on those days designated in the Law (cf. Leviticus 23; Amos 8:5). Prophets provided the few faithful people of the northern ten tribes with a substitute for the missing priests and Levites. By inviting Elisha into her home, the Shunammite had the privilege of sitting at the feet of the leader of all the prophets to bring his teachings and influence into her household. Such a great privilege and opportunity would not be overlooked by this wise and godly lady.

WHY DIDN'T THE SHUNAMMITE REQUEST A REWARD FOR HER HOSPITALITY?

When pressed for a favor that Elisha could do to show his gratefulness for the Shunammite's hospitality she responded, "I dwell among mine own people." (II Kings 4:13) She lived in peace and had no appeal to the king. Gehazi, the servant of Elisha, knew the real desire of her heart. Barrenness was often accompanied by the reproach of the husband and was considered a sign of judgment of the Lord (Genesis 29:32; II Samuel 6:23). The woman's husband was old; they had been unable to have children (II Kings 4:14). Although she believed in the Lord, she just could not muster the faith to ask for a son. She also did not want to raise her expectations again, merely to be disappointed. When her young son died she expressed this concern to Elisha by saying, "Did I desire a son of my lord? Did I not say, Do not deceive me?" (II Kings 4:28)

When Elisha, as God's spokesman, gave her this unspoken request, her response was similar to that of her godly ancestress, Sarah (Genesis 18:12). "And she said, Nay, my lord, thou man of God, do not lie unto thine handmaid." (II Kings 4:16) How blessed was this faithful woman of God. She had proved faithful in little and now was to have the opportunity to be faithful in much (cf. Luke 16:10).

WHAT WERE THE LASTING DIVIDENDS OF HER GENEROUS HOSPITALITY?

Because of the wickedness of the nation of Israel under the rule of King Jehoram, the Lord allowed the country to experience a seven-year famine to prod them to repentance. Elisha knew of the famine and told the Shunammite to take her household to Philistia for the duration. She returned to discover that her house and land had been illegally seized. It is almost certain that her husband had died by now (cf. II Kings 4:14,18; 8:2). She should have been able to appeal to the town elders, but they were unsympathetic to the Mosaic Law and easily bribed. Shunem was only three miles north of Jezreel where Naboth had been murdered for his land through the proceedings of a corrupt court (I Kings 21:8-14). When she appealed to King Jehoram, Gehazi had just told the king of the miracle of her son's restoration to life. As a result of this supernatural timing, the king restored all that was hers (II Kings 8:6). "The Lord will destroy the house of the proud, but he will establish the border of the widow." (Proverbs 15:25)

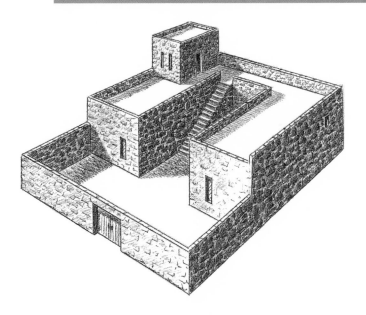

"Let us make a little chamber, *I pray thee, on the wall; and let us set for him there a bed, and a table, and a stool, and a candlestick. And it shall be, when he cometh to us, that he shall turn in thither."*

SHUNAMMITE WOMAN
shoo'năm-mīt

Hospitality

IS KNOWING HOW LONG A VISIT SHOULD LAST

"Withdraw thy foot from thy neighbors house; lest he be weary of thee, and so hate thee."

Proverbs 25:17

LIVING LESSONS ON HOSPITALITY . . .

FROM THE PAGES OF SCRIPTURE

Every father and mother have a responsibility to establish godly standards of conduct for their sons and daughters. Guests in their home should either demonstrate or desire to learn godliness. King David purposed that he would make the godly of the land his heroes and invite them into his home (Psalm 101).Hospitality ideally should include an agreed-upon schedule for both host and guest and clearly thought-out purposes for each visit. Idle conversation and overindulgences in eating are two dangers of entertaining without purpose. One of the most shocking crimes in Scripture took place because a host did not know how long a visit should last.

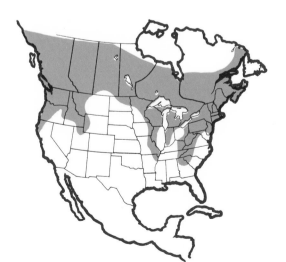

ILLUSTRATED IN THE WORLD OF NATURE

RUFFED GROUSE   *Bonasa umbellus*

The ruffed grouse, a native of North America, is known by many names—drumming pheasant, birch partridge, shoulder knot, grouse, and drumming grouse. It is approximately fifteen to twenty inches long and weighs between sixteen and twenty-eight ounces. The plump, succulent flesh of this bird is very delicious. The Indians of the northern United States and Canada relied heavily on it for food, and if the numbers of grouse were low in wintertime, it created a hardship for these northern tribes. The population of the ruffed grouse fluctuates; one year they may be in abundance—the next year, scarce. Grouse are believed to be at their peak every ten and a half years. The exact cause of the fluctuation is unknown, and hunting pressure does not seem to affect it. Even in refuges where hunting is prohibited grouse experience a periodic population decline.

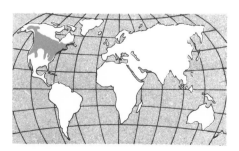

The range and habitat of the ruffed grouse

HOSPITALITY

HOW DOES THE RUFFED GROUSE ILLUSTRATE THE NEED TO KNOW HOW LONG A VISIT SHOULD LAST?

Large, fluffy snowflakes tumbled through the air. A blanket of white engulfed the forest, creating beautiful and spectacular sculptures. It was one of the first storms of the season, and the blizzard was so thick that it was almost impossible to see hemlocks fifty feet away. It had been snowing for only a little while, but during this time the white powder had accumulated several inches. The cold, north winds howled as they whipped and blew the snow into deep drifts.

Not yet accustomed to the biting cold, the few winter residents of the forest looked for shelter to protect themselves and gain a little warmth. Animals such as the bobcat, the white-tailed deer, and the snowshoe rabbit had grown thick coats. The grouse, too, had a warm, winter plumage to protect itself against the elements of cold. But even so, the frigid wind seemed to penetrate its insulated feathers. The bird sought refuge.

The grouse made its way through a curtain of falling snow as it left the protective bough of a spruce tree. It flew low to the ground and did something very unusual. With an explosion of flakes the flapping wings beat the snow as the bird dove down directly into a high snowdrift.

Here the grouse would find relief and comfort. By roosting here, the snow's insulation would provide a warm, cozy resting place and allow the grouse to escape the biting wind.

There the bird stayed, its feathers fluffed up to trap the maximum amount of air between its skin and plumage. The grouse could spend a few days without food and emerge from the snowdrift none the worse for the delay.

As the bird sat there sleeping, many hours passed. With time came a change in temperature. The sky cleared and the sun shone brightly on the following day. Warm rays of the sun caused the surface of the snow to melt throughout the afternoon. When darkness shrouded the forest, it began to grow cold once again. All the while the grouse remained beneath the drift, comfortably resting in its warm confines.

When night came, the temperature dropped lower and lower, falling well below freezing. In the morning the grouse began to venture from its dwelling place to forage for food, but as the bird tried to break through the surface of the snow, it was stopped. No matter how hard it struggled, its attempts were futile. The melting snow had refrozen during the night to form a hard, impenetrable crust over the drift's surface. The grouse's comfortable quarters had become a prison.

Because of its failure to leave at the right time, what was once a place of safety turned into a tomb. For here the trapped bird would eventually starve to death.

Bevert Andrewson

SCRIPTURAL REFERENCES TO THE GROUSE

"The king of Israel is come out to seek a flea, as when one doth hunt a partridge in the mountains."
I Samuel 26:20

This picture was used to describe David when he fled from Saul in the mountains.

"As the partridge sitteth on eggs, and hatcheth them not, so he that getteth riches, and not by right, shall leave them in the midst of his days, and at his end shall be a fool." Jeremiah 17:11

The struggle of a partridge or grouse to hatch its brood provides significant parallels to a man who tries to retain unjust riches. The partridge begins with a large number of eggs; between eight and twenty have been found in a single nest. After a short time the partridge rolls out of the nest those eggs it believes are infertile.

The eggs are laid in a depression on the ground and are subject to theft and destruction from hostile elements and prey. When a nest is disturbed or destroyed, the partridge must begin all over again. These later attempts to nest tend to produce a higher proportion of infertile eggs. When the eggs finally hatch, many of the chicks break out of their shells within minutes of each other. The mother takes these chicks and leaves the nest, abandoning the unhatched eggs. Some would have hatched if she had stayed longer, and others had already become infertile.

Thus the partridge, with much extra effort, has an unusually high nest mortality rate. In like manner, the rich man who walks in a vain show "heapeth up riches, and knoweth not who shall gather them." (Psalm 39:6) "The riches that he hath gotten are perished." (Jeremiah 48:36)

CHARACTERISTICS AND PHYSICAL FEATURES OF THE RUFFED GROUSE

Because the grouse did not know how long its visit should have lasted, the hospitality of the snow became a death trap. Many birds are lost each year in the snowy regions of the North because of this very problem. Not only may the sun cause a confining crust to form, but falling snow often turns to rain and then freezes, prohibiting the bird from burrowing out.

Another hazard of this form of escape is that the longer the grouse waits in its snow roost, the more likely a predator, such as a roving coyote, is to locate the bird. It is not difficult to detect a slight hump in the snow, the little breathing hole, or wing marks where the bird entered the drift. These direct the predator right to the spot.

Gray phase

Red phase

DOES THE GROUSE USE A SNOW ROOST EVERY TIME IT SNOWS?

The ruffed grouse seems to use snow drifts early in the season. Until the birds acclimatize to the snow and cold, they employ this risky survival technique. As the season progresses and they become accustomed to severe weather, they seek protection elsewhere and roost almost exclusively in the dense cover of evergreen boughs.

IN WHAT WAY IS THE GROUSE DESIGNED FOR SNOW?

The grouse is equipped with "snowshoes." Horny pectinations grow along the sides of its toes and act like snowshoes, enabling the bird to walk on the surface of the snow. These special growths appear in the autumn. In the spring when the snow has gone, the bird sheds the little appendages.

Another feature which enables it to cope with snow and cold weather is its aftershaft. These feathers are attached to its main body feathers but lack a stiff vein, hooklets, and barbicels. As a result, they are light and fluffy and provide added warmth and insulation.

DOES THE COLD WEATHER AFFECT THE BIRD'S COLORATION?

The cold is not believed to have a direct bearing on the grouse's color. It is interesting to note, though, that birds from the colder, northern regions where conifer trees abound tend to be more gray in appearance. Those of southern, deciduous forests tend to have a red tint to their plumage.

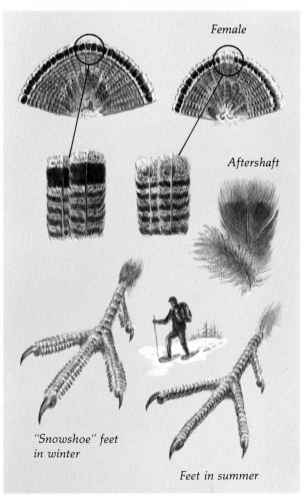

Female

Aftershaft

"Snowshoe" feet in winter

Feet in summer

With tail braced against a log, the grouse prepares for drumming.

Wings beat against air to produce sound

Worn drumming log

Strutting grouse

Wings go against air to produce sound.

Deceptive ventricular effect of sound makes it difficult for enemies such as the barred owl to prey upon the drumming bird.

WHAT DOES THE GROUSE'S TAIL REVEAL ABOUT THE BIRD?

It tells whether the bird is a male or female. If the dark, subterminal band of the tail is broken in the center, the bird is most likely a female. On a cock, this color band is continuous and unbroken.

There are other ways to distinguish the male from the female. The male is slightly larger and its feathers are brighter. The ruff feathers on the male's neck come together across the breast as opposed to the female's which show a break. These methods of identification are reliable, but there are always exceptions.

WHY WAS THE RUFFED GROUSE GIVEN THE SCIENTIFIC NAME BONASA UMBELLUS?

The name originates from Latin and Greek. *Bonasa* means "a bison." This name came from the grouse's drumming which resembles the sound of a bellowing buffalo. *Umbellus* refers to umbrella-like ruffs of dark feathers located on the bird's neck.

HOW DOES THE RUFFED GROUSE MAKE ITS DRUMMING NOISE?

For many years the exact means by which the bird produced this noise was debated. Many theories were given. Some thought the grouse beat its wings against its chest. Others throught that it beat them against a log. The movements of the grouse were so rapid that the process could not easily be determined. Only through the use of slow-motion photography was the secret unlocked.

The grouse chooses a fallen log and stands crosswise on it. Then it props its tail against the log, forming a brace for itself. The male lifts its wings upward and forward against the wind and begins to whirl, each time going faster and faster. The bird strikes neither its body nor the log—it strikes the air. This creates a miniature sonic boom.

WHY DOES THE GROUSE DRUM?

The bird has two reasons for drumming. First, it tells all grouse in the area, particularly males, that this territory is taken and they should not trespass. Second, it calls hens for mating.

The drumming is not always a call to the female, for the cock must be ready for mating. If it is not, the grouse will fight away a responding female. Both sexes have short periods of time when they are capable of mating interspersed with times when they are not.

During the height of the drumming season the male sleeps on its log. When walking through the woods at the end of the courtship season, one can easily identify these logs because of the well-worn drumming spot and piles of droppings.

DOESN'T THE DRUMMING SOUND EXPOSE THE GROUSE'S LOCATION?

The drumming noise created by the grouse carries for considerable distances and alerts the grouse's enemies—the barred owl, horned owl, coyote, and red fox. But the drummer has a slight advantage in that it is very difficult to determine the precise direction from which the sound is coming. As in ventriloquism, the sound source is deceptive. The bird can be far away and yet the sound can seem very close, and vice versa.

HOW PROTECTIVE OF THE NEST IS THE FEMALE?

The female grouse is a model parent. The male participates neither in the incubation nor the raising of the young. The female selects a concealed, protected spot alongside some obstacle such as a log, tree, or rock. The location of the nest is usually in young hardwoods where the area is relatively open. By nesting here, the grouse is able to watch for enemies and leave quickly if necessary.

She scrapes out a hollow in the ground and lines it with dead leaves and down. She lays eleven to twelve eggs which she carefully covers each time she leaves the nest.

The female begins incubation after all the eggs are laid. She sits on them continuously for approximately twenty-four days, leaving only to feed for short periods in the morning and afternoon. If an enemy approaches, she will flush, but as she progresses further with the incubation, she becomes more and more reluctant to leave. Towards the end of the twenty-four day period, she stays so long that a fox could actually catch her before she flew away.

WILL A FEMALE RENEST IF HER EGGS ARE DESTROYED?

Whether or not she will renest depends on when destruction strikes. If it should happen while the eggs are being laid or within the first two weeks of the incubation period, the eggs will probably be replaced. After this time the chances diminish. When the grouse does renest, she usually lays a smaller clutch with a higher proportion of infertile eggs.

WHAT MAJOR FACTOR DETERMINES WHETHER OR NOT A CHICK WILL SURVIVE?

One of the most critical times for the chicks is at birth. The factor which governs their survival is really the weather in early June when they hatch. If it is cold and wet, many will die. The female does all she can to protect her brood during these early hours and days of the chick's life. She waits for a warm, sunny day before she gathers her brood and leaves the nest for good. She takes them a short distance and then broods them, allowing them time to build up their strength.

The muted coloration of the female helps to camouflage the bird.

Eggs are covered when she leaves.

Female will build nest by a protective object.

Incubation period is 23-24 days.

Actual size of grouse egg

The mother must keep the chicks warm during the first days of their life if they are to survive.

Chicks stay close to parent. Should one wander, it will become lost and die.

Chick learns to find food for itself at an early age.

Varied contents of opened crop

Expandable crop allows bird to take in large quantities of food at one time.

Grouse systematically feeds on tree buds.

DOES THE YOUNG GROUSELET'S DIET DIFFER FROM THAT OF THE ADULT BIRD?

During the first few weeks of its life the young chick feeds almost entirely on insects and their larvae—flies, beetles, ants, spiders, and snails. First the mother catches the food for them, but as time goes on she teaches them how to catch insects themselves.

When summer arrives and wild fruits ripen, the grouselet's menu gradually shifts to strawberries, blueberries, and raspberries. By summer's end the birds maintain a diet quite similar to the omnivorous diet of the adult—ninety percent vegetation and ten percent insect. They eat almost any available vegetation growing above ground. Their choice includes seeds, buds, leaves, flowers, fruits, nuts, and twigs.

In the fall, the grouse feeds heavily on the abundant nuts and fruits of the season—acorns, beechnuts, and thorn apples—to prepare for winter. During cold months they eat fallen leaves and tree buds. Grouse which inhabit conifer forests feed on evergreen buds to such an extent that during this time their flesh takes on a peculiar taste which makes them less desirable as game.

WHAT IS UNIQUE ABOUT THE FEEDING HABITS OF THE GROUSE?

The walls of its crop are elastic in structure and can stretch, allowing the bird to take in large quantities of food at one time. With this feature the bird can leave protective cover, go to the food source, quickly gather in food, return to cover and there peacefully eat its meal with minimum exposure to enemies.

When feeding on tree buds, the grouse systematically works its way up the tree in a circular motion, feeding as it goes upward.

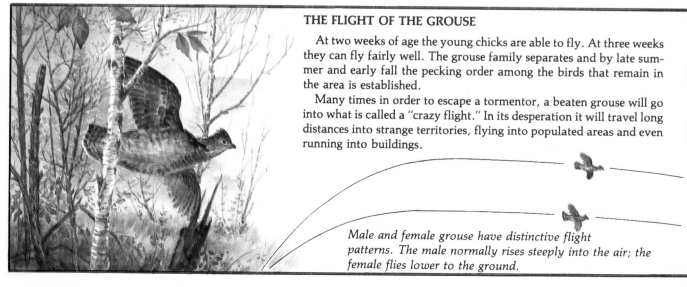

THE FLIGHT OF THE GROUSE

At two weeks of age the young chicks are able to fly. At three weeks they can fly fairly well. The grouse family separates and by late summer and early fall the pecking order among the birds that remain in the area is established.

Many times in order to escape a tormentor, a beaten grouse will go into what is called a "crazy flight." In its desperation it will travel long distances into strange territories, flying into populated areas and even running into buildings.

Male and female grouse have distinctive flight patterns. The male normally rises steeply into the air; the female flies lower to the ground.

HOW DOES SCRIPTURE ILLUSTRATE THE NEED TO KNOW HOW LONG A VISIT SHOULD LAST?

Scripture warns those who are guests in the homes of others not to overstay their visit. Where in Scripture did a man expose himself and his wife to great danger because he violated that counsel?

(Pause for a response —see page 20)

One day a wife left her husband and returned to her father's house. Four months later this husband visited the home of his father-in-law in an effort to win back his wife.

He stayed at her home for three days, enjoyed a pleasant visit, and achieved his objective. On the fourth morning he rose early and prepared to leave with his wife and servant, but his father-in-law insisted that he stay for breakfast. After breakfast, the girl's father pleaded with him to stay another day. He reluctantly agreed to do so. Little did they realize the consequences that were to come because they had not determined how long their visit should last or the further goals which they should have achieved during that time.

Early the next morning the son-in-law prepared to leave. Once again his father-in-law persuaded him to stay for another day of feasting and leave sometime later in the evening. When evening came, the father-in-law wanted him to stay overnight so he could get an early start in the morning. But the son-in-law purposed to leave then, even though it was growing late for travel. The son-in-law, his wife, and the servant began their trip home.

The dangers of the countryside increased with the lengthening shadows of evening. The three travelers hurried toward the safety of a city. Little did they realize that lurking behind the walls of that city was a danger far greater than anything they would experience along the lonely night paths.

When they entered the city a strange feeling of foreboding began to creep over them. The customary practice of hospitality was absent. No one invited them into their home for the night. Finally an old man walked through the city gate. He had been working in the field all day. He urged these three travelers to come into the safety of his home.

After he shut the heavy doors behind them, the darkness of night came over the city, and wicked men with perverted minds crept out of their houses. They pounded on the door of this old man's home and shouted their evil intentions to him. The old man attempted to reason with their corrupt minds. His shocked guests listened as these vile men refused to turn from their sinful demands.

The husband knew that only his life was in danger, but he purposed to save himself. To him this meant sacrificing his wife. In a shameful act of moral weakness, he pushed her out the door. The wicked mob turned upon her. She became the victim of their violence, and in the morning she was dead.

This husband had taken the journey to prove to his wife that he loved her. The truest test of his love would have been to lay down his life for her. Instead, he required his wife to lay down her life for him.

The visit of this husband in his father-in-law's home was not only the wrong length, it but failed to achieve the right purpose. The father-in-law seemed more concerned about eating and drinking than about discovering the true character of the one who was to protect his daughter. Before consenting to allow his daughter to leave, he should have spent time teaching his son-in-law how to love his wife. Ironically, this son-in-law was a Levite. It was his job to help teach the nation how to love God and how to love their neighbors as themselves.

From Judges 19:1-28

The Levites were appointed by God to help maintain and teach His standards of righteousness throughout the land. When they lowered their standards, it was not surprising that the standards of the people were lowered as well.

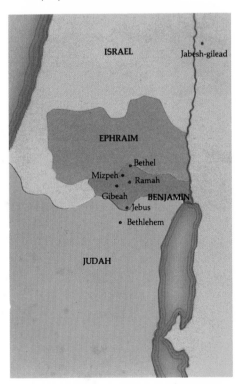

The Levite left Bethlehem in Judah, decided not to spend the night in the non-Israelite town of Jebus, but lodged in Gibeah of the tribe of Benjamin. The next day he returned with his dead concubine to his home in the tribe of Ephraim.

THE LEVITE FAILED TO REALIZE THAT HIS VISIT HAD LASTED TOO LONG

The story of the Levite and his concubine is one of the darker events in the history of Israel. "And it was so, that all who saw it said, There was no such deed done nor seen from the day that the children of Israel came up out of the land of Egypt unto this day." (Judges 19:30)

MORAL DECAY DESPITE A SURE SYSTEM OF INSTRUCTION

The most sobering part of the whole affair is that it happened so soon after the death of Joshua; for Phinehas, a contemporary of Joshua, was the high priest (Judges 20:28; cf. Numbers 25:7,13). How can we account for this breakdown in moral values in just one generation? One reason is that the fathers were not teaching their children the fear of the Lord (Deuteronomy 4:9, 10). But it was the responsibility of the priests and the Levites to teach the Law to these fathers. In fact, this should have been their full-time job.

THE LAW WAS NEVER MORE THAN TEN MILES AWAY

The Levites were required to serve at the central sanctuary for one week at a time and then only about twice a year. They were evenly distributed throughout the land for the remainder of the year in forty-eight Levitical cities (Joshua 21:41). Since copies of the Law were very scarce, there was a great need for oral instruction. This was the major assignment of the priests and Levites (cf. Leviticus 10:11; Deuteronomy 33:10). The forty-eight Levitical cities were so situated that no Israelite was more than ten miles away from at least one city. The Lord provided no excuse for ignorance of His Law.

THE LEVITE LOST RULE IN HIS OWN HOME

When we examine the life of the Levite in Judges 19-21, we can see why the national breakdown in morals was occurring. First we learn that he took to himself a concubine, a sort of second-class wife who could be dismissed with merely a present and whose children had no inheritance rights (Genesis 25:1-6). Such practices were not in accord with the highest principles of God's revelation (cf. Matthew 19:8).

The second fact is that this servant-wife became a harlot. We do not know the reasons, although we can be sure that she had become discontented with her husband's treatment. When the Levite discovered her actions, she fled to her father for protection. The New Testament says that a leader in the church must rule well in his own home. "For if a man know not how to rule his own house, how shall he take care of the church of God?" (I Timothy 3:5)

A RELIGIOUS MERCENARY

Third, his actions in the home of his father-in-law are less than exemplary. It seems that for four and a half days the Levite did little else than eat food and drink wine (cf. Judges 19:6; Proverbs 23:20,21).

It is curious that the Levite does not mention a Levitical city as his destination. He merely says that he lived "toward the side of Mount Ephraim" (Judges 19:18). We learn that he "got him unto his place" and "came into his house" (Judges 19:28, 29). The language is unusually similar to that which described the Levite also living in Mount Ephraim who hired himself out to Micah (Judges 17:7-10). It is very possible that this man was one of many Levites not satisfied with his appointed lot who became a wandering mercenary, selling his religious wares to the highest bidder.

How significant and tragic are the closing lines of the sordid account, "In those days there was no king in Israel; every man did that which was right in his own eyes." (Judges 21:25)

LEVITE CHARACTER SKETCH

WHAT WAS THE LEVITE'S MOTIVE IN RETRIEVING HIS UNFAITHFUL CONCUBINE?

Although we read that the Levite "went after her, to speak friendly unto her, and to bring her again," (Judges 19:3) there is evidence that he was not motivated by genuine love. First we must consider why his concubine was unfaithful to him. As a second-class wife, she felt that she would be treated better by her father than by her husband. In those days, harlotry was practiced for both mercenary and religious purposes. She may have become a harlot to earn money for food and clothing which her husband was not providing. A second consideration is that the Levite waited four months before he went after her (Judges 19:2). Third, his treatment of her in Gibeah was not the type of love which "is strong as death". (Song of Solomon 8:6) Fearing for his life, he allowed his own wife to be abused by worthless men while he went to bed in safety. Why was he not at least anxiously awaiting his wife's return so that he might comfort her? She may have spent hours before she died on the steps of the house while he remained in bed (Judges 19:27). His concern after arising seems to be impatience to leave rather than regard for his wife's safety. The evidence indicates that the Levite was motivated by a selfish desire for a concubine and servant rather than genuine love for her as a person.

WHY DID THE LEVITE'S FATHER-IN-LAW ALLOW THE VISIT TO LAST TOO LONG?

The Mosaic Law meted a most severe penalty for harlotry and adultery. The punishment was stoning until dead (Leviticus 20:10; Deuteronomy 22:21). It is likely that one reason the concubine went back home was to seek the protection of her relatives. The father-in-law would want to make sure that the Levite did not intend to bring his wife back for a quick trial and stoning. An entirely different reason is that he may have desired the Levite to stay in his home permanently. It seems that the Levites had strayed from their original calling, and some had sold their services and become personal priests for a fixed wage (Judges 17:10). The father-in-law may have felt that the blessing of the Lord would be upon his home with a Levite as his priest (Judges 17:13).

WHAT WAS THE LEVITE'S RESPONSE AFTER THE MURDER OF HIS CONCUBINE?

The Levite publically declared righteous indignation. "They have committed lewdness and folly in Israel." (Judges 20:6) His actions, however, seemed to reflect a desire for bloody revenge rather than righteous justice. Burial for a loved one normally occurred on the day of death. This was encouraged by the ceremonial laws which warned against touching a dead body (Numbers 19:11-14). The denial of proper burial indicated great disgrace (cf. Isaiah 14:18-20; Jeremiah 22:18,19). His gruesome actions attained the desired result. Four hundred thousand men gathered to hear the Levite's accusation against the men of Gibeah. The fact that over forty thousand men of Israel were killed in the war against the tribe of Benjamin indicates that neither the Levite's motives nor the motives of the men of Israel were entirely pure and that their intentions were less than honorable.

"And when he was come into his house, he took a knife, and laid hold on his concubine, and divided her, together with her bones, into twelve pieces, and sent her into all the coasts of Israel. And it was so, that all who saw it said, There was no such deed done nor seen from the day that the children of Israel came up out of the land of Egypt unto this day."

THE LEVITE
lē'vĭt

Hospitality

IS PROVIDING AN ATMOSPHERE WHICH CONTRIBUTES TO GROWTH

"Better is a dinner of herbs where love is, than a stalled ox and hatred therewith."

Proverbs 15:17

"In all things shewing thyself a pattern of good works: in doctrine shewing uncorruptness, gravity, sincerity ."

Titus 2:7

LIVING LESSONS ON HOSPITALITY . . .

FROM THE PAGES OF SCRIPTURE

The home is more a classroom than a castle. Each parent must be a learner as well as a leader, and one course every member must pass is how to demonstrate hospitality. Only then will there be an atmosphere in the home which is conducive to learning and living the principles of Scripture. One of the most outstanding couples in the New Testament was skilled in hospitality. They demonstrated it to each other and to every guest who entered their home. They made each visitor a vital member of a working team, including the apostle Paul who was one of their guests. Their home became a center for spiritual growth and greatly strengthened the outreach of the early Christian church.

ILLUSTRATED IN THE WORLD OF NATURE

MASSASAUGA RATTLESNAKE   *Sistrurus catenatus*

This species of rattlesnake is the only North American snake that still has as its common name the one given it by the Indians. In the spring these swamp rattlers are found along the shores of ponds, streams, marshes, swamps, and lakes. During the summer months they are more likely to be seen around the edges of fields and fencerows or under planks and stones. Even though the massasauga inhabits much of the midwestern United States, it is becoming very rare. It appears to be losing ground in its battle for survival as more and more land is developed. Unmolested, it can live fourteen years and grow twenty to forty inches in length. The massasauga is shy and non-aggressive and makes every attempt to avoid a confrontation.

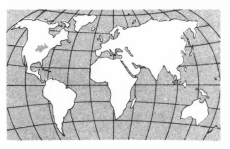

The range and habitat of the massasauga rattlesnake

HOSPITALITY

HOW DOES THE MASSASAUGA RATTLESNAKE ILLUSTRATE HOSPITALITY BY PROVIDING AN ATMOSPHERE FOR GROWTH?

Slithering among rocks and leaves, the long, slender creature slowly worked its way to a sunny knoll of the hardwood forest. Here it would bask in the rays of the warm sun. It was late August; the hot, muggy weather of summer had passed. Now the days were pleasingly cool and comfortable.

Like all snakes and reptiles, the massasauga rattlesnake avoids the cold. Lacking body mechanisms to maintain a constant temperature, it relies on outside sources such as the sun, shade, or burrows to regulate its body heat. At forty-five degrees it can barely move; at one hundred ten degrees it will die. The temperature for which it is best suited is between eighty and ninety degrees. In hot weather it cools off in a comfortable, shaded spot. To warm itself, the snake seeks out a sunny area and lies there to absorb the sun's warmth.

Today the temperature was about seventy degrees. The snake was by no means immobile, but neither was it at its peak of efficiency. By sunning itself in the afternoon it would be in better condition to hunt for food later. As it made its way along the ground, maneuvering around large, white oak trees, the snake suddenly encountered a large bird. Both became aware of each other's presence at the same instant.

Hoping to avoid any risk of attack, the snake attempted to conceal itself by sliding close to the base of large boulders. The wild turkey promptly came over to investigate. Quietly the snake waited for the gobbler to satisfy its curiosity and then leave, but suddenly the turkey's bill became a lethal weapon mercilessly jabbing at the snake's body.

The snake instinctively coiled, weaving its head back and forth in an attempt to avoid the jabs and to position itself to strike. Every time it tried, the bird jumped away. The turkey was too quick. Realizing that it was

no match for the bird, the snake desperately tried to escape. It had more at stake than just its own welfare.

With each attempt to retreat, the bird unleashed another hammer-like blow. The massasauga was beginning to feel the effects of this one-sided fight. Its half-coiled body now made wild, aimless strikes. As the snake waited for the bird's next attack, it caught sight of an opening between the large rocks. Feebly, it made a desperate effort to crawl inside.

It was able to get its head and part of its body to safety before the bird realized what was happening. Racing over, the turkey reached down, latched on to the base of the rattlers, and pulled furiously. The snake braced itself and wedged its muscular body against the stones. As both pulled harder and harder in opposite directions, the rattlers broke off. The massasauga quickly withdrew its battered tail before the bird had another opportunity to strike. There within the safety of the rocks, the snake's life would quietly slip away.

But it wasn't ready to die yet; it still had a mission to accomplish. Disregarding its own desperate condition, it began to exert all its remaining strength in a series of muscular contractions. Soon eight little sacs, one by one, were ejected from its body. As it lay dying, the sacs began to open.

Within the safety and comfort of the rocks occurred a phenomenon common to only a few snakes. In those last moments of its life the mother snake had given birth to eight, self-sustaining snakelets. By holding the snakelets within her body, she provided an atmosphere conducive to growth. She continued to do this until her dying moments when she provided an impenetrable fortress among the stones for her young, assuring their survival against the formidable bill of the turkey.

SCRIPTURAL REFERENCES TO THE SNAKE

"Now the serpent was more subtle than any beast of the field which the Lord God had made...."
Genesis 3:1

One of the more frequently mentioned creatures in Scripture is the serpent. In its original state it possessed a splendor and cunning quite unlike its present form. After Satan used it to tempt Eve, it was cursed.

"Upon thy belly shalt thou go, and dust shalt thou eat all the days of thy life."
Genesis 3:14

"They shall lick the dust like a serpent...."
Micah 7:17

Critics of Scripture have assumed an error in these verses. Further research, however, reveals that snakes do take dust into their mouth for a precise purpose, and only by dust shall they live. (See page 310.) It is ironic that Satan promised Eve she would have superior knowledge by tasting the forbidden fruit. Now the snake must gain knowledge for eating by taking dust into its mouth.

The serpent became a symbol of sin and God judged Israel with firey serpents in the wilderness. God told Moses to make a brass serpent and lift it up on a pole. Those who went out of the camp to look at it would be healed (Numbers 21).This symbol referred to Christ who was lifted up for our sin (John 3:14). The serpent is now included in the background for the symbol of medicine.

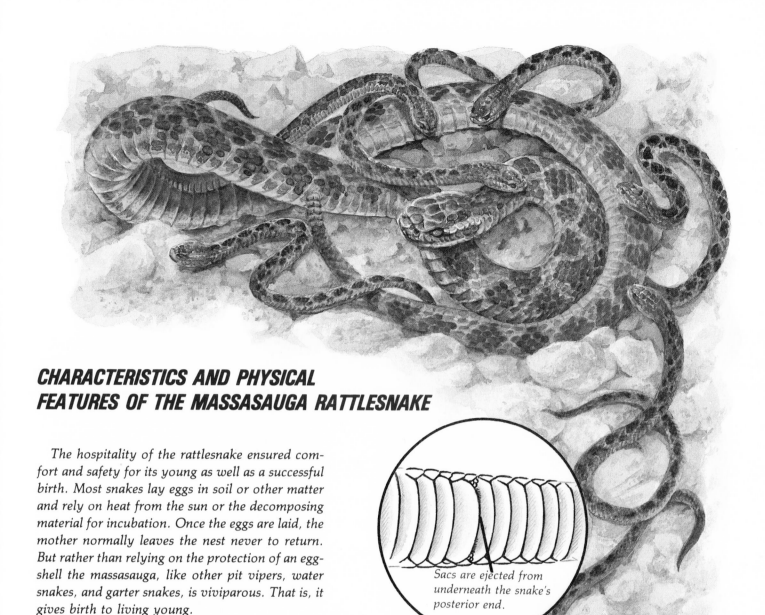

CHARACTERISTICS AND PHYSICAL FEATURES OF THE MASSASAUGA RATTLESNAKE

The hospitality of the rattlesnake ensured comfort and safety for its young as well as a successful birth. Most snakes lay eggs in soil or other matter and rely on heat from the sun or the decomposing material for incubation. Once the eggs are laid, the mother normally leaves the nest never to return. But rather than relying on the protection of an eggshell the massasauga, like other pit vipers, water snakes, and garter snakes, is viviparous. That is, it gives birth to living young.

Sacs are ejected from underneath the snake's posterior end.

DOES A VIVIPAROUS SNAKE HAVE AN ADVANTAGE OVER OTHERS?

The snakelets of the massasauga have a distinct advantage early in life over non-viviparous species. With either too little or too much moisture, snake eggs will desiccate or rot. When the female snake retains the embryos within her body, she can regulate their humidity. Furthermore, the parent can move away from the reach of hungry predators which would eat abandoned eggs. The mother is also able to control their temperature by seeking places either in the sun or shade which would accelerate the gestation period. This benefit can be crucial to species of northern climates where summers are shorter and temperatures cooler.

The birth of a viviparous snake is very simple. The female, either slowly or rapidly, ejects transparent sacs. The squirming snakelet then breaks through the delicate membrane and is born. From that moment the young snake is on its own, and the mother will pay no more attention to it.

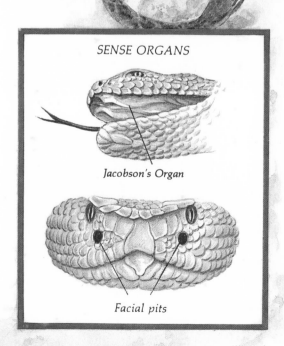

SENSE ORGANS

Jacobson's Organ

Facial pits

Jacobson's organ allows the rattler to "smell" with its tongue. The facial pits contain nerves sensitive to heat. These enable the snake to accurately strike warm-blooded prey at night.

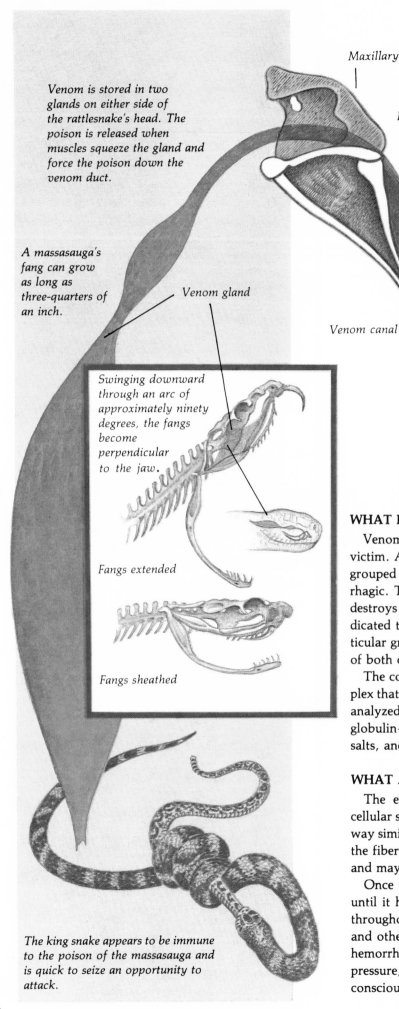

Venom is stored in two glands on either side of the rattlesnake's head. The poison is released when muscles squeeze the gland and force the poison down the venom duct.

A massasauga's fang can grow as long as three-quarters of an inch.

Venom gland

Swinging downward through an arc of approximately ninety degrees, the fangs become perpendicular to the jaw.

Fangs extended

Fangs sheathed

The king snake appears to be immune to the poison of the massasauga and is quick to seize an opportunity to attack.

Maxillary

Entrance lumen

Suture

Venom canal

Discharge orifice

The elongated fang is equipped with a suture or large cutting edge which allows the reptile to pierce through skin and flesh. The curved, needle-like structure injects venom into its intended victim beginning at the entrance lumen where the fang joins the skull. The fluid travels through the venom canal and is injected at the discharge orifice located above the tip of the fang. The size of the fang indicates how much venom a rattlesnake can inject. The smaller the fang the less chance of the snake injecting venom. When not in use, these fangs or maxillary teeth fold back and are encased in a protective sheath on the roof of the snake's mouth.

WHAT IS VENOM?

Venom is a deadly fluid which the snake injects into its victim. At one time it was thought that venom could be grouped into two categories: neurotoxic and hemorrhagic. The former destroys nerve tissues, and the latter destroys blood and other tissues. Further research indicated that venom does not fall precisely into two particular groups but rather is composed of varying degrees of both classes.

The composition of the rattlesnake's venom is so complex that its chemical components have not been precisely analyzed. It is known to include proteins—albumin and globulin—peptones, mucin, proteases, fats, inorganic salts, and ferments.

WHAT ARE THE EFFECTS OF VENOM?

The enzymes of venom break down the fiber and cellular structure of the snake's victim. Venom works in a way similar to certain meat tenderizers by breaking down the fibers. The venom destroys the flesh around the bite and may eventually cause gangrene.

Once the venom has been injected, it does not spread until it has been diluted under the skin. Then it travels throughout the lymphatic system until it reaches the heart and other vital organs. Venom produces pain, swelling, hemorrhaging, circulatory difficulties, lowering of blood pressure, weakening of pulse, allergic shock, unconsciousness, nausea, and increased temperature.

308

The venom of the massasauga is slower acting than other rattlers. Although it would be unusual, this rattlesnake could inject enough poison to kill a man.

DOES THE RATTLESNAKE JUST BITE HUMANS?

No. The massasauga is a mild-mannered rattlesnake and will use its venom on man only when cornered or if absolutely necessary. Otherwise, it will try to escape. The poison is primarily used to aid the snake in capturing its prey—rabbits, rats, and larger birds.

DOES THE RATTLESNAKE USE ALL ITS VENOM AT ONE TIME?

It is very careful not to waste its venom. When injecting its prey, it uses just enough to kill its victim—up to two-thirds of its supply. Approximately two weeks are required to replenish the poison. This is not too critical for the snake since it digests its food for quite a while.

The snake eats its prey whole. Gastric juices then begin to work and dissolve almost everything, including bones and teeth. When the snake is confronted with a large adversary such as a man, it may panic and inject larger amounts of venom, sometimes using it all in order to defend itself against the threat.

IS IT EVER POSSIBLE FOR A RATTLESNAKE TO LOSE ITS FANGS?

The smaller the fang, the more fragile it is. But the snake is designed in such a way that despite their fragility, fangs are always present. If the reptile loses a needle-like structure either by breakage in use or through periodic shedding, there is usually an immediate replacement waiting in storage. The snake is provided with as many as six additional "back-up" fangs at various stages of development. Should one break, the most developed fang takes its place.

It has been discovered that, for short periods of time, the one remaining fang can operate for both by injecting venom from both glands.

IS A BABY RATTLESNAKE POISONOUS?

When a baby rattlesnake is only two minutes old, it can instinctively coil and strike. Because its fangs are small, the amount of venom it could inject is limited, and therefore the bite probably would not be fatal to humans. It would, nonetheless, be serious and cause swelling and pain.

DOES A RATTLESNAKE HAVE TO BE COILED IN ORDER TO STRIKE?

No. This is a common misconception and one which could prove dangerous. A rattlesnake does not have to be coiled to strike. In reality, it can strike from any position. Even after death, when the head is severed from the body, it is capable of biting and discharging venom for up to six hours. It was found that the snake's heart can continue to beat for a day or two after death.

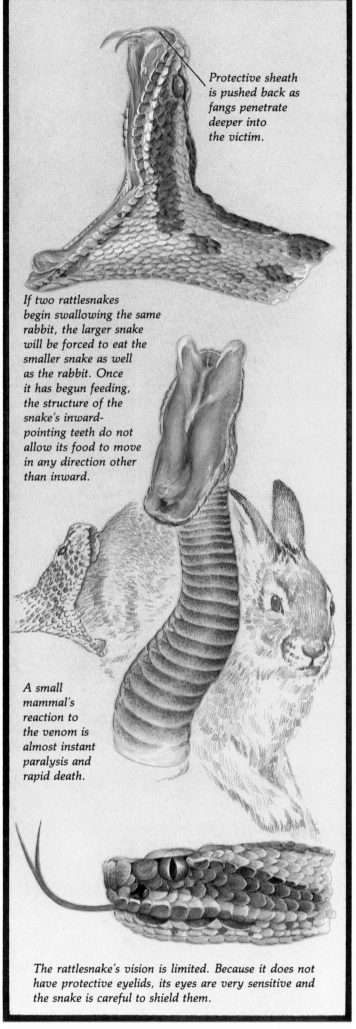

Protective sheath is pushed back as fangs penetrate deeper into the victim.

If two rattlesnakes begin swallowing the same rabbit, the larger snake will be forced to eat the smaller snake as well as the rabbit. Once it has begun feeding, the structure of the snake's inward-pointing teeth do not allow its food to move in any direction other than inward.

A small mammal's reaction to the venom is almost instant paralysis and rapid death.

The rattlesnake's vision is limited. Because it does not have protective eyelids, its eyes are very sensitive and the snake is careful to shield them.

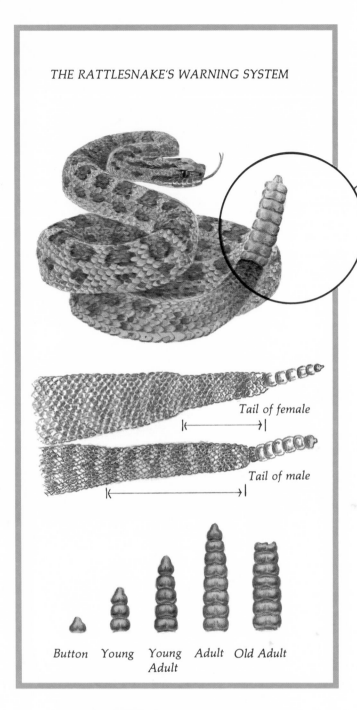

THE RATTLESNAKE'S WARNING SYSTEM

Tail of female

Tail of male

Button *Young* *Young Adult* *Adult* *Old Adult*

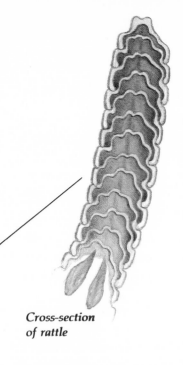

The "buttons" on the rattlesnake are not an accurate indication of the snake's age. Each time the snake sheds its skin a new segment is formed. This may occur one to four times a year for the adult. The rattles themselves are very fragile and rarely remain complete since they are often torn away or pulled off.

Cross-section of rattle

DOES A RATTLESNAKE ALWAYS WARN BEFORE IT STRIKES?

No. This is another misconception. The buzzing sound which the snake makes, similar to a group of locusts, is actually a sign of fear or anger. It is a noise made when the snake thinks it is going to be harmed or molested and is its attempt to intimidate and discourage the intruder.

The snake may not be able to rattle a warning. It might have been surprised or its rattles could be torn off. Generally speaking, though, it is customary for the snake to warn before striking.

When the rattlesnake is excited, it vibrates its rattles at a rate of fifty oscillations per second with such speed that a human cannot see the movement of the tip of the tail. The noise is produced by a chain of interlocking, nollow segments made of keratin, the same material of which the human fingernail is made.

The rattlesnake normally molts its skin three times a year. This shedding process is governed by growth and occurs more often if food and conditions are favorable for the rattlesnake.

WHAT IS THE MEANING OF GOD'S CURSE ON THE SNAKE—"DUST SHALT THOU EAT ALL THE DAYS OF THY LIFE"?

In a most unusual way, dust is essential to the life of the snake. Its eyesight is poor, and it has almost no hearing ability. Instead, the rattlesnake is forced to gain information by continually flicking its moist tongue into the air. By so doing, the snake collects tiny particles of dust. It transfers these particles to two specialized receptors or sacs in the roof of the mouth called the Jacobson's organ. This organ interprets what the particles are and relays the information to the brain. This gives the snake direction for food and allows it to sense danger.

HOW DOES SCRIPTURE ILLUSTRATE HOSPITALITY IN PROVIDING AN ATMOSPHERE THAT CONTRIBUTES TO GROWTH?

A famous guest experienced true hospitality in the home of a certain couple. They made him a working part of their family, and he made them a working part of his ministry. Who was this couple?

(Pause for a response—see page 20)

A shocked couple listened to the proclamation. The emperor Claudius had decided that certain people could not be included in the plans he had for his capital. These undesirable people were ordered to leave Rome, and this couple was included in the group.

They hastily packed their belongings, traveled to another city to find a home, and began to reestablish themselves. This experience may have been a motivation for them to learn and demonstrate hospitality to others.

One day a man knocked on their door. He explained that he practiced the same trade as they and that he was looking for lodging. This man was not particularly handsome, and his speech was not eloquent; but there was a power in his words and a humble graciousness in his spirit.

He found a warm welcome at the home of this couple. Soon he became a working member of the family. During their meals, he taught them the truths of Scripture. He worked diligently with them in making tents. It was a happy teamwork that often lasted far into the night.

This visitor was the apostle Paul. Each week he went to the local synagogue and boldly proclaimed the Gospel to those who were there. After weeks of his convincing ministry, there was a large following of believers in the city. A new dimension of hospitality was added to this couple's lives as they ministered to and strengthened the new converts.

Just as they had included Paul in the activities of their home, he included them in the further outreach of his ministry. These three Christians traveled to distant cities proclaiming the Gospel, demonstrating hospitality, and establishing churches.

One day this couple listened to a powerful speaker named Apollos. He was eloquent and sincere, but they recognized that he did not yet know vital truths which Paul had explained to them. They took him aside privately and taught him the way more perfectly. Then they demonstrated a further aspect of hospitality by introducing him to their friends in other cities.

The great influence of this couple is indicated in Scripture. Paul stated that they were his helpers in Christ Jesus, that they risked their lives for his, and that "unto whom not only he gave thanks but also all the churches of the Gentiles."

Aquila and Priscilla provided an atmosphere in their home which contributed to the growth of the early Christian church. That church continued to expand until one day the very city that rejected this couple became a major center for the Gospel.

From Acts 18:1-28

AQUILA AND PRISCILLA PROVIDED SPECIAL HOSPITALITY THAT CONTRIBUTED TO THE GROWTH OF THE EARLY CHURCH

Aquila and Priscilla are introduced to us in the pages of Scripture upon the Apostle Paul's arrival at Corinth. Paul was in need of money after his stay in Athens, and he sought an opportunity to apply his tentmaking craft. One of the tentmakers in Corinth was a Jew by the name of Aquila who worked with his wife, Priscilla.

TROUBLE IN ROME

Aquila and Priscilla had just been evicted from the capital of the Roman empire because "Claudius had commanded all Jews to depart from Rome." (Acts 18:2) The Roman historian, Seutonius, records that during the reign of Claudius Jews were expelled from Rome because of disturbances made at the instigation of "Chrestus." If this is, as many suppose, a reference to "Christus," the Latin form of Christ; then the disturbances were due to disputes between non-Christian Jews in Rome and Jewish Christians who claimed that Christ was the Messiah.

HOSPITABLE COUPLE GIVES PART-TIME EMPLOYMENT

Aquila and Priscilla readily befriended Paul, and since there is no record of their conversion, it is probable that they had become Christians at Rome. The hospitable couple not only gave Paul employment but also boarded him in their home (Acts 18:3). When Silas and Timothy arrived in Corinth with a gift of money from the newly established church at Philippi (Acts 18:5; II Corinthians 11:8,9), Paul was able to devote more time to preaching the Gospel. Aquila cooperated in providing part-time employment so that Paul was able to remain financially independent of the immature Corinthian church (II Corinthians 11:9).

A DECISION IS MADE TO MOVE THE BUSINESS

After one and a half years, Paul decided to begin a ministry in Ephesus. His relationship with Aquila and Priscilla had worked so well in Corinth that they agreed to move to Ephesus and establish their business while Paul visited Jerusalem (Acts 18:19). Since a church had not yet been formed in Ephesus, they attended worship services in the Jewish synagogue. Here they met Apollos, "an eloquent man, and mighty in the Scriptures." (Acts 18:24) He believed that Jesus was the promised Messiah and that He was the "Lamb of God, who taketh away the sin of the world." (John 1:29) But Apollos did not seem to have yet been informed of the complete significance of Christ's atoning death, His resurrection from the dead, and the coming of His Spirit. Both Priscilla and Aquila had the privilege of expounding "unto him the way of God more perfectly." (Acts 18:26)

WILLING TO GO WHEREVER THEY WERE NEEDED MOST

Aquila and Priscilla lived in Ephesus for three years (Acts 20:31). When Paul returned to the city on his third missionary journey, he once again worked with this couple in their common trade and lodged with them (cf. Acts 20:34; I Corinthians 16:19). At Ephesus, Paul began to make plans for a trip to Rome, the chief population center of the Roman empire. When Paul wrote his epistle to the Romans some months later, he sent greetings to "Priscilla and Aquila my fellow-workers in Christ Jesus." (Romans 16:3) It appears that Paul had again sent the faithful couple ahead of him to lay the groundwork for his ministry in Rome, just as they had done so successfully in Ephesus.

The last reference to this couple is found in Paul's second letter to Timothy. "Salute Priscilla and Aquila." (II Timothy 4:19) Since Paul was in Rome at the time, writing to Timothy in Ephesus, we gather that for some reason Aquila and Priscilla agreed with Paul that they were more needed there. Here they may have established a more permanent residence and helped build up the believers in the church at Ephesus.

Sculpture of the emperor Claudius *who ordered the Jews, including Aquila and Priscilla, to leave Rome*

As a tentmaker, *Aquila supplied the market's demand. The Roman army was a major consumer. Three kinds of tents used by the Roman soldiers are shown above.*

AQUILA AND PRISCILLA CHARACTER SKETCH

HOW DID AQUILA AND PRISCILLA CONTRIBUTE TO THE GROWTH OF THE GENTILE CHURCH?

Paul wrote these words to the church at Rome, "Greet Priscilla and Aquila, my helpers in Christ Jesus, who have for my life laid down their own necks; unto whom not only I give thanks, but also all the churches of the Gentiles." (Romans 16:3,4) Like Paul, this dedicated couple was ready to die for their faith. We do not know the details, but in an unknown incident, they voluntarily exposed their lives to some extreme peril in behalf of Paul. This may well have been related to one of the many dangerous encounters Paul experienced at Ephesus while staying in the home of this couple (cf. Acts 19:29,30; 20:19). Since the churches owed their spiritual lives to Paul, and Paul owed his life to Aquila and Priscilla, the churches were indebted to them as well. A further contribution this couple made to the church involved their ministry in the life of Apollos. Their instruction provided the basis for a more effective ministry on his part in his journeys to the various churches (cf. Acts 18:28; I Corinthians 3:6).

WHAT DID A CHRISTIAN COMMITMENT COST AQUILA AND PRISCILLA?

It cost them the love of their family and closest friends. As Jews, many in their family and many of their friends would condemn them as blasphemers because of their belief in Christ as the Son of God (cf. Matthew 10:35,36). It cost them their roots. . . from Rome, to Corinth, to Ephesus, back to Rome, and then back to Ephesus. The constant prospect of moving and reestablishing a home must have been especially difficult for Priscilla. The moves were costly from a monetary standpoint, for each time they relocated they had to reestablish their business. Their commitment cost them their privacy. Housing the apostle Paul meant crowds in their home well into the evening hours (cf. Acts 20:7,11). They also hosted the local church at Ephesus and at Rome (I Corinthians 16:19; Romans 16:5). Finally, it cost them their safety (Romans 16:3,4).

WHAT EXAMPLE DID AQUILA AND PRISCILLA LEAVE FOR CHRISTIAN COUPLES?

When Paul wrote from Ephesus to the church at Corinth, he may have had Aquila in mind. "The time is short; it remaineth that both they that have wives be as though they had none." (I Corinthians 7:29) The couple had probably just recently been sent to Rome. Their willingness to uproot again provides an example, especially to missionary couples, of flexibility and faith (cf. Hebrews 11:8-10). Contrary to the negative example of the infamous New Testament couple Ananias and Sapphira, they provide an example of generosity with the possessions entrusted to them. Finally, Aquila and Priscilla are an illustration of the benefits given to those who are given to hospitality. Because of their initial hospitality to Paul, they learned the great teachings the Lord had given him to proclaim. They heard firsthand reports of his missionary journeys and the amazing things God was doing through him. They established a friendship with Apollos, were able to see young believers grow up in Christ, and shared with them in the inestimable joys of Christian fellowship.

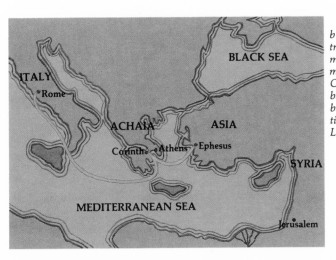

Aquila and Priscilla *became seasoned travelers through their many relocations. They moved from Rome to Corinth to Ephesus, back to Rome and then back to Ephesus in their tireless ministry for the Lord.*

AQUILA AND PRISCILLA
ăk'wĭ-là and prĭ-sĭl'à

313

Hospitality

IS PROVIDING LEADERSHIP FOR A PEACEFUL AND HARMONIOUS SURROUNDING

"Therefore if thine enemy hunger, feed him; if he thirsts, give him drink: for in so doing thou shalt heap coals of fire on his head."

Romans 12:20

LIVING LESSONS ON HOSPITALITY . . .

FROM THE PAGES OF SCRIPTURE

A person may open his home to many guests, share his belongings, and sacrifce for their comfort; but if his home does not have a spirit of harmony he has missed the real essence of hospitality. A harmonious atmosphere is aided by organized surroundings, restful music, pleasant conversation, and tasteful decor; but the major contributor will be the inner spirit of the host. He or she must provide the leadership for peace and harmony. On one occasion a king sent a large detachment from his army to capture a prophet. The prophet welcomed them as his guests and showed hospitality to them. The amazing results demonstrate the power of providing leadership for a peaceful and a harmonious surrounding.

ILLUSTRATED IN THE WORLD OF NATURE

BIGHORN SHEEP *Ovis canadensis*

It is unusual to see a solitary bighorn sheep. If an animal is by itself it is probably sick, injured, or old. Under normal conditions bighorns are very sociable and form two well-defined groups. One social group—the rams—is made up of six or more adult males in or just past their prime, averaging seven to eight years of age. The second group is composed of ewes, lambs, and young rams. This group numbers anywhere from twenty to forty. Bighorn sheep attain a length of approximately seven feet and a height of three and a half feet at the shoulder. The males, at two hundred and fifty pounds, are one hundred pounds heavier than females. Bighorns are extremely shy and suspicious creatures.

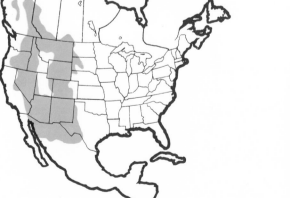

The range and habitat of the bighorn sheep

HOSPITALITY

HOW DOES THE BIGHORN SHEEP ILLUSTRATE HOSPITALITY BY PROVIDING LEADERSHIP?

Every fiber tensed in its sleek, muscular body as it maneuvered its low-slung frame to position. Like a loaded spring, the powerful beast suddenly sank its sharp claws into the loose gravel. With split-second timing the mechanism was triggered, hurling the beast through the air straight for its victim.

It had taken the mountain lion a long time to even come within striking range of the grazing lambs and ewes. One ever-present, unchanging factor made the mountain lion's job extremely difficult. If it was not for this handicap, the powerful cat would have feasted on mutton more often.

Past experience had painfully taught that if the cat was to be successful, it would have to outrun, outthink and outmaneuver the leadership of the bighorn herd. Ewes were always on guard and alert for any intruder or sign of danger. But in addition to and even more important than their watchfulness was the presence of one old, wise ewe—the main leader of the bighorns. She had been bellwether and was grandmother to most of the flock.

Having lived on the home range all her life, she was aware of all the choice places for food, especially in times of scarcity. She knew all the drinking holes as well as places of safety. But even more important than this, she knew every predator's trap and every route of escape. In emergencies, she knew exactly where she could or could not go. She would cooly and cleverly choose an escape from whatever threat the flock faced, and her wise leadership ensured protection. For this reason there was harmony among the flock even when danger approached. They had confidence in her judgment and were quick to respond to her warning and example.

The cat had taken every precaution and after a long, stealthy approach had precisely executed the attack. But its cunning was in vain. The predator's movements had not escaped the alert eye of the old ewe. Before it sprang from the ground, she had already warned the group.

The mountain lion watched as the last male bighorn easily scaled down the sheer cliff and disappeared out of sight. The path on which they fled was far too steep for the cat to even consider pursuit. Once again the old ewe's leadership had brought the herd to peaceful grazing where she resumed her watchful vigil.

SCRIPTURAL REFERENCES TO THE BIGHORN SHEEP

*"Then Saul took three thousand chosen men out of all
Israel, and went to seek David and his men upon the
rocks of the wild goats."*
I Samuel 24:2

The Scriptural counterpart of the bighorn sheep is the
mountain goat found in the ranges of Palestine. David
and his six hundred men fled to one of these mountain
ranges—the wilderness of En-gedi. Its name means "the
fountain of the goat." There in the highest and most
craggy part of the mountains he found safety and an
abundance of this animal.

It requires great skill to catch a goat. The animal leaps
from ledge to ledge recklessly, amazing a pursuer with
its surefootedness. It is reported to be able to slide down
the mountains, halt with all four feet drawn together on
a projection scarcely larger than a penny, and then leap
over a wide crevice, alighting with precision upon a
projecting piece of rock.

*"Knowest thou the time when the wild goats of the
rock bring forth? Or canst thou mark when the hinds
do calve?" Job 39:1*

The mother goat seeks privacy in which to have her
young and she will go a considerable distance to obtain
it. Usually the only way a hunter can find the kids is to
follow the mother to the rock cleft some time after they
are born.

CHARACTERISTICS AND PHYSICAL FEATURES OF THE BIGHORN SHEEP

The hospitality of the old ewe's leadership provided peace and harmony for the herd. In order to maintain a leadership position, a ewe must continually prove herself. She must be able to decoy an enemy away or usher the herd down a path impassable to a predator. Many times she must lead the sheep through terrain so treacherous that no enemy would even consider pursuit.

There is another criterion for this leadership position. The ewe must be capable of bearing young. When she loses this ability, the others no longer look to her for guidance. They then choose a new leader to guide them among the rocky cliffs and crevices.

HOW CAN THE BIGHORN CLIMB UP AND DOWN SUCH SHEER CLIFFS?

The quick coordination of the sheep enables the animal to respond rapidly, positioning its body in such a way as to use every crook and ledge to its benefit. Whether there are four feet or four inches of space, it uses them all to full advantage.

One of the most amazing assets of the bighorn is its strong, cushioned feet. Each foot is equipped with two rubber-like pads which enable the animal to hold on to any surface—wet, dry, sharp, smooth, hard, or soft.

In addition, its feet are equipped with a pair of built-in "brakes" in the form of sharp claws. The sheep applies these brakes by either bending or straightening its legs. As the animal drops down a steep cliff it controls the rate of its descent by a series of leaping, falling movements. At short intervals it grips and holds back with these specialized feet, slowing the fall as it eases its way to the bottom.

HAS THE BIGHORN ALWAYS USED HIGH CLIFFS FOR PROTECTION?

Data from ancient records indicate that the bighorn was not always a cliff dweller. Long ago it inhabited and grazed upon grassy foothills and bluffs. It was always on the alert and retreated to nearby rocky crags when danger approached. As civilization crept in and more and more pressure was placed on the animal, it gradually moved farther and farther into the mountains resorting to much more rugged terrain.

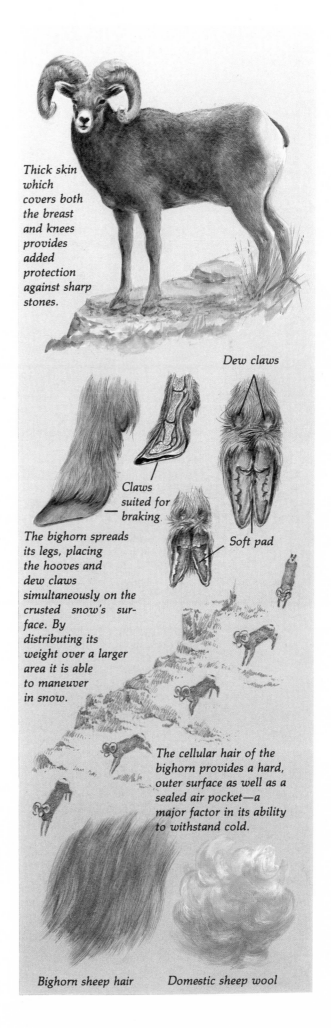

Thick skin which covers both the breast and knees provides added protection against sharp stones.

Dew claws

Claws suited for braking

Soft pad

The bighorn spreads its legs, placing the hooves and dew claws simultaneously on the crusted snow's surface. By distributing its weight over a larger area it is able to maneuver in snow.

The cellular hair of the bighorn provides a hard, outer surface as well as a sealed air pocket—a major factor in its ability to withstand cold.

Bighorn sheep hair   Domestic sheep wool

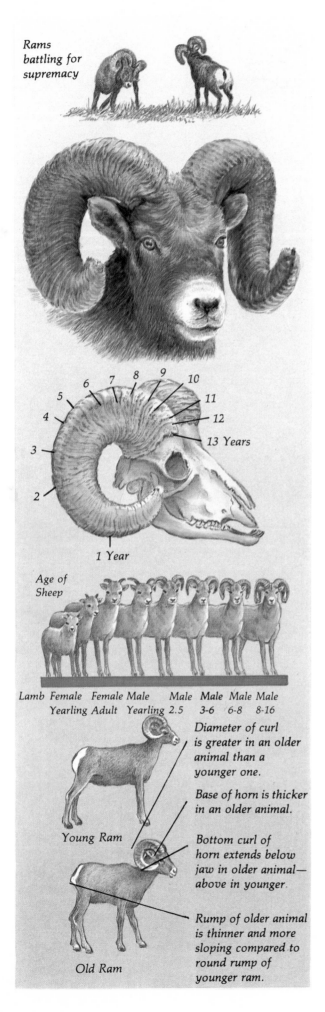

Rams battling for supremacy

Age of Sheep

5 4 3 2

6 7 8 9 10 11 12 13 Years

1 Year

Lamb | Female Yearling | Female Adult | Male Yearling | Male 2.5 | Male 3-6 | Male 6-8 | Male 8-16

Young Ram

Diameter of curl is greater in an older animal than a younger one.

Base of horn is thicker in an older animal.

Bottom curl of horn extends below jaw in older animal— above in younger.

Rump of older animal is thinner and more sloping compared to round rump of younger ram.

Old Ram

DO THE SHEEP'S HORNS HAVE ANY PURPOSE?

In December rams use their horns as weapons or a shield when they enter the mating or rutting season. Pacing away at about one hundred feet, two rams square off and then race back toward each other. They collide with tremendous impact. The crack of the slamming horns is so great that the sound can be heard as far away as two miles.

If opportunity permits, the ram uses the point of its horn to slash the body of its sparring partner. In this contest the name of the game is weight and endurance. With unwavering determination they inflict and receive blow after blow until one begins to stagger away in defeat.

A bighorn may also use its horn points as shovels to dig out roots among the rocks. This is true especially in times of drought when it searches for the sequaw root from which it derives liquid and food.

IS IT AN ADVANTAGE TO HAVE THE LARGEST HORNS?

The horns are a symbol of dominance, for it is usually the ram with the largest horns that is victorious in battle. The disadvantages appear to far outweigh the limited status which the larger horns bring. By having the largest horns the dominant ram is always subject to young hopefuls who challenge its supremacy. If it is to maintain this position, it must accept these challenges, and each time it does so, its body begins to show more wear and tear. When the animal is seven or eight years old and has passed its prime, its stamina and strength begin to wane also. The head adornment grows very heavy and cumbersome and becomes a burden from which there is no relief.

Another drawback occurs if the horns grow to immense proportions and form complete curls. The projecting ends do not permit the animal to feed properly. Gradually the animal's weight begins to decline, and it will eventually die.

CAN YOU TELL A SHEEP'S AGE BY ITS HORNS?

Yes. Unlike the white-tailed deer, both male and female sheep grow horns. The deer's antlers fall off in the winter whereas the bighorn's do not. The sheep's horns continue to grow throughout their lifetime although the female's are small and only slightly curved.

During the first eight years there is significant growth. After that, it tapers off. Like the growth rings of a tree, sheep's horns also have markings which indicate age. As the animal grows older and older the lines grow closer together. After ten years the markings are difficult to count because they are so close together.

DO RAMS ALWAYS FIGHT WITH EACH OTHER?

No. During most of the year small herds of rams group together, feeding and traveling in a peaceful coexistence. But as fall progresses and they draw closer and closer to the mating season, the males become agitated and excitable, polishing their horns as they prepare for combat and courtship. It has been observed that the fiercest battles occur with intruding rams which try to disrupt the social order. It is not uncommon for these battles to draw blood from both the nostrils and ears. Within a group of rams which have spent the summer together, there does not tend to be fighting. If there is, it is not as brutal. They generally divide the females among themselves.

WHAT IS MEANT BY THE TERM "OWNING" THE LAMB?

When a ewe feels the pains of birth, she leaves the company of the flock and seeks solitude. Finding a quiet spot in the cover of rocks and brush, she gives birth to either one or two young. Once the lambs are born, an important procedure takes place known as "owning" the lamb. The mother licks her newborn thoroughly clean, washing it from head to foot.

The ceremony takes about twenty to thirty minutes, but if it is not done, the lamb is doomed. During this washing the mother imprints herself on her young. From that point on, only she will accept the lamb when it comes to nurse. If she does not recognize it, she will turn it away. It is vital that the lamb know which ewe is its mother, for if it cannot identify its mother and go to her, it will be denied milk by the others and will eventually starve to death.

The licking also serves another purpose. At birth the lamb is warm. Exposure to cold air chills the lamb, and it is important that it be dried off as quickly as possible. By licking the lamb dry, the mother cleans it and fluffs its hair. The vigorous rubdown stimulates body circulation and is an encouragement to the lamb to rise to its feet and begin nursing, replenishing and building its food supply so that its body has energy to produce heat.

HOW MANY TYPES OF BIGHORN SHEEP ARE THERE IN NORTH AMERICA?

Originally, twenty-five subspecies of *Ovis canadensis* inhabited the North American continent. Several of these species are now extinct such as the *Ovis canadensis auduboni* which once inhabited the badlands of South Dakota. The remaining North American species are divided into four classifications.

The ewe is constantly on the lookout for possible danger.

The adult bighorn's eyes vary in color from pale amber to golden yellow. The lamb's eyes are brown.

The bighorn is one of the few animals which uses caves for shelter.

During the first days of a lamb's life the mother stays close, protecting it from such predators as the bald eagle.

ROCKY MOUNTAIN BIGHORN   *Ovis canadensis*

The Rocky Mountain bighorn is the largest of the American sheep. Its coloring is grayish-brown with a black tail. A white patch on its rump continues down the inside of the hind legs and also down the back of the forelegs. Its ears and nose are a paler brown than the rest of its head. The bighorn feeds on the tender grasses and plants found in the highest peaks and crags of its Rocky Mountain habitat.

STONE SHEEP   *Ovis dalli stonei*

The Stone Sheep, also called Blue Sheep or Black Sheep, is actually a subspecies of the Dall. With grizzlies, caribou, and some of the largest moose of North America, the Stone Sheep inhabit the wildest area of the continent. This may account for the fact that they were not even discovered until 1897. Their range extends from the Yukon to northern British Columbia. Except for striking white on their nose and patches of white on their rump and the backs of each leg, they are different shades of gray. Coloring varies among their members from medium gray to black. Often the shades vary on the individual animal. It is not unusual for one to have a face and neck of medium gray and a body of coal black. This animal weighs from 210 to 220 pounds. Its height at the shoulders measures from thirty-nine to forty inches.

DALL SHEEP   *Ovis dalli*

The comparatively small Dall Sheep were originally imported from Asia. They now inhabit most of the mountainous country of Alaska and the Yukon east to the Mackenzie Mountains of northwest Canada. Their coloring varies slightly according to their range. Generally, with the exception of their black hooves and amber eyes and horns, they are pure white—one of the few animals that remain white year round. The Dall Sheep, like other American bighorns, have excellent eyesight. They feed during the day and rest at night. Their shoulder height is thirty-six to forty-two inches and their weight averages from 125-200 pounds.

DESERT BIGHORN   *Ovis canadensis canadensis*

The desert bighorn, a subspecies of the Rocky Mountain bighorn, inhabits the dry, hot deserts of the southwestern United States where rainfall seldom exceeds nine inches a year. Its body is smaller and leaner than the Rocky Mountain bighorn, but its head is generally as large. Its coloring is also quite similar. If it weren't for their white nose, rump, and belly, they would hardly be noticed in the sandy, neutral-colored background of their habitat. Even desert animals need water to exist. Because of the scarcity of water and the extreme heat and cold of the desert climate, the numbers of these animals are slowly declining.

HOW DOES SCRIPTURE ILLUSTRATE HOSPITALITY IN PROVIDING LEADERSHIP FOR A PEACEFUL SURROUNDING?

Scripture teaches that if our enemy hungers we should feed him, and if he thirsts we should give him drink. What man obeyed this teaching and as a result conquered an entire army?

(Pause for a response—see page 20)

Early one morning the servant of a great prophet arose and went outside. What he saw caused him to stare in astonishment. During the night, a powerful detachment of cavalry and foot soldiers had surrounded the city. He knew why they were there. They had come to capture the prophet whom he served. Every time their king made secret plans to attack this country, the prophet reported them to his own king who was then able to out-maneuver the enemy.

Frightened and alarmed, the servant rushed to the prophet and reported what he had seen. The prophet listened and remained calm, almost unconcerned. This astonished his servant. He was soon to learn that the prophet whom he served had two secret weapons more powerful than any attacking army.

Spiritual vision was required to see the first weapon. The prophet prayed, "Lord, I pray thee, open his eyes that he may see." The Lord opened the eyes of that servant, and he suddenly saw a huge army of horses and chariots afire. They surrounded their enemy and could have easily destroyed them.

The prophet prayed a second time. His request was granted as God struck every one of those enemy soldiers with temporary blindness. Then he walked up to their general and said, "Follow me, and I will bring you to the one you seek."

The prophet's servant was about to witness one of the most unusual strategies ever employed to conquer an invading army. The blinded general and his men were led by the prophet straight to the capital city where the king and defending army were stationed.

The king could hardly believe his eyes. All the enemy soldiers had been brought right into his hands. Excitedly he asked the prophet, "Should we slay them?" "You shall not kill them," commanded the prophet. He knew that to destroy this military detachment would only result in others coming in their place. He would use a different strategy, one that would be even more effective.

The prophet instructed the king to prepare food and water for these captured soldiers and send them back to their land. The surprised king obeyed. He prepared a great feast for them, then sent them away.

By sitting down to eat a meal together, these armies were committing themselves to the tradition which is symbolized by sharing a meal—the friendship and protection of each other. So effective was this strategy that it marked the end of the marauding bands which had plundered the land. Elisha the prophet won a battle without bloodshed, and his leadership provided peaceful and harmonious surroundings for the people.

From II Kings 6:8-23

ELISHA'S UNUSUAL TACTICS PROVIDED A PEACEFUL ENVIRONMENT

The prophet Elisha had the rather unpopular job of being God's spokesman to Israel during the twelve-year reign of Jehoram. Although his major duty was to proclaim God's Word to the faithful few who had not yet bowed their knee to Baal (I Kings 19:18) and to instruct other prophets to help in this task, he was called upon by God at times to invade the realm of national politics.

The Assyrian chariot above *may have been similar to those which Elisha's frightened servant saw surrounding the city. Each chariot could carry a driver, an archer, and two shield bearers. It is no wonder that he cried, "Alas, my master! What shall we do?"*

FEAR PROMPTS JEHORAM TO OBEY

Such a command, of course, required involvement with King Jehoram, the reigning son of Ahab and Jezebel. The relationship between Elisha and Jehoram was always strained. Elisha was the successor of Elijah, the prophet who had proclaimed to Ahab that the Lord would take away his posterity (I Kings 21:21) and bring evil upon his house in his son's days (I Kings 21:29). Elijah had also correctly predicted the death of Jehoram's brother whom he succeeded to the throne (II Kings 1:17). Jehoram was afraid of Elisha and often accommodated his demands, but his sporadic cooperation was prompted more by fear of the consequences of disobedience than a genuine desire to please the Lord (cf. II Kings 3:2,3).

A STRAINED RELATIONSHIP

The first meeting between them was filled with tension. Elisha's first words to Jehoram were, "What have I to do with thee? Get thee to the prophets of thy father, and to the prophets of thy mother." (II Kings 3:13) When Jehoram claimed to be following the Lord's counsel, Elisha responded, "As the Lord of hosts liveth, before whom I stand, surely, were it not that I regard the presence of Jehoshaphat, the king of Judah, I would not look toward thee, nor see thee." (II Kings 3:14) Elisha was so upset by the encounter that he needed the music of a minstrel to calm his emotions before he was able to continue (II Kings 3:15).

BENHADAD CANNOT KEEP A SECRET FROM THE PROPHET

During the war between Syria and Israel, the Lord called upon his servant Elisha again to become involved with King Jehoram. Syria had decided to send small raiding parties against Israel in an effort to destroy selected cities before the Israeli army could respond. It was the strategem of Benhadad, Syria's king, and should have been extremely effective. But time after time Syrian raiding parties were met by Jehoram's soldiers at the target city. Benhadad naturally suspected a security leak among his generals. When interrogated, one of his generals boldly replied, "O king, but Elisha, the prophet that is in Israel, telleth the king of Israel the words that thou speakest in thy bedchamber." (II Kings 6:12) The king of Syria immediately directed his energies against Elisha.

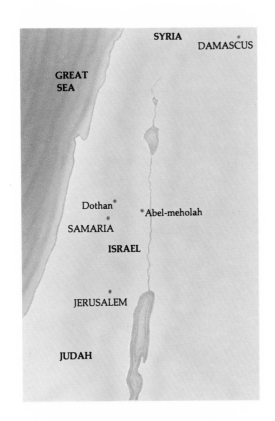

The economy of the Syrians *was related to their free access through Israel along the trade routes to Egypt and Phoenicia. This led to constant tension between the two countries and often exploded into open warfare.*

BLINDNESS SUBDUES AN ARMY

Soon Syrian horses, chariots, and a great host blockaded the city of Dothan where Elisha and his servant were. When Elisha's servant saw the very impressive Syrian forces surrounding the city, he exclaimed in fear, "Alas, my master, how shall we do?" (II Kings 6:15) Elisha prayed, "And the Lord opened the eyes of the young man, and he saw; and, behold, the mountain was full of horses and chariots of fire round about Elisha." (II Kings 6:17) Elisha prayed again, and the Lord smote the Syrian army with blindness. He then marched them right into the heavily fortified capital of Samaria eleven miles to the south.

King Jehoram recognized the golden opportunity to eliminate this portion of his enemy's forces, but Elisha forbid it. Instead, he commanded Jehoram to feed them at government expense and then set them free. Elisha's strange strategy was successful. The Syrian tactic of terror raids was halted, for we read, "So the bands of Syria came no more into the land of Israel." (II Kings 6:23)

ELISHA CHARACTER SKETCH

WHY DID ELISHA HELP THE WICKED KING OF ISRAEL?

Jehoram was a wicked king who "cleaved unto the sins of Jeroboam, the son of Nebat, who made Israel to sin; he departed not from them." (II Kings 3:3) He protected his idolatrous mother, Jezebel, in the capital city of Samaria and tolerated false worship. When Elisha helped him in the war against Syria, he was acting in accordance with the word of the Lord. The Syrian raids were not directed against the heavily defended capital where Jehoram dwelt. They were directed against smaller, unprotected cities. The Lord used Elisha to protect innocent people in the outlying countryside. The Lord was raising up other men—Jehu and Hazael—to replace Jehoram and the king of Syria (cf. I Kings 19:15-17). Jehu was to kill Jehoram, Jezebel, and the prophets of Baal in one sweep at the proper time (II Kings 9:24, 33; 10:17, 25). Until that time, it was the Lord's will that the nation be spared from the cruel and destructive raids of the Syrians (II Kings 6:23).

WHY DID ELISHA PRAY TO HAVE HIS SERVANT'S EYES OPENED?

Elisha wanted to train his servant just like his master, Elijah, had trained him. It was obvious that Elisha's former servant, Gehazi, would not succeed him. Although Gehazi had seen the prophet perform many miracles, he was never able to see past the miracles to the Lord Himself. Because of his focus on material things, Gehazi was punished with leprosy (II Kings 5:26, 27). Now Elisha desired that this new servant actually see a vision of the heavenly hosts. The servant must learn to be amazed at the resources of the Lord rather than merely the miracles of a man whom God chose to use. When Elisha and the servant led the Syrians through the gates of Samaria, the servant would not be filled with pride at his master's accomplishment but would be reverently awed by the Lord's mighty power.

HOW DID ELISHA PROVIDE THE NATION WITH A PEACEFUL AND HARMONIOUS SURROUNDING?

When Elisha marched the blinded band of Syrian soldiers into the Israeli capital, the king wanted to kill them. Elisha, however, knew that such a tactic would only provoke the Syrians' anger and prolong the terrorist raids. Elisha wanted to show the Syrians that they were dealing with a prophet of the true God that they might learn to fear Him. He decided to eat and drink with them instead.

Eating and drinking together among the people of the East signified a bond of friendship that was highly respected. When they ate together, there was bread and salt (cf. Numbers 18:19) between them. They were no longer strangers, regardless of their previous relationship—to share a meal was to forget past grievances. Eating a meal together was considered a sacred affair.

The strange tactic of Elisha was successful. The Syrian king realized that small raiding parties were no match for a nation under the Lord's protection and that his nation's honor was at stake because of the meal. The raiding stopped, and peace returned to the land.

"And he prepared **great provision for them.** *And when they had eaten and drunk, he sent them away, and they went to their master. So the bands of Syria came no more into the land of Israel."*

ELISHA
ē lī'sha

Generosity

"Greater love hath no man than this, that a man lay down his life for his friends. God so loved . . . that he gave . . ."

John 15:13; 3:16

PART SEVEN

Generosity

IS GIVING A GIFT THAT IS CHERISHED BY THE RECEIVER AND THE GIVER

"Lay not up for yourselves treasures upon earth, where moth and rust doth corrupt, and where thieves break through and steal."

Matthew 6:19

LIVING LESSONS ON GENEROSITY . . .

FROM THE PAGES OF SCRIPTURE

God has assumed a special care and protection for the fatherless and the widow. Anyone who gives to their needs is not only doing a special work for God but will receive a special reward from Him. The apostle James said that the truest sign of genuine religion is giving to the fatherless and the widows in their affliction and maintaining personal purity in every contact with the world (James 1:27). One woman in Scripture exemplified this mark of true Christianity by devoting herself to meeting the needs of widows. The gifts she gave represented that which she cherished the most and became lasting investments which produced greater dividends than she could have imagined.

ILLUSTRATED IN THE WORLD OF NATURE

BANNERTAIL KANGAROO RAT   *Dipodomys spectabilis*

The unsociable kangaroo rat is neither a kangaroo nor a rat. It is a close relative of the pocket mouse. But its appearance and the fact that it is one of the "jumping-est" creatures among all small mammals make its name appropriate. It is a native of the dry to semi-dry regions of North America, making its home in sandy soil where there is sparse vegetation. This rodent does not hibernate and, unlike some desert creatures, does not sleep away the hot, mid-summer periods either. The white stripe across the bannertail's flanks makes it one of the most handsome of all kangaroo rats. It is very clean and spends much time washing itself and taking dust baths. The bannertail is approximately fifteen inches long from its nose to the tip of its tail. It has a low annual birthrate and a life expectancy of approximately two years.

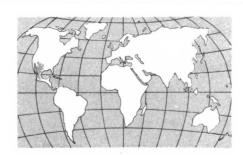

The range and habitat of the bannertail kangaroo rat

GENEROSITY

HOW DOES THE KANGAROO RAT ILLUSTRATE THE NEED TO GIVE?

Slipping through a cover of darkness, the strange creature scurried about in search of food. No other animal quite resembled it. This furry little ball with its large head, long tail, and big, black eyes was a sight to behold.

By using its tail and large, powerful legs to scamper about the desert floor, it hopped from place to place, chucking its cheeks full of food. Any variety of vegetation was quickly stuffed into these fur-lined pouches and taken back to the burrow for storage.

The kangaroo rat had quite a system. It gathered dry seeds and separated them according to type and size. It harvested edible leaves by cutting them into bite-size pieces. Rather than taking them immediately down to its burrow where they might spoil and decompose, the industrious bannertail dug shallow pits and placed them inside. The buried items would dry in the hot desert sun. Later it returned to take the dried morsels to its larder.

The kangaroo rat used every opportunity to gather supplies for its storehouse. It accumulated huge mounds of seeds and leaves. There was so much food that it had to dig and construct new chambers continually in order to house the harvest.

It had gathered more supplies than it could ever feasibly use. But in spite of this, it went out without fail night after night from dusk until dawn. It stopped only when danger or an intruder threatened. Having little use for visiting relatives, it would impudently inform them of its feelings about freeloaders by stomping its feet to create a thumping sound that told the visitor, "Keep out and stay away!"

One evening as it busily arranged produce in the burrow, it heard a noise. It stopped to listen. The noise sounded like little grinders going to work. Upon investigation, it realized that one of its cousins had come to pay a visit. It was a little Merriam kangaroo rat—smaller than the bannertail. This little rodent wasn't as industrious as its bigger cousin, but it was awfully friendly. It had stopped by to pick up a few kernels and socialize with its neighbor.

The bannertail was in no mood for this. It angrily raced over and with a powerful leap kicked the little rat, forcing it into a corner. Kick after kick was inflicted on its body. Soon the little creature lay still, lifeless. The bannertail had killed it.

It killed the visitor because its nature was to hoard everything. The kangaroo rat had no ability or willingness to give even from its overflowing, abundant harvest.

SCRIPTURAL REFERENCES TO THE KANGAROO RAT

The kangaroo rat is neither a kangaroo nor a rat. It is more closely related to the harvest mouse. As such it is included in the list of unclean, creeping things in Leviticus 11:29.

There are two characteristics of this kangaroo rat which are contrary to godly character—selfishness and unfriendliness. In the world of the kangaroo rat, as in the world of man, these two negative traits tend to go hand in hand.

The kangaroo rat is a hoarder, storing or burying every bit of food it can get. It does not share what it has but instead will attack any visitor. The consequence of a similar tendency in human nature is described in Ecclesiastes 5:13. "There is a sore evil which I have seen under the sun, namely, riches kept for the owners thereof to their hurt."

Riches attract friends and selfishness repels them. Those who would have genuine friends must follow the counsel of Proverbs 18:24. "A man who hath friends must show himself friendly; and there is a friend who sticketh closer than a brother."

CHARACTERISTICS AND PHYSICAL FEATURES OF THE KANGAROO RAT

The bannertail's lack of generosity did not permit it to share with the little Merriam. This hoarding action is typical of the species. It will quickly fight over food, grunting and growling all the while it tries to kick and defeat its opponent. It is not only selfish but totally unsociable. Put two of these in a cage and one will invariably be killed. During mating season they barely tolerate each other. Even then it is not long before one rat builds a partition in the burrow to separate the two. Because the kangaroo rat, or dipo, is such a shy and seclusive nocturnal creature, it is not easily seen in the wild. Despite its faults, it is a very interesting rodent, uniquely constructed and well-suited to live in its desert country home.

HOW ARE DIPO'S FEET SUITED FOR SANDY SOIL?

The kangaroo rat's long feet and powerful muscle and leg construction lend spring to its jump and enable it to bound up to twenty-four or more inches. By relying on jumping or hopping as its form of locomotion, it is able to travel across the soft sand with a minimum of resistance. Dipo may achieve a speed of seventeen feet per second! The hair that grows on the soles of its feet gives it further agility. This feature increases the animal's traction in the sand and enables it to make sharp turns to dodge obstacles or predators.

DOES DIPO RUN ON ALL FOURS?

No. The kangaroo rat is equipped for *bipedal saltatorial* locomotion. When it runs or hops at full speed it uses just the hind legs. Only the toes actually touch the ground. It can hop steadily for long periods of time without tiring. As it hops it carries its "arms" tucked close against its chest. As a result, the hind feet are very powerful; the forelimbs tend to be much weaker.

For feeding it uses all four feet to move slowly along the surface. The entire hind foot, as well as the heels of the hind legs are used at this slower pace.

DOES DIPO HAVE ANY DEFENSE AGAINST THE RATTLESNAKE?

If the kangaroo rat is in a favorable position, it may challenge an intruding rattlesnake and win. Turning its back on the snake, it uses its powerful hind feet and digs into the sand, kicking behind a steady stream of debris into the air. The snake does not have eyelids to protect its eyes. It is very sensitive and careful to keep foreign matter out of them. A short exposure to the mini "sandstorm" is enough to discourage the rattler.

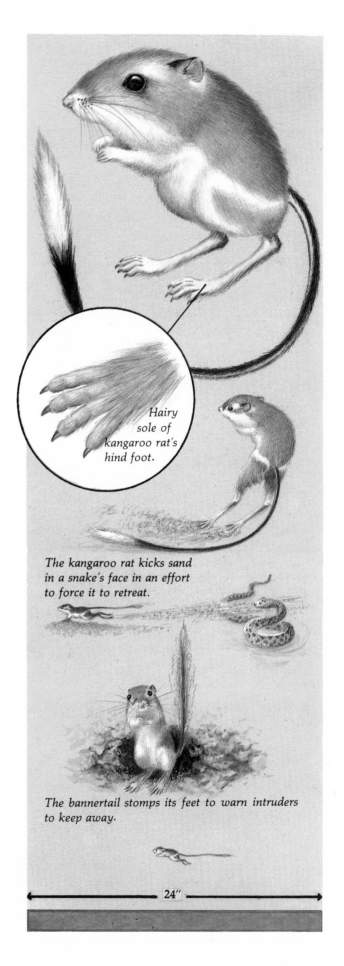

Hairy sole of kangaroo rat's hind foot.

The kangaroo rat kicks sand in a snake's face in an effort to force it to retreat.

The bannertail stomps its feet to warn intruders to keep away.

24"

Oil gland

The kangaroo rat protects its skin from the heat of the desert by lubricating it with oil.

The tufts of hair *on the kangaroo rat's tail function in much the same way as feathers on an arrow.*

With each jump *the kangaroo rat takes a zigzagging course in an effort to elude objects and pursuing predators.*

Dipo's nocturnal activities *are aided by nighttime vision.*

DOES THE DIPO'S LONG TAIL HELP IT IN ANY WAY?

The kangaroo rat's tail is a unique feature critical to the animal's survival. The white-tipped structure, longer than its body, serves as a prop to support it when it is resting on its haunches. It is of even greater importance when Dipo jumps. Without this balancing organ the bannertail would somersault uncontrollably through the air.

Similar in function to the feathers of an arrow, the long tufts of hair at the end of its tail cause the tail to "windmill" or twirl in a tight circle. This permits the kangaroo rat to maintain a straight course when it hops across the desert. As it hurtles through the air it resembles a missle with a rear prop. It zigzags with every jump. By using its specialized tail and the hairy soles of its feet, Dipo can achieve almost ninety degree turns in any direction.

When it touches the ground after jumping, its hind feet automatically return to a position from which the bannertail could immediately jump again. With rare agility it is able to elude and dodge its many predators. The slightest hint of danger sends it scurrying away not restrained in the least by the soft sand.

WHY DOESN'T THE KANGAROO RAT LOOK FORWARD TO A FULL MOON?

Because then there is too much light for safety. On nights when the moon is full, the adult kangaroo rat does not emerge from its burrow unless it is forced. They are most comfortable when it is completely dark and they feel their predators cannot see them. Generally, their activities are confined to the hours from sunset to sunrise. Even then, their venture outside the burrow is a very cautious one.

When leaving its home, the kangaroo rat stops just behind its doorway and drums out a series of thumping sounds. The reason for this prelude is not completely understood, but it is thought that the purpose of the action is to betray the presence of any lurking predator. The rat then waits for a few minutes. When it has decided it is safe, it hops outside. The big eyes of this creature, well-suited for night vision, tend to take on a red hue in darkness.

DOES THE KANGAROO RAT ALWAYS KNOW WHAT IT IS EATING?

The construction of the kangaroo rat's head and the position of its eyes enable the animal to have peripheral vision of 360 degrees. Each eye sees beyond the sweep of a half circle. However, Dipo does have one problem. This same construction and placement prevents the little animal from seeing the spot right beneath its nose. This is a bit inconvenient as it is unable to see what it is eating. The disadvantage is balanced, though, by the bannertail's very acute senses of smell, touch, and taste.

WHAT IS UNIQUE ABOUT THE KANGAROO RAT'S HEARING?

Dipo's ears are extremely sensitive to sound. In fact, they can pick up frequencies between 1,000 and 3,000 cycles per second. The unique mechanism which enables the rodent to have such acute hearing is three small bones of the inner ear. These bones serve two purposes. First, they transmit sound waves from the eardrum to the sense organs. Second, they amplify. It is estimated that the rat's sensitivity to sound is five times greater than man's.

Another factor contributing to the rodent's sensitive hearing is the tympanic bullae—dome shaped bones on either side of the head. Each of these contain a large, auditory chamber. It was once thought that the chambers were resonators, but research has shown that they enable the eardrum to vibrate more freely.

In a normal eardrum air pressure builds behind it in the middle ear causing it to resist movement. But the kangaroo rat's large chamber in the bullae allows increased pressure to be absorbed. This makes it possible for the inner eardrum to vibrate when stimulated by very weak vibrations. This is an important defense against one of its principal enemies, the screech owl. Dipo's sensitive ears are so acute that they can pick up the nearly silent wingbeats of this fearsome predator.

WHAT ENEMIES DOES THE KANGAROO RAT FACE?

Some of the enemies in a long list of predators are: the rattlesnake, bobcat, badger, gray fox, and kit fox. There are other creatures that are a nuisance to the bannertail such as the black widow spider and scorpion. It is interesting to note that one common pest—the flea—is rarely ever found on the clean kangaroo rat. Specimens that were held in captivity were free from fleas and other vermin that normally inflict animals.

HOW IS DIPO ABLE TO OUTMANEUVER ITS ENEMIES UNDERGROUND?

When faced with danger the kangaroo rat may choose from a number of alternative defenses. If a fox begins to dig at the bannertail's entrance when the rodent is home, Dipo's intricate maze of passageways offers many places in which to hide and find safety. It would be very difficult, if not impossible, for the fox to dig it out.

Another defense option would be to "dig in and fight." If a rattlesnake slithers into its home, the kangaroo rat may try to maneuver it into a corner and then throw up a dirt barricade with its powerful feet.

When a badger or other predator comes dangerously close, Dipo may decide to use an emergency exit. The bannertail's burrow has thin walls through which it can suddenly burst out, surprise its pursuer and race away to safety.

Dipo's sensitive ears are able to detect the owl.

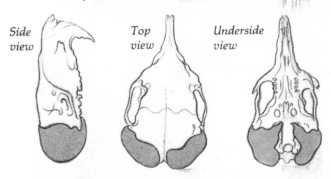

Side view   *Top view*   *Underside view*

The darkened bone structure *on the back of the kangaroo rat's skull is the tympanic bullae. These auditory chambers enable the eardrum to vibrate, giving acute hearing.*

Emergency shelters

Dipo escaping through emergency exit

Multi-chambered burrow for protection

335

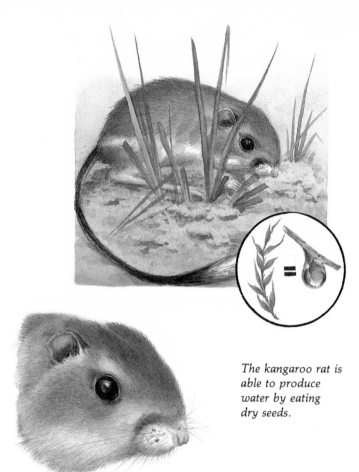

The kangaroo rat is
able to produce
water by eating
dry seeds.

The pouches located on either side of Dipo's mouth *are lined with fine, silken fur. This smooth lining enables the animal to fill and empty its food pouch quickly and prevents foreign matter from remaining there and causing infection.*

Large mounds *and extensive burrows are formed over many years by many generations.*

HOW IS THE KANGAROO RAT ABLE TO LIVE IN THE DESERT WITHOUT WATER?

The animal survives by extracting and storing hydrogen from dry seeds and other carbohydrates. Dipo combines this with the oxygen in the air to produce its own water. The bannertail is also able to survive because it is very efficient with waste. Its remarkable kidneys need very little water to function. They can contain as high as twenty-four percent urea as compared with man's six percent. Dipo also has very few sweat glands which further prevent the loss of water from its body.

Another remarkable feature of the kangaroo rat is evident during periods of drought. The animal can actually retain body fluid, eliminate the salt from it and then reabsorb the water through the walls of its bladder. This process is unique among animals. Because of this feature, the kangaroo rat is capable of drinking sea water. This liquid normally would quickly dehydrate an animal because its system would lose too much water trying to eliminate the high salt content.

Another water-producing feature, a more likely one, is found in Dipo's nose. When the little animal exhales, condensation takes place. Beads of water form on the cool membrane which lines its nose. This moisture is then swallowed, giving the animal one more resourceful means of meeting its water needs.

HOW DOES THE KANGAROO RAT COPE WITH THE HEAT?

Because Dipo is a nocturnal animal, it sleeps away the hottest daytime hours. But on extremely hot days even its underground burrow becomes uncomfortable. During these times the little rodent plugs the entrance with dirt from its other tunnels. By doing so, it is able to cool the chamber by as much as ten to twenty-five degrees. The humidity level is raised which is also very important. Being able to breathe high humidity air decreases Dipo's water loss. The little bannertail's surroundings are made comfortable despite the unbearable temperatures outside its home.

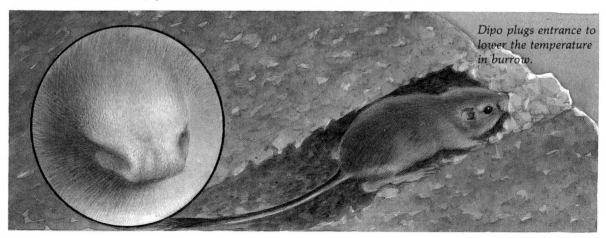

Dipo plugs entrance to lower the temperature in burrow.

The kangaroo rat is able to drink through its nose.

HOW DOES SCRIPTURE ILLUSTRATE GENEROSITY IN GIVING GIFTS THAT ARE CHERISHED BY BOTH THE GIVER AND THE RECEIVER?

If a man in a blue uniform stood in an intersection directing traffic, you would know he was a policeman. If a man walked from house to house in your neighborhood with letters in his hand, you would know he was a mailman. If you were asked to describe the truest "uniform" of genuine religion, what would that be? See John 13:35 and James 1:27.

(Pause for a response —see page 20)

A creaking ship edged toward the harbor as its billowing sails were drawn in. Men dashed about the deck. A plank was lowered, and soon precious cargo was being carried off the ship onto the dock. The seacoast city bustled with new activity. Curious shoppers studied merchandise from faraway places.

Among the busy inhabitants was one who had a deep concern that many in this influential city would believe on the Lord Jesus Christ. This dedicated Christian is not known for an ability to speak to crowds or perform miraculous deeds, but what this person did resulted in the salvation of many in that town. This Christian quietly demonstrated what the apostle James later described as the truest evidence of genuine religion.

One day this Christian became deathly ill. News of the sickness spread quickly. Then came the tragic report of death. The body was washed and laid in an upstairs room. It was then that the deep love of others for all that this one had done became evident. Many gathered together and wept.

Meanwhile, two men from that group left the city. In a nearby town they found one of the twelve apostles and urged him to come without delay. As the three men returned to that room, the apostle heard sobs and weeping. When he entered many widows showed him coats and garments which their friend had made and given to them.

Those in the room were asked to leave. Then the apostle knelt and prayed, turned to the body, and called her by name. Immediately her eyes opened, and she sat up. The apostle then gave her his hand, lifted her up and presented Dorcas alive to all the widows and friends who returned to the room. Now there were tears of joy and excitement. News of this miracle spread throughout the city and many believed on the Lord Jesus Christ.

There is a significant footnote to this account. The apostle who raised Dorcas from the dead was Peter. Until that time he had preached only to the Jews, but Dorcas lived in Joppa, a seaport city inhabited by both Jews and Gentiles. While he was there, Peter received the vision that God wanted him to proclaim the Gospel to the Gentile world as well. His example for doing so was Dorcas whose generosity was directed toward and cherished by both Jews and Gentiles.

From Acts 9:36-42

A hand spindle was made of wood *and was from nine to fifteen inches long.*

By using a yarn bowl and two spindles *an ambitious woman could double her production.*

A yarn bowl *with guides to separate the strands*

A loom was used to weave *the yarn into fabric for clothing.*

DORCAS GAVE CHERISHED GIFTS TO THE POOR AND NEEDY

The early church had just suffered a period of intense persecution, spearheaded by the misdirected efforts of Saul of Tarsus. But Saul had met the Lord and was now a believer. The immediate persecution was over, and Christians were able to minister to others and spread the good news of the Gospel in relative peace.

A JEWESS LIVING IN A ROMAN SEAPORT

One of these believers was Tabitha. Her name, when translated from Hebrew to Greek, is Dorcas. It means gazelle—an animal noted for its grace and beauty. Her Greek name implies that she was a Jewess who lived among the Greeks and spoke their language. Her home was in Joppa, a very beautiful and busy seaport on the eastern shore of the Mediterranean. It was Jerusalem's access to the western markets, located about thirty-five miles away. In Dorcas' day Joppa was ruled by Rome and, as an active port city, was marked especially by widows who had lost their husbands in accidents on the sea.

SHE GAVE TO THE WIDOWS AND FATHERLESS

The needs of the widows and fatherless children of Joppa were great. Neither Rome nor the general populace offered much assistance to these needy citizens. In fact, they were often abused and subjected to abject poverty by ruthless men. Dorcas, a disciple of Jesus Christ, followed the example of her Master by serving those in need (Matthew 20:28). She is not said to be a widow nor is there any mention of her husband. She may well have been a young woman who had postponed marriage in light of the unlimited opportunities to serve others.

NEWS OF HER DEATH SPREAD QUICKLY

We know little of her actual deeds other than "this woman was full of good works and almsdeeds which she did." (Acts 9:36) These good works included the many "coats and garments" which Dorcas made and distributed to those in need. We can only imagine that she mothered the needy, the lonely, and the helpless of her community. The widows in Joppa became Dorcas' special responsibility, and many came to depend on her. She took care of them and their children when they were sick. She distributed food when they were hungry, clothes when they were cold, and comfort when they were discouraged.

It is likely that in her endless errands of mercy, she exhausted the limits of her physical endurance. For reasons unmentioned, she became sick and died. The loss was felt immediately as news of her sudden death spread to her friends.

RAISED FROM THE DEAD TO CONTINUE HER GOOD WORKS

Reports had reached Joppa of what was happening in Lydda, an inland town some ten miles southeast of the city. In the name of Jesus, Peter had commanded an apparently incurable invalid to arise from the bed on which he had lain for eight years (Acts 9:33, 34). Peter was summoned and came to the assembly of mourners. His heart must have been touched with love for the woman who had served Christ so faithfully.

Peter sent everyone out of the room and began to pray. Unlike the actions of Elijah and Elisha when they raised the dead (I Kings 17:19-22; II Kings 4:33-36), Peter merely turned to her body and said, "Tabitha, arise." "And she opened her eyes; and when she saw Peter, she sat up. And he gave her his hand, and lifted her up; and when he had called the saints and widows, presented her alive." (Acts 10:40,41)

We are told nothing more of Dorcas in the New Testament, but we can be certain that she immediately resumed the work the Lord had called her to. She continued her ministry of comfort and help to the poor and helpless.

DORCAS CHARACTER SKETCH

HOW WAS DORCAS AN INSTRUMENT OF THE LORD IN GIVING?

The Lord has promised to help and guide all of His children, but His promises of special provision are more often directed to widows than any other group of people. The only other category that rivals them for special favor is the fatherless, often associated with them. Moses wrote concerning the Lord, "He doth execute the judgment of the fatherless and widow, and loveth the stranger, in giving him food and raiment." (Deuteronomy 10:18) The Lord curses those who mistreat her. "Cursed be he that perverteth the judgment of the stranger, fatherless, and widow." (Deuteronomy 27:19) David wrote, "A father of the fatherless, and a judge of the widows, is God in his holy habitation." (Psalm 68:5) Again we read, "The Lord preserveth the stranger; he relieveth the fatherless and widow." (Psalm 146:9) But how does the Lord in reality help the widow? He uses dedicated and willing disciples like Dorcas who are obedient to the promptings of His Spirit. Dorcas was an instrument of the Lord in fulfilling His special promises.

WHY WAS DORCAS SO DEEPLY LOVED BY THOSE WHO HAD RECEIVED AND CHERISHED HER GIFTS?

When Peter came to the chamber where Dorcas lay dead, "all the widows stood by him weeping." (Acts 9:39) Why were these women so deeply grieved? The first reason is found in the substance of Dorcas' charity. She had made them coats and garments. In other words, Dorcas gave these poor people what they needed most. So often our charity is based upon giving what we ourselves do not need, rather than what others do need. The second reason is found in the way she supplied her gifts. She made with her own hands the clothes that she lovingly gave. Her gifts were costly in time and labor. Most people are ready to give money, but few are willing to actually take the time and effort to "visit the fatherless and widows in their affliction." (James 1:27) Dorcas totally committed herself to these needy people and became personally involved with them. It is no wonder that she was so greatly mourned after her death.

WHY DID MANY PEOPLE BELIEVE IN CHRIST AFTER DORCAS' RESURRECTION?

"And it was known throughout all Joppa; and many believed in the Lord." (Acts 9:42) Such a miracle would naturally excite attention, but why belief in Christ? The reason they believed in Christ was because they were familiar with Dorcas' godly behavior and benevolence. They knew that Dorcas claimed to be a disciple of the Lord. When Peter, the spokesman for the entire movement, was able to restore her life, this confirmed two things. First, it was possible for a person to be raised from the dead. If Peter was able to raise Dorcas, then certainly the Lord Jesus, whom Peter served, was able to be raised from the dead. The resurrection of Jesus is, of course, the basis for our belief in Him (cf. I Corinthians 15:3, 4). Second, the identification of Dorcas with this movement confirmed that it was of God. Someone so kind and generous would not be of the Devil. These two things provided the evidence necessary for many to put their faith and trust in Jesus Christ as their Lord and Savior.

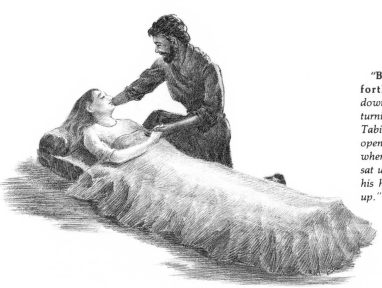

"But Peter put them all forth, *and kneeled down, and prayed; and turning to the body said, Tabitha, arise. And she opened her eyes; and when she saw Peter, she sat up. And he gave her his hand, and lifted her up."*

DORCAS
dôr'kăs

Generosity

IS WITHHOLDING A GIFT THAT WILL HURT THE ONE WHO RECEIVES IT

"But they that will be rich fall into temptation and a snare, and into many foolish and hurtful lusts, which drown men in destruction and perdition."

I Timothy 6:9

LIVING LESSONS ON GENEROSITY . . .

FROM THE PAGES OF SCRIPTURE

One of the valid concerns of a wealthy person is the possibility of corrupting those to whom he gives gifts. Scripture says that when riches increase the desires of those who have them increase. God further explains that those who desire to be rich fall into temptation and a snare and into many foolish and hurtful lusts, which drown men in destruction and perdition (I Timothy 6:9). These powerful truths emphasize the importance of knowing when giving will hurt the one who receives. One of the most famous generals in Scripture is well-known for his victorious battle, but few are aware of the final events of his life. He was generous with his family and friends, but the gift he gave brought harm to those who received it.

ILLUSTRATED IN THE WORLD OF NATURE

SAND WASP   *Bembix pruinosa*

Bembix, which means "buzzing insect" in Greek, is an appropriate name for this creature. The sand wasp creates sounds by using its wings and indicates its mood by various tones. When contentedly gathering food or feeding, it hums. Its tone is intensified while calling a mate and becomes a roar if attacked. The life-style and structure of the bembix pruinosa, a member of the order *Hymenoptera*, resemble man's characteristics in many ways and make the wasp an interesting subject for study. An inhabitant of North America, the wasp makes its home in sand dunes east of the Rocky Mountains.One-half inch in length, this insect weighs one one-hundreth of an ounce and has a life expectancy of three to four months. A female wasp does well to produce six young during its lifetime.

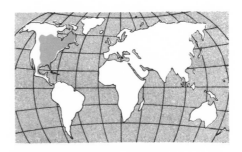

The range and habitat of the bembix wasp

(This is only an approximation. The exact range is not known.)

GENEROSITY

HOW DOES THE BEMBIX WASP ILLUSTRATE THE NEED TO WITHHOLD A GIFT?

Flying back and forth, the sand wasp tried to elude her quick opponent. But it was to no avail. She could not outmaneuver the adversary, and so she darted away in confusion.

Faithfully the wasp had brought dead flies to feed her newly-hatched larva. Its developing body needed constant nourishment in order to continue rapid growth. After burrowing below the surface of the sand, the mother wasp had tunneled out a passageway in which she laid one egg. Once it hatched, the young wasp began feeding on the flies that the mother provided.

Now the mother wasp returned to the nest cradling a large housefly between her legs which she would drag down the tunnel to her young. She scanned the area as she approached the entrance searching for her feared opponent—the tachina fly.

This fly isn't big. In fact, if she had been able to catch it, the wasp could easily kill it. Why then was the wasp so alarmed by the tachina fly?

The mother wasp wasn't concerned for herself, but rather for the safety of her young, and her fears were not unwarranted. The unwelcome threat emerged from behind a sand dune. The mother wasp tried to chase it away, but her effort was in vain. The fly was too quick and stayed just beyond reach, returning immediately to its watchful wait.

Realizing the futility of this tactic, the wasp darted away, her wings whining in frustration. The tachina fly did not pursue her because it knew she would return.

Camouflaged on a nearby dune, it settled back and patiently waited, all the while fixing its large, blood-red eyes on the entrance to the wasp's burrow.

After several attempts to return, the mother wasp's patience was wearing thin. This time she hoped that the fly had finally become discouraged and left. Even though the young, developing wasp still had plenty of food, the mother was motivated by a compelling drive to bring more.

As she approached the burrow this time, she was relieved to see no sign of the fly. Quickly she flew to the entrance. Once in the tunnel, she turned around and began to drag the limp housefly carcass behind her. She tried to maneuver as quickly as possible, but she wasn't quick enough. With incredible swiftness the tachina fly swept down and, unknown to the mother wasp, accomplished its destructive work.

The sand wasp was trying to make generous provision for her young, but no food at all would have been better than this. For in those few, split seconds when the mother wasp positioned herself in the tunnel, the efficient tachina had laid its deadly eggs in the carcass of the dead fly.

Soon, gluttonous maggots would hatch from the tachina's eggs. They would ravenously devour whatever food the mother wasp had provided in her underground nursery. The developing tachina would not only eat the stored provision but would eventually feed on the young wasp itself. Although the mother desired to provide for her young, her generosity destined it to death because she did not realize the destructiveness of her provision.

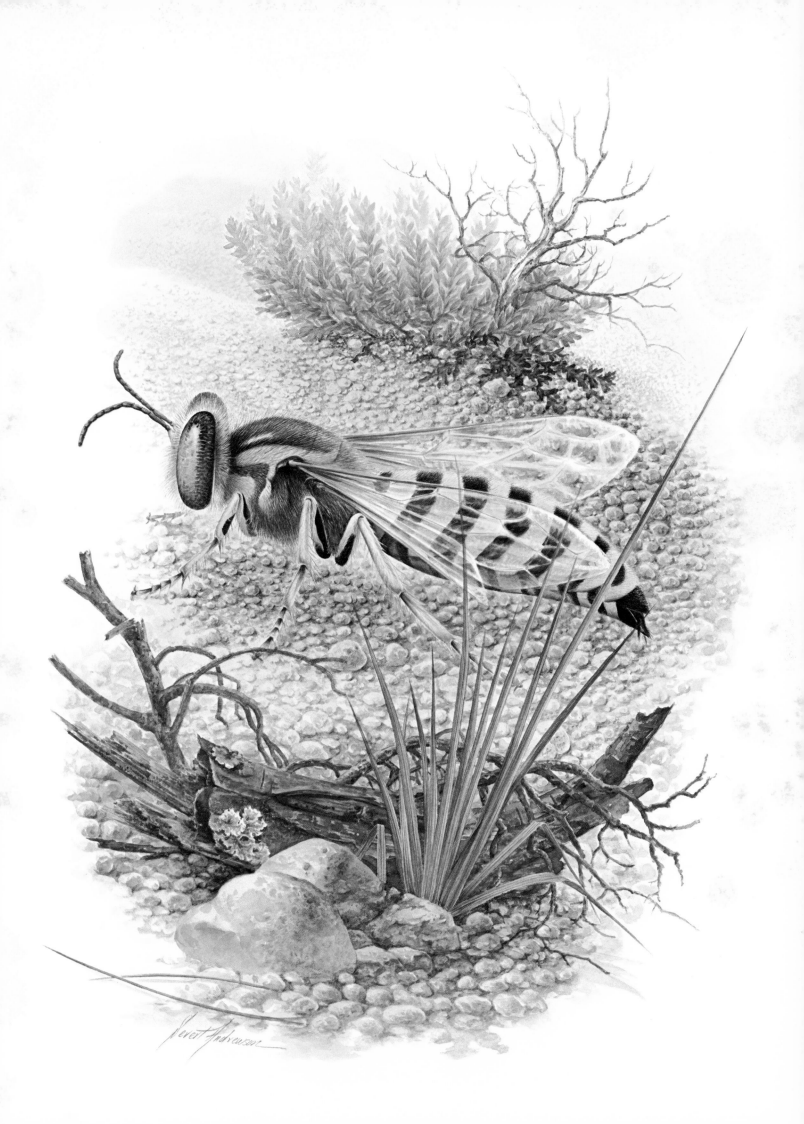

Scriptural references to the hornet

"Moreover the Lord thy God will send the hornet among them, until they that are left and hide themselves from thee, be destroyed."
Deuteronomy 7:20

Scriptural background

The Hebrew word for hornet includes its close relative, the social wasp. When the Israelites wandered in the wilderness, they probably encountered this insect. The wasp and hornet—easily angered if disturbed—were plentiful in Palestine. One city, Zoriath, means "place of hornets."

CHARACTERISTICS AND PHYSICAL FEATURES OF THE BEMBIX WASP

The generosity of the wasp was negated by the destructive force within its provision of food. It would have been better if the gift had never been given. The devotion and intensity of the bembix pruinosa in serving its young varies considerably among individual wasps. One wasp may be extremely energetic in carrying out the details of its life cycle, whereas another may be lazy and just barely perform. One may be patient and another impatient. One may be fastidiously clean and another sloppy in its ways. One may take extreme caution when bringing food to its young; another may be quite careless. One may be very generous, even overly generous, as was the case in this story; another may barely give enough to meet needs. Regardless of the individual personality, the general characteristics of this sand wasp are basically consistent. It is intriguing to observe the many precautions this insect takes, whether to a greater or lesser degree, against threats to its life and the life of its offspring.

PRECAUTIONS AGAINST INTENSE HEAT

In the hot, sandy regions where the bembix builds its nest, the wasp takes special precautions to ensure comfort for itself and its offspring. The insect escapes the heat by digging below the dry, hot layers of sand to deeper layers where it is cool and moist. The depth of the burrow is determined by the size of the dune and whether or not it is sheltered. If it is a shaded and smaller dune, the wasp digs approximately eight inches deep. If the dune is larger, she will dig deeper—for a very good reason. Since she makes her nest in the sand, she must fortify it against windstorms that might reach a shallow nest. The wind would blow away the top layers of sand and expose the nest to the scorching daytime heat.

PRECAUTIONS IN TESTING THE SOIL

The female undergoes an unusual ritual before she digs her burrow. She excavates a series of little pits. She does this by digging a shallow pit, backing up an inch or two, then digging another pit and continuing this process until she has dug an entire series—each pit connected by a straight line. It is believed that her purpose in doing so is to determine the texture of the soil and to decide whether or not the ground is suitable for constructing the burrow.

She begins the burrow by digging a horizontal tunnel which tapers down from the surface. She digs it directly beneath the series of shallow pits. The tested soil is safe from major cave-ins. The preliminary burrow, as it is called, extends as long as twenty inches.

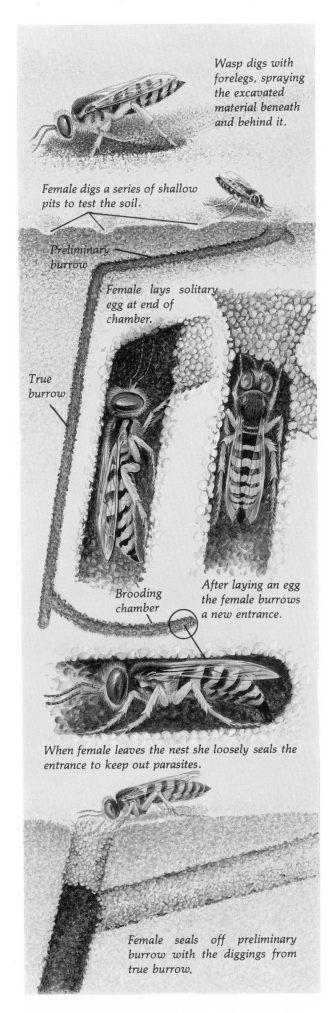

Wasp digs with forelegs, spraying the excavated material beneath and behind it.

Female digs a series of shallow pits to test the soil.

Preliminary burrow

Female lays solitary egg at end of chamber.

True burrow

Brooding chamber

After laying an egg the female burrows a new entrance.

When female leaves the nest she loosely seals the entrance to keep out parasites.

Female seals off preliminary burrow with the diggings from true burrow.

Bembix capturing fly in mid-air

Bembix stings and then positions fly so that it can be transported.

Enlargement of barbed dart

Sheath encasing darts

The stinger is made up of two barbed darts encased in a sheath. Powerful muscles at the base of this structure enable the wasp to puncture the skin and at the same time open the passageway for poison to be pumped into the wound.

Bembix returns to nest carrying insect to feed to her young.

PRECAUTIONS IN CONCEALING THE NEST

The wasp digs with its forelegs. Its legs are equipped with stiff, bristly hairs which act like tiny shovels. Bembix throws the excavated sand and material backward. If it encounters a small stone it carries it out, and if a root is in the way it clears the path by biting through it. Once the preliminary burrow is finished, she returns to the entrance and moves among the excavated piles to level them out.

When this job is complete, she again goes into the burrow and plugs the entrance from the inside. Then she makes her way to the end and digs obliquely downward, changing the course of the tunnel. The soil she excavates from this tunnel is pushed into the preliminary burrow. It eventually is completely plugged up. She digs this second burrow perhaps a yard and a half in length. It is as long, if not longer, than the preliminary one.

The new tunnel is called the true burrow. At the end of the true burrow the wasp changes its angle and digs a chamber approximately eight inches in length perpendicular to the surface. It is in this cell that she lays a single egg. The entire structure is used only once. When it is time for the sand wasp to renest, the female will construct a whole new burrow.

PRECAUTIONS TO ENSURE THE HATCH

The female does not leave after she has laid her single egg. Instead she guards and protects the egg for as long as two days until it is almost ready to hatch. At this time she leaves the nest to make another provision for her young—food. Since the preliminary burrow is filled by the second excavation, she makes her way up the true burrow. There she burrows an exit straight up and out to the surface and constructs another funnel-shaped entrance. Once this is made she lightly fills it in again, covering any telltale signs which might expose the nest's location.

PRECAUTIONS IN PROVIDING FOOD

The sand wasp brutally attacks its prey. It uses paralyzing venom as well as crushing mandibles which smash the head and thorax of insects. The wasp may bite off undesirable parts and chew the body up into pulp with its mandibles.

Bembix does not discriminate in the type of flies it captures. They include the housefly, green and blue bottle flies, or gadflies. She does, though, carefully choose the size of the insect. In the early stages of development she offers the larva a very small fly. The morsels become progressively larger as the larva grows.

In a five-day period a wasp larva may consume as many as forty-three flies. Each time the mother returns with a fly she re-excavates the entrance, slips in and out, and reseals the doorway upon her exit. She takes this precaution to protect against harmful parasites and predators that might enter the nest.

When approaching the nest she is watchful for the presence of the deadly tachina fly. If the coast is clear she quickly turns around and backs into the burrow, pulling the carcass behind her. She makes her many entrances and exits easier by eliminating pebbles and small obstacles that would be in her way as she hurriedly digs out. The wasp performs this function of sifting through the sand when it is not busy gathering meals for its young.

PRECAUTIONS IN KEEPING THE NEST CLEAN

The mother wasp stores supplies to feed her young larva in a unique way. She places dead flies in a row—one after the other. The larva moves from one fly to the next, consuming these morsels as it moves toward the entrance of the burrow. It does not always eat the entire fly but casts behind those parts it does not want.

At certain intervals the mother enters the nest and rakes up the debris, pushing it back toward the farthest part of the chamber. Then she seals that part of the chamber off by building a barricade of sand. It is believed that she does this to protect her young from parasites which might be attracted by these remains.

PRECAUTIONS IN BUILDING A COCOON

When the larva approaches the time of building its cocoon, the mother leaves the nest once and for all. She firmly seals the entrance, forcing the larva to finish its growth and spin the cocoon by itself.

The bembix larva is not equipped with large silk-producing glands. To compensate for this it uses grains of sand and cements them to the silky material.

The cocoon it weaves is cylindrical in shape and three-fourths of an inch in length. One end is round; the other is pointed. The materials are compacted together, and the inside wall is coated with a substance which completely waterproofs the cocoon.

This little structure is so strong that it is difficult for a man to crush it between his fingers. This strength protects the young insect from cave-ins and from being crushed underfoot.

PERPETUATING THE RACE

Once the wasp emerges from its cocoon, it makes its way to the surface. There it will dry its wings. When the wasp is able to fly, it ascends into the air and performs an intricate dance which is unique among the order Hymenoptera.

Many males congregate together to perform their "sun dance" in the air. Through this dance the male attracts a female. If a female is drawn to the humming group of males, it quickly acquires a mate with which to begin the life cycle again. A successful female can complete this process six times during her short lifespan.

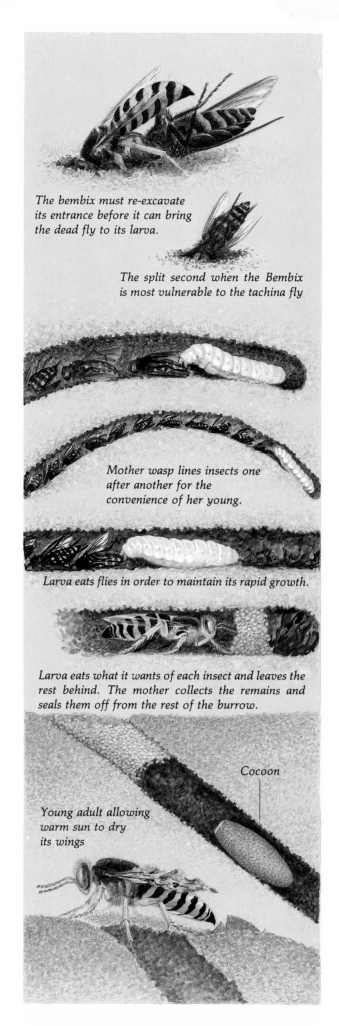

The bembix must re-excavate its entrance before it can bring the dead fly to its larva.

The split second when the Bembix is most vulnerable to the tachina fly

Mother wasp lines insects one after another for the convenience of her young.

Larva eats flies in order to maintain its rapid growth.

Larva eats what it wants of each insect and leaves the rest behind. The mother collects the remains and seals them off from the rest of the burrow.

Cocoon

Young adult allowing warm sun to dry its wings

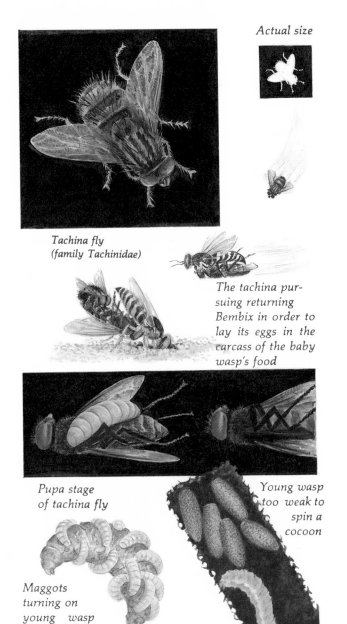

Actual size

Tachina fly
(family Tachinidae)

The tachina pursuing returning Bembix in order to lay its eggs in the carcass of the baby wasp's food

Pupa stage of tachina fly

Young wasp too weak to spin a cocoon

Maggots turning on young wasp larva and eating it

DOES THE SUCCESS OF THE TACHINA FLY ALWAYS MEAN DEATH TO THE YOUNG WASP?

Usually. It is interesting to note that it would be easy for the mother wasp to kill and remove the destructive maggots once they hatch inside the burrow. Yet she seems to tolerate these intruders. She is aware of their presence, for each time she brings food to the larva her sensitive limbs brush against these unwanted guests. Even if that direct contact did not occur, she would certainly be alerted by the high increase in food demand.

The mother kept constantly busy feeding one larva. Now she must assume the burden of meeting the demand of from one to twelve additional mouths. These rapidly-growing tachina fly maggots are quick to grab and consume the choicest morsels as soon as the mother brings them to the nest.

Even if she increased her activites to provide more food, it would be almost impossible for the wasp to take care of these and her own larva as well. As a result the young wasp is likely to suffer death in one of two ways.

The ravenous maggots of the tachina fly may turn their attentions to the young wasp itself when the food shortage becomes greater. They will eat the larva alive in order to satisfy their ravenous appetites.

A second possibility, if the young wasp survives to the cocoon-spinning stage of its life cycle, is just as tragic. What little food the young wasp was able to eat will not have sufficiently prepared it for the strenuous activity of producing the silk and materials for its cocoon. Its weakened condition will prevent the young wasp from continuing its life cycle. As a result, the starving insect will perish underground.

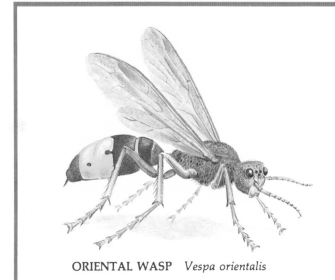

ORIENTAL WASP   *Vespa orientalis*

IS THE WASP MENTIONED IN SCRIPTURE?

When Moses assured the children of Israel that they would enter the Promised Land, he said, "Moreover the Lord thy God will send the hornet (wasp) among them, until they (the Canaanites) are left, and hide themselves from thee, be destroyed." (Deuteronomy 7:20)

One of the largest and most common wasps which inhabits Israel is the Oriental wasp. This brightly colored insect is easily agitated and has a very painful sting. Should one accidentally disturb its nest, the Oriental wasp will attack the intruder and try to drive it away.

HOW DOES SCRIPTURE ILLUSTRATE THE NEED TO WITHHOLD A GIFT THAT WILL HURT THE RECEIVER?

A young ruler was given a choice between gold and wise leadership. He chose wise leadership. His name was Solomon. Many years earlier another man was given the same choice, but he chose gold. Who was that man?

(Pause for a response —see page 20)

The battle he won was as unusual as it is famous. Three hundred carefully chosen men positioned themselves in the hills surrounding the armies of their enemy. On a given signal each one blew a trumpet and shattered a clay pot which covered a burning torch. The echoing sound of the trumpets and the sight of the burning torches startled their enemy.

They stumbled out of their tents, saw the flaming signals dotting the mountain rim, and concluded that they were surrounded by three hundred advancing companies of soldiers. They grabbed their swords and fled in the night, only to be met by fellow soldiers fleeing from torches on the opposite rim. In the confusion over 120,000 enemy soldiers killed each other or were killed as they tried to escape.

What happened next is not as well-known. The leader of this victorious army became a national hero. The people pleaded with him to become their king. He firmly and wisely declined, stating, "I will not rule over you. Neither shall my sons rule over you. The Lord shall rule over you."

His eye was not on leadership, but it was on something else. This general wanted the golden earrings which were worn by the enemy soldiers he and his men had conquered. He asked if they might be given to him as a reward. The grateful nation agreed.

A garment was spread on the ground, and the soldiers filed by and cast upon it the earrings which they had taken from their victims. With that gold this general made a lavish ephod. Then he gave the golden ephod to his city.

From the very beginning the gift had destructive results. People from far and near came to see it. They were drawn by more than curiosity. Soon they began worshipping the golden ephod.

The gift became a snare to this general and his household. Although he had refused to be king, one of his sons had aspirations to hold that position. After the general died, his son made a treacherous effort to seize power. He hired men to kill all his father's sons and then proclaimed himself the king. Later he was killed by a woman who cast a piece of a millstone upon his head and broke his skull.

This great general was Gideon. He had a generous heart and godly desires, but the gift he gave caused the nation to turn their attention to gold rather than to God and resulted in a heritage of destruction in his own family.

From Judges 7, 8

THE GIFT THAT BROUGHT HURT TO THE ONES GIDEON LOVED

"And the children of Israel did evil in the sight of the Lord; and the Lord delivered them into the hand of Midian seven years." (Judges 6:1) It is at the close of these seven years of intimidation and oppression that we find Gideon, the son of Joash, hiding his precious wheat from the eastern invaders.

GOD CHOOSES AN UNLIKELY CANDIDATE TO FREE HIS PEOPLE

The Lord announced to Gideon that he was to "save Israel from the hand of the Midianites." (Judges 6:14) Gideon protested immediately. He was from the small family of an unprestigious tribe. He could not visualize the tribes of Israel rallying about him. The strong son of a wealthy Ephraimite would have been Gideon's logical choice for a leader. But the Lord was patient with Gideon's doubts and convinced him with one sign after another that he was the man for the job.

HE HAD TO CLEAN HOUSE BEFORE HE COULD BE USED

Before Gideon could lead the nation, however, the Lord called upon him to be a leader in his own family. At night Gideon and ten of his servants destroyed the altar which his father Joash used to worship the Canaanite god named Baal. When Joash saw that his son remained unharmed after this bold act, he became Gideon's defense attorney. He argued with those who wanted to kill Gideon that if Baal was truly a god, he would be able to avenge himself. It may have been merely fear of reprisal that kept Joash from doing what his son did for him.

THIRTY-TWO THOUSAND CAME TO FIGHT BUT ONLY THREE HUNDRED WERE CHOSEN

The news of Gideon's victory over Baal spread quickly; and when Gideon blew his trumpet, 32,000 volunteered to fight against their enemy of 135,000. The Lord's plan, though, did not require 32,000 men. In accordance with Mosaic Law, Gideon allowed the fearful and fainthearted to return home (cf. Deuteronomy 20:8). The Lord now needed to separate the foolhardy, who feared neither man nor God, from the faithful who would obey the very strange tactics that were to be given. Sending the men down to some water near enemy lines, Gideon kept only the three hundred who drank with their heads erect. These men were neither foolhardy nor presumptuous; they were courageous but also cautious. They were alert men who proved to be obedient as well.

The battle which began at midnight became a rout. Gideon's band of three hundred men executed their instructions perfectly. Not one of them was killed (cf. Judges 8:4). Even after hours of exhaustive pursuit, Gideon and his men in their faint condition overcame and conquered 15,000 enemies (cf. Judges 8:10-12).

HIS MODEST REQUEST BECAME HIS FAMILY'S SNARE

Gideon became a hero overnight. The Israelites offered him the first hereditary crown. "Rule over us, both thou, and thy son, and thy son's son also; for thou hast delivered us from the hand of Midian." (Judges 8:22) Gideon refused, but their offer prompted him to make what seemed to be a modest request. He asked that all the soldiers, which included the thousands who had later joined the original three hundred, give him the golden earring they had spoiled from their enemy. The total amount of gold collected was 1700 shekels or about 42 pounds. At $150 per ounce, this would be the equivalent of $100,800. "And Gideon made an ephod thereof, and put it in his city, even in Ophrah: and all Israel went thither a whoring after it, which thing became a snare unto Gideon, and to his house." (Judges 8:27)

"But the Spirit of the Lord *came upon Gideon, and he blew a trumpet."*

This relief pictures the Assyrians *fighting against Midianite camel raiders. Using their trained camels, the Midianites could rapidly invade Israel before there was time to mount any resistance.*

"And the weight of the golden earrings *that he requested was a thousand and seven hundred shekels of gold; besides ornaments, and collars, and purple raiment that was on the kings of Midian, and beside the chains that were about their camel's necks."*

GIDEON CHARACTER SKETCH

WHY DID GIDEON WITHHOLD LEADERSHIP WHICH HE BELIEVED WOULD HARM THE ISRAELITES?

Gideon's explanation was, "I will not rule over you, neither shall my son rule over you; the Lord shall rule over you." (Judges 8:23) Gideon was convinced that the unique method of government which the Lord had established for Israel was more effective than a hereditary monarchy. The Lord had designated one particular tribe to judge issues of a local nature. The tribe of Levi was to be especially familiar with the Mosaic Law (cf. Deuteronomy 17:9). For issues on a national level, especially war, the Lord would appoint an individual at large in whom was the Spirit to lead the nation (cf. Numbers 27:18). Gideon had just demonstrated the effectiveness of this method during a national crisis. Three hundred men under the Lord's leadership had routed 135,000 Midianites. Gideon believed that God's plan of leadership—His rule over the nation—was superior to a kingship.

WHY DID GIDEON MAKE AN EPHOD?

The ephod was the shoulder dress of the high priest and probably included the breastplate, the Urim and Thummin, and the robe of the ephod. It required gold and precious stones (Exodus 28:6-35). The Urim and Thummin were used to discover the Lord's will in a matter (cf. Numbers 27:21). It appears that Gideon, so desirous of signs (Judges 6:13,17,37,39; 7:10,11), made an ephod with which to inquire of the Lord. He should have known that only the high priest, a descendant of Aaron, was permitted to inquire of the Lord in this manner. The result was that Gideon's ephod became an object used in the illegal practice of divination (Deuteronomy 18:10). It became a snare, leading the people away from the Lord and into Baal worship.

WHAT WERE THE CONSEQUENCES OF GIDEON'S HURTFUL GIFT?

Rather than encouraging and supporting the proper worship of the Lord at the tabernacle located at Shiloh, Gideon's ephod drew the people away from the legitimate sanctuary. The people came to Ophrah to worship rather than to the priests at Shiloh (Judges 8:27). This not only undermined the authority and respect of the priesthood, but it provided a precedent for further idolatrous practices. Gideon's own son used a gift of silver from the house of Baal and hired worthless mercenaries to kill his seventy brothers. This son was eventually judged by God for his wickedness (Judges 9:56). Gideon's gift of an ephod was the downfall of his family and the city (Judges 8:27).

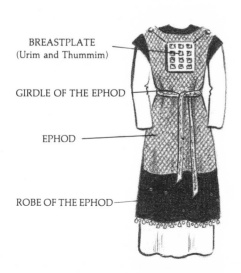

BREASTPLATE
(Urim and Thummim)

GIRDLE OF THE EPHOD

EPHOD

ROBE OF THE EPHOD

"And Gideon made an ephod thereof, *and put it in his city, even in Ophrah: and all Israel went thither a whoring after it, which thing became a snare unto Gideon, and to his house.*"

GIDEON
gĭd'ē̆ŏn

Generosity

IS GIVING A GIFT WHICH REQUIRES PERSONAL SACRIFICE

*". . . Neither will I offer . . . unto the Lord my God of
that which doth cost me nothing."*

II Samuel 24:24

LIVING LESSONS ON GENEROSITY . . .

FROM THE PAGES OF SCRIPTURE

The value of a gift is not measured by the amount of money which it cost but by the thoughtful effort that was involved in giving it. Many husbands and fathers forget this and are then disappointed when a wife or a child does not fully appreciate money or an expensive item given hastily without much forethought. Those who receive gifts look for evidence of personal sacrifice because it assures them that the gift truly represents the devotion of the person who gave it. In the same way God evaluates our gifts to Him. Scripture records the special honor that He gave to a godly widow whose gift represented such personal sacrifice.

ILLUSTRATED IN THE WORLD OF NATURE

EMPEROR PENGUIN   *Aptenodytes forsteri*

No one seems to know how the penguin acquired its name. One theory is that penguin is derived from the Welsh word *pengwyn* which means "whitehead." Others claim the name was inspired by its flightless wings which appear to be clipped or "pin winged." Another opinion suggests that its origin can be traced to seventeenth-century Spanish sailors who called the bird *pinguigo* or "greasy one", referring to the heavy coating of fat which insulates the penguin's body. The emperor penguin inhabits the ocean and ice of the Antarctic. It is one, if not the only bird, which never in its lifetime sets foot on land. With its weight of fifty to one hundred pounds and its length of four feet, the penguin is the heaviest and largest seabird in the world.

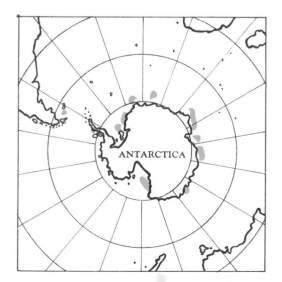

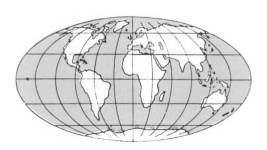

The range and habitat of the emperor penguin

GENEROSITY

HOW DOES THE EMPEROR PENGUIN ILLUSTRATE GENEROSITY IN GIVING THAT WHICH REQUIRES SACRIFICE?

Bitter, icy winds howled as they ripped across the barren wasteland. Lower and lower the temperatures plummeted—far lower than a normal thermometer could even record. An impenetrable darkness cloaked the ground. No creature, large or small, could possibly survive such frigid conditions. No creature, that is, except a large, unusual bird that never flies.

It was mid-winter in the frozen wasteland of the Antarctic. Literally thousands of these creatures had congregated together. What would cause a bird to subject itself to such hostile conditions?

The large mass of penguins stood still. Each one huddled against the next and faced inward in an effort to conserve energy and warmth.

The birds were prepared for this time. They had stored a large mass of fat which covered their bodies. In fact, this fat accounted for approximately one third of their body weight. The insulation of fat, together with its feathered coat, enabled the penguin to withstand the frigid air.

But the cold was not the only element with which to contend. Snow avalanches and ice break-ups were a constant threat which claimed the lives of many birds when they occurred. Still the penguins stood. The majority were males, and they would carefully stand in this position for a long, long time.

Why would these male penguins subject themselves to such rigor and sacrifice? The answer lay beneath the drooping folds of the emperor penguin's belly. Carefully cradled on its warm feet was a large, creamy white egg.

If the male was to succeed in giving life to its young, it would have to sacrifice. It could not consider its own personal needs or comfort but only those of the developing embryo inside the egg. If the egg should accidentally roll away, it would mean certain death for the embryo.

For this reason the male penguin restricts its activities. It sets aside its own personal needs and wants. Not only will it stop eating, but it will restrict all its movements to an absolute minimum for three and a half months! It is because of these sacrifices that the young are able to survive. In fact, the emperors have a survival rate greater than any other species of penguin—a tribute to the generous sacrifice of the male.

SCRIPTURAL REFERENCES TO THE PENGUIN

The penguin is not named in Scripture. There are, however, several verses which relate to the environment in which it lives.

"He giveth snow like wool; he scattereth the hoarfrost like ashes. He casteth forth his ice like morsels; who can stand before his cold?" Psalm 147:16,17

The ability of the penguin to survive the prolonged sub-zero and often violent weather of the Antarctic is only possible because of its heavy layers of fat, its thick downy plumage, and its practice of huddling together in large groups. Their method of gaining warmth by standing close together illustrates the truth of Ecclesiastes 4:11. If two be together "then they have heat; but how can one be warm alone?"

But the most amazing characteristic of the penguin is the role of the male in incubating the eggs of its young on its feet. The rigid discipline and self-sacrifice of the father is a beautiful illustration of the quality of dedication which God requires of a husband and father in Ephesians 5:25 and Proverbs 17:6.

CHARACTERISTICS AND PHYSICAL FEATURES OF THE EMPEROR PENGUIN

Because it was willing to give generously of itself the emperor penguin ensured life for its young. The emperor penguin's timetable for nesting is diametrically opposed to that of other birds. This penguin chooses the depths of the cold winter months for its long incubation. By doing so, it compensates for the slow growth and development of its young. At that time of year the sea ice is frozen so hard that it permits the bird to stand throughout the required sixty-two to sixty-eight days of incubation and also during the brooding period—the early weeks of the chick's life.

This peculiar schedule means that by the time the eggs hatch, the sea ice will have begun to melt, enabling the parents to gather food in near proximity. Toward the end of the fledgling period the immature chicks can fend for themselves without having to travel so far.

The penguin's frigid incubation schedule enables the young to shed their downy feathers and undergo their plumage changes during the warm days of summer.

So strong is the male emperor penguin's desire to give that the eggless members of the group often take a lost egg which accidentally rolled off another's foot and try to incubate the lifeless embryo. They may try to snatch a chick away from one of their neighbors in an effort to foster it. The birds have even been known to take a chunk of ice which resembles an egg and cradle it for extended periods of time.

The life cycle of this bird is unique. There is no other quite like it.

Emperor penguins bow when they meet each other by lowering their beak onto their breast.

Folds of fatty skin insulate the egg from bitter cold.

Actual size of egg 117-132 x 80-90 millimeters

Incubating males gather together for protection and warmth, forming huddles which can number in the thousands.

THE LIFE CYCLE OF THE EMPEROR PENGUIN

The relationship of the male and female emperor penguin is monogamous for the season. Each parent has its part in rearing the young. Unlike other birds, penguins do not build a nest. The simple reason for this is that there are no materials available on the barren sea ice.

JUNE—ANTARCTICA'S MID-WINTER

The penguin's breeding cycle occurs in mid-winter. The female lays a single egg 117-132 by 80-90 millimeters. Her mate immediately takes over by grasping the egg and cradling it on top of its feet.

The blood vessels in the penguin's feet are structured in such a way that they prevent loss of heat. Loose layers of skin around its stomach gently fold over the shell, keeping the egg warm.

JULY—AUGUST

Male penguins congregate together in huddles of as many as several thousand birds. The egg hatches in approximately sixty-four days. During this incubation period the female returns to feed at sea. She may travel one hundred miles over ice to reach her destination.

When the young chick hatches, the male continues to cradle it on its feet, feeding it from its own resources. The chick begs with a peeping call and vibrating movement of its bill. It also rubs the parent's bill, stimulating it to regurgitate a secretion from its crop. The male continues to brood the young chick until the mother returns from the sea.

Upon her return the female has no problem finding her mate and chick, even without a nest. When she assumes the brooding responsibilities, the male journeys to the sea to eat and recover its strength. It will be gone for approximately two to three weeks. When the male returns, it brings a new supply of food in its crop for the chick.

From that time on, both parents share the responsibilities of bringing food to the young penguin. The chick has an enormous appetite. In fifteen minutes it can eat its body weight.

The parents feed their young a formula high in fats and protein. The quality of this formula is such that the young penguin rapidly puts on weight. If the parent is late in returning with food, the formula will sustain the chick for several days.

Constant care is given to the chick during its first three weeks of life. Either parent carefully warms, feeds, and guards the little one. This period is crucial to the survival of the young one, for during this time a bond of recognition between the young penguin and its parents is established. This bond is of vital importance later in its life.

The development of the young emperor penguin is very slow but its appetite is great. In fifteen minutes a four-pound bird can eat its body weight.

After the egg hatches, the parent penguin continues to brood the chick.

The parent feeds its chick by regurgitating a secretion from its crop.

Young birds flock together in groups or "creches."

SEPTEMBER

By the time September arrives, the young chicks have achieved a degree of independence. They leave their parents and join other birds their own age. These groups of young birds are called creches. A creche can number anywhere from a few birds to several dozen.

Both parents continue to feed their chick, and at this time the bond of recognition, established during the first three months of life, is crucial. Parent penguins feed only their own young. Both parents and chick must recognize each other. It is believed that recognition is based on sight and sound. A penguin colony consists of many creches. The parents go from one group to another and search for their young chicks. They stand before the creche of birds and "sing out", continuing until their young one answers the call.

As months pass the penguin's juvenile down is molted, and the bird takes on its immature plumage.

When the rearing of their young is completed, the two parents return to the sea to care for their own needs. For the next few weeks they indulge in overeating and become very fat. They try to gain as much weight as possible in preparation for another yearly phase of their life cycle—the molt.

During the molt penguins drop their feathers and grow new ones in preparation for the coming winter. The birds are temporarily immobilized, and so they rest in some protected area until their plumage grows back. They may lose as much as fifty percent of their body weight when they molt.

DECEMBER

Once their plumage has grown again and is well-oiled, they travel once more to the sea to migrate, feed, and repeat their rigorous life cycle.

HOW DOES THE EMPEROR PENGUIN'S BODY STRUCTURE SUIT IT FOR WATER TRAVEL?

BODY SHAPE - The torpedo-like structure of its body enables the bird to weave agilely through the water with minimum resistance.

FEATHERS - The penguin's feathers grow almost solidly over its body, not in patches as most other birds. These feathers are smooth, thick, and grow very close together. Their insulating qualities provide great warmth for the bird. Built-in oil glands enable it to waterproof its plumage, reducing friction and promoting efficiency in the water.

WINGS - Rather than using its wings for flight, the penguin uses them as fins or paddles. Its wing stroke and powerful breast muscles enable the bird to swim on top as well as beneath the water's surface. It has been clocked at depths of sixty feet and speeds as fast as thirty feet per second.

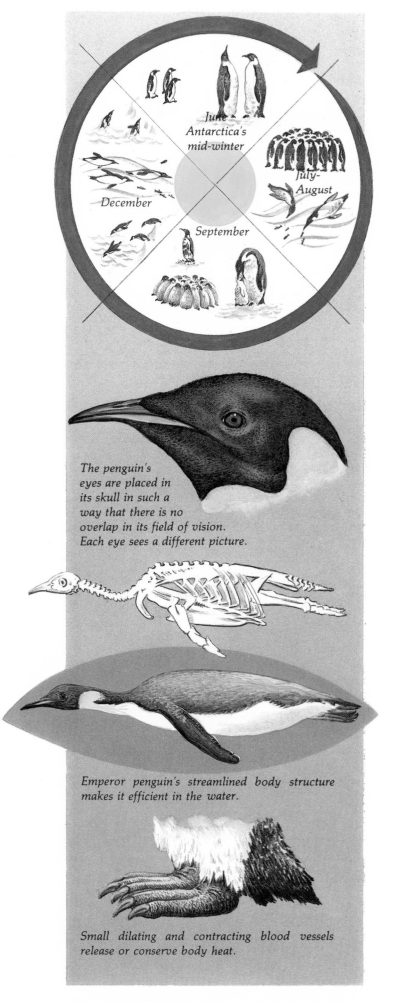

The penguin's eyes are placed in its skull in such a way that there is no overlap in its field of vision. Each eye sees a different picture.

Emperor penguin's streamlined body structure makes it efficient in the water.

Small dilating and contracting blood vessels release or conserve body heat.

Penguins "porpoise" out of water for sustaining air.

When approaching a steep bank, the emperor penguin has the amazing ability to jump straight out of the water as high as five feet and land upright.

The penguin normally walks upright, but when it wants to go faster it lays on its stomach and uses is flippers to toboggan across the ice.

IN WHAT WAY ARE A PENGUIN AND A PORPOISE ALIKE?

Their swimming habits are similar. In October and November the emperor penguin makes a limited northern migration. During this time hundreds, even thousands, of these birds can be seen in the sea. When swimming, the animal uses its flipper-like wings to stroke the water. Like a porpoise, it weaves in and out and surfaces periodically for air. Its streamlined form allows it to travel for long distances at a consistent speed.

The penguin is faster beneath the water than on the surface. On top of the water it maintains speeds of ten miles per hour, whereas underneath it can travel thirty miles per hour and faster. It needs this extra underwater diving speed in order to meet its heavy food demands.

During the breeding season and before its molt, the penguin has a limited time to store necessary fat. On these eating "binges" the bird gorges itself on sea life including fish, squid, and crustaceans. It migrates to areas where these creatures abound. There it is assured of meeting the food quota which is critical for its own survival and for the survival of its offspring.

HOW LONG DOES A PENGUIN LIVE?

The emperor penguin lives approximately thirty-five years. It begins to breed at the age of six. Especially during the early stages of its life it is vulnerable to destructive forces—primarily severe weather and predators.

The palatability of this bird's meat is not ranked very high. Although the penguin might have been a welcome sight to starving mariners, its heavy layers of fat make the bird very greasy, and the taste of the meat itself takes on the flavor of the fish it eats. When the meat is cut up and the blood and blubber are removed, it is said to make a wonderful soup. The nutritional value of penguin meat is exceptionally high, especially the liver, heart and kidneys.

Skua

Leopard Seal

PREDATORS OF THE EMPEROR PENGUIN

SKUA *Stercorarius skua*

The young emperor chick is preyed upon by the skua but not to the degree that other species of penguins are. This is due to the fact that by the time the skuas arrive, the majority of the chicks are too large for it to prey upon.

LEOPARD SEAL
Hydrurga leptonyx

This vicious seal which is ten to twelve feet long preys heavily upon penguins. Their powerful jaws and sharp teeth easily tear apart this virtually defenseless bird.

HOW DOES SCRIPTURE ILLUSTRATE GENEROSITY IN GIVING A GIFT WHICH REQUIRES PERSONAL SACRIFICE?

Jesus condemned the hypocrites who loudly proclaimed their sacrificial gifts to God. Years earlier a godly woman quietly demonstrated the true spirit of giving. She devoted her life to the Lord and was rewarded with greater spiritual perception than the religious leaders around her. Who was she?

(Pause for a response—see page 20)

This girl's childhood was spent in a time of political turbulence and national warfare. The news of the day was dim and often ugly.

Against the background of a corrupt and violent political scene, her life stands out in sharp contrast. This girl lived by God's standards and radiated the inward beauty of righteousness. Before long her vivacious spirit attracted the attention of a young man. His love for her grew, and one day he approached her father for permission to marry her. Their wedding followed the customs of the time, and for the next seven years they enjoyed a happy marriage.

Then this radiant young wife experienced the shock and sadness of her husband's death. The loss of her husband drew her closer to God, and she discovered a depth of fellowship with the Lord that she had never known before. She delighted in God's presence to such an extent that "she departed not from the temple but served God with fastings and prayer night and day." The result was an amazing increase in her spiritual alertness as well as a continuation of her vivacious youthfulness. Her concern for the pitiable condition of her own people grew with each political crisis.

One day news of an approaching enemy army brought panic to the city. After three months of fierce fighting, the invading army conquered the city. This marked the beginning of the strict Roman rule over her people. Taxation and oppression increased. There was no hope of human help in sight. As a result, many in the nation began to follow the example of this godly woman. With a new surge of interest they studied the Scriptures and looked for signs of the long awaited Messiah.

One day a young couple entered the temple. They had come to fulfill the requirements of the law for the firstborn son. This son was Jesus the Messiah. He was unnoticed on that day by the religious leaders. Only two people were given the spiritual discernment to recognize Him as the eternal Son of God. One was Simeon, a just and devout man. The other was Anna, this radiant and godly widow. When she saw Him, she rejoiced in her spirit and praised God for the gift of His Son.

Anna was over one hundred years old. For eighty-four years this godly widow had set aside personal gain to concentrate on serving the Lord and those around her. God honored her faithful giving by allowing her to be one of the very few who recognized the Messiah and received the foretaste of the hope and reward of every Christian—seeing her Savior face to face.

From Luke 2:21-38

Sculpture of the Roman general, **Pompey,** *who broke through the temple walls with battering rams after a three-month seige*

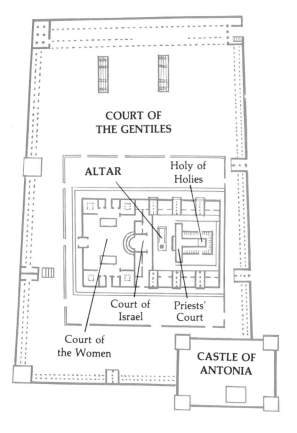

Floor plans of Herod's temple—*It was in this temple that Anna saw the baby Jesus.*

ANNA'S PERSONAL SACRIFICE OF EIGHTY-FOUR YEARS OF SERVICE

Anna, the godly prophetess who saw the baby Jesus, lived through periods of great upheaval in her homeland of Judea. During her life, which spanned the entire first century before Christ, she saw the rise and fall of six Judean rulers before the Roman general, Pompey, conquered Judea in behalf of the Roman empire in 63 B.C.

A PROPHETESS CONCENTRATES ON SERVING GOD

During the second half century of her life, she saw her country divide into bitterly rival political and religious groups, all reacting and responding differently toward Roman rule. But for some reason, Anna was not attracted to any of these activist and outspoken groups. Her way of life was completely different from those around her. Her life was spent for the most part within the temple of the Lord in Jerusalem. We read that she "departed not from the temple, but served God with fastings and prayers night and day." (Luke 2:37)

THE TEMPLE—SCENE OF WORSHIP AND WARFARE

Even at the temple, however, she was not free from political turmoil. Anna remembered when open rebellion broke out at a memorable Feast of Tabernacles. Jannaeus, while officiating in the temple as Priest-King, showed his contempt for the Pharisees by pouring out a libation at his feet, instead of on the altar as prescribed. The people pelted him with citrons that they were carrying in honor of the feast. Soldiers were called; and before order was restored, six thousand people were killed.

Anna also recalled when Pompey entered Jerusalem and found the temple being used as a military fortress. It took him three months to break through the temple walls with battering rams. Once inside, he slaughtered the officiating priests and twelve thousand other Jews. Anna remembered with horror how Pompey profaned the Holy of Holies by entering it to satisfy his curiosity. Her worship would also have been periodically disturbed when Herod the Great began his extensive work of remodeling the entire temple.

THE MOST MEMORABLE EVENT

But of all the activities she observed during her many years in the temple the one that stood out as the most significant was the day a poor carpenter, his young wife, and her firstborn son humbly entered. They came to fulfill the Law of Moses in two ways. First, they came to present their baby boy to the Lord. When the Israelites left Egypt, the Lord said to Moses, "Sanctify unto me all the firstborn, whatsoever openeth the womb...is mine." (Exodus 13:2) Second, they came to offer the prescribed sacrifice for Mary's purification. The proper sacrifice was a lamb for a burnt offering and a turtle-dove or young pigeon for a sin offering. The poor could substitute a turtle-dove or pigeon for the lamb (Leviticus 12:6-8). The offering of the birds indicates that Joseph and Mary were poor (Luke 2:24).

A BABY FULFILLS A LONG-AWAITED PREDICTION

When Anna entered the temple that day, she saw the righteous and devout Simeon holding the holy babe in his arms saying, "Lord, now lettest thou thy servant depart in peace, according to thy word; for mine eyes have seen thy salvation, which thou hast prepared before the face of all people; a light to lighten the Gentiles, and the glory of thy people, Israel." (Luke 2:29-32) Anna knew in her heart that this little baby was the promised Redeemer. "And she, coming in that instant, gave thanks likewise unto the Lord, and spoke of him to all those who looked for redemption in Jerusalem." (Luke 2:38)

ANNA CHARACTER SKETCH

WHAT PERSONAL SACRIFICE DID ANNA MAKE IN ORDER TO SERVE THE LORD?

The only thing worse for a Jewish woman than being a widow was to be childless (cf. I Samuel 1:2,10). Since Anna spent all of her time in the temple after her husband died, we must assume that she had no responsibility as a mother. As a young widow, Anna could have turned from the Lord in bitterness. She could have agonized over her loss and desperately tried to find another husband (cf. Romans 7:2), but she responded differently. She went to the Lord to find joy, strength, and to have Him meet her needs. The apostle Paul stated the benefits which could result for a childless widow if she responded properly. "The unmarried woman careth for the things of the Lord, that she may be holy both in body and in spirit; but she that is married careth for the things of the world, how she may please her husband." (I Corinthians 7:34) Anna had experienced the wonderful joys of human love for seven years; now she was privileged to experience the matchless joys of an intimate relationship with the Lord for over eighty-four years. And Anna "gave thanks likewise unto the Lord." (Luke 2:38)

HOW DID ANNA KEEP FROM BECOMING A BUSYBODY?

Paul instructed Timothy regarding widows: "But the younger widows refuse; for when they have begun to wax wanton against Christ, they will marry, having damnation, because they have cast off their first faith. And, withal, they learn to be idle, wandering about from house to house, and not only idle but tattlers also, and busybodies, speaking things which they ought not." (I Timothy 5:11-13) Paul realized that young and lonely widows who are engaged in the work of the local church may have mixed motives. One motive is to help and counsel others; another may be to have others meet their needs of friendship and acceptance. Some, however, had no message to give. As a result, they listened to gossip and spread it to others, doing more harm than good. Anna chose to seek the Lord for fellowship and acceptance. She learned His secrets. After eighty-four years, the Lord gave her a message worth sharing. And she "spoke of him to all those who looked for redemption in Jerusalem." (Luke 2:38)

HOW IS ANNA AN EXAMPLE TO US OF GIVING THROUGH SERVICE?

First, she is an example to unmarried believers that the Lord can meet their deepest social needs. Second, she is an example to widows. The Scriptural instruction to "Honor widows that are widows indeed," certainly applied to Anna. "Now she that is a widow indeed, and desolate, trusteth in God, and continueth in supplications and prayers night and day." (I Timothy 5:3,5) Anna was proof of Paul's good judgment concerning unmarried widows. "But she is happier if she so abide, after my judgment, and I think also that I have the Spirit of God." (I Corinthians 7:40) She also provides an example for believers with family responsibilities to set apart time to fellowship with the Lord. Anna must have experienced great periods of joy and refreshment of spirit for her to remain so disciplined for so many years. And finally she provides incentive for us all to be ready for the return of the Lord. Anna waited patiently for His first coming and was spiritually prepared to discern the significance of what was happening that day in the temple. We also should look for the coming of our Lord the second time. "For our conversation is in heaven, from where also we look for the Savior, the Lord Jesus Christ." (Philippians 3:20)

"And she, coming in that instant, *gave thanks likewise unto the Lord, and spoke of him to all those who looked for redemption in Jerusalem."*

ANNA
ăn'ȧ

Generosity

IS GIVING THE RIGHT AMOUNT AT THE RIGHT TIME

"As we have therefore opportunity, let us do good unto all men, especially unto them who are of the household of faith."

Galatians 6:10

LIVING LESSONS ON GENEROSITY . . .

FROM THE PAGES OF SCRIPTURE

Faith and giving go hand in hand. True generosity is a result of faith, and true faith results from generosity. The greater our faith is, the more we can see spiritual realities and the more free we are to let go of temporal possessions. Giving what we have to God sets in motion spiritual laws which return to us more than we gave and demonstrate to us the reality of God—the true source of all provision. One of the greatest men in Scripture was not only a great man of faith, but he was also a great man of giving. His generosity was rewarded by God and used to establish a basic precedent in giving.

ILLUSTRATED IN THE WORLD OF NATURE

AMERICAN ALLIGATOR *Alligator mississipiensis*

The alligator is endowed with a constant grin. The curvature of its jawbone gives the impression that the reptile is continually smiling and content. Whether in fact it is or not, it should be. For as an adult this large, powerful reptile is master of its domain and has few enemies—except for man. The American alligator inhabits the swamps and wetlands of North America's southeastern regions. Lazily, this contented-looking creature sprawls out on the shore or in open water to bask in the warm sun. It does this for a reason. Like other reptiles, the alligator is not equipped to warm itself, and it is therefore classified as a cold-blooded animal. Records indicate that the alligator can live as long as fifty years and can attain a length of nineteen feet.

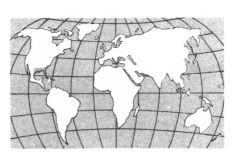

The range and habitat of the American alligator

GENEROSITY

HOW DOES THE ALLIGATOR ILLUSTRATE GENEROSITY BY GIVING THE RIGHT AMOUNT AT THE RIGHT TIME?

Sprawled awkwardly on a heap of decaying vegetation, the large, scaly-skinned creature crawled in circles, working its low-slung body over a soggy mass of material. The Spanish called this reptile a lizard or "el largato." The English adopted the name but ran the two words together to form "alligarter." Mispronunciation changed the name further, and from this distortion came alligator—the name by which it is known today.

This particular alligator had a definite reason for its strange behavior. The female had just laid twenty eggs and covered them with loose material. Now she smoothed out the rough mass of vegetation and added the final touches to complete the nest. Once this was accomplished, she slipped back into the water to wait.

Unlike most reptiles, the female alligator has not completed the responsibility of parenthood after laying its eggs. She maintains a long and constant vigil over her nest against predators such as snakes, raccoons, and even man. She is aggressive and has little tolerance for unwanted intruders. The alligator is not afraid to use sharp teeth and a very powerful tail against any enemy.

For the next two months the female will stay very close to the nest, maintaining and repairing the structure when necessary. She keeps a constant vigil against any threat. Meanwhile, deep within the mass of decomposing vegetation, heat is being generated to warm and incubate the eggs.

Then one day, weeks later, the female will do another strange thing. She will return to the nest and actually tear it apart with her mouth until she reaches the eggs. Then she will carefully grip each one, one at a time, and gently release it from the heavy mass of material. She also helps the young escape from the leathery-like confinement of their eggshell.

How could the alligator know when to return? How could she have known when they were ready to hatch? The answer is simple. She asked the eggs!

As time grows near for the alligators to hatch, the mother returns to the nest and, laying her head next to the structure, gives a low grunt. Then she waits to see if the young inside the eggs answer. If there is no reply, she will go back into the water and wait for a day or two before she returns to inquire again.

If the mother is not aware of the right timing and uncovers them too soon, the eggs will lose the heat necessary for incubation and will not hatch. If she returns too late, the young may have been able to cut themselves free from the eggshells without assistance, but the heavy mass of vegetation would have suffocated them. This ability of the alligator to give the right amount of assistance at the right time helps ensure that the young will hatch successfully.

SCRIPTURAL REFERENCES TO THE ALLIGATOR

The alligator and the crocodile may be considered cousins. The crocodile was the master and terror of the Nile in Egypt. It was ravenous, crafty, fierce, relentless, keen-eyed, and swift in devouring its prey. In spite of these deadly traits the Egyptians venerated it, pampered it, and paid divine honors to it.

There is evidence that Pharaoh thought he became invincible like the crocodile by wearing scaly armor. Thus, the prophecy against him by Ezekiel, "Behold, I am against thee, Pharaoh, king of Egypt, the great dragon (tannian crocodile) that lieth in the midst of his rivers, which hath said, My river is mine own, and I have made it for myself. But I will put hooks in thy jaws, and I will cause the fish of thy rivers to stick unto thy scales, and I will bring thee up out of the midst of thy rivers...." (Ezekiel 29:3,4)

This prophecy has a background in the description of the crocodile given by God to Job. "Canst thou draw out leviathan (crocodile) with an hook...canst thou put an hook into his nose...Who can open the doors of his face? His teeth are terrible round about. His scales are his pride." (Job 41:1,2,14,15)

CHARACTERISTICS AND PHYSICAL FEATURES OF THE AMERICAN ALLIGATOR

The generosity of the female alligator in giving the right amount of help at the right time is critical to the survival of its offspring. Giving the right amount at the right time pertains to the protection and aid of the hatching eggs and also applies to early stages of the nest's construction. It is most important that the nest is built in a proper way and in the proper place to ensure the survival of the alligator eggs.

HOW DOES THE ALLIGATOR BUILD ITS NEST?

When its time arrives, the female leaves the company of other alligators and quietly slips away. It selects a site on high ground—a spot where the alligator can be free from the worry of floods.

Once the location is chosen, it busily clears an eight to ten foot space. The alligator accomplishes this by using its strong jaws, sharp teeth, and forepaws in bulldozer fashion. With these tools it snaps and tears out brush, twigs, and sticks that clutter the nesting site. Its heavy weight helps to smooth the vegetation. Finally the area is cleared.

Next the female proceeds to stack both damp and dry vegetation pile upon pile. With her snout she moves and pushes this material to form a mound. In the center of the structure she hollows out an opening and refills this excavated space with plants and mud. She continues to fill and shape the mound until it meets her approval.

Following this procedure the alligator lays her eggs—twenty to seventy in number. Afterwards, she completely fills the hole and smooths the surface, putting her finishing touches on the structure. The entire process takes approximately three days. The mass of soggy vegetation doesn't look impressive, but to the alligator's young it will mean the difference between life and death.

OF ALL PLACES, WHY WOULD AN ALLIGATOR LAY ITS EGGS IN ROTTEN VEGETATION?

When damp vegetation is exposed to the warm rays of the sun, the growth of bacteria is encouraged. In fact, it thrives. As a result, decomposition takes place. During the chemical process of decomposition sufficient heat is generated—between eighty and one hundred degrees Fahrenheit—to incubate the alligator's eggs. The female keeps the nest moist by watering it during hot, dry days.

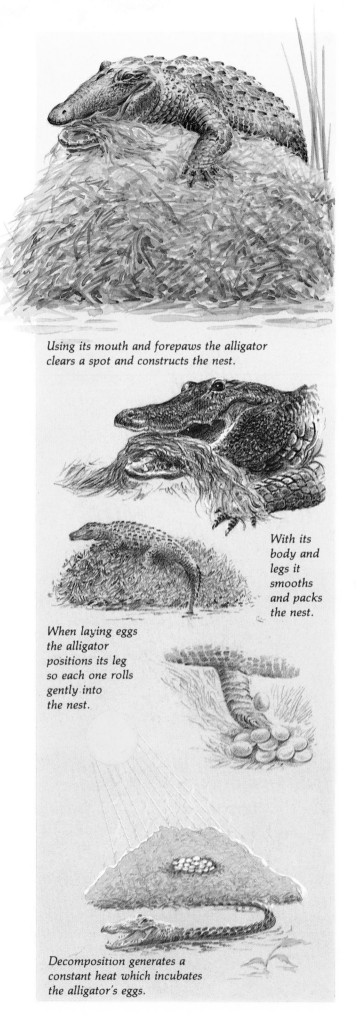

Using its mouth and forepaws the alligator clears a spot and constructs the nest.

With its body and legs it smooths and packs the nest.

When laying eggs the alligator positions its leg so each one rolls gently into the nest.

Decomposition generates a constant heat which incubates the alligator's eggs.

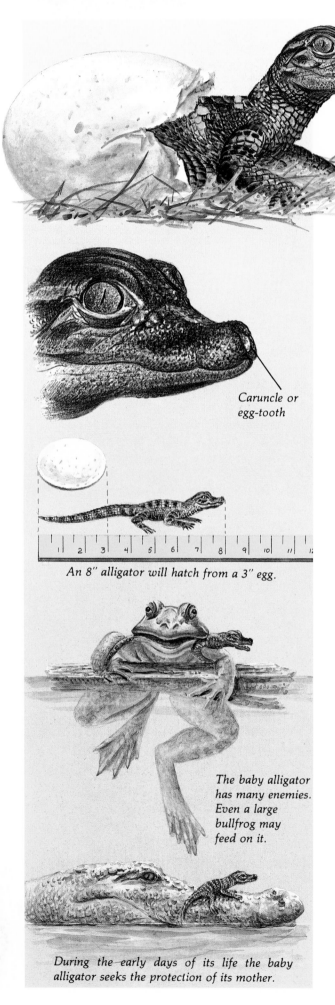

The eggs which the female lays require approximately nine to ten weeks of incubation. These tough-shelled eggs measure nearly three inches in length; they are about the size of a goose egg. When the reptile hatches, it emerges as an eight-inch alligator. It is amazing to think that something as long as eight inches is coiled up within a shell only three inches in length!

Caruncle or egg-tooth

An 8" alligator will hatch from a 3" egg.

The baby alligator has many enemies. Even a large bullfrog may feed on it.

During the early days of its life the baby alligator seeks the protection of its mother.

HOW MANY SHELLS DOES AN ALLIGATOR EGG HAVE?

Two. The egg is comprised of a hard and tough outer shell as well as a soft, rubbery inner shell. The inner shell is much thinner than the outer.

When it is time for the young alligator to hatch, the outer shell will have been cracked already, but the inner shell must be split open by the emerging reptile. To accomplish this task, the infant alligator is equipped with a caruncle or egg-tooth. This bony protrusion comes to a point on the young alligator's nose. With this tooth the unhatched alligator splits open the shell. Once the egg-tooth has been used for this purpose it gradually disappears.

The alligator emerges from the shell headfirst and immediately looks for the nearest body of water, even if it is a considerable distance away. When the young alligator hatches, it is hungry and wants to eat. It has many needle-like teeth with which to capture food and it is extremely aggressive. Its diet consists of varied marine life such as small fish, insects, snails and other crustaceans. When the young are about two years old they usually set out in search of a place of their own, leaving the pond or pool in which their mother lives.

The young alligator is most vulnerable during the early days of its life. Raccoons, herons, egrets, snakes, large fish, and even bullfrogs prey on them. It is estimated that only one alligator out of one hundred lives to the ripe old age of three.

HOW FAST DOES AN ALLIGATOR GROW?

Under normal conditions, the alligator grows approximately one foot a year. At twenty years of age the average length of a male is approximately sixteen feet; the average female is ten feet long. They may live to be fifty-six years of age.

The growth of any cold-blooded animal, including an alligator, can be controlled. If it is fed well, given plenty of room to grow, and kept in an atmosphere with the right temperature, it will grow to record lengths. On the other hand, its growth can be stunted if it is fed just enough to maintain its health and kept in a cooler temperature. It is impossible to achieve such variance in length and weight with warm-blooded animals.

WHAT'S UNUSUAL ABOUT THE ALLIGATOR'S EYES?

Their placement is unusual. The alligator's eyes are raised on either side near the top of its head. This reptile relies heavily on its ability to ambush in order to capture food. Because its eyes are positioned in this way, the reptile is able to lie in the water and submerge its entire body. Yet, like a periscope, its eyes remain above the surface, constantly watching for some unsuspecting prey.

The alligator's eyes have another unusual feature. The reptile is equipped with three eyelids. The upper and lower lids permit the alligator to shut out light. This is convenient and necessary since the alligator enjoys long hours of napping in the warm sun's rays. Underneath these eyelids is a third, transparent lid. The protective lid is of great benefit to the alligator when it dives beneath the water. Because it is transparent the eyelid has the same effect as goggles do on a skin diver. It protects the eye and allows the alligator to see under water.

A third unusual factor is the color of the eyes themselves. In the daytime the pupils of its eyes are the shape of vertical slits. But when the beam of a flashlight is directed to the eyes at night, they appear to be round and to have a bright, red color. This feature has proved detrimental to the alligator as "gator" hunters, interested in the reptile's skin, can therefore easily locate the alligator at night.

WHAT HAPPENS WHEN AN ALLIGATOR'S TEETH WEAR OUT?

The reptile receives another set. When a tooth wears out, or even begins to wear out, another pushes its way up through the center of the old tooth.

The alligator has many sets of teeth; the exact number is not known. When an alligator grows very old, these new replacement teeth finally stop growing. The reptile eventually loses all its teeth.

CAN AN ALLIGATOR STICK OUT ITS TONGUE?

No, it can't. Its well-developed tongue is attached to the bottom of its mouth the full length of its lower jaw. This attachment prevents the tongue from protruding outside the mouth. What might be thought a restriction is really of great benefit to the alligator, though. When its mouth is opened under water, the tongue blocks off its throat to prevent the alligator from swallowing water.

The alligator not only closes off its throat but is also able to close the valves in its nose and ears as well. These abilities aid the alligator in securing its food. One way the alligator kills its prey is by drowning. With these built-in valves the powerful reptile can hold its prey under water indefinitely.

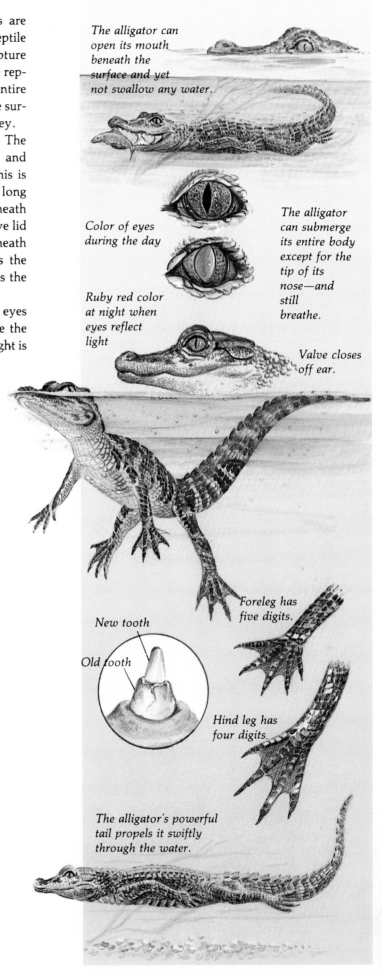

The alligator can open its mouth beneath the surface and yet not swallow any water.

Color of eyes during the day

Ruby red color at night when eyes reflect light

The alligator can submerge its entire body except for the tip of its nose—and still breathe.

Valve closes off ear.

New tooth

Old tooth

Foreleg has five digits.

Hind leg has four digits.

The alligator's powerful tail propels it swiftly through the water.

The alligator is able to dine on poisonous snakes without harmful effects.

IS THE ALLIGATOR A FUSSY EATER?

Not exactly. One is likely to find almost anything in an alligator's stomach. Since the pointed teeth of the reptile are not designed for grinding it must swallow its food whole. Its stomach is large and can hold huge amounts of food. One examination of a twelve-foot alligator's stomach revealed three, whole pigs weighing approximately thirty pounds each. The alligator is also very fond of turtles. Their hard shells have little chance to resist the crushing power of the alligator's strong jaws.

Few animals are beyond the appetite of the alligator. It has been reported that it will even feed on cows foolish enough to drink at a 'gator hole. When the cow lowers its head to drink, the alligator lunges at the animal, catching it by the nose. It seizes the cow with a vice-like grip and begins rolling over and over while it backs into the water. This action is so violent that it actually twists the animal's head off its body.

Its diet is not limited to flesh but even includes large stones, bottles, and chunks of wood. It is believed that these large, indigestible objects keep the digestive organs in working order during periods of hibernation.

If no water hole exists, *the alligator will dig ponds for itself in swampy areas. These ponds are called 'gator holes. They benefit the alligator and the rest of the wildlife in the area, attracting all varieties of animal life. During periods of drought when natural, shallow ponds have dried, these deep 'gator holes are often the only places where water may be found.*

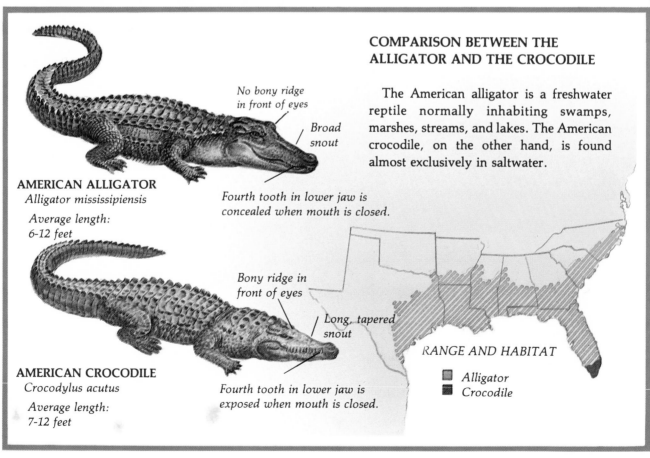

COMPARISON BETWEEN THE ALLIGATOR AND THE CROCODILE

The American alligator is a freshwater reptile normally inhabiting swamps, marshes, streams, and lakes. The American crocodile, on the other hand, is found almost exclusively in saltwater.

No bony ridge in front of eyes

Broad snout

AMERICAN ALLIGATOR
Alligator mississipiensis

Average length: 6-12 feet

Fourth tooth in lower jaw is concealed when mouth is closed.

Bony ridge in front of eyes

Long, tapered snout

AMERICAN CROCODILE
Crocodylus acutus

Average length: 7-12 feet

Fourth tooth in lower jaw is exposed when mouth is closed.

RANGE AND HABITAT

☐ *Alligator*
■ *Crocodile*

HOW DOES SCRIPTURE ILLUSTRATE GENEROSITY BY GIVING THE RIGHT AMOUNT AT THE RIGHT TIME?

There is a time when giving money results in gain and a time when keeping money results in loss. Who gave a gift that resulted in God's blessing and then refused a gift that would have diminished God's glory?

(Pause for a response—see page 20)

Five terrified kings lost all sense of dignity. They fled from battle and stumbled into treacherous slime pits. They had gone out in pride but retreated in disgrace. The invading army shouted with delight as they watched these kings and their men fall in the slime or scramble up the mountains to hide in rocky crags. Many were taken captive.

A breathless runner raced from the battlefield. Soon he reached his destination—the encampment of a very influential man. The runner poured out his story of the kings' defeat. Then he said, "Your nephew has been taken captive." The words stung like a whip. This great man quickly assembled his servants and armed them for battle.

Their hastily formed army pursued the plundering invaders. They neared the enemy camp and waited until nightfall. Then they divided into three groups for an attack. The unsuspecting enemy was totally surprised and fled in panic, leaving behind all the captives, wealth, and possessions. This victory was one more blessing of God upon the life of a very generous man.

Years earlier, a conflict had arisen between him and the nephew whom he now rescued. There had been insufficient grazing lands for both of their flocks. This great man demonstrated his generous spirit by inviting his nephew to choose whatever lands he wanted. Then he took the lands in the opposite direction. Now two more tests of generosity faced him.

As he and his men returned to his nephew's city, the priest of the Most High God came out to meet him. This priest, who was also the king of Salem, gave him refreshment and blessed him. Immediately this great man took a gift of his own and gave it to this priest of the Most High God.

Then a king of one of the five cities which had been defeated said to this man. "Return to me only the captives that belong to me and keep all the goods for yourself."

Quickly and wisely this great man refused that gift. He explained why he did so. He said, "Lest thou shouldst say, I have made Abram rich." The one who offered the gift was the king of that wicked city, Sodom. Abraham did not want anyone to rob God of His rightful glory as the true source of his wealth.

Meanwhile, the gift which he gave to Melchizedek was an action which illustrated giving the right amount at the right time. All of his physical and spiritual descendants were to follow his example. Abraham gave a tenth of all that he had and established the principle of tithing.

From Genesis 14

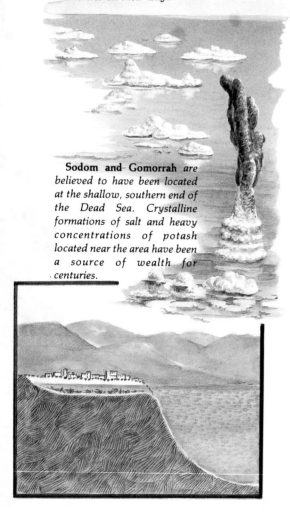

THE
GREAT
SEA

Damascus

Karnaim • Ashtaroth
REPHAIM
Ham •

SUSIM

Jerusalem •   • Kiriathaim
DEAD
Hebron •   SEA
                   EMMIM
Sodom
Gomorrah   • Zoar
AMORITES
          • Tamar
Kadesh   AMALEKITES
barnea
              HORITES

El-paran •

Chedorlaomer and his allies *came down the trade route east of the Jordan, swept around the southern boundary of the Dead Sea, and then attacked Sodom from the west. They smote the Rephaim, Zuzim, Emim, Horites, Amalekites, and Amorites on their way.*

Sodom and Gomorrah *are believed to have been located at the shallow, southern end of the Dead Sea. Crystalline formations of salt and heavy concentrations of potash located near the area have been a source of wealth for centuries.*

BY GIVING THE RIGHT AMOUNT AT THE RIGHT TIME ABRAHAM FREED HIS NEPHEW

The Middle-East was just as volatile two thousand years before Christ as it is today. Reasons for the instability of the area, though, were quite different centuries ago.

THE PROMISED LAND BORDERED TRADE CENTERS

There were two concentrations of civilization in Abram's day. The first and more powerful was located in the area surrounding two great rivers—the Tigris and the Euphrates. This area tended to produce aggressive leaders who were interested in demonstrating and expanding their power. The second concentration of people was located along the Nile River. These people, the ancient Egyptians, were usually content to live by themselves in peace. The land which lay between these two great centers of trade was the land which the Lord had promised to Abram and his descendants.

FIVE CITIES REFUSED TO PAY THEIR TAXES

It was economically expedient for the kings of the north to control various trade routes through the Promised Land into Egypt. The area around Sodom and Gomorrah was rich in minerals. Copper mining was carried on in the gulf of Aqaba, and the five cities mentioned in Genesis 14 may have controlled these mines. For these reasons, and no doubt for many others, the Elamite king, Chedorlaomer—evidently the most powerful king in the north—had subdued these cities and the surrounding region for twelve years. For reasons unknown, possibly a military setback for Chedorlaomer, the five cities in Canaan refused to pay tribute (Genesis 14:4).

A RUTHLESS REPRISAL AND A NEPHEW TAKEN CAPTIVE

One year later, when Chedorlaomer decided to act, his reprisal was ruthless. With three allied kings he marched down one of the famous trade routes called the King's Highway, destroying everything in his path. After disposing of the nomads who might have sided with the rebellious cities, they attacked.

The battle was a rout. Petrified with fear, the inhabitants of the five cities which included Sodom and Gomorrah appeared to offer no resistance other than running for cover in the hill country. Bera, the king of Sodom, seems to have been killed after falling into a tar pit. His pre-appointed successor evidently escaped into the hills (Genesis 14:10, 17). Abram's nephew Lot, however, was not so fortunate. As a non-fighting civilian, he was taken captive with the women and children. The treatment of prisoners of war in those days has become infamous. Lot's future was not a bright one.

AFTER THE DARING RAID, A SPECIAL BLESSING

Abram, located north of this area in Hebron (Genesis 13:18), had not been disturbed. When he heard of his nephew's situation, he immediately acknowledged his responsibility. Gathering his forces, he pursued the powerful confederacy of northern kings. His strategy was perfect.

Because Chedorlaomer believed that he had eliminated all threats on his way to attack, his forces felt no need to fear and had probably begun to celebrate by drinking the wine confiscated from the conquered cities. It is very likely that they were already drunk when Abram attacked them at night and that he routed them without losing a man.

With his nephew rescued, Abram proceeded back to the land which the Lord had promised him. Upon his return, he was welcomed by the new king of Sodom and also the king of Salem whose name was Melchizedek. Abram very respectfully received the offer of physical refreshment and spiritual blessing from Melchizedek, but he very firmly refused the offer of spoil from the king of Sodom. Abram then returned to his temporary home in Hebron. His nephew Lot, ignoring the reproof of the Lord, returned to help in the rebuilding of the wicked city of Sodom.

ABRAHAM CHARACTER SKETCH

WHY WAS ABRAM SO PROMPT TO GIVE AID TO HIS NEPHEW, LOT?

Abram's faith in God is evident in his decision to rescue Lot. Considering that this northern confederacy of kings had just conquered every obstacle in its path, it would be foolish to a natural mind to try to overpower them with only 318 men and a few Amorite allies. Not only did they risk immediate defeat, but they also risked retaliatory action in the case of an indecisive victory. There are two good reasons for Abram's decision. First, the Lord had promised to give the land to him and his descendants (Genesis 13:14-17). By faith, Abram was protecting his descendants from northern oppression by breaking their yoke from the present possessors of the land. Second, he was committed to the welfare of not only a member of his own family but also a fellow believer in the Lord (II Peter 2:7). As the father of our faith, he demonstrated the New Testament teaching of loyalty and commitment to one's natural and also to one's spiritual family. Lot was a member of both.

HOW DID ABRAM GIVE AT THE RIGHT TIME?

When Melchizedek, the priest-king of Jerusalem, learned of the important victory that the Lord had given Abram, he desired to express his gratitude. He did so in two ways. First, he brought a tangible expression of food and drink for Abram's hungry, tired soldiers. Second, through his office of priest of the Most High God, he pronounced a blessing upon Abram. In an expression of fellowship, Abram received the physical refreshment; and in an act of faith and humility, he received the blessing.

Abram recognized that it was the right time for him to give a gift to Melchizedek. He gave him a tenth of his share of the spoil and by this act acknowledged Melchizedek's right to bless him. He knew that Melchizedek was one of the few priests who remained true to God and desired to share in the support of his ministry.

HOW DID ABRAM GIVE THE RIGHT AMOUNT?

Abram had taken an oath, swearing that he would not take a thread or a sandal thong from the king of Sodom lest he should say that he had made Abram rich (Genesis 14:23). This vow may have been motivated by two different experiences.

The first occurred recently in Egypt when he went to obtain food. Because of his need and desire for provisions, he compromised his integrity by deceiving the king. As a result of that compromise, he received much. When Abram was dismissed from Egypt with his questionable gain, he was probably distressed over the fact that he had dishonored his name and hence the name and reputation of his Lord as well. His disgust may have prompted him to promise himself never again to accept favor from a heathen king.

A second reason may have been the example of his nephew. Lot seems to have been motivated by the desire for material gain. He chose the best and most productive land. His association with the city of Sodom was in all likelihood motivated by the same desire for gain. Abram, observing Lot's increasing tolerance of the sinfulness about him, may have sworn not to let this temptation master him, too. He knew that the right amount to give Melchizedek was ten percent. The right amount to give the king of Sodom was one hundred percent. He refused to accept anything from him. The Lord's reputation was more important than his own personal gain.

"**And he brought** *back all the goods, and also brought again his brother, Lot, and his goods, and the women also, and the people.*"

The Lord changed Abram's name to Abraham when he was 99 years old (Genesis 17:1-5).

ABRAHAM
ā'brà-hăm

379

INDEX OF SCRIPTURAL REFERENCES